2/13

The Early Medieval World

The Early Medieval World

FROM THE FALL OF ROME TO THE TIME OF CHARLEMAGNE

VOLUME TWO: L–Z

Michael Frassetto

ABC-CLIO

Santa Barbara, California • Denver, Colorado • Oxford, England

Library of Congress Cataloging-in-Publication Data

Frassetto, Michael.
    The early medieval world : from the fall of Rome to the time of Charlemagne / Michael Frassetto.
        p. cm.
    Includes bibliographical references and index.
    ISBN 978-1-59884-995-0 (hardcopy : alk. paper) — ISBN 978-1-59884-996-7 (ebook) 1. Europe—History—392-814—Encyclopedias. 2. Middle Ages—Encyclopedias. 3. Civilization, Medieval—Encyclopedias. I. Title.
    D114.F83 2013
    940.1'2—dc23   2012031995

ISBN: 978-1-59884-995-0
EISBN: 978-1-59884-996-7

17   16   15   14   13   1   2   3   4   5

This book is also available on the World Wide Web as an eBook.
Visit www.abc-clio.com for details.

ABC-CLIO, LLC
130 Cremona Drive, P.O. Box 1911
Santa Barbara, California 93116-1911

This book is printed on acid-free paper ∞
Manufactured in the United States of America

Contents

L

Law and Law Codes

Prior to their contacts with the Roman Empire in the migration period, the Germanic, or barbarian, peoples of Europe had no written laws or legal codes. The nature of the law was customary. Law was remembered and passed along through an oral tradition that stretched back for generations. Although customary, the law was not simplistic; it included a well-defined set of procedures, such as the use of the oath. Although the extent of influence varied, depending upon when and where the invaders made contact with the Romans, who had a great legal tradition and had prepared important legal codes already in the third century, profoundly altered the nature of the laws of the various barbarian tribes. The Germanic peoples who entered the empire learned the tradition of written law and the practice of codifying the law, and kings of the Franks, Visigoths, and other peoples issued laws and law codes as their kingdoms were established. Exposure to the Romans and other barbarian peoples also led to the emergence of the principle of the law, a development that remained important long after the initial contact with the empire. According to this principle, each person was bound by the laws of his own group.

Like the conquest of the Roman territories on the Continent by various barbarian peoples, the conquest of England by the Anglo-Saxons in the fifth century introduced important challenges for the tradition of the law. The Anglo-Saxon accomplishment, however, is unique among the various peoples that created kingdoms in the former Western Empire because Roman contact and influence had been on the wane even before the arrival of the invaders, and in the fifth century little of the Roman legacy survived. There were no Roman jurists, and there was no Roman legal inheritance to speak of. As a result, Anglo-Saxon laws were issued in the vernacular, were little influenced by Roman traditions, and reflected long-standing Germanic customary law. Furthermore, the Anglo-Saxon kings of England issued no special laws for the Romans, as did their contemporaries on the continent. Aethelberht of Kent was one of the early kings to issue important laws in the vernacular, and his laws were recognized as statements of his royal authority. They were the king's laws and were to be followed as such. The early laws dealt with such matters as the wergeld, feud, personal injury, and payment of fines to keep the peace. They also addressed the nature of royal and local courts and instituted the necessary regulations that emerged from the conversion to Christianity. Beginning with Alfred the Great, however, Anglo-Saxon kings showed Roman influence issue written laws, called *belagines* (although these are sometimes thought to have been Ostrogothic laws only).

As the Visigoths became more settled and expanded into Spain, creating the kingdom of Toulouse (418–507), a more sophisticated legal code became necessary, in part to regulate the relationship between the Goths and the Romans living in the kingdom. There is some evidence to suggest that the legal code took shape by the mid-fifth century, when the king, Theodoric II (d. 466), issued written legal statutes. Although once associated with the Ostrogothic king Theodoric the Great, the *Edictum Theodorici* (Edict of Theodoric) now is believed to have been issued around 458 by the Visigothic king. The edict was intended to resolve various issues between Romans and Goths, but was in no sense a complete code of laws. It was under Theodoric's brother and successor, Euric, that the legal code now known as the *Codex Euricianus* (Code of Euric) most likely appeared. Sometime around the year 475 and possibly as late as 483, Euric, or perhaps his son Alaric II a generation later, issued this code of laws, which remained influential into the eighth century. The code, written in Latin, became the personal law of the Visigoths thus establishing the principle of personality, and it dealt with disputes between Romans and Goths that arose out of their cohabitation in the same kingdom. It addressed such matters as loans, gifts, purchases, wills, interest payments, and charters.

The *Codex Euricianus* was not, however, a universal legal instrument that was territorial like the Code of Justinian, nor was it a complete compilation of all Gothic law, but rather a collection of royal statutes. Consequently, a second legal document was necessary and was issued by Alaric, probably in 506, to be applied to his Roman subjects. The *Breviarium Alaricianum* (Breviary of Alaric), or the *Lex Romana Visigothorum* (Roman Law of the Visigoths), was compiled by a number of jurists commissioned by Alaric who borrowed from the imperial Theodosian Code of 438. These two codes were in effect throughout the Visigothic realm by the early sixth century and were replaced only in the mid-seventh century, when King Recceswinth issued a unified code for Romans and Visigoths. Nonetheless, the *Codex Euricianus* and the *Breviarium Alaricianum* are the most important and influential of the early Germanic legal codes and are in many ways as significant an achievement as the Bible of Ulfilas, the translation of the scriptures into Gothic that laid the foundation for the written language.

Less influential but still important laws and legal codes were issued by the Burgundians, Ostrogoths, and Vandals. The Burgundians entered the Roman Empire and settled for a time along the Rhine River, and then for a much longer period along the Rhone River, where they were heavily exposed to Roman influence. Like the Visigoths, the Burgundians had followed the tradition of customary law and were now faced with the need to provide a legal tradition for a mixed population of Burgundians and Romans. In the late fifth and early sixth centuries, two Burgundian kings, Gundobad and his son Sigismund, issued legal codes intended to resolve that problem. Gundobad, around the year 500 or slightly before, issued the *Lex Gundobada* (Law of Gundobad), or *Liber constitutionem* (Book of Constitutions), which applied to the Burgundian peoples of the kingdom and was further refined by Sigismund. In 517 or 518, Sigismund issued the *Lex Romana Burgundionum* (Roman Law of the Burgundians), which, following Visigothic precedent, applied to the king's Roman subjects and was most likely drawn up by Roman legal scholars. The existence of these two codes thus confirmed the principle of personality.

The codes had a mixed fate once the Burgundians were conquered by the Frankish king Clovis (r. 481–511). The *Lex Gundobada* remained the personal law of the Burgundian peoples under Frankish rule for centuries, but the Roman law was quickly replaced by the Breviary of Alaric. In similar fashion, the laws and legal compilations that had been issued in Ostrogothic Italy and Vandal Africa were replaced by their conquerors. In Italy, Theodoric the Great preserved what he could of Roman administration and law, and in Africa, the Vandals faced the problem of ruling a mixed barbarian and Roman population. In each case, however, the conquests of Justinian eradicated whatever legal reforms took place in the kingdoms. With the exception of the personal law of the Burgundians, the laws of the Burgundians, Ostrogoths, and Vandals had a lesser impact than did the laws of the Visigoths.

Despite their important legacy in many areas, the Ostrogoths had a much less significant impact on the history of law in Italy than the Lombards, who entered Italy not long after the end of the wars between the Goths and Byzantines. Like the Visigoths and other peoples who established themselves in former imperial territory, the Lombards were faced with the challenge of ruling over a diverse population. The solution the Lombards seem to have adopted, like that of their predecessors throughout the former Western Empire, followed the principle of personality; the Roman population followed Roman law and the Lombards followed Lombard customary law. The king remained the source of new law and continued to produce new laws and legal traditions. In the seventh century, however, the Lombards went beyond what other peoples had done. Lombard law was codified by King Rothari; and he produced the most complete set of laws of any of the barbarian kings, including nearly all of the royal law and codified Lombard legal principles nearly in full. In 643, Rothari published, with the help of Roman jurists, the *Edictus Rothari* (Edict of Rothari), which addressed family and property law and civil laws concerning personal injury and property damage. Rothari's code was clearly influenced by Roman law, and many of the prologues of the laws followed the formula of imperial legal preambles.

The *Edictus Rothari* remained the fundamental legal code of the Lombard king-dom until the kingdom was conquered by Charlemagne, and Rothari's successors preserved the code and added new laws to it as needs arose. These new laws too show the influence of Roman law, as well as the growing influence of the Catholic church on the Lombards and their legal tradition. Moreover, even after Charlemagne's conquest of the kingdom, Lombard law continued to be the law for most of the population of Italy and was only supplemented by Carolingian law. The laws of the Lombards remained an important legal tradition even after the collapse of the Carolingian Empire, and became one of the important traditions studied by lawyers in the High Middle Ages.

As in many other areas, the Franks left a lasting impact on medieval law and law codes. The most famous of Frankish law codes is the Salic law, which was compiled by the first great Merovingian king, Clovis, in the early sixth century. It is a collection of the laws of the Salian Franks, although it does not include all the laws of the Franks. Like the laws of the Visigoths and others, the Salic law was most likely codified by a team of Frankish officials and Roman lawyers; it included Frankish custom and the royal edicts of Clovis. The Salic law is not an orderly codification of the law, but a collection of important laws and customs that was intended, among other things, to preserve the peace in the Merovingian kingdom. The law also concerns royal rights and prerogatives and imposes higher fines for crimes against the king, his property, and agents. Moreover, although designed to cover all those living in the Merovingian kingdom, the Salic law, like the laws of the Visigoths and others, recognizes the principle of personality. The code im-poses different penalties for crimes, depending on whether they are committed by Franks or by Romans and provides a legal distinction between Romans and bar-barians. Originally compiled before 511, the Salic law was revised and expanded by later Merovingian kings, including Chlotar I and Chilperic I, in the later sixth and seventh centuries, and a prologue and epilogue were added in later versions. It was also revised by the Carolingians and was much studied in the eighth and ninth centuries.

The Carolingians inherited the Salic law, just as they inherited the kingdom from the Merovingian kings. The first Carolingian king, Pippin the Short, was also the first Carolingian to reform the law. In 763–764, Pippin produced a law book of 100 titles—and often called the 100-Title Text—that included all Frankish law. Char-lemagne too produced a shorter version of the code, in 70 titles, in 798, and ordered, according to a contemporary source, a revision of all the laws of the empire made in 802, two years after his imperial coronation. The Carolingian version of the Salic law seems to have lost its personal character, no longer to have been based on the principle of personality; rather it had assumed territorial status; that is, the law was now over all peoples living in the empire and not just the Franks, presenting itself as applying equally to all peoples in the empire and making no distinction between Franks and others. It continued to be concerned with peace and order and assessing fines and wergelds, but it gave much greater weight to the authority of the king than earlier revisions had. It also expressed a number of Roman legal ideas, including the idea that royal land belonged to the office, not the person, of the king.

Charlemagne's legal reforms were not limited to revisions of the Salic law. He also oversaw the codification of the laws of the Alemanni and the Bavarians, probably in 788, after they had been conquered by the great Carolingian king. Charlemagne, and his successors Louis the Pious and Charles the Bald, also issued new laws in the capitularies, which contained the word of the law as expressed by the king. The capitularies were often stated at royal councils and then written down and disseminated throughout the kingdom.

See also: Aethelberht I of Kent; Alemanni; Alaric II; Alfred the Great; Anglo-Saxons; Breviary of Alaric; Burgundian Code; Capitularies; Carolingian Dynasty; Charles the Bald; Clovis; Charlemagne; Code of Justinian; Euric; Gundobad; Justinian; Lombards; Louis the Pious; Merovingian Dynasty; Ostrogoths; Pippin III, Called Pippin the Short; Rothari; Salic Law; Sigismund, St.; Theodosian Code; Ulfilas; Vandals; Visigoths

Bibliography

Attenborough, Frederick L., ed. and trans. *The Laws of the Earliest English Kings.* Cambridge: Cambridge University Press, 1922.

Drew, Katherine Fisher, trans. *The Burgundian Code: The Book of Constitutions or Law of Gundobad and Additional Enactments.* Philadelphia: University of Pennsylvania Press, 1972.

Drew, Katherine Fisher, trans. *The Lombard Laws.* Philadelphia: University of Pennsylvania Press, 1973.

Ganshof, François Louis. *Frankish Institutions under Charlemagne.* Trans. Bryce Lyon and Mary Lyon. Providence, RI: Brown University Press, 1968.

Heather, Peter. *The Goths.* Oxford: Blackwell, 1996.

King, Peter D. *Law and Society in the Visigothic Kingdom.* Cambridge: Cambridge University Press, 1972.

McKitterick, Rosamond. *The Carolingians and the Written Word.* Cambridge: Cambridge University Press, 1989.

Pollock, Frederick, and Frederic W. Maitland. *The History of English Law before the Time of Edward I.* 2nd ed. 2 Vols. London: Cambridge University Press, 1968.

Rivers, Theodore J., trans. *Laws of the Alamans and Bavarians.* Philadelphia: University of Pennsylvania Press, 1977.

Rivers, Theodore J, trans. *The Laws of the Salian and Ripuarian Franks.* New York: AMS, 1986.

Wallace-Hadrill, J. M. *The Long-Haired Kings.* Toronto: Toronto University Press, 1982.

Wood, Ian. *The Merovingian Kingdoms, 450–751.* London: Longman, 1994.

Wolfram, Herwig. *The Roman Empire and Its Barbarian Peoples.* Trans. Thomas J. Dunlap. Berkeley: University of California Press, 1997.

Wormald, Patrick. "*Lex Scripta* and *Verbum Regis:* Legislation and Germanic Kingship from Euric to Cnut." In *Early Medieval Kingship.* Ed. Peter Sawyer and Ian N. Wood. Leeds, UK: University of Leeds Press, 1977, pp. 105–38.

Leander, St. *See* Isidore of Seville

Leo I, the Great, Pope (r. 440–461)

One of the most important early popes and, with Gregory the Great, Leo was the founder of the medieval papacy. During his reign, Leo endured the crumbling of the Western Empire, facing the invasion of Huns and Vandals and negotiating with Roman emperors. He was also a staunch defender of orthodoxy and sought to enhance the status of the spiritual primacy of Rome.

Leo was probably born in the late fourth century, perhaps at Rome, and served as deacon for pope Celestine I and Sixtus III. Leo's election as pope in 440 came while he was in Gaul on mission for the emperor, and he quickly made his mark on the papacy. During his reign, Leo composed some 143 letters and 96 sermons that helped solidify his position as the leader of the church and laid the foundation for the growth of the medieval papacy. They also helped define the teachings of medieval Christianity, and it is as a defender of orthodoxy that Leo made a particularly important mark. The pope suppressed the Manichaeans in Rome and the Priscillianist heretics in Spain. He also involved himself in the dispute over the nature of Christ, approving the condemnation of Euthyches who taught monophysitism (the belief that Jesus Christ had one nature). The pope also repudiated the council of Ephesus in 449 that defended Eutyches and called it the "Robber Council." He further appealed to the emperors Theodosius II and Valentianian III to call a council to decide the matter. The Council of Chalcedon in 451 was the result of his appeal, and it was Leo's work, *Tomus,* that was accepted at the council and provided what would become the orthodox teaching that Christ possessed two natures, one human and one divine. Leo delayed approving the decisions of Chalcedon, however, because the council proclaimed the parity of Constantinople and Rome. Leo had consistently maintained the universal authority of the bishop of Rome and primacy in the church.

Leo's challenges were not limited to matters of dogma and organization but included threats to the security of Rome and its inhabitants. The pope was forced on two occasions to defend his flock from barbarian invaders. In 452, Attila the Hun and his great army invaded Italy and threatened to besiege Rome. Leo met Attila near Mantua and persuaded the Hun to depart from Italy, perhaps encouraged by a "divine disease" that struck his army or, as popularized by Raphael, by the heavenly host led by saints Peter and Paul that appeared with Leo. Three years later, in 455, Leo was forced to negotiate with the Vandal king Gaiseric for the safety of Rome again. This time Leo was less successful as the Vandals pillaged and plundered the city, but Leo did obtain the promise from Gaiseric that the people of the city would not be harmed.

See also: Attila the Hun; Gaiseric; Gregory I, the Great, Pope; Huns; Rome; Vandals

Bibliography

*The Book of Pontiffs (*Liber Pontificalis*): The Ancient Biographies of the First Ninety Roman Bishops to* A.D. *715.* Raymond Davis, trans. Liverpool, UK: Liverpool University Press, 1989.

Herrin, Judith. *The Formation of Christendom.* Princeton, NJ: Princeton University Press, 1987.

Wessel, Susan. *Leo the Great and the Spiritual Rebuilding of Rome.* Leiden: Brill Academic Publishers, 2008.

Wolfram, Herwig. *The Roman Empire and Its Germanic Peoples.* Trans. Thomas J. Dunlap. Berkeley: University of California Press, 1997.

Leo III, Pope (d. 816)

The long and important reign of Pope Leo III (r. 795–816) witnessed a number of significant developments in papal policy and diplomatic relations. He was an active builder and restorer of churches and public structures such as aqueducts and a great benefactor of the city. He negotiated a difficult theological issue between the churches of Jerusalem and the east and the western, especially Frankish, churches. He also faced and suppressed two serious revolts in Rome during his reign. Despite his numerous accomplishments, Leo is best known for the imperial coronation of Charlemagne on Christmas Day, 800.

Although lacking the family connections of his predecessor, Hadrian I (r. 772–795), Leo III had long been known to the papal establishment and the people of Rome when he was made pope. He was raised and educated in the papal administration, served as a high-level bureaucrat, and was the cardinal priest of the church of St. Susanna in Rome before his election on December 27, 795, the day after the death of Hadrian. The *Book of the Popes* (*Liber Pontificalis*) describes him as "chaste, eloquent and of resolute mind" (Davis 1992, 179). He is also described as a "defender of the church" (179) and as a papal administrator he took active care of the poor and the sick. His rapid election demonstrates the high regard the clergy and people of Rome had for Leo. Although he was a faithful servant of the people and church of Rome, Leo's lack of important family connections caused him difficulty throughout his reign as pope.

Perhaps aware of his weak position in Rome, Leo immediately sought to strengthen the papacy's ties to the Carolingian king Charlemagne. Indeed, unlike his predecessor, Leo had no desire to pursue the alliance with the papacy's traditional protector in Constantinople, and in 796 he sent the keys of St. Peter and the banner of the city of Rome to Charlemagne. The great king called for a new treaty between himself and the pope, in which the king would defend the church against internal and external enemies and the pope would, like Moses, stand with arms upheld in prayer for victory. Leo began to date his official documents from the time of Charlemagne's conquest of the Lombards in 774, and he also promoted the see of Salzburg to metropolitan status at the king's request in 798. Leo clearly tied the papacy to the great power to the north.

Although he secured a protector and diplomatic ally, Leo still faced problems in Rome from a rival faction, an aristocratic one that included relatives of Pope Hadrian. On April 25, 799, the turmoil in Rome reached a crisis. On that day Leo left the Lateran palace to lead a major religious procession throughout the city of Rome and was attacked in front of the monastery of Saints Sylvester and Stephen by two nephews and a former ally of Hadrian. Although the accounts vary, it is clear that Leo was roughly handled by his attackers and may have been blinded and had his tongue cut out by them. The *Book of the Popes* notes also that his attackers "left him half-dead and drenched in blood." He was then placed under a sort of house arrest, being put into a monastery by his enemies, but he was rescued by his chamberlain, who lowered him from the monastery walls by a rope. The pope was then safely returned to St. Peter, where his enemies would not harm him. He was then escorted to Charlemagne's court at Paderborn (now in Germany) by the king's ally Winichis, duke of Spoleto.

At Charlemagne's court, according to some accounts, Leo miraculously regained the powers of sight and speech and defended himself against the accusations of his attackers. Leo was accused of adultery, perjury, and simony (the buying and selling of church offices), serious crimes that would have rendered him unfit for office. Uncertain of how to proceed, Charlemagne kept Leo at court until the situation at Rome quieted down before returning him to the city. In November 799, Leo was returned with a Frankish escort to protect him and was enthusiastically welcomed back by the people of Rome. On the day after his arrival, his attackers were tried before Leo and his Frankish escort and were found guilty, but sentencing was deferred until the arrival of Charlemagne.

Despite the importance of the situation, or perhaps because of it, Charlemagne did not arrive in Rome for a year after Leo's return, an indication of continued uncertainty among the king and his advisors of how to proceed. Charlemagne left his kingdom in August 800 and, according to the *Royal Frankish Annals,* was met by the pope and his entourage 12 miles from the city of Rome. King and pope dined together and entered Rome the following day, November 24, 800. Charlemagne was welcomed by enthusiastic crowds and was led by the pope to the basilica of St. Peter, where they prayed together. On December 23, before Charlemagne and an assembly of Frankish and Roman secular and religious nobles, Leo swore an oath of purgation and declared his innocence of the crimes of which he was accused. Leo's oath was accepted as proof of innocence because no one at the assembly could prove otherwise. Leo was restored to his place. The fate of the rebels against him was also decided. They were condemned to death, but the sentence was reduced to exile for life on the request of the pope himself.

Two days after his trial, Leo performed the most famous act of his reign. On Christmas Day, 800, at the shrine of St. Peter, Leo crowned Charlemagne emperor. According to the *Royal Frankish Annals,* when Charlemagne rose from prayer Leo "placed a crown on his head, and he was hailed by the whole Roman people: To august Charles, crowned by God, the great and peaceful emperor of the Romans, life and victory!" (Scholz 1972, 81). The *Book of Pontiffs* adds that the acclamation was repeated three times and that Leo then anointed Charles emperor. Although the exact meaning of the coronation to the various participants in the act will probably never be known, we need not accept Einhard's remark that Charlemagne would have avoided mass had he known what was going to happen. It is likely that the new emperor was not at all pleased by the way the coronation—which he surely knew about—had taken place, and may have thought that Leo sought to put him in the pope's debt. Indeed, it is possible that Leo sought to reassert his authority after his rescue by Charlemagne, or he may have intended to bind the Carolingian ruler even more closely to himself. It may also be that Leo had less self-serving motives and sought to reward the king with the imperial crown as thanks for all his efforts on behalf of the papacy and church. Whatever the case, the imperial coronation on December 25, 800, was Leo's most important act and one that shaped political thought and practice for the next 1,000 years.

The remainder of Leo's reign was relatively secure, no doubt as a result of Charlemagne's support. He was an able administrator and active builder, which benefited the city greatly. He did find himself at cross-purposes with his benefactor in 809, however, over a matter of liturgical practice in which the Western church differed from the church in the Holy Lands. Although Leo supported Frankish practice, he recommended that the Frankish version not be publicly recited. And in 808, Leo complained to the emperor about Charlemagne's representatives in Italy.

Leo did face one final crisis after the death of Charlemagne; long-simmering resentments that had not been eradicated in 800 boiled over, and the Roman aristocracy revolted for a second time in 814. The pope acted promptly and had the leaders of the rebellion executed. Charlemagne's successor, Louis the Pious, was concerned by Leo's harsh response and ordered his nephew, King Bernard of Italy, to investigate the situation. Leo's explanation proved satisfactory to the Carolingian emperor, but not to the Roman nobles who in 815 sought to take lands away from the papacy. Once again Louis, through his nephew Bernard, intervened, and this time on behalf of the pope. The situation in Rome remained unsettled, but it was Leo's successor as pope who addressed the situation. Leo died June 12, 816, after a long reign in which he drew the papacy closer to the Carolingians and, most importantly, crowned Charlemagne emperor.

See also: Carolingian Dynasty; Charlemagne; Lombards; Louis the Pious; *Royal Frankish Annals*

Bibliography

Davis, Raymond, trans. *The Lives of the Eighth-Century Popes* (Liber Pontificalis): *The Ancient Biographies of Nine Popes from A.D. 715 to A.D. 817*. Liverpool, UK: Liverpool University Press, 1992.

Einhard and Notker the Stammerer. *Two Lives of Charlemagne*. Trans. Lewis Thorpe. Harmondsworth, UK: Penguin, 1981.

Halphen, Louis. *Charlemagne and the Carolingian Empire*. Trans. Giselle de Nie. Amsterdam: North-Holland, 1977.

Herrin, Judith. *The Formation of Christendom*. Princeton, NJ: Princeton University Press, 1987.

Llewellyn, Peter. *Rome in the Dark Ages*. New York: Barnes and Noble, 1971.

McKitterick, Rosamond. *The Frankish Kingdoms under the Carolingians, 751–987*. London: Longman, 1983.

Noble, Thomas F. X. *The Republic of St. Peter: The Birth of the Papal State, 680–825*. Philadelphia: University of Pennsylvania Press, 1984.

Riché, Pierre. *The Carolingians: A Family Who Forged Europe*. Trans. Michael Idomir Allen. Philadelphia: University of Pennsylvania Press, 1993.

Scholz, Bernhard Walter, trans. *Carolingian Chronicles: Royal Frankish Annals and Nithard's History*. Ann Arbor: University of Michigan Press, 1972.

Leo III, the Isaurian (c. 680–741)

The Byzantine emperor Leo III (r. 717–741) was founder of a dynasty whose religious policy caused great dissension in the empire. His policy, known as iconoclasm, contributed to a growing schism between the church in Rome and the church in the Byzantine Empire. The antagonism that existed between the popes and Leo III, who also increased the burden of taxation in Italy without improving his defense of the papacy against the Lombards, reinforced the tendency of the popes to look to western European leaders for protection. Indeed, Leo's iconoclastic policy drove

Pope Gregory III to appeal to the Carolingian mayor of the palace, the power behind the throne in the kingdom of the Franks, for aid. The ongoing iconoclastic controversy after Leo's death attracted the attention of Charlemagne and his court scholars, especially Theodulf of Orléans.

Leo took the throne in 717 in a bloody coup that eliminated the last of the Heraclian dynasty, which had been established a century earlier. Although he managed to take the throne, Leo was immediately faced with a great crisis—Muslim soldiers were besieging the great capital of the Eastern Empire, Constantinople. By a combination of luck, skill, and superior technology, including Greek fire, a type of napalm that destroyed the attackers' ships, Leo managed to save the city by 718. Over much of the next decade, Leo continued to expel Muslim invaders from Byzantine territory. Indeed, his efforts were critical to the long-term survival of the empire, which did not fall to the Muslims until 1453, and to the preservation of three distinct cultural regions around the medieval Mediterranean—a Latin Christian, a Greek Christian, and a Muslim region. For many of his subjects, however, Leo's efforts at defending the empire were only secondary to the more important efforts of the monks and priests of the realm. During the assault on Constantinople, the patriarch marched around the city walls bearing a religious image, or icon, of Mary, which many believed saved the city. Faith in the icon was something that Leo did not share, and the widespread belief in them may have offended the religious sensibilities of the emperor, who most likely recalled the Mosaic prohibition against graven images. Although Leo introduced a number of governmental, military, and administrative reforms that would greatly strengthen the empire, he is remembered mostly for the almost disastrous religious policy that arose out of his hostility to icon worship.

Leo, either because of religious conviction or animosity toward the priests who promoted veneration of images, instituted a policy of iconoclasm in 727. The policy may have also been motivated by a terrible volcanic eruption in the Aegean Sea, which Leo interpreted as divine disfavor caused by the use of icons. Whatever his motive, Leo pronounced an imperial decree against the use of icons in the Byzantine church and also began to attack the monasteries. Leo was exercising what he thought was his divine right as emperor to intervene in religious matters, but the monks had traditionally criticized religious policy making by the emperors. His efforts were at first modest, but they became increasingly harsh, and as early as 730 there are records of the destruction of icons. Defenders of the use of icons, mostly monks, were harshly treated and sometimes martyred, which only hardened the determination of those opposed to the new policy. Leo's son and successor, Constantine V (r. 741–775), took an even harder line against icons. Ultimately, the iconoclastic policy was overturned, but not before contributing to increased tensions between the church in the east and the west.

Leo's foray into religious policy making was not well received at Rome by Pope Gregory II or Gregory III. Whatever the merits of the policy were, and there alone

Leo's actions would have received condemnation from Rome, the popes would have opposed Leo purely on the grounds of principle. It was not the responsibility of the emperor to determine matters of the faith; rather he was to protect the church and its ministers. In many ways, the emperors in Constantinople had failed to protect the church in Italy—a responsibility many centuries old by Leo's time. Moreover, not only did Leo fail to protect the pope and his church in Italy, especially from the Lombards who had been seeking to conquer the peninsula since 568, but he had increased the administrative demands on the popes and had significantly increased taxation in Italy. As a result, relations between Rome and Constantinople worsened to the point that Gregory III turned for help to the great rising power in the north, the Carolingian Franks and their leader Charles Martel, for aid against the Lombards. Charles needed his alliance with the Lombards and was unable to help, but an important precedent was set for both the Carolingians and the papacy. Over the next generation an alliance between the two was established, and a break between Rome and Constantinople occurred. Indeed, Leo's intervention in religious policy and reorganization of administration in Italy drove the popes into an alliance with the Carolingians, an alliance that contributed to the Carolingian usurpation of the royal power from the last of the Merovingian kings in 751.

Leo's iconoclastic policy continued to have repercussions into the late eighth and even early ninth century, long after the emperor's death. In the late eighth century, the empress Irene and her son Constantine V presided over the Second Council of Nicaea, which decreed the restoration of the veneration of icons. A second wave of iconcoclasm was initiated by a series of emperors from 815 to 842, but once again the policy was overturned and the veneration of icons was formally restored in a ceremony that continues to be celebrated in the Orthodox Church as the Triumph of Orthodoxy. Despite the ultimate failure of his religious policy and the dissension it caused within the empire and with the pope in Rome, Leo left an important legacy for the Byzantine Empire and saved it during its darkest hour.

See also: Alcuin of York; Carolingian Dynasty; Charlemagne; Charles Martel; Gregory II, Pope; Gregory III, Pope; Iconoclastic Controversy; Irene; *Libri Carolini*; Lombards; Louis the Pious; Merovingian Dynasty; Rome; Theodulf of Orléans

Bibliography

Davis, Raymond, trans. *The Lives of the Eighth-Century Popes* (Liber Pontificalis): *The Ancient Biographies of Nine Popes from A.D. 715 to A.D. 817.* Liverpool, UK: Liverpool University Press, 1992.

Herrin, Judith. *The Formation of Christendom.* Princeton, NJ: Princeton University Press, 1989.

Llewellyn, Peter. *Rome in the Dark Ages.* New York: Barnes and Noble, 1993.

McKitterick, Rosamond. *The Frankish Kingdoms under the Carolingians.* Longman: London, 1983.

Obolensky, Dmitri. *The Byzantine Commonwealth: Eastern Europe, 500–1543.* New York: Praeger, 1971.

Riché, Pierre. *The Carolingians: A Family Who Forged Europe.* Trans. Michael Idomir Allen. Philadelphia: University of Pennsylvania Press, 1993.

Sullivan, Richard. *Heirs of the Roman Empire.* Ithaca, NY: Cornell University Press, 1974.

Leovigild (r. 568/569–586)

Visigothic king of Spain (r. 568/569–586), Leovigild enjoyed great military success against a variety of rivals, including the Byzantine Empire as well as other barbarian peoples. His power was recognized by other kings in Europe, and his son Hermenegild married a Merovingian princess. But Hermenegild also sought to overthrow his father and rebelled. Hermenegild's revolt and marriage also revealed one of the fundamental tensions of Leovigild's reign, the tension between Catholic and Arian Christians. Although Leovigild took great steps to unify the kingdom religiously as well as politically, the great religious dilemma was resolved only during the reign of his other son, Reccared. Leovigild did attempt to establish common ground between his Arian beliefs and those of the Catholic majority in Spain, but ultimately failed in his efforts. Both Hermenegild and Reccared converted to Catholic Christianity, and it was Reccared who provided the solution of the great religious question that Leovigild tried so hard to answer.

Raised to the status of coruler and given charge of Spain by his brother Liuva I (r. 568/569–573), Leovigild was one of the great kings of the sixth century. He sought to unify Spain, both politically and religiously, under his authority. To secure that end, he modeled royal ceremonial rites more closely after the practices of the Eastern Empire and abolished the law forbidding intermarriage between Goths and Romans. He also undertook frequent campaigns to suppress rebels and rivals for power. As one contemporary chronicler noted, Leovigild restored Gothic territory in Spain to its traditional boundaries. He led his armies in annual campaigns against a variety of foes including Byzantines, Basques, and other barbarian peoples. The king also suppressed a number of independent cities, including Córdoba, and extended his kingdom into the northeast. He thus incorporated most of the peninsula into his kingdom. As a sign of his growing power and self-confidence, Leovigild founded the city Reccopolis, an action usually reserved for Roman emperors, and in 573 made his sons Hermenegild and Reccared coregents to help administer the kingdom. Moreover, his efforts brought him recognition outside the kingdom, including an important marriage between his son Hermenegild and the Merovingian princess Ingunde in 579. Of course, his military success also generated dissension within the kingdom, and

Hermenegild's marriage to the Catholic Ingunde, as well as his close relationship with Leander, leader of the Catholic church and brother of the important author Isidore of Seville, eventually led the young king to convert to Catholicism from his father's Arianism.

Despite the marriage alliance between his son and the Catholic Merovingian princess, Leovigild was committed to the Arian faith and sought to unify his kingdom under the Arian banner. He took a number of steps to ensure the success of his version of the Christian faith at the expense of the Catholic church in Spain, including banishing a number of bishops. His efforts, however, did not turn to persecution; instead he promoted conversion. To accomplish that end and the triumph of Arianism in Spain, he held a council at Toledo in 580. The council promoted the Arian faith of Leovigild but also sought to convert Catholic Christians in Spain, passing several decrees that were intended to make conversion more likely. The council introduced theological changes that brought Spanish Arianism closer to Catholic teaching by recognizing that the Son of God was equal (*aequalis*) to the Father, not just similar (*similis*), as the Arian church in Spain had taught. The council also recognized the Catholic sacrament of baptism and abolished the law mandating rebaptism for converts, thus eliminating an impediment to conversion. Leovigild's council also adopted a more conciliatory policy toward the veneration of relics, which was unknown to Arian Christians. The more tolerant and open attitude of Leovigild's church enjoyed some success, and at least one bishop, Vincent of Saragossa, converted. His effort failed nonetheless, because of the strength of the Catholic faith among his Roman subjects and because of the intellectual weakness of the Arian church.

The failure of Leovigild's religious policy is no better illustrated than in the actions of his two sons Hermenegild and Reccared, both of whom converted to Catholic Christianity. The more serious conversion for Leovigild was that of Hermenegild, which was accompanied by a revolt against his father. In 579, Hermenegild made his conversion and broke with his father. He actively sought allies against Leovigild and found them in Constantinople and among the people his father had conquered. He also found a friend and supporter in Pope Gregory I the Great, who later promoted Hermenegild as a martyr to the faith. Indeed, Hermenegild portrayed himself as a victim of persecution and used that as justification for rebellion against his father. His efforts ultimately failed, and his rebellion was put down by 584. Leovigild exiled his son to Valencia in 584 and then to Tarragona, where Hermenegild was murdered in 585. Despite Gregory's support for Hermenegild, most contemporary Catholic writers, including Isidore of Seville and the Frankish historian Gregory of Tours, had little sympathy for him or his revolt.

Reccared too converted to Catholic Christianity, but only after his father's death, and in other ways he shared in the important legacy Leovigild left. Although not successful in his religious policy, Leovigild left his successor with a powerful and unified kingdom. Leovigild had conquered much of the peninsula and had reformed the royal administration in a way that borrowed from Roman imperial practices, including celebrating his victories on the coins he minted. He also elevated the status of the king above his noble and non-noble subjects and introduced a number of new officials to the royal administration. These reforms benefited Leovigild's successor, as did his efforts to unify the kingdom religiously. Though Leovigild's attempts failed in that regard, the notion of unifying the kingdom religiously was a powerful one and needed only Reccared's recognition that it could only be unified by the Catholic Christian faith.

See also: Arianism; Gregory I, the Great, Pope; Gregory of Tours; Hermenegild; Merovingian Dynasty; Reccared I; Toledo; Visigoths

Bibliography

Bury, John B. *History of the Later Roman Empire: From the Death of Theodosius I to the Death of Justinian.* 2 Vols. 1923. Reprint, New York: Dover, 1959.

Collins, Roger. *Early Medieval Spain: Unity in Diversity, 400–1000.* New York: St. Martin's Press, 1983.

Gregory of Tours. *History of the Franks.* Trans. Lewis Thorpe. Harmondsworth, UK: Penguin, 1974.

Heather, Peter. *The Goths.* Oxford: Blackwell, 1996.

Isidore of Seville. *Isidore of Seville's History of the Goths, Vandals, and Suevi.* 2nd rev. ed. Trans. Guido Donini and Gordon B. Ford. Leiden: Brill, 1970.

Thompson, Edward A. *The Goths in Spain.* Oxford: Clarendon, 1969.

Wolfram, Herwig. *History of the Goths.* Trans. Thomas J. Dunlap. Berkeley: University of California Press, 1988.

Wolfram, Herwig. *The Roman Empire and Its Germanic Peoples.* Trans. Thomas J. Dunlap. Berkeley: University of California Press, 1997.

Letter to Baugulf

The circular letter on learning to the abbot Baugulf of Fulda, or *De litteris colendis,* was, with the capitulary *Admonitio Generalis* of 789, the cornerstone of Charlemagne's program of intellectual and cultural reform. Although he addressed it only to the abbot Baugulf, Charlemagne ordered that the letter be circulated among various Carolingian ecclesiastics, and it thus contributed to the development of the Carolingian Renaissance. The letter outlines Charlemagne's desire to provide basic education for the boys of his kingdom and reveals his notion that providing a basic Christian education was essential to his duty as king.

Despite its importance, the exact date of the letter remains uncertain, and modern knowledge of it is the result of mere chance. The composition of the letter, probably at Charlemagne's own dictation, is traditionally dated to the period 780 to 800. Some scholars have proposed a more specific dating to the years 781 to 791 or even to 794 to 796, but the broadest range remains the most generally accepted of the dates of the document. The letter itself is known only from two manuscripts. One manuscript from the 12fth century was destroyed in a bombing raid during World War II, and the other one, which was discovered only in 1927, is from the eighth century. Although only one copy of the letter is still extant, it was most likely copied and sent some time later with some additions to many monasteries by Baugulf.

The letter includes Charlemagne's desire that the monks and secular clergy of his realm should devote themselves to follow the "life set out in their rule and their practice of holy religion" (279). But more than that, they "ought also to be zealous in the cultivation of learning and in teaching those who by the gift of God are able to learn" (279). He encourages learning and education so that his subjects can better follow the will of God and praise God without error in speech or practice. He notes in the document that although he has received many letters with expressions of good pious belief, he has noticed many errors of speech in them. Charlemagne, therefore, encourages Baugulf and the clergy to study the Scriptures and literature in general so that they may better know God's message and better do God's will. The king's appeal to the monks and clergy of the realm to devote themselves to study and teaching was an important stimulus to the growth of the Carolingian Renaissance.

See also: Admonitio Generalis; Capitularies; Carolingian Renaissance; Charlemagne

Bibliography

Brown, Giles. "Introduction: The Carolingian Renaissance." In *Carolingian Culture: Emulation and Innovation.* Ed. Rosamond McKitterick. Cambridge: Cambridge University Press, 1994, pp. 1–51.

Charlemagne. "A Letter of Charles on the Cultivation of Learning, 780–800." In *Carolingian Civilization: A Reader.* Ed. Paul Edward Dutton. Peterborough, ON: Broadview, 1993, pp. 79–80.

Laistner, Max L.W. *Thought and Letters in Western Europe, A.D. 500 to 900.* 2nd ed. Ithaca, NY: Cornell University Press, 1976.

McKitterick, Rosamond. *The Frankish Kingdoms under the Carolingians, 751–987.* London: Longman, 1983.

Libri Carolini

The official Carolingian response to the Second Council of Nicaea (787), which restored the veneration of icons in the Byzantine Church, the *Libri Carolini* (Caroline Books), or as it is more formally known, the *Opus Caroli Regis* (Work of

King Charles), offers a sophisticated theory of religious art and a formal rejection of Byzantine icondulism. The work, long held to have been produced by the great scholar Alcuin, is now generally held to have been written by Theodulf of Orléans but with some editorial assistance from Alcuin.

Written in Charlemagne's name in response to the decisions of Second Nicaea, which was held without representation from the Carolingian church, the *Libri Carolini* demonstrates the wide patristic and biblical learning of its main author, Theodulf of Orléans. Composed from 790 to 793 and presented at the Council of Frankfurt in 794, the *Libri*, which were never formally promulgated, present the Carolingian view of the use of images and the role of art in religious practice. Divided into four books, which address the various decisions of the council, the *Libri* asserts the aesthetic and didactic value of art. For Theodulf, as for Pope Gregory the Great, art could help instruct the laity in the lessons of the Bible. Paintings and other art could also be admired for their beauty and elegance. Theodulf, however, rejected the use of classical imagery of pagan gods or the personification of the sun and moon as contrary to the teachings of the Scriptures. Moreover, as a result of a faulty translation of the decisions of Nicaea which used *adoratio* (a type of veneration reserved for God alone) to translate the term used for veneration of sacred images, Theodulf forcefully denounced the council's and denied that images possessed any spiritual qualities. The *Libri* thus offered a theory of art that stressed the talent of the artist and beauty of his creation and denied that images had any mystic function.

See also: Alcuin; Charlemagne; Gregory I, the Great, Pope; Iconoclastic Controversy; Irene; Theodulf of Orléans

Bibliography

Chazelle, Celia. *The Crucified God in the Carolingian Era: Theology and Art of Christ's Passion.* Cambridge: Cambridge University Press, 2001.

Freeman, Ann. *Theodulf of Orleans: Charlemagne's Spokesman against the Second Council of Nicaea.* London: Variorum, 2003.

Noble, Thomas F. X. *Images, Iconoclasm, and the Carolingians.* Philadelphia: University of Pennsylvania Press, 2009.

Lindisfarne Gospels

One of the great works of medieval book illumination, the Lindisfarne Gospels (British Library, MS Cotton Nero D.iv) was produced in the late seventh or early eighth centuries in Northumbria and is an important example of the Insular or Hiberno-Saxon style, which mixed Anglo-Saxon and Celtic artistic traditions. The manuscript includes the complete text of the four canonical Gospels—Matthew,

Mark, Luke, and John—which are preceded by a letter of Jerome's to Pope Damasus and canon tables of Eusebius. The text of the Gospels is a pure version of the Vulgate compiled by Jerome, and the entire manuscript is lavishly decorated. The Lindisfarne Gospels, according to an insertion from the 10th century and based on an oral tradition, were written and illustrated in 698 by the monk Eadfrith, who later became bishop of Northumbria. The binding of the manuscript was supplied by Eadrith's successor, Ethelwald, in 721, and the cover was decorated with precious gems and metals by the anchorite Billfrith. According to the 10th-century insertion, the manuscript was prepared to honor St. Cuthbert, former bishop of Lindisfarne, who died in 687 and whose relics were translated in 689.

The manuscript is extensively and beautifully illuminated, each Gospel opens with a miniature of the evangelist, a major illustrated initial, and a cross-carpet page (a page devoted solely to decoration). Decorated initials are found throughout the manuscript along with numerous other illuminations that recall the artistic motifs found in the Sutton Hoo collection. The illustrations include interlaced

Title page of St. John's Gospel from the Lindisfarne Gospels, from around 698. (The British Library Board)

ribbons and other geometric designs, birds and beasts and other images from nature, and spaces in between are often filled with red dots. The illustrator used a wide variety of colors. In response to the Viking invasions in the 10th century, the community fled with its treasures, including the Lindisfarne Gospels, to county Durham. At this point, the priest Aldred added the insertion concerning the composition of the manuscript and added an interlinear translation into Old English of the text.

See also: Anglo-Saxons; Jerome; Kells, Book of; Monasticism; Northumbrian Renaissance; Sutton Hoo

Bibliography

Backhouse, Janet. *The Lindisfarne Gospels.* Oxford: Phaidon, 1981.

Brown, Michelle. *The Lindisfarne Gospels and the Early Medieval World.* London: British Library, 2010.

Brown, Michelle. *The Lindisfarne Gospels: Society, Spirituality, and the Scribe.* Toronto: University of Toronto Press, 2003.

Liutprand (d. 744)

The greatest of the Lombard kings of Italy, Liutprand ruled during a time of great prosperity and growth for the Lombard kingdom (r. 712–744). He expanded the boundaries of the kingdom in Italy and sought to bring the entire peninsula under his authority. The Lombard duchies of the south were brought to heel by Liutprand, and he conquered many of the possessions of the Byzantine Empire in Italy. He also enjoyed success against the papacy, which owned extensive estates in central Italy coveted by Liutprand. His advances in central Italy were watched closely by the popes of his age, and his successes in Italy, paradoxically, laid the foundation for the later invasions of the Carolingian king Pippin and the conquest of the kingdom by Charlemagne. Although Carolingian rulers ultimately brought about the demise of the Lombard kingdom, Liutprand was a trusted ally of the Franks. He was also a skilled ruler who introduced important legal and administrative reforms in the kingdom.

Although vilified in the *Liber Pontificalis* (The Book of the Popes), Liutprand was most likely a devout Christian, who came to the throne after the Lombards had converted from Arian Christianity to Catholic Christianity. He took the throne in 712, following a period of disarray in the Lombard kingdom, and shortly thereafter pursued the traditional Lombard policy of striving to unite Italy. His efforts led him into conflict with the popes of his day—Gregory II, Gregory III, and Zachary—but he did attempt to maintain good relations with the popes and, as Paul the Deacon notes, made pious donations to the church in his kingdom. He defended the Italian peninsula against attacks from Saracen pirates and declared himself the defender of the church and orthodoxy in response to the policy of iconoclasm instituted by the Byzantine emperor Leo III, the Isaurian. Indeed, he took the opportunity to combine his desires to unify Italy under his authority and to establish himself as defender of the church when he seized imperial territory in Italy during the turmoil of the iconoclastic controversy. He also reached a diplomatic settlement with Pope Zachary shortly after the pope ascended the throne, as part of which he returned four towns previously seized from papal territory. It seems, then, that Liutprand was not the enemy of the papacy he is sometimes styled by hostile sources, and he clearly was not the threat to the papacy that his predecessors were.

Although not an open enemy of the institution of the papacy, Liutprand did threaten papal territories, just as he threatened the rest of the peninsula. During his long reign as king, Liutprand gradually extended the boundaries of the kingdom and the extent of Lombard power. In the 720s, in coordination with the Frankish mayor of the palace Charles Martel, Liutprand secured his northern border at the expense of the duchy of Bavaria. He also exploited Byzantine weakness in the 720s when he seized several cities in Italy, an action that unsettled Pope Gregory II, with whom Liutprand had previously had good relations. The pope in turn arranged an alliance with the Lombard duchies in the south, Spoleto and Benevento, which angered the king and may have forced him to attack papal territory in defense of Lombard interests. Although a treaty was negotiated between Rome and the king, the attack led to ill feelings, as well as Liutprand's subjugation of the southern duchies to his authority. After a period of quiet in the 730s, Liutprand was once again forced into action against the pope, now Gregory III, who had supported rebellion in the duchy of Spoleto and had called for the defense of Ravenna against Lombard aggression and conquest.

It was during the hostilities at the end of the late 730s that Pope Gregory III laid the foundation for the later destruction of the Lombard kingdom. After Liutprand's renewed aggression and conquest of papal territories, Gregory sent a note to the Carolingian mayor Charles Martel, seeking aid against the Lombard king. This appeal by the pope proved fruitless for several reasons. The Lombards and Franks had long been allies, and Paul the Deacon tells the story of Charles sending his son Pippin to Liutprand to receive the traditional gift of the king's hair. Liutprand sent both his hair and many gifts to confirm the friendship between the two rulers and their peoples. It was also important at that time for Charles to preserve the alliance with Liutprand because Muslim armies from Spain continued to threaten the Frankish kingdom. Despite the failure of this attempt by Gregory, later popes did seek and receive aid from the Carolingians against the Lombards. Hostility between the pope and the king survived Gregory's reign, but it was eased during the early years of Pope Zachary, who personally met with Liutprand and negotiated the return of several papal towns. Indeed, it was Liutprand's devotion to the Catholic faith and respect for the holy see that contributed to Zachary's success.

Although Liutprand's dream of uniting all of Italy ultimately was not realized, he exercised great influence over events on the peninsula and greatly enhanced Lombard royal authority in Italy. He also strengthened royal power within the Lombard kingdom. He strengthened his ties with the dukes and other nobles throughout the kingdom. He also enhanced his ties with all free people in the kingdom by imposing an oath that bound them all to him. He improved royal bureaucracy and the administration of justice. He also cultivated a more sophisticated concept of power. Finally, Liutprand revised the Lombard code of law. Although his struggles with the papacy led in the end to an alliance that brought about the end of the Lombard kingdom, Liutprand clearly presided over a highly successful period in Lombard history and left his successors, both Lombard and Frankish, an important legacy.

See also: Arianism; Carolingian Dynasty; Charles Martel; Franks; Gregory II, Pope; Gregory III, Pope; Lombards; Paul the Deacon; Pavia; Rome; Zachary, St.

Bibliography

Christie, Neil. *The Lombards: The Ancient Langobards.* Oxford: Blackwell, 1998.

Davis, Raymond, trans. *The Lives of the Eighth-Century Popes* (Liber Pontificalis): *The Ancient Biographies of Nine Popes from* A.D. *715 to* A.D. *817.* Liverpool, UK: Liverpool University Press, 1992.

Herrin, Judith. *The Formation of Christendom.* Princeton, NJ: Princeton University Press, 1989.

Llewellyn, Peter. *Rome in the Dark Ages.* New York: Barnes and Noble, 1993.

Noble, Thomas X. F. *The Republic of St. Peter: The Birth of the Papal State, 680–825.* Philadelphia: University of Pennsylvania Press, 1984.

Paul the Deacon. *History of the Lombards.* Trans. William Dudley Foulke. Philadelphia: University of Pennsylvania Press, 1974.

Riché, Pierre. *The Carolingians: A Family Who Forged Europe.* Trans. Michael Idomir Allen. Philadelphia: University of Pennsylvania Press, 1993.

Lombards

A Germanic people who first appear in the sources in the first-century AD, settling along the Elbe River, the Lombards, or Langobardi (Long Beards), developed a reputation for being an especially fierce people. Although they suffered occasional setbacks, they won numerous victories over other barbarian peoples, and at the same time were skilled diplomats, able to maintain good relations with the Avars, Byzantines, and Franks. They are best known, however, for their invasion and conquest of much of Italy, which undermined the efforts of the emperor Justinian to reestablish imperial power in Italy. Although pagan or Arian at the time of the invasion, the Lombards were able to establish good relations with the bishops of Italy and eventually converted to Catholic Christianity. Their efforts to unify the Italian peninsula under a Lombard king caused the popes in Rome great anxiety. The Lombard struggle with the papacy contributed to the formation of the papal states and the destruction of the Lombard kingdom in 774 by Charlemagne, whose aid had been sought by the pope.

The origins of the Lombards remain obscure, and the early Roman and medieval texts add little to our knowledge of the earliest period. The first mention of the Lombards was made by Tacitus (c. 56–117) in the *Germania,* who placed them along the lower Elbe River. Later Roman and early medieval writers placed them in lower Austria by the fifth century and then south of the Danube River in Pannonia (modern western Hungary and eastern Austria) in the sixth century. Paul the Deacon, the eighth-century historian of the Lombards, placed their origins in Scandinavia and then traced their migrations into Pannonia. His version of the history, however, follows the standard pattern of migration that most late Roman and early medieval historians ascribed to various barbarian tribes. The period between the first appearance of the Lombards and their settlement in Pannonia is uncertain; the archeological records suggest that theirs was a pastoral existence. They also seem to have developed a fairly well-organized tribal structure and a reputation for fierceness that was later justified in their contacts with Rome and other barbarian peoples.

However, that may be, by the end of the fifth century it is most likely that the Lombards had moved into Pannonia; in the next century they were led by the vigorous king Audoin (r. 546–560/561). By the time of Audoin, the Lombards had become a force to be reckoned with and had defeated the Heruls and Gepids in battle. Audoin had gained such renown that he was able to arrange his marriage to a grandniece of Theodoric the Great, the Ostrogothic king of Italy, a marriage that may have been the inspiration for the Lombard invasion of Italy. Indeed, it was Audoin's son, Alboin, who led the Lombards into Italy.

After distinguishing himself in battle against the Gepids during his father's lifetime, Alboin continued to wage war as king in his own name. Although defeated by the Gepids in 565, Alboin rejoined battle two years later after forming an alliance with the Avars. His victory led to the destruction of the Gepids and death of their king at the hand of Alboin, who made a goblet of his rival's skull and then married his rival's daughter. After his victory over the Gepids, according to tradition, Alboin entered Italy at the invitation of the disgruntled Byzantine general Narses. Although Narses's invitation may have played a part in the invasion, Lombard awareness of the weakened state of Italy, brought about by the Gothic Wars and divisions in the church, as well as possible family connections, surely also played a role. After settling affairs in Pannonia, Alboin entered the peninsula in 568 with up to 150,000 followers; he quickly conquered much of northern Italy and may have even threatened Rome. Alboin's success in Italy, however, was cut short by an assassination plot involving his wife, who had grown tired of seeing her husband drink from her father's skull.

The death of Alboin reveals two of the weaknesses of the Lombard system, the tradition of elective kingship and a powerful noble class. A new king did emerge immediately in the wake of the assassination; Cleph (r. 572–574) was elected, but he was then assassinated in his turn. This was followed by a 10-year period in which no king was elected and the dukes ruled throughout Lombard Italy. The dukes also continued the subjugation of Italy, spreading south into Tuscany, Beneventum, and Spoleto. There was, however, little effort to intermingle with the Italian population, and the Lombards both kept themselves separate from and continued to oppress the native population. Their warlike tendencies also led them north in an attempt to conquer Burgundy, an almost fatal mistake. The Lombard dukes faced the might of the Merovingian Franks in Burgundy, a might enhanced by an alliance with the Byzantine Empire. The Lombards paid dearly for their expedition north and were nearly destroyed by the Merovingians. It was this experience, at least in part, that led to a restoration of the kingship, as the dukes joined together to elect Cleph's son Authari (r. 584–590) as king. His reign was noteworthy for his marriage to Theudelinda, a Bavarian Catholic princess, recovery of much of the territory lost to the Franks and Byzantines, and efforts to strengthen the Lombard kingship.

During the seventh century, Authari's successors built on his legacy, continuing to strengthen the monarchy and to preserve their ethnic identity. They also expanded Lombard control in Italy, but introduced important changes in the government and religion of the Lombards. Both developments are evident already during the reign of Authari's immediate successor, Agilulf (r. 590–616), whom Authari's widow, Theudelinda, chose to be king and her new husband. Agilulf stabilized the Lombard frontiers in Italy, limiting imperial territory in the process. He also introduced the practice of early designation of royal successors, identifying his son, Aldoald (616–626), as the heir while the boy was still young. Although an Arian Christian, Agilulf had his son baptized a Catholic and allowed his Lombard subjects to baptize their children as Catholics.

This concession was surely made in deference to Theudelinda, who exercised great power and influence, was courted by Pope Gregory I, and was a patron of the Irish Catholic missionary, St. Columban. Indeed, it was during the reign of Theudelinda and Agilulf that Columban established the famous monastery of Bobbio. Theudelinda's efforts on behalf of the Catholic faith failed, however, and when, according to Paul the Deacon, her son went insane, the new king, Ariald (r. 626–636), was an Arian Christian. Indeed, the reaction against Theudelinda, which may have been motivated by the Lombards' desire to maintain their own identity, lasted two generations and continued into the following reign. The reign of Rothari was characterized not only by the promotion of Arian Christianity, but also—and more importantly—by the codification of the Lombard laws. The laws revealed both Germanic tradition and Roman legal practice and show the ambivalent attitude the Lombards had toward the Romans.

Although indebted to both their Ostrogothic and Roman predecessors in ruling Italy, the Lombards introduced their own customs and social and political arrangements in Italy, as Rothari's laws demonstrate. The most significant aspect of the Lombards' rule in Italy was their effort to retain their ethnic identity, which led to their limited intermingling with the native Italian population as well as their preference for Arian Christianity. Their political system was organized around a king, whose capital was, eventually, established in the city of Pavia. The king came increasingly to rely on taxes and revenues from his royal estates and remained the leading figure in the kingdom, assisted at court by a growing bureaucracy and a number of officials appointed by the king. The dukes were the next most important power in the kingdom and numbered as many as 35 during the kingdom's existence. They were sometimes independent of the king, as were the dukes of Spoleto and Beneventum, and were great powers in their own right, who were often elected to the kingship. At the bottom of the social hierarchy were half-free peasants, slaves, and freedmen, but the most important class was that of the *arimmani* (Lombard word for soldiers). The *arimmani* were free men who were responsible for serving in the Lombard military and were essential to the success of the Lombard kings.

Despite the successes of Rothari and other early seventh-century kings, the Lombards faced turmoil during the latter part of the century. They suffered from internal dissent brought on by religious differences and the ambition of the dukes. Moreover, the Lombards faced foreign invasion by the Merovingians and the Byzantines during the reign of King Grimoald (r. 662–671), who also had to evict invading Avars from part of Lombard Italy. There was a major rebellion in the north during the reign of King Cuncipert (r. 680–700), which the king suppressed, enabling him to bring a group of northern bishops under his control. It was also during this period, that the Lombards, under King Aripert I (r. 653–661), converted to Catholic Christianity from the Arian faith of Rothari and some earlier Lombard kings.

The turmoil of the late seventh century gave way to the high point of Lombard history in the eighth, under the great kings Liutprand, Aistulf, and Desiderius, whose very success led paradoxically to the demise of the Lombard kingdom. The first of these kings, Liutprand, exploited the turmoil in Italy brought on by the Iconoclastic Controversy in the Byzantine Empire. The controversy emerged because of the decision of Leo III, the Isaurian, to eliminate the use of icons in worship, alienating the papacy, which was already disenchanted with the empire for its failure to protect Italy. Liutprand moved quickly to improve his control of the kingdom and expand its boundaries at the expense of the empire. Although an aggressive and expansionist king, Liutprand strove to maintain good relations with the pope. A Catholic Christian, the king tried to cooperate with Rome even though the popes felt threatened by his efforts to control Italy. His mixed success is demonstrated by the efforts of Pope Gregory III to forge an alliance with the Carolingian mayor, Charles Martel, against the Lombards—Charles was reluctant because of his own ties with Liutprand—and the treaty Liutprand signed with Pope Zachary, who nonetheless promoted ties with the Carolingians.

Liutprand's successor, Aistulf, was the most aggressive and bloodthirsty of the Lombard kings. According to one contemporary source, Aistulf was a "shameless Lombard king" who possessed "pernicious savagery" and cruelty (Davis 1992, 55). In keeping with Lombard tradition, he sought to unify the peninsula under his authority, and therefore posed a great threat to papal territories in central Italy. He seized Ravenna, the imperial stronghold in Italy, from the Byzantines and ended the imperial presence there. The victory over the empire, however, forced the popes to find a new protector and brought about the beginning of the end of the Lombard kingdom. Pippin the Short, recently crowned king of the Franks, agreed to come to the aid of the pope and invaded Italy twice in the 750s to restrain Aistulf. Although Aistulf signed treaties guaranteeing the safety of the pope and his lands, the Lombard king nonetheless frequently broke them. He surely would have violated his last agreement with Pippin had Aistulf not died in a hunting accident in 756.

Aistulf was succeeded by Desiderius, the final Lombard king of Italy. His reign began well and was supported by the pope himself. Moreover, Desiderius enjoyed good relations with the Carolingians, who formed an alliance with the Lombard king against the duke of Bavaria. Benefiting from the unrest in the Frankish kingdom at the death of Pippin, Desiderius forged a marriage alliance with the Carolingians, joining his daughter to Charlemagne. But the marriage was repudiated by the great king shortly after, and the growing threat posed by Desiderius to the papacy led Pope Hadrian I to seek aid from Charlemagne, who invaded Italy in 773 and by the next year had conquered the kingdom. Charlemagne assumed the iron crown of the Lombard kingdom and incorporated Lombard Italy into his growing empire. Although the Lombard kingdom came to an end in 774, its memory is preserved in the region of Italy that still bears the name Lombardy.

See also: Aistulf; Alboin; Arianism; Avars; Carolingian Dynasty; Charlemagne; Charles Martel; Desiderius; Franks; Gothic Wars; Gregory I, the Great, Pope; Gregory III, Pope; Hadrian I, Pope; Justinian; Liutprand; Merovingian Dynasty; Narses; Ostrogoths; Paul the Deacon; Pavia; Pippin III, Called the Short; Ravenna; Rome; Rothari; Theodoric the Great; Theudelinda; Zachary, St.

Bibliography

Christie, Neil. *The Lombards: The Ancient Langobards.* Oxford: Blackwell, 1998.

Davis, Raymond, trans. *The Lives of the Eighth-Century Popes* (Liber Pontificalis): *The Ancient Biographies of Nine Popes from* A.D. *715 to* A.D. *817.* Liverpool, UK: Liverpool University Press, 1992.

Drew, Katherine Fisher, trans. *The Lombard Laws.* Philadelphia: University of Pennsylvania Press, 1973.

Goffart, Walter. *Barbarians and Romans, A.D. 418–584: The Techniques of Accommodation.* Princeton: Princeton University Press, 1980.

Hallenback, Jan T. *Pavia and Rome: The Lombard Monarchy and the Papacy in the Eighth Century.* Philadelphia, PA: American Philosophical Society, 1982.

Herrin, Judith. *The Formation of Christendom.* Princeton, NJ: Princeton University Press, 1987.

Llewellyn, Peter. *Rome in the Dark Ages.* New York: Barnes and Noble, 1996.

Paul the Deacon. *History of the Lombards.* Trans. William Dudley Foulke. Philadelphia: University of Pennsylvania Press, 1974.

Riché, Pierre. *The Carolingians: A Family Who Forged Europe.* Trans. Michael Idomir Allen. Philadelphia: University of Pennsylvania Press, 1993.

Scholz, Bernhard Walter, trans. *Carolingian Chronicles: Royal Frankish Annals and Nithard's History.* Ann Arbor: University of Michigan Press, 1972.

Wallace-Hadrill, J. M. *The Barbarian West, A.D. 400–1000.* New York: Harper and Row, 1962.

Wickham, Chris. *Early Medieval Italy: Central Power and Local Society, 400–1000.* Ann Arbor: University of Michigan Press, 1981.

Wolfram, Herwig. *The Roman Empire and Its Germanic Peoples.* Trans. Thomas J. Dunlap. Berkeley: University of California Press, 1997.

Lothar (795–855)

Carolingian king and emperor, Lothar was the son and successor of Louis the Pious and brother of Charles the Bald and Louis the German. As the oldest son of Louis the Pious, Lothar was recognized early in his father's reign as the heir designate and was associated with his father as emperor in 817. In the 820s he played an important role in Italy as his father's representative and formalized a long-standing relationship between the Carolingian dynasty and the papacy. The remarriage of Louis to Judith and the birth of Charles the Bald complicated the relationship between Lothar and his father. In the 830s Lothar led two revolts against his father, both of which failed, leaving Lothar in disgrace. He ultimately was restored to his father's good graces, but after the death of Louis the Pious the empire was torn apart by civil war. Lothar, although bested by his brothers, came to terms with them and ruled as emperor until his death in 855.

The firstborn son of Louis the Pious and his wife Irmengard (d. 818), Lothar had reached adulthood in 814 when his grandfather Charlemagne died, and Louis assumed the throne. His maturity benefited Louis by making Lothar an important associate in government, but it also plagued Louis, because Lothar became the focus of opposition to the new emperor. In the opening years of his reign, however, Louis was well served by Lothar, who ruled in Bavaria from 814 to 817. In 817, when Louis implemented the *Ordinatio imperii,* his plan of succession for the empire, Lothar was made coemperor and recognized as Louis's successor, while Lothar's brothers, Louis the German and Pippin, were made subkings, subject to the authority of Louis and Lothar. Lothar was given the responsibility of ruling Italy, which led to the revolt of his cousin, Bernard, king of Italy. The revolt was brutally suppressed by Louis, and Lothar assumed his responsibilities in Italy.

In the 820s, Lothar played an important role in Italy and in the relations of the Carolingian Empire and the papacy in Rome. He exercised a number of royal, or imperial, functions in Italy by calling councils and issuing capitularies. Aware that Judith, his father's second wife, was about to give birth, Lothar called on the pope, Paschal I, to crown him emperor in 823. In this way he was able to assert his place in the empire and confirm his title of emperor, because papal coronation was becoming the official means to assume the imperial title. Although this action may have been an effort to counter any efforts by Louis the Pious to limit his authority, Lothar remained an important figure in the family and the state. He had previously stood as godfather to Judith and Louis's first child, Gisele, and now stood as godfather for his new half-brother, later known as Charles the Bald. Indeed, godparentage had become a very significant responsibility in Carolingian society.

Lothar also played an important role in regularizing relations between the papacy and the Carolingian dynasty. In 824, Lothar issued the *Constitutio Romana* (Roman Constitution) on his father's behalf. This constitution was issued after a period of turmoil in the city of Rome and confirmed Carolingian rights in Rome and papal territories. The constitution legislated that the Frankish rulers were to be notified upon the election of a new pope and that the people of Rome were to swear an oath of loyalty to the Carolingian emperor. The Carolingians also enforced loyalty to the pope and promised to protect papal territories in central Italy.

Although he remained an important figure in government, Lothar, along with his brothers Pippin and Louis the German, became increasingly concerned about the place of their newest brother Charles, a concern that eventually led them into rebellion against their father. Their concerns were found to be justified in 827, when their father reorganized the succession plan to include Charles. For many ecclesiastics, the *Ordinatio* of 817 was sacred, and consequently any violation of it was regarded as an act against God. For others in the empire, especially members of the nobility, its sacred character was less of an issue, but nevertheless the restructuring of the succession plan provided an excuse to revolt. And in the late 820s and early 830s, Lothar and his brothers did revolt against their father and Charles. Lothar was motivated by his desire to rule as well as by the encouragement of ambitious

Frankish Emperor from his psalter, ninth century.
(The British Library Board)

members of the nobility. He was also supported by leaders in the church who believed in the sacred nature of government and the *Ordinatio* and often reminded Lothar about these ideas.

Lothar was involved in two rebellions against his father Louis. The first revolt occurred in 830; it was initiated by his brother Pippin who had the most to lose in the new succession plan. Lothar quickly joined the rebellion from Italy, entering it because of his dissatisfaction over his father's promotion of Bernard of Septimania to high rank at the court, a move that threatened Lothar's own position. Lothar quickly took charge of the situation and placed Louis and Charles under house arrest. His efforts at ruling, however, met with little success, and, as the chronicler Nithard noted, "the state of the empire grew worse from day to day, since all were driven by greed and sought only their own advantage" (Scholz 1972, 131). Lothar's position was undermined by Louis, who secretly negotiated with both Pippin and Louis the German. By Easter 831, Louis had been restored to the throne. Lothar was returned to Italy in disgrace, and his supporters were jailed, but he was permitted to remain as king in Italy. Louis also restructured the plan of succession once again and created four equal kingdoms out of the empire for his four sons.

Louis, however, failed to keep his bargain with his sons and faced a revolt again, one that was much more serious than the revolt of 830. In 833 Lothar and Louis and Pippin formed an alliance against their father. The four and their armies met on the so-called Field of Lies, where Louis the Pious's armies abandoned him for Lothar, who took his father into custody. Judith was sent to Italy, Charles was sent off to a monastery, and in October, Lothar forced his father to perform an act of penance and abdicate at a great council. Lothar's rough treatment of his father, however, alienated his brothers, especially Louis, who came to the aid of the older Louis. By February 834 the tide had turned, and Louis the Pious was restored to the throne. The emperor and his allies defeated Lothar's army, and Lothar surrendered and was once again returned to Italy.

Turmoil in the Carolingian Empire, however, continued during Louis's last years and into the early 840s. Lothar remained quietly in Italy for several years while his father secured his position once again. On the death of Pippin, Louis restructured the succession yet again, establishing a large kingdom for his son Charles. Lothar was restored to his father's good graces, largely thanks to the efforts of Judith who desired a good relationship between Charles and Lothar, shortly before the older Louis's death. Lothar and Charles were to share the empire, and, although placed on equal footing with Charles, Lothar inherited the imperial title. His claims to this title, as well as his claims to territory drove his efforts in the following years. Indeed, almost immediately after Louis's death, his sons once again fell into civil war, as in various combinations they struggled to enforce their claims to power and territory. Although he reconciled with his godson Charles, Lothar soon turned against him and was then faced by a hostile alliance from his two brothers. Open warfare took place, which culminated in the bloody Battle of Fontenoy in 841, which was marked by massive losses for all combatants. Although weakened, Lothar struggled on, but his brothers reaffirmed their alliance against him with the famous Oath of Strasbourg in 842, and in 843 Lothar agreed to a division of the empire in the Treaty of Verdun.

From the end of the civil war in 843 until his death in 855, Lothar ruled as emperor over the central portion of the empire, which included the imperial capital of Aix-la-Chapelle (modern Aachen, in Germany) and Italy. Although tensions remained and Lothar was constantly attempting to assert his position in the realm, the brothers did manage to rule peacefully during Lothar's lifetime. They held an important council in 844 that sought to reorganize the church, as well as councils in 847 and 851 that emphasized brotherly rule and the unity of the empire. At the same time, however, Lothar attempted to keep his two brothers apart and sought to forge alliances with one against the other. He found little success in that until his reconciliation with Charles in 849, which was commemorated by the commissioning of a new illuminated Gospel from Tours and a magnificent gem, the Lothar Crystal, which told the story of Susannah and the Elders. On September 22, 855, Lothar retired to a monastery, where he died six days later. He was succeeded in the northern section of his territory by his son Lothar II (d. 869), and in Italy by his son Louis (d. 875), who assumed the title of emperor. Although he successfully maintained his position in the empire during his life, Lothar's middle kingdom, especially the inheritance of Lothar II, remained a source of contention for many years to come.

See also: Aix-la-Chapelle; Capitularies; Carolingian Dynasty; Charlemagne; Charles the Bald; Fontenoy, Battle of; Franks; Judith; Louis the German; Louis the Pious; Nithard; Rome; Strasbourg, Oath of; Verdun, Treaty of

Bibliography

Godman, Peter, and Roger Collins, eds. *Charlemagne's Heir: New Perspectives on the Reign of Louis the Pious.* Oxford: Clarendon, 1990.

Llewellyn, Peter. *Rome in the Dark Ages.* New York: Barnes and Noble, 1993.

McKitterick, Rosamond. *The Frankish Kingdoms under the Carolingians, 751–987.* London: Longman, 1983.

Nelson, Janet. *Charles the Bald.* London: Longman, 1992.

Reuter, Timothy. *Germany in the Early Middle Ages, c. 800–1056.* London: Longman, 1991.

Riché, Pierre. *The Carolingians: A Family Who Forged Europe.* Trans. Michael Idomir Allen. Philadelphia: University of Pennsylvania Press, 1993.

Scholz, Bernhard Walter, trans. *Carolingian Chronicles: Royal Frankish Annals and Nithard's History.* Ann Arbor: University of Michigan Press, 1972.

Louis the German (d. 876)

Third son of Louis the Pious, who inherited the eastern portion of the Carolingian Empire on his father's death. A participant in the civil wars against his father, Louis the German also supported his father at key moments when his older brother, Lothar, seemed too harsh in his treatment of the elder Louis. After his father's death, Louis the German was involved in fratricidal warfare with Lothar and Charles the Bald that led to the fragmentation of the empire of Charlemagne. Although there was at least nominal cooperation between the brothers and nominal recognition of the imperial authority, the empire was essentially divided into three separate kingdoms ruled by Louis and his brothers. The kingdoms created by the sons of Louis the Pious established the outlines of later medieval and even modern France and Germany, and Louis the German himself set important precedents for later rulers of medieval Germany.

Born probably in Aquitaine circa 804, Louis was raised to prominence in Louis the Pious's reorganization of the empire in 817. In that division of the realm, which made Lothar coemperor and heir to the imperial throne, Louis was made king of Bavaria, the base of power for Louis that lasted throughout his entire life. In the 820s Louis served his father in his assigned region of Bavaria, but in the 830s, perhaps in response to his father's efforts to create a region in the kingdom for Charles the Bald, the son of his second wife, Louis took part in two rebellions against Louis the Pious. Indeed, Louis the German, with his brother Pippin, initiated the revolt of 830, intending to "liberate" his father from the pernicious influence of his stepmother Judith and his father's close advisor Bernard of Septimania. After the initial success of the revolt, Lothar took control of it and alienated his younger brothers. Louis the Pious, under house arrest, secretly sent messengers to Louis and Pippin, encouraging their support in exchange for greater territories in the empire. The younger Louis readily accepted, and his support for his father was essential to the collapse of the rebellion of 830.

The empire continued to face turmoil over the next several years, and once again Louis the German took an active role in revolt against his father. In 833, Louis and his brothers Lothar and Pippin revolted against the elder Louis, deposing him and placing him, Judith, and Charles the Bald in monasteries. Lothar's bad treatment of his father, however, and his efforts to gain greater control of the empire angered Louis. As he had in 830, Louis the German played a key role in restoring his father to the imperial throne. His efforts were rewarded in 839 when, after the death of Pippin, Louis the Pious sought to restrict his son Louis to Bavaria and favored both Charles the Bald and the rehabilitated Lothar. The younger Louis quite naturally struggled to maintain his authority in the eastern part of the Carolingian Empire.

On the death of Louis the Pious in 840, the difficult situation in the empire exploded into open civil war between his three surviving sons. Lothar sought to gain control of the entire empire, and his ambition drove his younger brothers Louis and Charles into an alliance against him. The two brothers formed an alliance in the spring of 841 and fought a terrible, bloody battle against Lothar at Fontenoy on June 25, 841. Louis and Charles triumphed over Lothar and remained firm in their alliance, despite Lothar's efforts to divide them. In the following year, Louis and Charles confirmed their alliance in the famed Oath of Strasbourg, which was sworn and recorded in early forms of the Romance and German languages. Lothar was gradually worn down by his younger brothers and came to terms with them in 843 with the Treaty of Verdun, which assigned Lothar the imperial title and central kingdom of the empire. Charles was assigned the western kingdom, and Louis received the eastern kingdom, including territories that extended east of the Rhine River and north of the Alps.

Although the three brothers had come to terms and continued to meet and to appear on the surface to cooperate with each other, none of the three were content with the settlement, and each conspired to enlarge his share at his brothers' expense. As king of East Francia, Louis was the sole binding force in a newly created territory and sought to solidify his authority throughout his kingdom, in part by establishing or favoring monasteries—a policy used effectively by his successors in the 10th century. As ever, Bavaria remained his power base and the starting point for his expansionist tendencies to the east and west. His efforts to expand his eastern frontier met with little success, but he did send forth missionaries in an effort to extend both religious and political authority. He also made several attempts to seize West Francia from his half brother and former ally, Charles the Bald. In 853 a group of west Frankish nobles sought his aid, and in 854 he sent his son to Aquitaine. In 858, Louis himself invaded his half brother's kingdom, but on neither occasion was he able to unseat his brother, in part because Charles the Bald received the full support of the bishops of his realm.

Louis also cast covetous eyes on the kingdom of his older brother Lothar, or least that of Lothar's heirs. When Lothar died in 855, his kingdom was divided among his sons, with his son Louis inheriting the imperial crown. The other son, Lothar, inherited much of the northern part of his father's kingdom, Lotharingia, but died without heir. Louis the German and Charles each sought to acquire the territory. Louis invaded in 870, and he and his brother came to terms in the treaty of Meerssen in that year. They divided the realm of Lotharingia between themselves, with both brothers gaining important territory and Louis obtaining the capital, Aachen. Louis also attempted to seize the imperial title after the death of his nephew Louis in 875, but was outmaneuvered by Charles the Bald, who was crowned emperor.

Along with his struggles against his brothers, Louis the German faced challenges to his power from his sons, Carloman (d. 880) and Louis the Younger (d. 882), but not Charles the Fat (d. 888). As early as 856 he faced rebellion from his son Carloman, who built up his power in Bavaria at his father's expense. In 860 Louis sought to curtail his son's advances, and in 863 an open power struggle developed between the two. By 865 the two had been reconciled, but Carloman's brother, Louis the Younger, suspicious of his older brother, revolted. The revolt was brought to a close by 866, thanks in part to the efforts of Charles the Bald to reconcile his brother and his nephew. Although Louis the Younger quarreled with his father on occasion after 866 and continued to be mistrustful of his brother, Louis the German never faced the kinds of revolt that his brother Lothar or his father Louis the Pious had faced. In part, this was due to his ability to reconcile with his sons after disputes broke out. It was also due to his willingness, perhaps as a result of his awareness of potential problems from his sons, to bestow power on his sons. In the late 850s and early 860s, Louis granted land and authority to his sons—they were given power to rule that was less than that of a king but more than that of a noble. They were granted important territorial regions, and in that way they were the precursors of the territorial dukes of the later Middle Ages.

At his death, Louis's three sons divided the realm among themselves. One of them, Charles the Fat, went on to assume the imperial title that his father had at times pursued, only to lose it when deposed in 887.

Louis the German's reign was marked by relative stability in his own kingdom and efforts, not always successful, to expand his western and eastern frontiers. In a good Carolingian fashion, he promoted missionary activity among the pagan folk on his eastern frontier. His efforts to convert the pagan and expand his border prefigured the activities of 10th-century rulers, and his arrangement with his sons also foreshadowed later medieval developments. Although in many ways a traditional Carolingian ruler, Louis laid the foundation for developments in later medieval Germany.

See also: Carolingian Dynasty; Charlemagne; Charles the Bald; Charles III, the Fat; Fontenoy, Battle of; Franks; Judith; Lothar; Louis the Pious; Nithard; Strasbourg, Oath of; Verdun, Treaty of

Bibliography

Fichtenau, Heinrich. *The Carolingian Empire.* Trans. Peter Munz. Toronto: University of Toronto Press, 1979.

Ganshof, François L. *The Carolingians and the Frankish Monarchy: Studies in Carolingian History.* Trans. Janet L. Sondheimer. London: Longman, 1971.

Halphen, Louis. *Charlemagne and the Carolingian Empire.* Trans. Giselle de Nie. Amsterdam: North-Holland, 1977.

McKitterick, Rosamond. *The Frankish Kingdoms under the Carolingians, 751–987.* London: Longman, 1983.

Nelson, Janet. *Charles the Bald.* London: Longman, 1992.

Reuter, Timothy. *Germany in the Early Middle Ages, c. 800–1056.* London: Longman, 1991.

Riché, Pierre. *The Carolingians: A Family Who Forged Europe.* Trans. Michael Idomir Allen. Philadelphia: University of Pennsylvania Press, 1993.

Scholz, Bernhard Walter, trans. *Carolingian Chronicles: Royal Frankish Annals and Nithard's History.* Ann Arbor: University of Michigan Press, 1972.

Louis the Pious (778–840)

The only surviving son and heir of the great Carolingian king, Charlemagne, Louis the Pious ruled the empire from 814 until his death in 840. As emperor he introduced important reforms of the structure and organization of the empire and continued the religious and cultural reforms associated with the Carolingian Renaissance. Traditionally accused of causing the collapse of the Carolingian Empire because of his excessive devotion to the church and his domination by his wife and other advisors, Louis is no longer blamed for the empire's collapse. Instead his reign and his understanding of his office are seen in a more positive light, especially the first decade, when he instituted a number of far-reaching political and religious reforms.

Although the empire did not fall because of Louis but because of fundamental flaws in its structure that had already emerged in Charlemagne's last years, its fortunes did suffer during Louis's reign because of the revolts his sons waged against him.

Louis's youth was marked by his early introduction to power. In 781, when not quite three years old, Louis was crowned and anointed king of Aquitaine by Pope Hadrian I. This crowning has traditionally been seen as Charlemagne's concession to demands for independence in Aquitaine, a territory incorporated into the empire by Pippin the Short, but more likely he intended it as an effective means to govern the province and provide practical experience for Louis. Aquitaine did provide important lessons for Louis, who faced revolts from native Gascons and repeated raids from Muslim Spain. Louis effectively responded to both these threats during his reign as king and even undertook counteroffensives into Spain. Although he frequently communicated with his father, Louis ruled Aquitaine on his own and was never visited by Charlemagne in the subkingdom. He also participated in military campaigns outside Aquitaine, including campaigns in Italy and Saxony. Moreover, while king of Aquitaine, Louis had a number of experiences that shaped his later life. In 794, Louis married Irmengard, the daughter of a powerful noble, who bore him three sons and two daughters. He also initiated a program of church reform with Benedict of Aniane. Finally, Louis's future was shaped by his father's ordering of the succession. In 806, Charlemagne implemented a plan of succession that divided the realm among his sons, a long-standing Frankish tradition, in which Louis would continue to be king of Aquitaine. On September 11, 813, after his other brothers had died, Louis was crowned emperor by his father at a great assembly in Aix-la-Chapelle.

In 814, following his father's death, Louis succeeded to the throne as the sole emperor of the Frankish realm and brought a more profound understanding of the office of Christian king or emperor than his father had had. Like his father, Louis was filled with the sense of Christian mission that his position entailed, perhaps best demonstrated by his expulsion of prostitutes and actors from the imperial court and his dismissal of his sisters, none of whom had been allowed by his father to marry, to religious communities. Unlike his father, however, Louis understood his position strictly in imperial terms, an understanding reflected in his official title: "Louis, by Order of Divine Providence, Emperor and Augustus." Unlike his father who made reference to his royal dignities in his official imperial title, Louis dispensed with royal dignities in his official title from the beginning of his reign and provided a solid foundation for the empire in 817. In that year, following a serious accident while crossing a bridge in which several were injured, Louis held a council at Aachen. At the council, Louis established a new framework for the Frankish empire, whose territorial integrity would remain inviolate. In the *Ordinatio imperii,* Louis instituted a plan that would have allowed the empire to continue as a political and spiritual unit forever. His eldest son, Lothar, was associated with Louis and would ultimately succeed him as emperor over the entire Frankish realm. Louis's younger sons, Louis the German and Pippin of Aquitaine, would receive subking-doms—a concession to Frankish tradition—but would be subject to their father and then their brother. This bold new design was rooted in Louis's firm convictions that God had bestowed upon him the burden of government and that the empire itself was a divinely ordained unit.

Equally important steps were taken by Louis to reorganize and strengthen rela-tions with the pope in Rome. In 816 he was crowned by Pope Stephen IV in the city of Rheims, a coronation that has traditionally been seen as a concession to papal authority and an abdication of sovereignty. Louis, in fact, gave nothing up by accepting coronation from Stephen, but merely solidified relations between the pope and emperor and confirmed what was implicit in the coronation of 813. Furthermore, because the pope was the highest spiritual power and the represen-tative of Peter, the great patron saint of the Carolingians, it was only logical that Louis should receive papal blessing. But more important than the coronation was the new constitutional and legal settlement that Louis imposed on Rome in two stages, in 816/817 and 824. Starting with the unwritten rules that had guided re-lations between the Carolingians and the pope for the previous two generations, Louis issued the *Pactum Ludovicianum* in 816 and confirmed it the following year with the new pope, Paschal I. This document identified the territories under papal control and precisely defined the relationship between Rome and the Frankish rulers. Although recognizing papal autonomy, the pact proclaimed the duty of Carolingian rulers to protect Rome. This agreement provided a written basis for the relationship between the pope and the Carolingian emperors and regularized the relationship between them by incorporating it into traditional Carolingian gov-ernmental structures.

An even greater step in the development of the relationship between Louis and Rome occurred with the publication of the *Constitutio Romana* in 824. In 823, following a period of turmoil in Rome involving the pope and high-ranking of-ficials of the city's administration, Lothar, acting as his father's representative, issued the *Constitutio,* which confirmed the long-standing relationship between the Carolingian rulers and the popes. The *Constitutio* was intended to protect the pope and people of Rome and to provide a clear written framework for the place of Rome in the empire. The *Constitutio* stated the obligation of the pope to swear on oath of friendship to the emperor after his election as pope but before his consecration. The people living in the papal territories were also to swear an oath of loyalty to the emperor. The Carolingians claimed the right to establish courts in Rome to hear appeals against papal administrators. The *Constitutio* summarized, in writing, the customary rights and obligations of three genera-tions of Frankish rulers, providing a more solid foundation for the exercise of Carolingian power in Italy.

Louis also instituted important reforms of the church in his empire during his reign as emperor, building upon reforms that were begun while he was still king of Aquitaine. With his close friend and advisor, Benedict of Aniane, Louis implemented monastic reforms that attempted to standardize monastic life in the empire. The reforms were intended to establish a uniform monastic practice in an empire in which a variety of monastic rules were followed. The reforms, implemented in 816–817, introduced the Rule of Benedict of Nursia, or at least Benedict of Aniane's understanding of it, as the standard rule of the empire. Louis's reform legislation also sought to improve further the morality and education of the clergy.

Louis's political and religious reforms were not uniformly popular in the empire, and in 817 a revolt broke out that affected the shape of the emperor's reign. His nephew, Bernard, king of Italy, with the support of bishops and nobles, revolted against the settlement of 817. Louis quickly, and ruthlessly, suppressed the revolt. Bernard was sentenced to death. His sentence was commuted to blinding—a particularly unpleasant punishment that led to Bernard's death soon after it occurred. The nobles were exiled, and the bishops, including Theodulf of Orléans, were deposed from their sees. Four years after the revolt, in 821, Louis issued a general amnesty, recalling and restoring the exiles and bishops. As part of this reconciliation, Louis underwent voluntary penance for the death of Bernard. Although the act, undertaken from a position of strength, was regarded as meritorious at the time, it set a bad precedent for later in Louis's reign.

Louis clearly made substantial improvements on the organization of the empire and on Carolingian relations with Rome in the first half of his reign, but in the second half he suffered from the revolts of his sons and the near collapse of the empire. The difficulties Louis faced were the result, in part, of his second marriage to Judith, a member of the Welf family, which had extensive holdings in Bavaria and other parts of Germany. The birth of a son on June 13, 823, the future Charles the Bald, and the promotion of Bernard of Septimania further complicated matters for Louis. He also suffered from the death of his closest advisor, Benedict of Aniane, in 821. These problems were made more serious by the ambitions of Louis's older sons, especially Lothar, as well as those of the nobility, who could no longer count on the spoils of foreign wars of conquest to enrich themselves or their reputations. In fact, the end of Carolingian expansion, with the exception of missionary activity among the Danes and other peoples along the eastern frontier, limited the beneficence of the Carolingian rulers and allowed the warrior aristocracy to exploit the tensions within the ruling family for their own gain.

The situation came to a head in the late 820s and early 830s and led to almost 10 years of civil strife throughout the empire. A revolt broke out in 830 after Louis had promoted Bernard of Septimania to the office of chamberlain and granted territory to Charles in the previous year. With the support of various noble factions, the older sons of Louis rebelled against their father in April and accused Bernard and Judith of adultery, sorcery, and conspiracy against the emperor. Lothar, although not originally involved, joined the rebellion from Italy and quickly asserted his authority over his younger brothers. Lothar took his father and half-brother into custody, deposed Bernard, who fled, and sent Judith to a convent. But his own greed disturbed his brothers, who were secretly reconciled with their father. At a council in October, Louis rallied his supporters and took control of the kingdom back from Lothar. Judith took an oath that she was innocent. Louis reorganized the empire, dividing it into three kingdoms and Italy, which Lothar ruled. The sons of Louis would rule independently after their father's death, and no mention of empire was made in this settlement.

Although Louis was restored, the situation was not resolved in 830, and problems remained that caused a more serious revolt in 833–834. Along with the question of how to provide for Charles, the problem of the ambitions of Lothar and his brothers remained, as did that of an acquisitive nobility. Furthermore, certain leading ecclesiastics, including Agobard of Lyons and Ebbo of Rheims, argued that Louis had violated God's will by overturning the settlement of 817 when he restructured the plan of succession in 830. The older sons formed a conspiracy against their father that led to a general revolt in 833. Meeting his sons and Pope Gregory IV (r. 827–844) at the so-called Field of Lies, Louis was betrayed and abandoned by his army and captured by his sons. Once again, the emperor was subjected to humiliating treatment at the hands of Lothar. Judith was sent to Rome with the pope, and both Charles and Louis were sent to monasteries. In October Lothar held a council of nobles and bishops at which Louis was declared a tyrant, and then Lothar visited his father in the monastery of St. Médard in Soissons and compelled Louis to "voluntarily" confess to a wide variety of crimes, including murder and sacrilege, to renounce his imperial title, and to accept perpetual penance. Lothar's actions, however, alienated his brothers Louis and Pippin, who rallied to their father's side. In early 834 Louis the German and Pippin revolted against their brother and were joined by their father, who had regained his freedom. Lothar was forced to submit and returned in disgrace to Italy. In 835 Louis made a triumphant return. He was once again crowned emperor, by his half-brother Bishop Drogo of Metz, and he restored Judith and Charles to their rightful places by his side. The bishops who had joined the revolt against Louis were deposed from their offices by Louis at this time.

Louis remained in power until his death, but his remaining years were not peaceful ones; familial tensions remained. It was important to Louis, and especially to Judith, that Charles be included in the succession, but Louis recognized at the same time that it was necessary not to alienate his other sons too completely in the process. And, of course, Lothar's ambitions remained even though he remained out of favor for several years after 834. Louis faced further revolts from Louis the German

Emperor Louis the Pious in the dress of a Christian Roman Roman ruler from *De laudibus sanctae crucis* by Hrabanus Mauris. (The British Library Board)

as well as the son of Pippin; after Pippin died in 838, his portion of the realm was bestowed on Charles rather than Pippin's own heirs. One of Louis's last important acts was his reconciliation with Lothar, who pledged his support for Charles and was rewarded with the imperial title. Louis also divided most of the empire between Lothar and Charles, an act that almost certainly guaranteed further civil war after Louis's death on June 20, 840.

Despite the very real breakup of the empire in the generation after his death, Louis should not be blamed for the collapse of the Carolingian Empire, which had revealed its flaws already in the last years of Charlemagne's life. Louis's reign, particularly the first part before 830, was a period of growth for the empire, or at least the idea of empire. In fact, his elevation of the idea of empire as the ultimate political entity and his own understanding that the empire was established by God was a significant advancement in political thought and remained an important political idea for his own line and for the line of his successors. His codification of Carolingian relations with Rome was equally important, creating a written document that strengthened and defined imperial-papal ties for the ninth and tenth centuries. Although he faced difficulties in the last decade of his life that prefigured the breakup of the empire in the next generation, Louis was a farsighted ruler, whose reign provided many important and lasting contributions to early medieval government and society.

See also: Aix-la-Chapelle; Astronomer; Benedict of Aniane; Carolingian Dynasty; Carolingian Renaissance; Charlemagne; Charles the Bald; Louis the German; *Ordinatio Imperii*; Pippin III, Called Pippin the Short; Rome

Bibliography

Cabaniss, Allen, trans. *Son of Charlemagne: A Contemporary Life of Louis the Pious.* Syracuse, NY: Syracuse University Press, 1961.

Ganshof, François Louis. *The Carolingians and the Frankish Monarchy.* Trans. Janet Sondheimer. London: Longman, 1971.

Godman, Peter, and Roger Collins, eds. *Charlemagne's Heir: New Perspectives on the Reign of Louis the Pious.* Oxford: Clarendon, 1990.

Halphen, Louis. *Charlemagne and the Carolingian Empire.* Trans. Giselle de Nie. Amsterdam: North-Holland, 1977.

McKitterick, Rosamond. *The Frankish Kingdoms under the Carolingians, 751–987.* London: Longman, 1983.

Noble, Thomas X. F. *The Republic of St. Peter: The Birth of the Papal State, 680–825.* Philadelphia: University of Pennsylvania Press, 1984.

Scholz, Bernhard Walter, trans. *Carolingian Chronicles: Royal Frankish Annals and Nithard's History.* Ann Arbor: University of Michigan Press, 1972.

Louis the Stammerer (846–879)

The son and successor of the Carolingian king Charles the Bald, Louis had a short and undistinguished reign that followed a lifetime of disappointing his father. Born in 846, Louis would find himself frequently involved in his father's struggles to secure personal control over his West Frankish kingdom and maintain the continuity of the dynasty. Louis, however, often joined with his father's rivals in the 860s. In 862, Louis married his concubine, Ansgard, without his father's approval or even knowledge. Despite this tension, Charles made his son king of Aquitaine in 867 and made him lay abbot of several monasteries.

In 877, as Charles prepared to depart for Rome, the king issued the capitulary of Quierzy, which made Louis the regent but one to be advised by a special group of advisors. Charles also ordered his son to join him in Rome to receive imperial coronation. Louis faced the threat of rebellion following his father's death in October, 877, but the efforts of the archbishop Hincmar of Rheims secured Louis's succession and Hincmar crowned Louis king at Compiègne on December 8, 877. Louis's coronation as king was repeated by Pope John VIII the following year in preparation for eventual imperial coronation and to strengthen the ties between the pope and the West Frankish ruler. In 878, Louis repudiated his first wife and married Adelaide, who would bear the future Charles III, the Simple in 879 after the death of Louis on April 10.

See also: Carolingian Dynasty; Charles the Bald; Hincmar of Rheims

Bibliography

Nelson, Janet. *Charles the Bald*. London: Longman, 1992.

Riché, Pierre. *The Carolingians: A Family Who Forged Europe*. Trans. Michael Idomir Allen. Philadelphia: University of Pennsylvania Press, 1993.

M

Marriage

One of the most important and central institutions in any society, marriage was a custom that underwent profound and lasting change during late antiquity and the early Middle Ages. Traditions common among the Germanic peoples, including polygyny and concubinage, were gradually worn away by the influence of Roman civilization, and especially Christianity. Certain Germanic customs continued, but the institution of marriage came to be defined as an indissoluble union between two people. Although women lost a degree of social mobility as a consequence of the new practice of marriage, they gained greater security and a more important role in the family.

Perhaps the earliest account of the marriage practices of the Germanic peoples is to be found in the *Germania* of the great first-century Roman historian, Tacitus. He explains that the German peoples possess a very strict marriage code that is most worthy of praise. The barbarians, as he calls them, each take only one wife, with the exception of those whose status brings them many offers of marriage. The dowry, he says, is brought to the wife from the husband and not, as it in Rome, to the husband from the wife. The gifts presented are quite revealing of the attitudes of the barbarians, according to Tacitus. The dowry generally consists of oxen, a horse and bridle, or a shield, spear, and sword. The bride bestows gifts of arms on her husband, thus establishing a bond between the two in which they willingly share hardships and good times. The new bride joins her husband's household and shares in all its labors.

Tacitus explains that the marriage is a permanent bond, and that secret love letters are unknown. Adultery, he says, is seldom practiced and severely punished. And women generally remain committed to one man; Tacitus does not mention the fidelity of men, making it likely that men were less faithful than women. Tacitus's view of Germanic marriage, however, must be accepted only with extreme caution; he was, after all, as much a moralist as a historian. For Tacitus, the Germanic people were noble savages, whose moral and ethical behavior stood in stark contrast to the immorality of the Romans of the first century. His moralistic agenda notwithstanding, Tacitus's depiction of marriage among the Germanic tribes on Rome's frontiers offers at least a glimpse into early Germanic marital customs.

It is generally held that the early Germans recognized two forms of legitimate marriage, one that involved parental participation and one that did not. The latter form has been traditionally known as *Friedelehe,* a practice in which a free woman entered a relationship with a free man. (Marriage between slaves was not recognized as legitimate and marriage between the free and unfree was strictly forbidden in law.) Although the romantic nature of this form of marriage has been rightly questioned, it most likely existed as a form of quasi-marriage, in which the rights and economic security of the woman involved were relatively unprotected. Of course, this marriage custom was not approved, and the man involved could be forced to pay heavy fines if the bride's family pressed charges. Another form of marriage that occurred without parental involvement was *Raubehe,* marriage by abduction. The most famous example of this type of marriage was the kidnapping of the Thuringian princess, Radegund, whose hand in marriage was fought over by the sons of the great Frankish king Clovis (r. 481–511). The legal codes of the various Germanic peoples, however, came to punish this practice severely—at least when it took place within the individual kingdoms.

Although there were exceptions, the most common type of marriage was a formal arrangement between a suitor and the prospective bride's parents. Marriages were contracted when the couple involved reached the *legitima aetas* (legitimate age) or *perfecta aetas* (perfect age). This age varied among the various Germanic peoples: 20 for the Burgundians, 12 or 15 for the Franks, and 25 for the Visigoths. First marriages are believed to have taken place generally when couples were in their mid-teens, although some scholars suggest that first marriages took place when the couples involved were in their mid-twenties.

The arrangement of the marriage of a daughter involved three specific steps: the *petitio* (formal marriage proposal), the *desponsatio* (betrothal), and the *nuptiae* (wedding ceremony). The suitor offered a formal pledge, the *arrha,* which could include payment to the parents. If the pledge was accepted, then the suitor and the woman's parents entered a legally binding contract, followed by the exchange of rings before witnesses. Penalties for breaking the contract were quite severe for the woman and her family but less severe for the man. Betrothed women could be executed if they married someone else, and parents could be fined heavily. Penalties for the groom were modest; at worst they involved payment of the dowry. Following the betrothal, the bride was delivered to her spouse's household, which symbolized the transfer of legal authority from the father to the husband.

Marriages were also important economic transactions, especially for the woman. The bride was entitled to two significant monetary grants from her new husband, which were granted to guarantee her financial security now that she was released from her father's legal custody. The bride, as Tacitus notes, received the *dos* (dowry, bridegift). The dowry could be quite substantial, particularly among the elite of Germanic society. Visigothic law set the maximum dowry at one-tenth of the husband's property, but it could include up to 20 slaves and 20 horses. Among the

Franks and Lombards the dowry was even larger: one-third of the husband's property among the Franks and one-quarter of the property among the Lombards. The bride was also entitled to the *morgengabe* (morning gift). This gift was customarily given by the husband to his wife following the consummation of the marriage and was generally less substantial than the dowry. Although it could be as extravagant as the five cities Chilperic gave to Galswintha, the *morgengabe* was usually more modest in value and involved money, jewelry, and clothing. The bride, however, did not come empty-handed to the marriage but contributed her trousseau, which included personal items (dresses, bracelets, earrings, and other jewelry) and household items (linens, a bed, benches, and stools). The bride's contribution to the marriage could be quite substantial, as was that of Rigunth, a Frankish princess, whose trousseau amounted to 50 wagonloads of goods. And Galswintha's was so great that Chilperic murdered her rather than divorce her and return it.

The institution of marriage from the fifth to eighth centuries was relatively unstable and marked by ease of divorce, polygyny, and concubinage among the German peoples who took over the Roman Empire. Divorce was a fairly simple affair, at least for the man. A wife could be repudiated for a variety of things, including adultery, inability to bear children, and "bad" behavior. She could also be divorced for no reason, provided the husband was willing to give up control of her property. The woman had to endure the worst behavior; she could not even divorce her husband for adultery. Moreover, as Tacitus notes, the wealthier Germans practiced polygyny, and this practice became increasingly popular among the Germanic peoples who took over the Western Roman Empire. Although not practiced by all Germanic peoples in the post-Roman world, polygyny was quite common among the Franks. Ingunde, the wife of Chlotar I, asked her husband to find a husband for her sister and, liking his sister-in-law so well, Chlotar married her himself. And he may have married others as well while still married to Ingunde. Chilperic was expected to renounce Fredegund and his other wives to marry Galswintha, and Dagobert I had many wives and concubines. There is evidence that even the early Carolingians practiced polygyny before they implemented the rule of monogamy. Along with multiple wives, Frankish rulers possessed concubines, and they were emulated in this practice by members of the nobility.

The instability of marriage among the Germanic peoples, especially the Franks, was particularly disadvantageous to women. Women were particularly vulnerable to divorce and had an insecure position in the marriage. But the instability of marriage did offer some women the opportunity of social advancement, particularly lower class or slave women like Fredegund. Women did have rights to the property they brought into the marriage, and a wife could keep this property if she were divorced through no fault of her own. Unlike their ancient Roman counterparts, Germanic women had greater economic and legal independence from their husbands, and like Roman women they were released from paternal authority when they married.

Marriage customs, however, underwent dramatic change during the eighth and ninth centuries as a result of reforms implemented by the Carolingian dynasty. The church had long struggled to limit multiple marriages, concubinage, and divorce among the Franks and other Germans, with only marginal success. Beginning with Pippin and, with greater force, his son Charlemagne, Frankish law came to conform to church law. The Carolingians instituted a reform of marriage laws and custom that established marriage as an indissoluble bond between two people. The Carolingian rulers continued the practice of concubinage, but they practiced serial marriage instead of multiple marriage. Charlemagne himself had several concubines and a series of wives, but he remained with each until her death. His personal example of monogamous marriage was translated into law. In his *Admonitio Generalis* he forbade remarriage after divorce, and in a law passed in 796 eliminated adultery as a reason for divorce. A man could separate from an adulterous spouse according to this law, but he could not remarry while his wife lived. Although Carolingian legislation limited the social mobility open to some women, it made marriage a more stable and secure institution and strengthened the role of the woman in the family.

See also: Admonitio Generalis; Carolingian Dynasty; Charlemagne; Chilperic I; Clovis; Dagobert; Fredegund; Galswintha; Merovingian Dynasty; Radegund

Bibliography

Gies, Frances, and Joseph Gies. *Marriage and Family in the Middle Ages.* 2nd. ed. New York: Harper and Row, 1987.

Herlihy, David. *Medieval Households.* Cambridge, MA: Harvard University Press, 1985.

Reynolds, Philip L. *Marriage in the Western Church: The Christianization of Marriage.* Leiden: Brill, 1994.

Tacitus. *The Agricola and the Germania.* Trans. H. Mattingly. Trans. Rev. S.A. Handford. Harmondsworth, UK: Penguin, 1970.

Wemple, Suzanne. *Women in Frankish Society: Marriage and the Cloister, 500–900.* Philadelphia: University of Pennsylvania Press, 1985.

Martin of Tours, St. (c. 316–397/400)

A former Roman soldier and convert to Christianity, St. Martin was an important figure in the history of Christianity in Gaul in the fourth century. He was an active preacher, miracle worker, bishop of Tours, and founder of monasticism in Gaul. His tomb became a popular pilgrimage site, famed for its miracles, and his relics, especially the cloak of St. Martin, were highly venerated. The Merovingian and Carolingian kings were devoted to Martin, and the bishops of Tours, most notably

Gregory of Tours, actively promoted his cult. *The Life of St. Martin,* written by Sulpicius Severus, also helped promote the cult of the saint and is a model of early medieval Christian hagiography.

The son of a Roman soldier, Martin was born in Sabaria in Pannonia (modern Szombathely, Hungary) at about 316 and later joined the Roman military. While serving as a soldier, Martin encountered a naked beggar near Amiens on a cold winter's day. Martin took off his cloak, cut it in half, and gave part to the beggar. That night, Jesus, wearing the cloak, appeared in Martin's dream and praised him for taking care of the poor. Martin then accepted baptism as a Christian while remaining in the Roman army for another two years before deciding that as a Christian he could not fight. After his release from the army, Martin went to Tours, where he became a disciple of Hilary of Poitiers and preached against Arianism. He then went to Italy and entered into opposition to Arians there before undertaking the life of a hermit.

In 360 he returned to Gaul with Hilary, who had been exiled by the Arian emperor, and founded Marmoutier, the first monastery in Gaul. In 372, Martin was consecrated bishop of Tours, a position he accepted reluctantly and continued to live the life of an ascetic. As bishop he continued the fight against heresy and preached Catholic orthodoxy. He destroyed pagan temples, built new churches, and performed miraculous cures and two resurrections from the dead. He died in 397 (possibly 400), and his relics were finally entombed in Tours and became the center of an important pilgrimage and cult site.

See also: Arianism; Monasticism; Tours

Bibliography

Donaldson, Christopher William. *Martin of Tours: Parish Priest, Mystic, and Exorcist.* New York: Routledge and Kegan Paul, 1980.

Gregory of Tours. *The History of the Franks.* Trans. Lewis Thorpe. Harmondsworth, UK: Penguin, 1974.

Sulpicius Severus. "Life of Saint Martin of Tours." In *Soldiers of Christ: Saints and Saints' Lives from Late Antiquity and the Early Middle Ages.* Ed. Thomas F. X. Noble and Thomas Head. University Park, PA: Pennsylvania State University Press, 1995, pp. 1–29.

Mercia

An Anglo-Saxon kingdom of the English Midlands, Mercia rose to prominence under Penda in the seventh century and then dominated southern English politics in the eighth and ninth centuries. The kingdom included modern Derbyshire, Leicestershire, Nottinghamshire, Stafforshire, and Warkwickshire and was bordered by Northumbrian to the north, East Anglia and Essex to the east, and Wales to the west. The kingdom's name came from the Old English word *mierce* (border) and may indicate that it was a border territory between the invading Anglo-Saxons and the native Britons.

Little is known about the earliest period of the Anglo-Saxon conquest of Mercia, but the first kings of Mercia were most likely leaders of tribes that settled along the Tame river and established royal sites at Tamworth and Repton. The first king of Mercia known by name is Cearl whose daughter married the king of Northumbria. The first king of note was Penda (r. 632/633–654) who transformed the kingdom into a major power and fought with Northumbria for dominance in the north. He also extended his influence into southern England, defeating rival kingdoms in the south without formally establishing his authority over those kingdoms. A pagan king, Penda nonetheless allowed his son Paedao to introduce Christianity into Mercia. It was another of Penda's sons, Aethelred (675–704), who ended Northumbrian influence south of the Humber River and laid the foundation for the subsequent expansion of Mercian power. It was under Offa (r. 757–796) that Mercia enjoyed some of its greatest successes and extended its hegemony throughout southern England. Offa managed to take control of Kent in the 760s and then imposed his authority on Sussex and then spread his influence into Wessex. He is also credited with building an earthwork, Offa's Dyke, along the Welsh frontier. His power was recognized by Pope Hadrian I and by Charlemagne, with whom Offa corresponded and negotiated a trade agreement in 796.

Mercian power declined, however, as the power Wessex grew in the ninth century and suffered as well from the attacks of the Danes. In 874, the last independent Mercian king, Burgred (r. 852–874), was driven from the kingdom by the Danes, and appointed Ceolwulf II (r. 874–881) who served the interests of the Danes. After the disappearance of Ceolwulf, the eastern half of the kingdom was controlled by the Danes and the western land came under the influence of the West Saxon kings. The Danes were driven out by the West Saxons, especially during the reign of Aethelflaed, Lady of the Mercians (r. 911–918). Thereafter, Mercia was ruled by the West Saxon kings and was incorporated into the kingdom of the English. Mercia maintained an important position in the new kingdom and was a powerful earldom in the 10th and 11th centuries.

See also: Anglo-Saxons; Bede; Charlemagne; Hadrian I, Pope; Offa of Mercia; Penda

Bibliography

Brown, Michelle, and Carol Ann Farr, eds. *Mercia: An Anglo-Saxon Kingdom in Europe.* London: Continuum, 2001.

Campbell, James. *The Anglo-Saxons.* New York: Penguin, 1991.

Whitelock, Dorothy, ed. *The Anglo-Saxon Chronicle.* Westport, CT: Greenwood, 1986.

Yorke, Barbara. *Kings and Kingdoms of Early Anglo-Saxon England.* New York: Routledge, 1997.

Merovingian Dynasty (450–751)

Ruling family of Frankish Gaul from the mid-fifth to the mid-eighth centuries, when it was replaced by Pippin the Short and the Carolingian dynasty. Creators of the most effective and longest lasting successor state to emerge in the post-Roman world, the Merovingians rose to prominence under their greatest king, Clovis (r. 481–511), who first forged various Frankish peoples into a unified kingdom. Although his successors were generally not his equals, they managed to expand the boundaries of the realm and strengthen the dynasty's hold on the kingdom. For most of the two centuries after the death of Clovis, the Merovingian kings were the among the most powerful and important of the rulers who came to power in Europe after the fall of the Western Roman Empire. They were plagued, however, by internal strife, as each of the various descendants of Clovis strove to seize control of the kingdom under his own authority and at the expense of his brothers or other male relatives. Indeed, the central weakness of the dynasty was the tradition of dividing the realm among all legitimate, and sometimes illegitimate, male heirs. This often led to civil war, including the truly bitter competition between the Merovingian queens Brunhilde and Fredegund in the late sixth century. Despite this underlying structural weakness, the dynasty prospered in the seventh century under the kings Chlotar and Dagobert. By the late seventh century, however, the dynasty faced internal discord, early death and weakness of several kings, and an increasingly acquisitive nobility. Although certainly not the "do-nothing kings" (*rois fainéants*) of popular tradition, the late Merovingians became increasingly irrelevant in the kingdom by the late seventh and early eighth centuries. Their authority was severely curtailed by the rising power of the Carolingian mayors of the palace, who deposed the last Merovingian king, Childeric III, in 750.

The dynasty traditionally traced its origins to a certain Merovech, the son of a sea god, but the first historical king of note was Childeric I (d. 481), the father of Clovis. Little is known of Childeric's reign other than what Gregory of Tours reported in his history and what appears in the later chronicle of Fredegar. According to Gregory, Childeric was a successful warlord from northeastern Gaul and Germany—modern Belgium and the Rhineland—who fought battles at Orléans and Angers, and also seized several islands from the Saxons when they fought the Romans. Childeric also negotiated a treaty with the Saxon leader Odovacar, possibly the same leader who deposed Romulus Augustulus in 476. Although a great warrior and successful conqueror, Childeric, according to Fredegar, was deposed for profligacy. Childeric, however, made an arrangement with one of his faithful followers, who was to agitate for Childeric's return and then send the king half of a coin they had divided when it was safe to return. While in exile, Childeric stayed with a Thuringian king, whose wife Basina followed Childeric back to the Franks and became his queen because she saw in him a ruler of great power.

Two other sources, the king's tomb at Tournai and a letter from Bishop Remigius of Rheims, provide information on Childeric's reign. The burial site provides important information on the cultural sophistication and Romanization of the Franks already in the mid-fifth century. Although there is ample evidence of the "barbarian" nature of the Franks in the tomb, there is also evidence of Roman influence. The tomb was built near a Roman cemetery and Roman road and contains a brooch and Byzantine coins that suggest contacts with the imperial capital at Constantinople. Moreover, there was other jewelry of high quality. The bishop's letter to Childeric's son Clovis reveals the extent of Childeric's domain and suggests that Childeric was in contact with the Catholic Christian bishops of Gaul.

On the death of Childeric in 481, his son Clovis ascended the throne, and it is with Clovis that the history of the Merovingian dynasty truly begins. Although well known from the pages of the history of Gregory of Tours, Clovis must remain a shadowy figure; the portrait offered by Gregory is very much the creation of the bishop of Tours himself. Gregory's king is depicted as having been in many ways God's instrument, one that punished the wicked; expelled God's enemies, the Arians, from Gaul; protected the saints, bishops, and church; and converted directly to Catholic Christianity from paganism. Indeed, one of the most famous tales of Clovis's reign involves his conversion. His wife Clotilda, a Burgundian Catholic, sought to convert her husband to her faith, but with little success. Her efforts were hindered when their first son died after she had him baptized; Clovis questioned the power of the Christian God and preferred the power of the traditional gods of the Franks. Ultimately, Clovis converted, as Gregory tells us, during a battle that he was losing. He offered to convert to his wife's faith if he should win the battle, which he did. Gregory then describes how Clovis accepted baptism, like a new Constantine, from the hands of Bishop Remigius, and with him 3,000 of his followers converted as well.

Gregory also describes the great conquests of Clovis over rival Franks, Romans, Visigoths (an almost crusade-like battle against Arian Christians), Burgundians (to avenge injuries against his wife), and others. Clovis occasionally employed great trickery to defeat his rivals, but all, in Gregory's eyes, in a good cause. Perhaps the best illustration of the character of Clovis is given in Gregory's tale of the ewer of Soissons. After defeating the Roman "king" Syagrius of Soissons, Clovis came into possession of great booty, part of which was a sacred vessel of importance to the bishop of Soissons. Honoring a request from the bishop, Clovis asked if the follower to whom he had given the vessel would return it. But the follower refused and cut the vessel in half, offering the king only his share. Later, Clovis cut his follower in half with a great blow with his broadsword, declaring that this was what the warrior had done to his cup at Soissons. The tale was designed to demonstrate

Clovis's authority and, more importantly, his devotion to the Catholic bishops even before his conversion.

Although a marvelous and memorable portrait, the image presented by Gregory of Tours is most likely not a portrait of the historic Clovis. Rather, Gregory's portrait was intended for Clovis's descendants, who failed to obey the bishops and the church and divided the kingdom in civil war. The historic Clovis was rather different from Gregory's portrait. Although he was a good friend of the bishops, Clovis most likely did not convert directly to Catholic Christianity; at the very least he leaned toward Arianism before receiving baptism from the Catholic Remigius. Moreover, he was most likely not the ruthless barbarian Gregory made him out to be. He was most certainly a successful warrior king, but he also seems to have been influenced by Roman culture. Most notably, his codification of Frankish law in the *Lex Salica* (Salic law), a written Latin version of Frankish custom, suggests the influence of Roman legal traditions. Clovis also borrowed Roman administrative techniques, particularly those involving collecting taxes. In 511, Clovis divided his kingdom among his sons, which traditionally has been understood as an example of the personal nature of Merovingian kingship (so that division of the kingdom would simply be the division of his personal property among his heirs). This division, however, followed Roman administrative boundaries, with each region having a Roman city as capital, and may have been influenced as much by Roman as Frankish traditions.

The legacy of Clovis was undoubtedly a mixed one, however. Although he had established a great kingdom and forged important connections with the bishops of Gaul, he also established the tradition of the division of the realm—traditionally recognized as the fatal flaw in the history of the Merovingian dynasty. The division practically guaranteed that civil war between the descendants of Clovis would occur regularly, and within a decade of his death civil war had indeed broken out. The sixth century was particularly plagued by this problem, which was exacerbated by the Merovingian practice of polygyny and serial marriage. As a result of royal marriage practices, only little influenced by the increasing Christianization of the Merovingians and their kingdom, there were numerous claimants to the throne, especially since both legitimate and illegitimate sons could succeed their fathers. Moreover, heirs to the throne had to be recognized by all other Merovingian kings, and often war was the only means to enforce a claim or depose a pretender. Although certainly a problem, civil war did have the benefit of eliminating those with weak claims to the throne and strengthening the ties between the Merovingian kings and the Frankish aristocracy and episcopacy.

The most famous example of a civil war, or blood feud, among the Merovingians was that of the queens Fredegund and Brunhilde, the wives of Chilperic I (r. 561–584) and Sigebert (r. 561–575), respectively. The traditional competition between rival Merovingian kings may have been worsened by the hatred that existed between their queens, who were motivated by a thirst for power, the concern to protect their families, and possibly, in Brunhilde's case, the desire for revenge. Although the Merovingian kings had been in the habit of marrying lowborn women, Sigebert married a Visigothic princess, Brunhilde, which inspired Chilperic to do the same. Perhaps already married to Fredegund, who was at least an important concubine, Chilperic married Brunhilde's sister, Galswintha, whom he murdered, possibly at Fredegund's instigation, shortly after the marriage. This led to the promotion of Fredegund and the beginning of several decades of assassinations and attempted assassinations of bishops, kings, and queens. Fredegund engineered the murder of Sigebert, Chilperic, and several bishops, and attempted to murder Brunhilde. Despite her best efforts, Fredegund was survived by Brunhilde—often just as ruthless as her rival in promoting the interests of her male heirs—who ruled the Merovingian kingdom through her sons and grandsons during the last decade of the sixth century and the first decade of the seventh. In 613, however, the nobility of Austrasia—one of the three subkingdoms that emerged in the sixth century, along with Neustria and Burgundy—rallied behind Fredegund's son Chlotar to depose Brunhilde, try and condemn her for numerous crimes, and execute her in the most brutal fashion.

The two generations following the fall of Brunhilde, from 613 to 638, were times of the resurgence of the dynasty and in many ways its high point, as well as the moment of the first appearance of members of the family that became the Carolingian dynasty. In gratitude for his support, Chlotar II (r. 613–629) made Pippin of Landen, an early Carolingian, mayor of the palace and granted other concessions to his family and that of Arnulf of Metz, who had formed a marriage alliance with Pippin. Balancing the interests of the major aristocratic families of the realm would be one of the chief concerns of Chlotar and his son Dagobert (r. 629–638/639). They did this by promoting the status of the monarchy as a sacral institution against the nobility, and also by legislating actively. Chlotar issued numerous diplomas and charters. He passed the Edict of Paris in 614, which has often been seen as a surrender of royal power but may be better understood as a means by the king to force the aristocracy to ensure law and order throughout the kingdom. Clearly the king was successful in this. Fredegar notes that Chlotar reigned happily (*feliciter*), suggesting a time of peace and order. Chlotar, and Dagobert after him, laid the foundations for a chancery—an essential tool for the diplomatic activities of the kings—and built up a sort of school at the royal palace, to which the sons of nobles were invited to be educated, strengthening ties between the monarchs and the nobles. Moreover, to further their hold on the kingdom and to establish a counterweight to the power of the nobles, Chlotar and, especially, Dagobert drew closer to the church. Dagobert, for example, strengthened the dynasty's ties with the powerful abbey of St. Denis near Paris.

Despite the successes of Chlotar and Dagobert, the Merovingians suffered a period of decline after Dagobert's death. Although the dynasty suffered over the course of the next century, the decline was not as precipitous as is traditionally

Merovingian-Frankish king Dagobert I, 605–639, flanked by noblemen, from a 14th-century manuscript. (The British Library Board)

held. Indeed, the dynasty kept a firm hold on the throne until the usurpation of Pippin the Short in 751, and even then the first Carolingian king faced opposition and took very cautious steps to secure the throne. An earlier attempt at usurpation by the Carolingian mayor Grimoald in the 650s failed, a failure that demonstrates the continued authority of the Merovingian line. In the 650s and 660s, Clovis II and his wife Balthild had a successful reign, and Balthild after her husband's death was an effective regent who refashioned the dynasty's relations with the church and reformed the church in the kingdom. At the same time, however, the Merovingians faced increasing competition from various factions of the nobility, particularly from the later Carolingian line. The nobility of the subkingdoms came more and more to compete for access to and control of the monarchs, many of whom were weakened by youth or incompetence. The office of mayor of the palace became increasingly important in the late seventh century, and the mayors of the two main subkingdoms, Austrasia and Neustria, competed for control of the kingdom. In 687, the Neustrian mayor of the palace, Berthar, and the Merovingian king Theuderic III (r. 675–691) invaded Austrasia. The Austrasian mayor, Pippin of Herstal, met and defeated his rival at the battle of Tetry and then deposed Berthar from office, replacing him with Pippin's own man. Theuderic was forced to accept Pippin as mayor and both the power of Pippin's family and the authority of Austrasia over Neustria were confirmed following the battle.

By the late seventh and early eighth centuries, the Merovingian dynasty was being gradually replaced by the Carolingian dynasty. Effective control of the kingdom had been taken by Pippin and his successor Charles Martel, even though the Merovingians continued to issue charters and remained on the throne. During Charles Martel's reign as mayor of the palace, the various Merovingian kings who held the throne were increasingly marginalized, even if not to the extent portrayed by Einhard in his description of the last of the line (who owned only one estate, were maintained by the Carolingians, and trotted out once a year in a donkey cart to appear at a council of state). In fact, the Merovingians had become so irrelevant to Martel's ability to rule that during the last four years of his life he ruled without a king on the throne and divided the realm between his two sons, Pippin the Short and Carloman, just as the Merovingian kings had done. His successors were forced to restore a Merovingian, Childeric III, to the throne in 743 because of political unrest in the kingdom, but he was little more than a figurehead. In 750, Pippin felt secure enough to take the step Grimoald had taken in the previous century. He sent a petition to the pope—perhaps feeling it necessary to substitute the sanction of the church and the Christian God for the divine aura that Childeric could claim as the descendant of a sea god—asking whether the person with the title or the person with the power should rule as king in Francia. The pope answered as Pippin had hoped, and in 751 the last of the Merovingian kings was deposed and the Carolingian dynasty was established on the Frankish throne.

See also: Austrasia; Balthild, St.; Brunhilde; Carloman, Mayor of the Palace; Carolingian Dynasty; Charles Martel; Childeric III; Chlotar II; Clothilda; Clovis; Dagobert; Fredegar; Fredegund; Gregory of Tours; Neustria; Odovacar; Pippin of Herstal; Pippin I, Called Pippin of Landen; Pippin III, Called Pippin the Short; *Rois Fainéants*; Romulus Augustulus; Saint-Denis, Abbey of; Tertry, Battle of; Tournai; Tours, Battle of; Visigoths

Bibliography

Dill, Samuel. *Roman Society in Gaul in the Merovingian Age.* 1926. Reprint, London: Allen and Unwin, 1966.

Fouracre, Paul, and Richard A. Gerberding. *Late Merovingian France: History and Hagiography, 640–720.* Manchester, UK: University of Manchester Press, 1996.

Geary, Patrick. *Before France and Germany: The Creation and Transformation of the Merovingian World.* Oxford: Oxford University Press, 1988.

Gregory of Tours. *History of the Franks.* Trans. Lewis Thorpe. Harmondsworth, UK: Penguin, 1974.

Harmondsworth, UK: Bachrach, Bernard S. *Merovingian Military Organization, 481–751.* Minneapolis: University of Minnesota Press, 1972.

James, Edward. *The Franks.* Oxford: Blackwell, 1991.

Lasko, Peter. *The Kingdom of the Franks: North-West Europe before Charlemagne.* New York: McGraw Hill, 1971.

Wallace-Hadrill, J. M. *The Long-Haired Kings.* Toronto: Toronto University Press, 1982.

Wallace-Hadrill, J. M. *The Frankish Church.* Oxford: Clarendon, 1983.

Wallace-Hadrill, J. M., ed. and trans. *The Fourth Book of the Chronicle of Fredegar with Its Continuations.* London: Nelson, 1960.

Wemple, Suzanne. *Women in Frankish Society: Marriage and the Cloister, 500–900.* Philadelphia: University of Pennsylvania Press, 1985.

Wood, Ian. *The Merovingian Kingdoms, 450–751.* London: Longman, 1994.

Milan

Situated between the Ticino and Adda rivers in the Po Valley in northern Italy, Milan, or Mediolanum as the Romans called it, became an important city and a Roman imperial capital from the late third to fifth centuries. Milan's geographic location contributed to its rising importance because it provided Roman rulers easy access to Italy and imperial territories north of the Alps. The site of the conversion of St. Augustine, Milan earned a reputation as an important Christian center, especially under its greatest bishop, Ambrose. Although the city's status declined in the early Middle Ages, it would rise to prominence once again in the 11th century and the later Middle Ages.

Founded by Celtic tribes around 400 BC, Milan became a Roman settlement in the third century BC and quickly grew into one of the major centers in northern Italy. The most important phase of Milan's history began in the late third century when the emperor Diocletian (r. 284–305) established the city as one of the main administrative centers for the western half of the empire. Diocletian's coemperor, Maximian (r. 286–305), undertook major renovations of the city, building baths, a circus, and great new palace. He also erected massive walls to secure the defense of the new political and military capital. The emperor Constantine declared the city the Vicar of Italy and issued the Edict of Milan (313), which legalized Christianity, in the city. Later fourth century emperors used the city as a base to enforce their authority in the Western Empire and to keep a watchful eye of the barbarian peoples of the north. Milan's importance was reinforced by the great Christian bishop Ambrose, whose sermons and personal example inspired numerous Christians, including Augustine. Ambrose oversaw construction of a cathedral and baptistery and other churches in Milan and used his position as bishop of the imperial capital of the west to defend and spread Catholic Christianity and to ensure that even emperors understood their place as Christians.

Milan suffered during the barbarian invasions of the fifth century and lost its position of leadership in the Western Empire. In 402, the city was sacked by the Visigoths during their invasion of Italy, and in 404, the capital of the Western Empire was moved to Ravenna, which contributed to the city's decline. Matters worsened for Milan during the fifth and sixth centuries. In 452 Attila sacked the city. During the Gothic Wars of the sixth century, Milan was seized by the Byzantine general Belisarius in 538 but then retaken and destroyed by the Goths in 539. The remnants of the city were taken by the Lombards in 569 when they invaded and seized control of much of Italy. Although fleeing from the Lombards, Milan's clergy returned in the early seventh century and contributed to a modest revival of the city's fortunes. New building took places, and the city's walls seem to have been reinforced. In 604 the Lombard ruler Agilulf crowned his son there, and a Lituprand's brother was enthroned as bishop in the eighth century. When the Lombard kingdom fell to Charlemagne in 774, Milan became part of the Carolingian empire and continued on its path of revival and would reemerge as a major city in the 11th and 12th centuries.

See also: Ambrose of Milan; Augustine of Hippo, St.; Belisarius; Charlemagne; Constantine; Gothic Wars; Lombards; Ostrogoths; Ravenna; Rome; Theodosius the Great; Visigoths

Bibliography

Krautheimer, Richard. *Three Christian Capitals: Topography and Politics*. Berkeley: University of California Press, 1983.

La Rocca, Cristina. *Italy in the Early Middle Ages: 476–1000*. New York: Oxford University Press, 2002.

McLynn, Neil B. *Ambrose of Milan: Church and Court in a Christian Capital*. Berkeley: University of California Press, 1994.

Moorhead, John. *Ambrose: Church and Society in the Late Roman World*. New York: Longman, 1999.

Missi Dominici

Carolingian royal officials who represented the king's interests in specified regions. The *missi dominici* (singular: *missus dominici*), or messengers of the lord king, were responsible for announcing the king's will on the local level and for ensuring that justice was done throughout the realm. The *missi dominici* were specially chosen by the king, and the office was used as a means to establish royal control in a large and growing empire.

Although *missi dominici* seem to have been used by the kings of the Merovingian dynasty as well as by the early Carolingian mayors of the palace, the office was only fully exploited by Charlemagne, who turned it into a regular and important part of his administration. At first even Charlemagne used the office on an occasional basis, but as his reign progressed the *missi dominici* became a more formal and regular tool of government. By 802, at the latest, the *missi dominici* had become a normal tool of Charlemagne's government and were sent out to all parts of the empire on an annual basis to perform their various services for the king. But there is evidence to suggest that they were used much earlier; they were probably used to disseminate the capitulary of Herstal in 779 and were also most likely used to administer oaths of fidelity to Charlemagne in 789 and 792–793. The *missi dominici* remained an important part of Carolingian government, at least through the reigns of Louis the Pious and Charles the Bald.

There were two categories of *missi dominici*: the *missi ad hoc,* or "special" *missi,* and the "ordinary" *missi.* The powers of the two were not different, but the special missi were used for specific missions to examine particular circumstances or injustices. The more important office, however, was that of the "ordinary" *missi dominici*. Although early in Charlemagne's reign they were chosen from many of the king's retainers, regardless of social rank, after 802, they were chosen only from the secular and ecclesiastical nobility, to reduce the possibility of corruption. Indeed, the classic format of the *missi dominici* included a lay aristocrat, such as a count, and an ecclesiastical noble, such as an abbot or bishop. They were given responsibility for exercising royal authority in a specific geographic area within the kingdom known as a *missaticum.*

The *missi dominici* held numerous responsibilities as the king's official representatives. Their primary duty was to enforce the royal will. They were charged with transmitting new capitularies throughout the kingdom, enforcing the new laws laid out in those capitularies, investigating the conduct of counts and other royal agents, and collecting revenues. They were to ensure that justice was done properly in the royal and local courts, and they could hear judicial appeals. They were also employed to administer oaths of fidelity to the king and to prepare the army for military campaigns. The counts throughout the realm were expected to provide food and lodging for the *missi dominici*, and legislation was enacted to ensure they were properly received when they reached their *missaticum.* Although an often effective tool of government, the *missi dominici* were not above corruption themselves, as the reforms of 802 suggest. And Theodulf of Orléans noted the difficulties faced by the *missi dominici,* who were frequently offered bribes. The *missi dominici* were, nonetheless, an important element of Carolingian administration.

See also: Capitularies; Carolingian Dynasty; Charlemagne; Charles the Bald; Louis the Pious; Merovingian Dynasty

Bibliography

Fichtenau, Heinrich. *The Carolingian Empire.* Trans. Peter Munz. Toronto: University of Toronto Press, 1979.

Ganshof, François Louis. *Frankish Institutions under Charlemagne.* Trans. Bryce Lyon and Mary Lyon. Providence, RI: Brown University Press, 1968.

Halphen, Louis. *Charlemagne and the Carolingian Empire.* Trans. Giselle de Nie. Amsterdam: North-Holland, 1977.

McKitterick, Rosamond. *The Frankish Kingdoms under the Carolingian, 751–987.* London: Longman 1983.

McKitterick, Rosamond. *The Carolingians and the Written Word.* Cambridge: Cambridge University Press, 1989.

Monasticism

Among the most important institutions of late antiquity and the early Middle Ages, monasticism represented the highest form of religious life in the period. It offered a highly structured and well-regulated means of pursuing the religious life, either as an isolated ascetic or as a member of a larger community. The monastic life, which was patterned after the life of Jesus and the Apostles, involved the work of God, prayer, asceticism, chastity, and a path to salvation in a community set apart from the rest of society. Although isolated, monasteries themselves often made important contributions to the broader society and were often important to the economic, intellectual–cultural, and political life of the early Middle Ages.

The origins of Christian monasticism can be traced to the deserts of Egypt in the third century when St. Antony (c. 251–356) accepted Jesus' call to the wilderness and undertook the life of a religious solitary (the word "monk" comes from the Greek meaning "living alone") at about the year 270. Renouncing wealth and family and seeking to defeat personal temptation and worldliness by living a life a seclusion and rigid asceticism, Antony went out into the desert and eventually developed a reputation as a holy man, attracting many followers. Soon there were numerous anchorites, or solitary hermits, living in colonies and seeking the spiritual life in the deserts along the Nile. At times, these early hermits found themselves in a sort of competition—"spiritual athletes" attempting to follow ever more rigorous devotions to God, depriving themselves of food and sleep and remaining constantly at prayer. To temper the excesses of these spiritual athletes and eliminate the problem of spiritual pride, St. Pachomius (c. 292–346) and, especially, St. Basil the Great (330–379) introduced coenobitical or communal monasticism. These communities included a large population of monks under the direction of an abbot who guided them in their daily routine. The daily life as defined by Pachomius and Basil included times of prayer and meditation, communal worship, and manual labor. The communities also clearly separated its members from the outside world and included dormitories, a refectory, a church, an infirmary, and other structures. It was coenobitical monasticism and the formal written rules associated with it that would be the predominant form of monastic life throughout the late antiquity and the early Middle Ages.

The foundation set by Antony, Pachomius, and Basil would be developed over the fourth and fifth centuries by religious/monastic leaders in the Eastern Church and exported to western church. A central figure in both these developments was St. John Cassian (c. 360–435) whose personal example and writings greatly influenced monastic life. A monk in Bethlehem, Cassian toured the Egyptian communities in 385 and later moved to southern Gaul and established two monasteries—one for males and one for females—near Marseilles. He also wrote *Conferences*, a spiritual guidebook, and *Institutes*, a monastic rule, or book of instruction, for the community he founded. Cassian was not alone in transferring monastic practices to the west. St. Hillary of Poitiers (c. 315–67) was sent into exile in the east and returned to establish a community of ascetics in Poitiers, and Honoratus (d. 429) following a pilgrimage to the Holy Land established the important community of Lérins. Perhaps of even greater significance was St. Jerome who traveled back and forth between Rome and the Holy Land and actively encouraged the monastic life in both places. He lived for a time as a hermit in Syria and later established religious communities in Rome, where he oversaw a community of women led by the noblewomen Marcella and Paula, and Jerusalem, where Paula financed the building of communities for men and women.

Originating in the east, monasticism sunk deep roots in Gaul and other parts of the Western Church and its successor states. In the later fourth century, the former Roman soldier and bishop, St. Martin of Tours, dedicated himself to the ascetic life and founded a community in Marmoutiers. St. Augustine of Hippo (354–430) established a community dedicated to religious living and prayer and study in North Africa, and Cassiodorus (c. 490–585) founded a community at Vivarium that was dedicated to the study of sacred and secular learning in the pursuit of God. In Ireland, monasticism was particularly dynamic, and the structure of the Irish church was patterned around monastic communities. Isolated cells along the stark Irish coastline were centers of lonely ascetics who stood for hours in the icy North Sea, arms outstretched in a cross, in prayer as a means to humble the flesh and honor God. Monastic communities were often associated with royal families and were centers of learning and literacy and produced some of the most magnificent manuscripts of the early Middle Ages, including the Book of Kells. Irish monks also helped spread monasticism to England and the Continent. Irish missionaries founded communities in northern England and on the continent at Luxueil and Bobbio, which became some of the most important early medieval religious centers. The most influential of the Irish monks and missionaries was St. Columban (d. 615), whose rule was widely followed in Ireland and on the Continent.

Beehive-shaped cells of the early Christian monastery at the top of Skellig Michael, a remote island off the coast of Ireland. Founded in the sixth century. (Anthony Patterson)

The most influential figure and the father of Western monasticism, however, was St. Benedict of Nursia (c. 480–547). Born into a noble Roman family and well educated, Benedict heard the call of the desert and took up the religious life, settled in a cave in Subiaco. Attracting a substantial following, Benedict established a formal community, which he left after an attempted poisoning. He eventually established a monastery on Monte Cassino that would be one of the great monastic centers of the early Middle Ages. As important as Monte Cassino was, Benedict's most important contribution was his Rule. Drawn from a variety of sources, including the Rule of the Master, Benedict's rule is noteworthy for its simplicity, flexibility, and humanity. As with other rules, Benedict's outlined the daily activities of the monks, stressing equal parts prayer and manual labor, and established guidelines for the recruitment and training of new monks. It not only stressed the importance of humility, chastity, and obedience but also offered exceptions for the novice, sick or the elderly. The Rule of Benedict also outlined the duties of the abbot, who was responsible for his monks and was expected to offer both stern discipline and compassion and comfort as the situation warranted.

The wisdom and humanity of the Rule of Benedict account for its ultimate triumph in Western monasticism, but in the first two centuries of its existence it competed with other monastic rules or was used in combination with them. Indeed, there are few references to Benedict and his Rule in the sixth century beyond the important account by Gregory the Great. Benedict surely had influence in the sixth century, however, because Gregory composed part of his life of Benedict with the aid of four monks who knew the saint, and it is possible that St. Columban knew Benedict's Rule. But in general in the seventh and eighth centuries, Benedict shared influence with Columban and the monks associated with the Irish tradition and other monastic lawgivers such as Caesarius of Arles. It was commonplace to combine elements from the Benedictine, Celtic, and other monastic traditions in the so-called *regula mixta* (mixed rule) in the monasteries of barbarian Europe.

It is possible that Benedictine monasticism was exported to England by the mission Gregory sent under the direction of St. Augustine of Canterbury, but this is widely disputed by scholars today. But even if Augustine did not bring the Rule, it did arrive by the mid-seventh century. There is evidence for its introduction to Northumbria in 660, and both Benedict Biscop, founder of Wearmouth and Jarrow, and the Venerable Bede, the great Anglo-Saxon scholar, were greatly influenced by the Rule of Benedict. The Anglo-Saxon missionaries of the eighth century, especially St. Boniface, brought the Rule with them on their evangelical missions to the continent. The reform activities of these missionaries greatly influenced the Frankish church and the leaders of Frankish society, especially the great rulers Charlemagne and Louis the Pious.

Under Charlemagne, the Benedictine Rule was increasingly important in the empire he established, and it was recognized by the great ruler as the best rule for the monastic life. His esteem for the Rule was so great that he sent an abbot from the realm to Monte Cassino in 787 to obtain an authentic copy. Although important to Charlemagne, the Rule of Benedict was established throughout the realm as the official monastic rule only by his son Louis the Pious. With the help of his close friend and advisor, Benedict of Aniane, Louis imposed the Rule on all monasteries of the empire by the decrees of two councils held in Aachen in 816 and 817. Over the next several centuries, the Rule of Benedict was the official standard of all monasteries, and it was the foundation for major monastic forms at Cluny in the 10th century and at Cîteaux in the 12th.

See also: Augustine of Hippo, St.; Basil the Great; Benedict of Aniane; Benedict of Nursia; Cassian, St. John; Cassiodorus; Charlemagne; Carolingian dynasty; Gregory I, the Great, Pope; Jerome, St.; Monte Cassino

Bibliography

Brooke, Christopher. *The Age of the Cloister: The Story of Monastic Life in the Middle Ages.* Mahwah, NJ: Hiddenspring, 2003.

Clark, James G. *The Benedictines in the Middle Ages.* Woodbridge, UK: Boydell and Brewer, 2008.

Dunn, Marilyn. *Emergence of Monasticism: From the Desert Fathers to the Early Middle Ages.* Oxford: Wiley Blackwell, 2003.

Farmer, David Hugh, ed. *Benedict's Disciples.* Leominster, UK: Fowler Wright, 1980.

Fry, Timothy, ed. and trans. *RB 1980: The Rule of Benedict in Latin and English with Notes.* Collegeville, MN: Liturgical Press, 1981.

Gregory the Great. *Life and Miracles of St. Benedict (Book Two of the Dialogues).* Trans. Odo J. Zimmerman and Benedict Avery. Collegeville, MN: St. John's Abbey Press, 1949.

Harmless, J. William. "Monasticism." In *The Oxford Handbook of Early Christian Studies.* Eds. Susan Ashbrook Harvey and David G. Hunter. Oxford: Oxford University Press, 2008, pp. 493–517.

Lawrence, Clifford H. *Medieval Monasticism: Forms of Religious Life in Western Europe in the Middle Ages.* 2nd ed. London: Longman, 1989.

Russel, Norman, trans. *The Lives of the Desert Fathers: Historia Monachorum in Aegypto.* Collegeville, MN: Cistercian Publications, 2006.

Wallace-Hadrill, J. M. *The Frankish Church.* Oxford: Clarendon Press, 1983.

Monte Cassino

One of the most important religious communities of the Middle Ages, Monte Cassino was founded in 529 by the father of western monasticism, Benedict of Nursia. Roughly 80 miles southeast of Rome and on a mountain some 1,500 feet high, Benedict's establishment was built on an old pagan shrine and was the place where Benedict first implemented his monastic rule. In the late sixth century, 577 or 580, the monastery was destroyed by the Lombards during their invasion of Italy.

The remains of Benedict were removed to Fleury after the monastery's destruction and its monks fled to Rome. Monte Cassino's fame endured, however, and in 718 Pope Gregory III sent monks from nearby communities to rebuild the monastery.

During the eighth century the community attracted a number of notable figures, including the Carolingian mayor of the palace, Carloman, and the great historian of the Lombards, Paul the Deacon. In the later eighth century, with the support of the Carolingians, Abbot Gisulf (796–817) oversaw the complete restoration of the monastery and further enhanced its fame and a growing number of pilgrims. In 883, however, the monastery was destroyed again, this time by marauding Muslims from North Africa. In 952 the monks returned and rebuilt the monastery, which would remain one of the great centers of monastic life for the rest of the Middle Ages.

See also: Benedict of Nursia, St.; Carloman, Mayor of the Palace; Carolingian Dynasty; Gregory III, Pope; Lombards; Monasticism; Paul the Deacon

Bibliography

Bloch, Herbert. *Monte Cassino in the Middle Ages.* 3 Vols. Cambridge, MA: Harvard University Press, 1988.

N

Narses (c. 480–574)

Byzantine general and eunuch, Narses was an important figure in the administration of the emperor Justinian (r. 527–565) and his wife Theodora. A highly loyal member of the court, who may have shared Theodora's faith, Narses played a key role in support of the emperor during the Nika Revolt of 532. He later took charge of Byzantine forces during the reconquest of Italy. Taking over from Belisarius, Narses brought the Gothic Wars to a close and achieved final victory for Justinian. He also played a key role in the reorganization of the administration of the peninsula after the conquest and then struggled against the Lombards as they advanced into Italy.

Narses was probably already in his forties when he arrived at court at the beginning of Justinian's reign. He came from Armenia, a slave eunuch who entered imperial service and by the later 520s was commander of the emperor's bodyguard. He was probably close to Justinian as a result, and his loyalty to the emperor brought him into the confidence of Theodora. Although not an educated man, Narses could unravel a problem quickly and was noted for his humanity and dignity in all situations. Indeed, he was a man of such decency that the fifth-century Byzantine historian Procopius never mentions him in his *Secret History*. His loyalty and many talents were displayed most clearly during the Nika Revolt in 532, when he joined Belisarius and others to bring an end to the revolt. His role as the commander of the imperial bodyguard was of particular importance, and he and his guard helped in the massacre that brought an end to the rebellion.

His service in the Nika Revolt led to advancement for Narses, and, in 538, he was sent to Italy to determine whether the war could be ended more quickly. His appointment essentially made him Belisarius's commander, and the two fell into repeated conflict. These disagreements, along with Belisarius's prominence, led to the appointment of Narses as commander of the armies in Italy and the recall of Belisarius. Narses, having witnessed the troubles of Belisarius, insisted that he himself be granted the tools necessary to complete the job. In 551, Narses was given command of the war in Italy, and in 552 he invaded with a large force that included a substantial number of Lombards as mercenaries. Although opposed by the armies of the Ostrogothic king Totila, Narses proceeded along the coast to Ravenna. He was joined by a second Byzantine army and then met the Gothic king at a decisive battle in late June or early July. The Battle of Busta Gallorum, on a plain in the northern Apennines, was a complete disaster for the Goths, who left 6,000 dead on the battlefield and withdrew with their king mortally wounded. In October, Narses again met in battle with the Goths and again defeated them. This time, however, an armistice was settled between the two sides. But the war was still not at an end, and Narses and various Gothic leaders met in battle several more times in 554 and 555. For the next several years, Narses was able to restore imperial authority over Italy. In 561, the Ostrogoths once again rose up and once again were defeated by Narses, and this time it was the final defeat of the Goths, who disappeared from history at that point.

Narses remained in Italy after the final defeat of the Ostrogoths and after the death of Justinian. As conquering general, Narses remained in authority for the next several years, but he was deposed from office, after enriching himself greatly, because the Italian population complained that his rule was worse than that of the Goths. His position might have remained secure had he not lost the favor of Justinian's successor, Justin II (r. 565–578), who sacked the old general. After losing his military command, Narses retired from imperial service. The invasion of the Lombards in 568 under their king, Alboin, led to the recall of Narses, even though, according to the Lombard historian Paul the Deacon, the general himself had invited the Lombards because of the treatment he received from Justin. Whatever the case, the Lombards proved too powerful even for Narses, who had little success against them. He once again retired from public life and died a few years later, after a career of long and effective service to the empire.

See also: Alboin; Belisarius; Gothic Wars; Justinian; Lombards; Ostrogoths; Theodora

Bibliography

Barker. J. W. *Justinian and the Later Roman Empire.* Madison: University of Wisconsin Press, 1960.

Browning, Robert. *Justinian and Theodora.* London: Thames and Hudson, 1987.

Burns, Thomas S. *A History of the Ostrogoths.* Bloomington: Indiana University Press, 1984.

Bury, John B. *History of the Later Roman Empire: From the Death of Theodosius I to the Death of Justinian.* 2 Vols. 1923. Reprint, New York: Dover, 1959.

Christie, Neil. *The Lombards: The Ancient Langobards.* Oxford: Blackwell, 1998.

Heather, Peter. *The Goths.* Oxford: Blackwell, 1996.

Llewellyn, Peter. *Rome in the Dark Ages.* New York: Barnes and Noble, 1993.

Paul the Deacon. *History of the Lombards.* Trans. William Dudley Foulke. Philadelphia: University of Pennsylvania Press, 1974.

Procopius. *The History of the Wars; Secret History.* 4 Vols. Trans. H. B. Dewing. Cambridge, MA: Harvard University Press, 1914–1924.

Wickham, Chris. *Early Medieval Italy: Central Power and Local Society, 400–1000.* Ann Arbor: University of Michigan Press, 1981.

Nennius (fl. early ninth century)

Along with the sixth-century monk Gildas, Nennius was one of the most important early contributors to the legend of King Arthur. His work, the *Historia Brittonum* (History of the Britons), contains the earliest mention of king Arthur and greatly influenced the 12th-century writer Geoffrey of Monmouth, who elaborated on the earlier Arthurian tales.

Nennius was a Welsh historian and antiquary who wrote at the end of the eighth or the beginning of the ninth century. His famous *Historia Brittonum* is traditionally dated between circa 800 and 829/830 and appeared originally in Wales. It remains uncertain, however, whether Nennius wrote the *Historia* himself or merely copied it from an earlier source or sources. Although best known for its treatment of the legendary Arthur, the *Historia* is not without reliable historical information; it includes details on the early residents and Anglo-Saxon invaders of the island, material on the kingdom of Bernicia, and topographical information. The descriptions of the struggles in Bernicia accord well with the tradition recorded by Bede and appear to follow Gildas, who noted that victory sometimes went to the invaders and sometimes to the Britons.

Nennius's work is most famous for his account of the Britons' struggle against the Anglo-Saxon invaders, particularly his description of the one great leader, whom he named Arthur. Most significantly, the history of Nennius includes a list of the 12 great victories, culminating with the Battle of Badon Hill, that Arthur won against the invaders. The *Historia* also contains the history of the world in six ages, tales of miracles and prodigies in England, and details of the life of St. Patrick. The work exists in some 35 manuscripts from the 10th to the 13th centuries and was a popular and influential work.

See also: Anglo-Saxons; Badon Hill, Battle of; Bede; Gildas; King Arthur

Bibliography

Alcock, Leslie. *Arthur's Britain: History and Archeology, A.D. 367–634.* Harmondsworth, UK: Penguin, 1971.

Barber, Richard. *The Figure of Arthur.* Totowa, NJ: Rowman and Littlefield, 1972.

Nennius. *Nennius: British History and the Welsh Annals.* Ed. John Morris. Totowa, NJ: Rowan and Littlefield, 1980.

Stenton, Frank M. *Anglo-Saxon England.* 3rd ed. Oxford: Clarendon, 1971.

Neustria

The "new land" or "new western land," Neustria was one of the three subkingdoms, along with Austrasia and Burgundy that emerged under Merovingian rule and comprised much of northwestern Gaul. Under the Merovingians, Neustria included lands from north of the Loire and west of the Meuse but under the Carolingians in included only the territory between the Loire and the Seine. Its main cities were Soisson and Paris, Neustria's capital beginning in the sixth century.

Neustria emerged in the mid-sixth century following the death of Chlothar I (d. 561) and came to dominate political affairs for much of the sixth and seventh centuries. Under the ambitious queen Fredegund and then later under her son Chlothar II, Neustria controlled Frankish affairs, and under Dagobert, Chlothar's son, the kingdoms of Neustria and Austrasia were reunited. In the late seventh century, as Merovingian power waned, Ebroin the mayor of the palace assumed leadership of Neustria, and the kingdom suffered division again. At the battle of Tertry, the Austrasian mayor of the palace, Pippin I of Landen defeated his Neustrian rival and brought to an end the ascendancy of Neustria and joined it to Austrasia.

During the reign of the Carolingians, Neustria was reconstituted as a smaller subkingdom than it had been under the Merovingians. Charlemagne established it as a subkingdom when he gave it as a kingdom to his son Charles the Younger in 790. Under Louis the Pious, Neustria was granted first to Lothar and then to Charles the Bald. It formed an important component, along with Aquitaine, of the West Frankish kingdom and was granted by Charles the Bald to Robert the Strong as a marcher region to help defend it against the Vikings. It would form the core of the domains of Robert's descendants, the future Capetian kings.

The culture and customs of Neustria were distinct from its sometime rival Austrasia. The population of Neustria was predominantly Gallo-Roman, in contrast to the more Germanic Franks of Austrasia, and spoke a form of Latin known as "*Langue d'oil*," which was the ancestor of modern French. The Neustrians also followed customary law, inherited from Germanic practice, rather than the written law of the Austrasians and others.

See also: Austrasia; Carolingian Dynasty; Charlemagne; Chlothar II; Fredegund; Merovingian Dynasty; Pippin I, Called Pippin of Landen

Bibliography

Geary, Patrick J. *Before France and Germany the Transformation of the Merovingian World.* Oxford: Oxford University Press, 1988.

James, Edward. *The Franks*. Oxford: Basil Blackwell, 1991.

Riché, Pierre. *The Carolingians: A Family Who Forged Europe*. Trans. Michael Idomir Allen. Philadelphia: University of Pennsylvania Press, 1993.

Wood, Ian. *The Merovingian Kingdoms, 450–751*. London: Longman, 1994.

Nithard (c. 800–844)

Carolingian count and historian, Nithard was an active figure in the affairs of his days. A lay abbot, grandson of the great king and emperor Charlemagne, and participant in the civil wars between the sons of Louis the Pious, Nithard is best known as the chronicler of the wars of Lothar, Louis the German, and Charles the Bald. His account provides our best account of the wars and important insights into the character of his hero, Charles the Bald, as well as into the nature and ideal of Carolingian kingship.

Little is known of Nithard's life, other than what he reveals in his work of history, and even the date of his death is uncertain. He is traditionally thought to have died on June 14, 844, in battle against Pippin II of Aquitaine (d. 864), but it has been suggested that he died fighting the Vikings on May 15, 845. In either case, his death occurred in battle, and it followed a life active in public affairs and close to the great powers of the day. He was the son of Charlemagne's daughter Bertha (779/780–after 823) and her lover, the court scholar Angilbert. He was raised at court, where he received an excellent education, as indicated in his observations on the movement of a comet in 841–842 and his ability to quote Scripture and Virgil. Later in life he became a partisan of Charles the Bald and joined the king in the fratricidal struggles of the early 840s. Nithard served as an envoy to Lothar for Charles in 840, seeking unsuccessfully to make peace with the emperor. In 841, he fought on Charles's side in the Battle of Fontenoy, and in 842 Nithard served on a commission to determine the division of the empire between Charles and Louis the German. In 843, in return for his faithful service, Nithard was made lay abbot of St. Riquier by Charles the Bald. He was buried in the monastery after his death in battle in 844 or 845, and was memorialized in an epitaph that celebrates his wisdom and mourns his death and the brevity of his term as abbot.

Nithard was also the court historian of Charles the Bald, at whose request he wrote his famous work, *Four Books of Histories* (*Historiarum Libri VI*). Although clearly partisan, Nithard's work provides the best view of the events of the 830s and 840s. It begins with an introduction to the wars that outlines events from the death of Charlemagne through the death of Louis the Pious. This book describes the civil turmoil in the 830s, which set the stage of the wars of the early 840s, and in it Nithard, as he does throughout the work, sides with Charles and portrays Lothar in the worst possible light. Books two through four describe the wars of Charles, Louis, and Lothar. These books contain valuable information about the partisans in the wars, the various battles, and related material, including two versions of the Oath of Strasbourg (842), one in an early form of Romance, the other in an early form of German. The *Histories* also contain a sympathetic portrait of Charles the Bald, commentary on ideal Christian kingship, and an eyewitness perspective on the events Nithard describes. Although not elegantly written, the *Histories* remain compelling reading; Nithard could capture scenes effectively and often wrote passionately. The fourth book, which Nithard wrote reluctantly because of his shame over the course of the civil war, ends rather abruptly. It may have been left unfinished by the author.

See also: Angilbert; Carolingian Dynasty; Charlemagne; Charles the Bald; Fontenoy, Battle of; Lothar; Louis the German; Louis the Pious; Strasbourg, Oath of

Bibliography

Laistner, Max L. W. *Thought and Letters in Western Europe,* A.D. *500 to 900.* 2nd ed. Ithaca, NY: Cornell University Press, 1976.

McKitterick, Rosamond. *The Frankish Kingdoms under the Carolingians, 751–987.* London: Longman, 1983.

Nelson, Janet. *Charles the Bald.* London: Longman, 1992.

Scholz, Bernhard Walter, trans. *Carolingian Chronicles: Royal Frankish Annals and Nithard's History.* Ann Arbor: University of Michigan Press, 1972.

Northumbrian Renaissance

Also known as the Northumbrian Golden Age, the Northumbrian Renaissance was an important cultural artistic movement in the northern Anglo-Saxon kingdom of Northumbria. Lasting from the mid-seventh to the mid-eight centuries, the renaissance made important contributions to the development of Christian learning and culture and reflected the deep roots the Christian faith had sunk by that time. Important centers of the renaissance were the many monasteries of Northumbria, especially Jarrow and Wearmouth, which were centers of study as well as of book copying and illumination. Numerous works of Christian and classical Latin learning were produced during the renaissance, and the study and teaching of the liberal arts formed the heart of the movement.

Among the most representative and impressive examples of Northumbrian Renaissance culture is the Lindisfarne Gospels, which reflects the focus on Christian learning and the insular style of book illumination that was popular at this time. Another important contribution of the movements is the Codex Amiatinus, an illuminated manuscript and the earliest extant complete copy of Jerome's Vulgate. The movement was stimulated, in part, by the activities of Benedict Biscop, whose interests in book culture and acquisition of numerous manuscripts during his trips to Rome provided the material resources for the renaissance. Perhaps the most celebrated figure of the renaissance is Bede, a monk and scholar who wrote works of computus, history (notably the *History of the English Church and People*), and hagiography. His tradition of scholarship was carried to the continent by Alcuin, whose teaching and learning helped shaped the Carolingian Renaissance of the late eighth and ninth centuries.

See also: Alcuin; Anglo-Saxons; Bede, Benedict Biscop; Carolingian Renaissance; Jerome; Lindisfarne Gospels

Bibliography

Blair, Hunter. *The World of Bede*. Cambridge: Cambridge University Press, 1991.

Hawkes, Jane and Susan Mills. *Northumbria's Golden Age*. Stroud, UK: Sutton Publishing, Ltd., 1999.

Neuman de Vegvar, Carol. *The Northumbrian Renaissance: A Study in the Transmission of Style*. Cranbury, NJ: Associated University Presses, 1987.

Notker the Stammerer (c. 840–912)

Poet, liturgist, historian, and monk of St. Gall, Notker the Stammerer (Latin: *Balbulus*) is an important figure of the Carolingian renaissance. His liturgical compositions had a major influence on the development of medieval chant, but he is perhaps best known for his *Gesta Karoli Magni* (Deeds of Charlemagne), an anecdotal biography of the great Carolingian ruler that helped shape the emerging legend of Charlemagne and offered the late Carolingians a guide for proper Christian kingship.

Born near the monastery of St. Gall in Switzerland, Notker would join that community, where his brother was a chief official. Notker, who would later describe himself as "toothless and stammering," remained in the monastery all his life, dedicating himself to prayer and scholarship. As a young monk, he listened to the stories of the warrior Adalbert, who had served in Charlemagne's armies. He himself would later serve as a teacher at the monastery; his students included, later bishops and abbots of the Carolingian Empire, and his contacts were widespread as indicated by his letters and other literary works. His surviving corpus demonstrates his learning and talents as a writer, even if at times he appears uncomfortable when writing in certain verse forms. Among his many works was a history of the East Frankish kingdom from 827 to 881, a martyrology, and a life of St. Gall written in verse and prose. A number of charters of the monastery were copied by Notker, and the monk wrote numerous letters, including one in which he outlined a plan of study for the young. His reputation in the ninth century and throughout much of the Middle Ages, however, rested on his talents as a poet. Notker wrote poems on friendship and other secular themes that displayed great depth of emotion and literary talent. Even greater were his religious poems, including four hymns he wrote in honor of St. Stephen and some 50 verse works with melodies for the cycle of the church year. Notker was also an influential composer of early medieval music and introduced the sequence, a choral work that follows the Alleluia in the mass, into Germany.

Although best known in the Middle Ages for his verse, Notker is best known today for his *Gesta Karoli*, written most likely between 885 and 887. The work, which was never finished, was composed for the Carolingian ruler, Charles the Fat

(r. 876–887), and was designed to provide a guide to kingship by citing examples from the Life of Charlemagne. Drawing from the tales told of the Carolingian ruler by Adalbert, Notker provides an image of Charlemagne as a great king and hero who defeated his enemies abroad and humbled the proud at home. Anecdotal in nature, the *Gesta* includes scenes of Charlemagne mocking proud bishops and arrogant noble youth who fail to learn their lessons as well as their fellow students of more modest means. The king is shown as a supporter of education and the church, encouraging his subjects to learn the Scriptures and bishops to perform the mass properly. Charles is compared with the great biblical kings David and Solomon and is praised for his deep religious piety. In contrast to Einhard's Life of Charlemagne, Notker's life emphasizes the Christian nature of the king's rule and his deep concern of God's plan and church. Charlemagne's martial side, however, is not neglected, and he is portrayed as a courageous warrior whose empire knows almost no bounds. The king is depicted as a fierce warrior who defeated the Avars, Saxons, and Slavs, and Notker hoped to encourage Charles the Fat to emulate his great grandfather, the Iron Charles. Along with the recollections of Adalbert, the *Gesta* was shaped by a variety of literary works. There are numerous biblical allusions throughout the text, and Notker also cites the Roman poet Virgil and the Christian poet Prudentius as well as saints' lives by Athanasius and others, letters of contemporaries like Alcuin and Walafrid Strabo, and the works of Augustine of Hippo. The *Gesta* is thus an important example of the achievements of the Carolingian Renaissance and a life of Charles that portrays him as the ideal Christian king.

See also: Augustine of Hippo, St.; Carolingian Renaissance; Charlemagne; Charles III, the Fat; Einhard

Bibliography

Crocker, Richard. *The Early Medieval Sequence*. Berkeley: University of California Press, 1976.

Einhard and Notker the Stammerer. *Two Lives of Charlemagne*. Trans. David Ganz. London: Penguin Books, 2008.

Ganz, David. "Humour as History in Notkers's *Gesta Karoli Magni.*" In *Monks, Nuns, and Friars in Medieval Society*. Eds. E. King, J. Schaefer, and W. Wadley. Sewanee, TN: University of the South Press, 1989, pp. 171–83.

Laistner, M.L.W. *Thought and Letters in Western Europe, A.D. 500 to 900*. 2nd ed. Ithaca, NY: Cornell University Press, 1951.

MaClean, Simon. *Kingship and Politics in the Late Ninth Century: Charles the Fat and the End of the Carolingian Empire*. Cambridge: Cambridge University Press, 2003.

Odovacar (c. 433–493)

Odovacar was a Germanic warrior of the Scirian tribe who rebelled against the last western Roman emperor, Romulus Augustulus, and Romulus's father, the master of the soldiers, Orestes. Odovacar deposed Romulus and is thus traditionally said to have ended the line of emperors ruling the Western Empire. Unlike earlier rebellious military commanders, he neither declared himself emperor nor promoted someone else as emperor. Instead, he recognized the authority of the emperor in Constantinople, Zeno, and established himself as king in Italy. His reign of 17 years was plagued by a long war with his eventual successor, Theodoric the Great, who murdered Odovacar but benefited from the traditions of Odovacar's monarchy.

Odovacar was born probably in 433, and was the son of Edica-Edikon, a servant of the great Hunnish ruler, Attila. Edica-Edikon prospered greatly under Attila, and created an independent Germanic kingdom after the death of the Hun and collapse of his empire. The kingdom did not last long, however, as Edica-Edikon was killed in battle in 469. Odovacar and his brother Hunnulf both fled the kingdom, with Odovacar going to Italy, followed by many of his father's supporters. In Italy, Odovacar entered the service of the western emperor as a member of the imperial guard, but sided with the emperor's powerful general, Ricimer, when civil war broke out between them in 472. His support for Ricimer was crucial to Ricimer's victory, and Odovacar learned much from his example, even though Ricimer died shortly after his victory.

In 476, Odovacar led a revolt of Germanic soldiers against the emperor, Romulus Augustulus, the son and puppet of Orestes. Orestes had earlier forced the emperor Julius Nepos into exile and declared his son emperor. The claim was not recognized in Constantinople, but Orestes strove to make it effective in Italy. He faced the rebellion led by Odovacar because he was unwilling to grant Germanic soldiers in the army equal status with Roman soldiers. Odovacar defeated Orestes and executed him on August 28, 476. Odovacar deposed and exiled Romulus rather than execute him because, according to a contemporary, of his youth and beauty. But Odovacar compelled Romulus to send a delegation of senators to Zeno, the emperor in Constantinople, declaring that no new emperor was needed and that they welcomed the rule of Odovacar. The Germanic warrior was willing to give up the title king for patrician and authority to rule in Italy. Zeno was in an awkward position, since the legitimate western emperor still lived, but he addressed Odovacar as patrician nonetheless. Odovacar sought accommodation with the emperor during his reign, and as a sign of good faith executed the murderer of Julius Nepos. Despite his best efforts, and willingness to recognize the sovereignty of the emperor in the east, Odovacar was not able to sign a treaty with the emperor. He did, however, establish peace in Italy and an important and effective royal administration that was built on cooperation with the senatorial aristocracy.

Although somewhat eased by the death of Julius Nepos in 480, relations between Zeno and Odovacar remained tense; they became highly strained in 486. The emperor faced a rebellion, and Odovacar, if not openly supporting the rebel, seems at least to have been in negotiations with him. In response, Zeno encouraged the Rugians, who had settled just north of Italy, to attack Odovacar. In 487, however, Odovacar struck first and destroyed the kingdom, thus ending the possibility of the establishment of a rival kingdom in Italy. His victory, however, had very negative consequences for Odovacar; the king's wife was an Ostrogoth, and her death and the flight of her children came to the attention of Theodoric the Great.

In 488, Theodoric negotiated a secret treaty with Zeno that granted Theodoric the right to rule Italy in the emperor's place if he defeated Odovacar. In the following year, Theodoric's armies reached Italy, and Odovacar, sensing treachery on Zeno's part, took steps to break formally with the emperor. He established his son as caesar and hoped that the break would be welcomed by the aristocracy, which had become increasingly alienated from the emperor over religious issues. Odovacar and Theodoric fought two bloody battles, in 489 and 490, which cost both sides numerous casualties but which were both won by Theodoric. The second victory was, in some ways, a worse defeat for Odovacar, because the senatorial aristocracy shifted its support to Theodoric. But the invader's victory was not sealed; Odovacar made a stand in Ravenna, a near impregnable stronghold. Theodoric besieged the city, and Odovacar held fast from August 490 until February 493. In July 491, Odovacar launched a ferocious but unsuccessful assault on the besiegers. Finally, the bishop of Ravenna negotiated a treaty between the two rulers that would allow the two to rule Italy together. Odovacar submitted, and Theodoric entered Ravenna on March 5, 493. A few days later, Theodoric murdered Odovacar, claiming that his rival was plotting against him. On that same day, according to a contemporary chronicler, "all Odovacar's soldiers were slain wherever they could be found, and all his kin" (Bury 1959, 426). Odovacar and his family and people were thus annihilated by Theodoric, but Odovacar left his murderer an important foundation for the establishment of a great kingdom in Italy.

See also: Attila the Hun; Huns; Orestes; Ostrogoths; Ravenna; Ricimer; Rome; Romulus Augustulus; Theodoric the Great; Zeno

Bibliography

Bury, John B. *History of the Later Roman Empire: From the Death of Theodosius I to the Death of Justinian.* 2 Vols. 1923. Reprint, New York: Dover, 1959.

Lot, Ferdinand. *The End of the Ancient World and the Beginning of the Middle Ages.* 1931. Reprint, New York: Harper and Row, 1961.

Randers-Pehrson, Justine Davis. *Barbarians and Romans: The Birth Struggle of Europe,* A.D. *400–700.* Norman: University of Oklahoma Press, 1983.

Wolfram, Herwig. *History of the Goths.* Trans. Thomas J. Dunlap. Los Angeles: University of California Press, 1988.

Wolfram, Herwig. *The Roman Empire and Its Germanic Peoples.* Trans. Thomas J. Dunlap. Berkeley: University of California Press, 1997.

Offa of Mercia (d. 796)

One of the greatest and longest ruling kings of Anglo-Saxon England, Offa (r. 757–796) is also the great king about whom the least is known. The only information about Offa and his reigns come from outside the kingdom of Mercia. It includes charters and chronicles written in Northumbria, Wessex, and elsewhere in England. Although possibly as great a ruler as Alfred, who clearly respected Offa, the Mercian king lacks a contemporary Mercian biographer to announce and record his greatness. Despite this lack of information, it is clear that Offa had a profound impact on England during his long reign, and his power and organizational ability are demonstrated by the famed earthwork he built, Offa's Dyke, along the Welsh frontier. Alfred himself praised Offa as a king and adopted laws, now lost, from Offa. And the pope and the greatest king of the early Middle Ages, Charlemagne, treated Offa with respect and recognized his power.

Offa came to power in 757 by driving his rival Beornred into exile by force of arms. His military success at the beginning characterized the rest of his long reign; it was the key to his success, but it was also the key to the demise of the kingdom in the following generation. Indeed, the great Anglo-Saxon scholar and friend of Charlemagne, Alcuin of York, recognized that it was Offa's ruthlessness that secured not only his success but also his untimely death. It was this ruthlessness that secured his power inside and outside of Mercia, restoring the kingdom of Mercia to a position of preeminence in England. After conquering Mercia by the sword, Offa extended his authority over other kingdoms in England. The first to fall victim to Offa was Kent, in the 760s. The struggle to control the kingdom of Kent was long lasting and brought Offa the bitter enmity of the archbishop of Canterbury. The Kentish kings were able to restore their independence for nearly a decade after 776, but they were finally suppressed in 785.

In the 770s, Offa brought the kingdom of Sussex under his control by defeating, according to a Northumbrian chronicle, the "men of Hastings" in battle. In the 780s he asserted his authority over Wessex, when that kingdom fell into civil war after a prolonged period of peace under one of its kings. Offa was able to exploit

Offa's Dyke passes through the Shropshire countryside. The earthwork formed a boundary, albeit discontinuous, between England and Wales. (Andrew Fogg)

the situation when a usurper revolted and both he and the king died in battle. Further claimants to the throne of Wessex rose up, including Beorhtric, who received support from Offa and married one of Offa's daughters. The Mercian king's support was essential for Beorhtric's victory, and this support allowed Offa to extend his influence and authority over Wessex. His influence was also felt in Northumbria, and his political authority extended far to the south, where several lesser kingdoms also succumbed to his advance. He also extended his authority westward at the expense of the Welsh, and an expansion borne witness to by Offa's greatest extant legacy, Offa's Dyke, an engineering and organizational marvel of the eighth century that extends some 150 miles over mountainous terrain. Indeed, this fortification may have been part of a military system of fortified towns of the kind later made famous by Alfred the Great. By the 780s Offa could claim to be king of the English, a title recognized in the charters of contemporaries. Perhaps in recognition of his power and in emulation of the Carolingian dynasty, Offa had his son consecrated as king in 787.

Offa's political power was recognized and respected on the continent. He corresponded with Pope Hadrian (r. 772–795) and received legates in the mid-780s from the pope. He also convinced Hadrian to establish a new archiepiscopal see in his kingdom at Lichfield in 787. The new archbishop proved a counterbalance to the hostile archbishop of Canterbury, but he did not last long after the death of Offa. Nonetheless, Offa sought to establish the ecclesiastical independence of the church in his kingdom and empowered it by the foundation of monasteries, including St. Albans. His representatives also participated in church councils in England and on the continent, including the Council of Frankfurt in 794.

It was not only the pope who recognized Offa; the great Frankish king, Charlemagne, also corresponded with Offa and respected his power. Always courteous in correspondence with Offa, Charlemagne wrote seeking advice or mercy from Offa in regard to exiles from Mercia in the Frankish kingdom. Charlemagne's opinion of Offa was most likely influenced by the Mercian king's participation through his clergy at the Council of Frankfurt and by the active trade that existed between the two kingdoms. In 796 a trade agreement was forged between the two kings, in which merchants from both kingdoms were to be protected by both kings. The extent of trade is demonstrated by the improvement in English coinage under Offa, who was likely influenced by the coinage of his Carolingian contemporary. Offa's coin, the penny, remained the basis of English coinage until the 13th century and surpassed all other coins in England in his day. The coins also demonstrate further the political shrewdness of the king; they often bore Offa's image or that of his wife, Cynethryth, in imitation of Byzantine or late Roman practice.

Offa was clearly a king of wide-ranging influence in England and the continent. He was also a brutal king, who managed to rule much of England by suppressing or eliminating the sovereigns of the other English kingdoms. It was this brutality that proved the undoing of his kingdom in the generations following his death on July 26, 795, and that ended the revival of the power of Wessex. Although the political power of his kingdom was short lived, his influence lasted well beyond his death in the coinage he introduced to England, his military construction, and the laws he implemented that were adopted by Alfred.

See also: Alcuin of York; Alfred the Great; Anglo-Saxons; Carolingian Dynasty; Charlemagne; Hadrian I, Pope; Mercia; Wessex

Bibliography

Keynes, Simon. "The British Isles: England, 700–900." In *The New Cambridge Medieval History.* Vol. 2. Ed. Rosamond McKitterick. Cambridge: Cambridge University Press, 1995, pp. 18–42.

Levison, Wilhelm. *England and the Continent in the Eighth Century.* Oxford: Clarendon, 1946.

Stenton, Frank M. *Anglo-Saxon England.* 3rd ed. Oxford: Clarendon, 1971.

Ordinatio Imperii

Succession plan designed by Louis the Pious in 817. The *Ordinatio Imperii* (Disposition for the Empire) was intended to establish a unified empire, while still recognizing the long Frankish tradition of dividing the realm between the king's heirs. It was thought to be divinely inspired by contemporaries, especially the members of the church. It shaped Louis's policies for much of the next decade, but it was gradually undermined by the birth of another son to Louis and his second wife, Judith. Violation of the *Ordinatio* then became a justification for rebellion for Louis's opponents.

In 817, Louis the Pious met with the leaders of the realm to determine the empire's fate. He may have been inspired to do this because of an accident he had near Easter. As he was leaving the church he had attended for services on Maundy Thursday, the arcade through which he walked collapsed and injured the emperor and several of his companions. Shortly thereafter, Louis held a great assembly at his capital, Aix-la-Chapelle (modern Aachen, in Germany), at which he established a succession plan, the *Ordinatio Imperii,* based upon the idea of the empire's unity. Louis sought divine inspiration, holding a three-day vigil of prayer and fasting before promulgating the *Ordinatio.* At the assembly, he bestowed the imperial title upon his eldest son, Lothar, made him coemperor, and granted him the duty of ruling Italy. He granted his other sons, Louis the German and Pippin, royal authority over subkingdoms in the eastern and western parts of the empire. Sovereign in their own territory, the younger sons would be subject to the authority of Lothar once Louis died.

This attempt at establishing the empire's unity was not met with uniform support. Although Louis made an attempt to recognize Frankish tradition, his settlement was met by passive resistance from the Franks, whose tradition favored divided succession. He also faced opposition from his nephew Bernard, king in Italy, who was ignored in the settlement and in fact was essentially stripped of his authority by the appointment of Lothar to rule in Italy. Bernard rose up in rebellion against his uncle, a rebellion that was quickly suppressed by Louis. Bernard was blinded for his rebellion and died from the punishment. The *Ordinatio*'s later history was troubling for Louis, who revised the plan of succession to include a fourth son, Charles the Bald, and was accused of violating the document, and thus violating God's will. Having provided this justification for rebellion, Louis found himself the target of revolts in 830 and 833–834, as members of the nobility and the church supported the uprisings of Louis's older sons.

See also: Aix-la-Chapelle; Carolingian Dynasty; Charles the Bald; Judith; Lothar; Louis the German; Louis the Pious

Bibliography

Dutton, Paul Edward, trans. "The Ordinatio Imperii of 817." In *Carolingian Civilization: A Reader.* Trans. Paul Edward Dutton. Peterborough, ON: Broadview, 1993, pp. 176–79.

Ganshof, François Louis. *The Carolingians and the Frankish Monarchy.* Trans. Janet Sondheimer. London: Longman, 1971.

Pullan, Brian, trans. *Sources of Medieval Europe from the Mid-Eighth to the Mid-Thirteenth Century.* New York: Barnes & Noble, 1966.

Riché, Pierre. *The Carolingians: A Family Who Forged Europe.* Trans. Michael Idomir Allen. Philadelphia: University of Pennsylvania Press, 1993.

Scholz, Bernhard Walter, trans. *Carolingian Chronicles: Royal Frankish Annals and Nithard's History.* Ann Arbor: University of Michigan Press, 1972.

Orestes (d. 476)

Roman military commander and father of Romulus Augustulus, who is traditionally recognized as the last western Roman emperor. Orestes, whose son was still a boy when he was promoted to the imperial dignity, was the real power behind the throne, as Ricimer had been before him. His efforts to seize power failed, however, because of the unwillingness of Zeno, the emperor in Constantinople, to recognize Romulus, and because of the opposition of Odovacar.

Orestes, a Roman but a subject of the Huns, rose to prominence in the service of the greatest Hunnish king, Attila. He was the Latin secretary of Attila, and sometime rival of another of Attila's aides, Edica-Edikon, the father of Odovacar. According to some accounts, the rivalry between the two nearly brought about Edica-Edikon's demise, and surely created tensions between Orestes and Odovacar. After the collapse of the empire of Attila, Orestes offered his services elsewhere and was raised to the rank of master of soldiers and given the rank of patrician by the emperor Julius Nepos. The emperor saw in Orestes a Roman with connections with leading aristocratic families and also with important experience and contacts with the barbarians, who served in Rome's army in great numbers or settled along Rome's frontiers as friend or foe.

The emperor ordered Orestes to Gaul to protect the province from the threat of various German tribes, but the new master of soldiers had other plans. Instead of going to Gaul, Orestes marched on the capital of the Western Empire at Ravenna. In the face of the advance, Julius Nepos fled to Dalmatia on August 28, 475. In control of Italy and the capital, Orestes chose not to assume the imperial dignity himself, but instead conferred it on his young son Romulus Augustulus on October 31, 475. Orestes, however, remained the real power in Italy, ruling through his son.

Although he successfully seized control, Orestes's usurpation was not recognized by the emperor Zeno in Constantinople, who maintained that the legitimate emperor of the Western Empire was the exile Julius Nepos and not Romulus Augustulus. Despite this lack of recognition, Orestes kept control of Italy for a year after his rebellion against Julius Nepos. His downfall was the result, not of the refusal of Zeno to recognize Romulus but of Orestes's inability to preserve the loyalty of his troops. The vast majority of his army was made up of German soldiers of various tribes. They demanded grants of land in Italy as reward for their service in the Roman army. Grants of land had been a traditional reward for military service, and other barbarian peoples had received these grants, but never in Italy. True to his Roman roots, Orestes refused to grant his Germanic soldiers land in Italy, and as a consequence, he faced a revolt led by Odovacar, who declared that he would make this concession if he ever obtained power. Orestes was quickly overwhelmed by Odovacar and the Germans in the imperial army. Orestes was executed on Odovacar's orders on August 28, 476, and shortly thereafter Odovacar forced Romulus Augustulus to abdicate, but allowed him to retire and did not kill him. Odovacar did not resurrect the system established by Orestes; instead he refused to establish a new puppet emperor in the west and ruled over Italy under the sovereignty of the emperor in Constantinople. The death of Orestes and deposition of his son Romulus is thus traditionally seen as the end of the Roman Empire in the west, even though much that was Roman survived long after their deaths.

See also: Attila the Hun; Huns; Odovacar; Ricimer; Rome; Romulus Augustulus; Zeno

Bibliography

Bury, John B. *History of the Later Roman Empire: From the Death of Theodosius I to the Death of Justinian.* 2 Vols. 1923. Reprint, New York: Dover, 1959.

Bury, John B. *The Invasion of Europe by the Barbarians.* New York: W. W. Norton, 1967.

Lot, Ferdinand. *The End of the Ancient World and the Beginning of the Middle Ages.* 1931. Reprint, New York: Harper and Row, 1961.

Randers-Pehrson, Justine Davis. *Barbarians and Romans: The Birth Struggle of Europe,* A.D. *400–700.* Norman: University of Oklahoma Press, 1983.

Wolfram, Herwig. *The Roman Empire and Its Germanic Peoples.* Trans. Thomas J. Dunlap. Berkeley: University of California Press, 1997.

Ostrogoths

As barbarian people whose name means "Goths of the rising sun," or "Goths glorified by the rising sun," or simply "East Goths," the Ostrogoths played an important role in the history of the later Roman Empire. Identified as early as the first century by Roman writers, the Ostrogoths were at first part of a larger population of Goths that included the Visigoths. During the third century, the larger Gothic population came into contact, often violent, with the Roman Empire. Defeated by the empire, with which they then cultivated better relations, the Goths divided into eastern and western groups, the Ostrogoths and the Visigoths, and their subsequent histories diverged. For the Ostrogoths, as well as the Visigoths, history in the fourth and fifth centuries was shaped by the movements of the Huns and the rise and fall of the great Hunnish empire of Attila. In the fifth century, a reconstituted Ostrogothic tribe formed into a powerful group led by kings. The most famous and important of these kings, Theodoric the Great, participated in political life in the Eastern Roman

Empire and created a successor kingdom in Italy in the late fifth and early sixth centuries. Despite the qualities of Theodoric and the strength of his kingdom, the Ostrogothic kingdom of Italy did not long survive the death of Theodoric. In the 530s, the great emperor Justinian sought to conquer the Western Empire, which had fallen under barbarian control in 476. For some 20 years, Justinian's soldiers and generals fought Ostrogothic armies before finally defeating them, destroying Theodoric's creation, and essentially eliminating the Ostrogoths as a people and a force in history.

Ancient accounts record that Gothic history began in 1490 BC, when a Gothic king led his people in three boats from Scandinavia to the mouth of the Vistula River. Eventually the Goths moved to the area between the Don and Danube Rivers, before being forced out in the mid-third century AD by the Huns. The traditional accounts of the origins of the Goths by ancient historians like Jordanes, however, are not generally accepted. The origins of the Goths are no longer traced to Scandinavia but rather to Poland, where archeological discoveries place a sophisticated, but nonliterate, culture. It was from there that the Goths moved, after which move they made contact with the Roman Empire. In the third century the Goths had repeated clashes with the empire, winning some and putting the empire, already in serious straits, into even greater jeopardy. Roman emperors gradually turned the tide and nearly destroyed the Goths. In the wake of these defeats, however, tradition holds that a great king emerged, Ostrogotha, in circa 290, who founded the kingdom of the Ostrogoths. Although it is unlikely that Ostrogotha existed, it is at that point that the division of the Goths into two groups occurred.

In the fourth century, the two groups, the Tervingi, or Visigoths, and Greuthingi, or Ostrogoths, had more or less come to terms with the empire. By the 370s, however, the relationship between the various Gothic groups and the empire changed as they faced the threat of the Huns. Prior to the arrival of the Huns, King Ermanaric, a member of the Amal clan, had created a substantial kingdom in eastern Europe. He led the struggle against the Huns but was defeated by them, and in 375 he sacrificed himself to the gods in the hopes of saving his people from the Huns. His successor and some of the Goths continued the struggle against the Huns for another year before they were conquered and absorbed by them. From the end of the fourth to the middle of the fifth century, the Greuthingi/Ostrogoths remained part of the Hunnish empire and fought in the armies of the greatest Hun, Attila.

After the death of Attila, however, the fortune and composition of the Ostrogoths underwent a change. Most scholars believe that the Ostrogoths of this period are unrelated to earlier groups identified as Ostrogoths. Whatever the relationship is, in the mid-fifth century under the king Valamir, an Amal, the Ostrogoths emerged from domination by the Huns. Valamir exploited the confused situation in the empire of the Huns after Attila's death in 453 and the defeat of Attila's successor at the Battle of Nedao in 454. Although Valamir and his Goths most likely fought with the Huns against other subject peoples, the Ostrogoths emerged as an independent people because of the collapse of the Huns not long after the battle. Valamir then faced other rivals and endured further attacks by the Huns before their ultimate demise; he died in battle against the Gepids in 468/469.

Valamir was succeeded by his brother Thiudimer, who moved his followers into Roman territory, where they became *foederati* (federated allies) of the empire and came into contact with another group led by the Ostrogothic king Theodoric Strabo, or the Squinter. The two groups struggled against each other for preeminence and for preference before the emperor. The empire itself, however, underwent important changes during this period. In the 470s a new emperor, Zeno, came to power in Constantinople, and the emperor in Italy was deposed and the imperial line ended by the barbarian Odovacar in 476. These changes among the Ostrogoths and within the empire had an important bearing on the future of the Ostrogothic people.

In 473, Thiudimer died and was succeeded by his son Theodoric the Amal, or later known as the Great, who had been named successor in 471. Prior to his nomination, Theodoric had spent 10 years in Constantinople as a hostage of the emperor. During that period Theodoric learned a great deal about the empire and its customs and culture, even though it appears that he did not learn to write. Upon assuming power, he found himself in competition with the other Theodoric, whose followers had revolted against the emperor in 471 and again in 474. The later revolt was part of a palace coup against the new emperor, Zeno, who turned to the Amal for support. To ensure that neither group of Ostrogoths or their leaders became too powerful, Zeno also began to negotiate with Theodoric Strabo and settled a treaty with him in 478. But Zeno's duplicity backfired and angered Theodoric the Amal, who rose against the emperor and settled a treaty with Theodoric Strabo in 479. The hostilities between the two Theodorics were settled for a time, too, as the two closed ranks against the emperor. In 481, Strabo attacked Constantinople but failed to take it or depose the emperor. Shortly thereafter he was killed when his horse reared and threw him onto a rack of spears. Theodoric the Amal was the beneficiary of his occasional ally and rival's death. Although Strabo was succeeded by Rechitach, his followers gradually joined with Theodoric the Amal, who had Rechitach murdered in 484.

Theodoric the Amal, or the Great, to give him his more familiar name, was able to create a great Ostrogothic power that quickly threatened the power of Emperor Zeno. The Ostrogothic king continued the struggle with Zeno, which was resolved for a time in 483, with the emperor making great concessions to the king. Indeed, Theodoric was made a Roman citizen, given the title of patrician, and awarded a consulship for the next year. The Ostrogoths were given a grant of land within the empire. But it occurred to Zeno that he could not trust the rising power of Theodoric, and he replaced him as consul, an event followed by renewed hostilities between the Ostrogoths and the empire. Theodoric's revolt in 485 put further pressure on Zeno, who responded by offering Theodoric the opportunity to lead the assault on Odovacar, the barbarian king in Italy since 476. This assignment, which Theodoric himself had first suggested in 479, was beneficial to both king and emperor and one that Theodoric quickly accepted.

In 488–489, Theodoric led his Ostrogoths, probably numbering some 100,000 people, against Odovacar in Italy. The struggle between the two leaders lasted until 493. It was a hard fought war, with Theodoric winning the battles but unable to take his rival's capital of Ravenna. Indeed, after losing two battles Odovacar established himself in the capital, from which he ventured out to meet Theodoric on the field of battle. Odovacar's hand was strengthened by one of his generals, who joined Theodoric but then rejoined Odovacar, slaying the Gothic warriors who were with him. As a result Odovacar was able to take the offensive, but only for a short while, until Theodoric was reinforced by a Visigothic army. In the early 490s Theodoric gradually took control of Italy and forced Odovacar to come to terms. On February 25, 493, the two leaders agreed to terms that were to be celebrated at a great banquet. Theodoric apparently agreed to share power with his rival, but at the banquet he killed Odovacar, and Theodoric's followers killed the followers of Odovacar in a bloody massacre that ended the war and brought control of Italy to Theodoric.

After his victory, Theodoric was hailed king of Italy, but at first he had to refuse the title in favor of patrician of Italy. The new emperor Anastasius I (r. 491–518) refused to recognize the title of king, with its implications of Theodoric's independence, reminding him that he held power at the discretion of the emperor. Ultimately, however, Theodoric was recognized as king in Constantinople and ruled Italy until his death in 526. His reign was highly beneficial for Italy, and his relationship with the native Roman population was generally good, despite his Arianism and the Romans' Catholicism. He preserved much of the traditional Roman administration, as had Odovacar, and cooperated with the Senate. He ensured the food supply to Italy and patronized Boethius and Cassiodorus as part of a cultural revival. He was also an active builder throughout Italy, erecting public monuments and churches as well as his famous palace and mausoleum in Ravenna. His activities were not limited to Italy, but included an ambitious foreign policy that saw him establish hegemony over the Vandals in Africa and the Visigoths in Spain. In competition with Clovis in northern Europe, Theodosius was able to limit the Merovingian king's expansion into southern Gaul. Although in name only a king, Theodoric, as contemporaries admitted, ruled as effectively as any emperor.

Theodoric's later years and the years following his death were marked by increasing turmoil, leading to the eventual fall of the Ostrogothic kingdom. This situation was due in part to changes in the Eastern Empire, as well as to mistakes on his own part. In 518 a new emperor, Justin, assumed the throne and brought an end to a period of doctrinal uncertainty in the empire. He was a Catholic Christian who promoted traditional orthodox teaching, and in 523 he prohibited Arianism in the

Theodoric's mausoleum, Ravenna. (Daderot)

empire. The support for orthodox teaching and stability in doctrine restored the Italian population's faith in imperial leadership. Moreover, Theodoric was further challenged in matters of religion by the success of the Catholic Clovis against the Visigoths. His concerns were heightened by an alleged plot involving a number of senators, including his advisor Boethius. He ordered Boethius executed and at the same time imprisoned the pope, who had just returned from an embassy to Constantinople. These actions strained relations with his Roman subjects and darkened an otherwise enlightened reign.

Theodoric's situation was worsened by his lack of a male heir, and just prior to his death he encouraged his followers to accept his widowed daughter, Amalswintha, as regent for his grandson Athalaric. At first Theodoric's wishes were accepted, but gradually the Ostrogothic nobility turned against Amalaswintha. Although she was praised for her intelligence and courage, the nobility were divided over her guidance of Athalaric and her pro-Roman foreign policy. When Athalaric reached his majority in 533, a number of nobles sought to persuade him to turn on his mother. The rebellion was nearly successful. Amalaswintha requested a ship from Emperor Justinian to take her to Constantinople, but ultimately stayed and triumphed over her rivals. She married a cousin, Theodohad, in 534 to stabilize the throne, but her husband failed to remain loyal to her, and Athalaric died that same year. Her arrest and murder, which was inspired, according to the fifth-century Byzantine historian Procopius, by Justinian's wife Theodora out of jealousy, provided the emperor with the pretext for his invasion of Italy.

Justinian's invasion of Italy, led at first by Belisarius and later Narses, opened the final chapter of the history of the Ostrogoths. The Gothic Wars, which lasted from 534 to 552, were devastating for both Italy and the Ostrogoths. The opening phase of the war saw rapid victories and much success for the invading armies, in part because of the weakness of Theodohad. Belisarius reached Rome in 536, and Theodohad was deposed in favor of Witigis. The rise of Witigis and the arrival of a second Byzantine general, Narses, slowed imperial progress. When Narses was recalled, Belisarius went on the offensive again and may have forced Witigis to take desperate measures, which possibly included Belisarius's acceptance of the imperial title. Although this remains uncertain, Belisarius was recalled in 540 and took the Ostrogothic king with him. In 541, Witigis was replaced as king by Totila.

Under Totila's leadership, the Ostrogoths fought back successfully and prolonged the war for another 11 years. Totila was able to win back territory in Italy from Byzantine armies and forced the return of Belisarius in 544. In 545 Totila began a siege of Rome; he occupied it in 546, laying waste to the city in the process. Control of the city swung back and forth between the two sides for the rest of the war, which Belisarius was unable to conclude, despite putting great pressure on his rival, because of inadequate supplies and soldiers. Belisarius was recalled in 548, at his own request, and replaced by Narses two years later. Narses demanded sufficient resources to bring the war to a swift conclusion and got them. In 552 Narses won the Battle of Busta Gallorum, at which Totila was killed and organized Gothic resistance was ended. Although Totila had a successor as king and pockets of Ostrogoths resisted until 562, the Ostrogothic kingdom in Italy was crushed by the Byzantine invasion. The Ostrogoths ceased to be an independent people, and the last of the Ostrogoths were probably absorbed by the Lombards during their invasion of Italy in 568.

See also: Amalaswintha; Arianism; Attila the Hun; Belisarius; Boethius; Clovis; Constantinople; Gothic Wars; Huns; Justinian; Lombards; Merovingian Dynasty; Narses; Odovacar; Rome; Theodora; Theodoric the Great; Totila; Vandals; Visigoths; Zeno

Bibliography

Amory, Patrick. *People and Identity in Ostrogothic Italy, 489–554.* Cambridge: Cambridge University Press, 1997.

Browning, Robert. *Justinian and Theodora.* Rev. ed. London: Thames and Hudson, 1987.

Burns, Thomas. *The Ostrogoths: Kingship and Society.* Bloomington: Indiana University Press, 1980.

Burns, Thomas. *A History of the Ostrogoths.* Bloomington: University of Indiana Press, 1984.

Bury, John B. *History of the Later Roman Empire: From the Death of Theodosius I to the Death of Justinian.* 2 Vols. 1923. Reprint, New York: Dover, 1959.

Goffart, Walter. *Barbarians and Romans A.D. 418–584: The Techniques of Accommodation.* Princeton, NJ: Princeton University Press, 1980.

Heather, Peter. *The Goths.* Oxford: Blackwell, 1996.

Jordanes. *The Gothic History of Jordanes.* Trans. Charles C. Mierow. New York: Barnes and Noble, 1985.

Moorhead, John. *Theodoric in Italy.* Oxford: Clarendon, 1992.

Procopius. *History of the Wars.* Trans H. B. Dewing. Cambridge, MA: Harvard University Press, 1969–1993.

Wolfram, Herwig. *History of the Goths.* Trans. Thomas J. Dunlap. Berkeley: University of California Press, 1988.

Wolfram, Herwig. *The Roman Empire and Its Germanic Peoples.* Trans. Thomas J. Dunlap. Berkeley: University of California Press, 1997.

Wood, Ian. *The Merovingian Kingdoms, 450–751.* London: Longman, 1994.

P

Paris

A Roman town originally known as Lutece or Lutetia, Paris, which took its name from a local Celtic tribe, emerged as an important Merovingian site in the late fifth and sixth centuries. It would remain an important Merovingian city throughout the dynasty's reign but would decline as a political capital during the rule of the Carolingians. Despite its political decline, Paris remained an important religious and commercial center and would become the capital of the Capetian line, which ruled from 987 to 1328.

With its convenient location on the Seine River, the future city of Paris attracted settlement by local native tribes before it was taken by the Romans who built baths and other public structures and made the town known as Lutece an important market center. In the third century, Christianity was introduced to the region with the arrival of St. Denis, the apostle to Gaul who was the first bishop of the town. A Christian community sprung up and by the fourth century a Christian cemetery and church had been built. It was also in the fourth century that the town came to be known as Paris, after the local tribe the Parisi.

As Roman rule decline in the west, Paris suffered threats from various barbarian peoples. According to tradition, the city was defended by St. Genevieve on several occasions. Arriving in the city she was given permission to found a religious community and her piety was recognized by the local population. In 451, Genevieve called on the people of Paris to pray that God would protect them against Attila, who was preparing to lay siege to the city. Her efforts were successful and the great Hun turned away to move against Orleans. As the Franks began to move into the region, Genevieve again offered comfort and support to the people of Paris, arranging the delivery of food when Childeric moved against Paris.

Despite Genevieve's efforts, the city would fall to the Franks who would oversee the cities growth into the eighth century. It was Childeric's son, Clovis, who would take control of Paris and make it the capital of the Merovingian kingdom he would forge beginning in the early 480s. The first Catholic Christian barbarian king, Clovis oversaw the construction of a church dedicated to the Holy Apostles and founded a monastery in honor of St. Genevieve. His successors in the sixth century would continue his political and religious association with Paris. Throughout the sixth century a series of church councils were held in Paris and a number of important monasteries, including St. Germian-de-Pres and St. Victor, were established in the city, and just outside Paris the royal abbey of St. Denis was founded. During the reign of King Dagobert (628–38/639), St. Denis became a royal necropolis and both Merovingian and Carolingian kings would find their final resting place in the crypt of the monastery. Paris was not only the political and religious center of the Merovingian kingdom but was also a commercial center, especially after Dagobert instituted a trade fair for the city.

By the eighth century, Paris had grown to a population of between 20,000 and 30,000 people but had begun to lose its place as a political capital. When the new Carolingian dynasty took control of the Frankish kingdom, the political center moved to the east even though early members of the family forged close ties to the monastery of St. Denis—the first Carolingian king, Pippin, was crowned king in the monastery and all Carolingians except Charlemagne were buried there. During the reign of the Carolingians, the local counts were charged with the defense and administration of the city, and the bishops came to exercise more and more authority. The bishops contributed to the reputation of Paris as a center of learning and oversaw two important councils in the ninth century. Its place along the Seine contributed to the city's continued importance as a trade center, but it also led to increasing difficulties for Paris as Viking invaders exploited the waterways of France. Carolingian kings or their representatives were forced to fight off Viking attacks; and the defense of the city in 885–885 by Robert the Strong laid the foundation for his family's rise to power and eventually usurpation of the throne from the Carolingians in 987. Although effective royal power was much reduced, the new Capetian dynasty would rule from Paris until their own demise in 1328.

See also: Attila; Carolingian Dynasty; Charlemagne; Clovis; Dagobert; Denis, St.; Genevieve, St.; Merovingian Dynasty; Pippin III, Called Pippin the Short

Bibliography

McNamara, Jo Ann, John E. Holberg, and Gordon Whatley, eds. *Sainted Women of the Dark Ages.* Durham, NC: Duke University Press, 1992.

Riché, Pierre. *The Carolingians: A Family Who Forged Europe.* Trans. Michael Idomir Allen. Philadelphia: University of Pennsylvania Press, 1993.

Velay, Phiippe. *From Lutetia to Paris: The Island and the Two Banks.* Paris: CNRS, 1992.

Wood, Ian. *The Merovingian Kingdoms, 450–751.* London: Longman, 1994.

Paul the Deacon (c. 720–799)

Best known for his important work of history, *Historia Langobardorum* (The History of the Lombards), Paul the Deacon was also a teacher and monk who wrote a life of Pope Gregory the Great, poetry, and works on pedagogy and monastic life. He was an influential figure at two royal courts, that of his own Lombard people and that of the great Carolingian king, Charlemagne. As a Lombard he benefited from the support of learning and culture initiated by King Liutprand, but also suffered from the collapse of the Lombard kingdom in Italy under the advance of Charlemagne. His learning, however, attracted the attention of the great and powerful, and his history of his people was very popular and influential in the Middle Ages. It remains the best source for the history of the Lombards from their origins to the mid-eighth century.

Paul was born at around 720 to a noble Lombard family. His father, Warnefrid, and mother, Theodolinda, were of sufficient wealth and prominence and were able to send their son to a fashionable court for his education. It is unclear whether he was sent to the royal court at Pavia of King Ratchis (r. 744–749), or possibly that of his famous predecessor Liutprand, or to Cividale, the court of the duke of Friuli. In any case, he was most likely taught by a leading scholar of his day, one who was able to teach the young Paul some Greek and Hebrew as well as the curriculum of traditional Christian and Roman Latin authors. By 770, Paul had come to the attention of the Lombard King Desiderius and was made the tutor of the king's daughter, Adelperga. In 774, when the Lombard kingdom in Italy fell to Charlemagne, Paul retired to the community of Monte Cassino and, perhaps unwillingly, became a monk. He remained there until 783, when he journeyed to the court of Charlemagne to plead for the release of his brother, who had been involved in a conspiracy against the great Frankish king, and for the return of his property. The mission ultimately proved successful, and Paul remained at court as an honored guest for the next several years, where he joined other leading scholars such as the Anglo-Saxon Alcuin of York and tutored one of the king's daughters. He returned to Monte Cassino in 785, perhaps with greater commitment to the monastic life, thanks to his experience at Charlemagne's court, and remained there until his death in 799.

Paul wrote a wide variety of works during his career. His earliest composition may have been a poem composed for Adelperga around 770. He wrote other poems during his life, although their number was not great. He wrote a poem in praise of St. Benedict of Nursia and verses in his correspondence with other members of Charlemagne's court. His finest poems include one that is a delightful description of Lake Como and another that is a moving plea to Charlemagne for his brother's freedom. He edited a fourth-century history of Rome and continued it down to the age of Justinian, and wrote a life of Pope Gregory I and a history of the bishops of Metz. His writings also included more religious works, among them was a collection of homilies that Charlemagne recommended for use by the clergy in his kingdom and a commentary on the Rule of Benedict that influenced the monastic reforms of the early ninth century.

His most famous and important work, however, was the *Historia Langobardorum,* which traces the history of the Lombards from their origins to the death of King Liutprand in 744. The work exists in over one hundred manuscripts and was imitated and used by writers down to the 15th century. Paul borrowed from earlier historians, including Gregory of Tours, Isidore of Seville, and Bede, but his most important sources—the anonymous *Origo Gentis Langobardorum* (The Origin of the Lombard People) and the chronicle of Secundus—are now lost. Although relatively weak on exact chronology, the *History* is a simple but powerful narrative of the Lombard people. Paul describes the Lombards' origin and their entry into Italy, as well as the many invasions the Lombards were forced to fight off. He writes of the great kings and dukes of the Lombards and tells of the exciting escape of the young king Grimoald from the Avars. He discusses the affairs of popes, bishops, and monks, as well as supernatural events and miracles. His work is a source of great value, and it is regrettable that death kept him from including in his *History* the tale of the defeat of his people by Charlemagne, whom he admired.

See also: Alcuin of York; Avars; Bede; Benedict of Nursia, St.; Carolingian Dynasty; Carolingian Renaissance; Charlemagne; Desiderius; Franks; Gregory I, the Great, Pope; Gregory of Tours; Isidore of Seville; Liutprand; Lombards; Pavia; Rome

Bibliography

Christie, Neil. *The Lombards.* Oxford: Blackwell, 1998.

Laistner, Max L. W. *Thought and Letters in Western Europe, A.D. 500 to 900.* 2nd ed. Ithaca, NY: Cornell University Press, 1976.

McKitterick, Rosamond. *The Frankish Kingdoms under the Carolingians, 951–987.* London: Longman, 1983.

Paul the Deacon. *History of the Lombards.* Trans. William Dudley Foulke. Ed. Edward Peters. Philadelphia: University of Pennsylvania Press, 1974.

Riché, Pierre. *Education and Culture in the Barbarian West: From the Sixth through the Eighth Century.* Trans. John Contreni. Columbia: University of South Carolina Press, 1976.

Pavia

A northern Italian town on the Ticino River, Pavia was a prominent city under the Romans, Ostrogoths, Lombards, and Carolingian Franks. Throughout late antiquity and the early Middle Ages, Pavia was key military and political center as well as an important center of religion and commerce.

Founded by the Romans in the first-century BC, Pavia, or Ticinum as the Romans called it, was originally a military encampment and evolved into an important commercial center. In the fifth century, Pavia suffered from the barbarian invasions and was sacked by Attila the Hun in 452. In 476, the Roman Empire is said to have fallen when Orestes was defeated and killed by Odovacar at Pavia. Under the Ostrogoths, who established a citadel there, Pavia became a major stronghold as well as a leading commercial center. Pavia was also a center of Gothic resistance to Belisarius and the Byzantine army during the Gothic Wars. Although captured by the Byzantines, along with the rest of Italy, Pavia was taken by the Lombards in 568 as part of their invasion of Italy. Pavia became the capital of the Lombard kingdom until its fall in 774. Under King Liutprand, Pavia flourished and became a major religious site when Liutprand had the relics of St. Augustine of Hippo transferred to the church of San Pietro in Ciel d'Oro, which had been built in the sixth century. The saint's relics were laid alongside the important early Christian philosopher, Boethius, and Liutprand himself would be buried there.

Lombard rule came to an end in 774 when Charlemagne defeated the last Lombard king, Desiderius, and seized control of the kingdom and its capital Pavia. Carolingian control of Pavia helped establish their legitimacy in Italy and remained important in the eighth and ninth centuries. In the 10th century, the city was sacked by the Magyars but was revived under the Ottonian dynasty and remained an important city throughout the rest of the Middle Ages.

See also: Attila the Hun; Augustine of Hippo, St.; Belisarius; Boethius; Carolingian Dynasty; Charlemagne; Desiderius; Gothic Wars; Liutprand; Lombards; Odovacar; Orestes; Ostrogoths

Bibliography

Christie, Neil. *The Lombards: The Ancient Longobards.* Oxford: Wiley-Blackwell, 1999.

Hallenback, Jan T. *Pavia and Rome: The Lombard Monarchy and the Papacy in the Eighth Century.* Philadelphia, PA: American Philosophical Society.

La Rocca, Cristina. *Italy in the Early Middle Ages: 476–1000.* New York: Oxford University Press, 2002.

Paul the Deacon. *History of the Lombards.* Trans. William Dudley Foulke. Ed. Edward Peters. Philadelphia: University of Pennsylvania Press, 1975.

Peasants

Throughout late antiquity and the early Middle Ages, society was divided into a number of legal and social classes. Society was ruled by kings and powerful landed nobles and was served by slaves; between the ranks of the great free and the unfree were the peasants. The peasants, descendants of the ancient *coloni* (plural of *colonus,* Latin for farmer), remained essentially legally free until after the year 1000 and were the most important figures in the economic life of the period. The peasants, or *coloni* as they are often called in contemporary sources, were also the most numerous members of society. Although they were the largest part of the population, it is impossible to get a complete picture of the peasants because they figure in so few contemporary documents, and those that do portray them often present a misleading picture. The most famous of the sources for early medieval peasant life are the polyptychs of Charlemagne and the Carolingian dynasty.

In all likelihood, the great majority of residents in the countryside of barbarian Europe were free, landholding peasants, but the terms on which the land was held and the economic wealth of the peasants varied greatly. Most peasants and their families lived on small properties, of one *mansus,* or Anglo-Saxon hide, which were large enough to support a family. These properties could be freely disposed of by the peasants, who could buy and sell their lots and pass them along to their children. Of course, as small proprietors, the peasants were constantly under the pressure of wealthy and powerful figures who sought to acquire the *mansi* of the peasants. As a defense, peasants sometimes made a grant of their holding or part of it to a local church or monastery, which then allowed the peasant to receive it back and work it for his family's benefit. Peasants were also sometimes forced to squeeze several families on a parcel of land designed for one family. Moreover, rural families sometimes held land in tenancy and were obligated to offer payment or service to the landowner. Their tenant holdings were part of a large estate and were often not contiguous but scattered across the estate. The size and number of holdings varied as well, and some tenants had quite extensive lots to work. Both tenant farmers and small freeholders often hired themselves out to other landowners to supplement their incomes. Some peasants, however, were able to acquire several *mansi* of their own and teams of animals to work the fields, and thus became relatively comfortable. The owners of four or more *mansi* were expected to do service at the lord's court.

The *mansus* was made up of a number of parts, and the peasants were members of a large community, the village. The individual holding, whether free or tenant in whatever form, included, among other things, a simple hut of stone, wood, or clay where the peasant family lived. Although some were larger and more elaborate, these homes generally had a single room divided into sections, a dirt floor, a bed, benches, and tables. Around the hut were fields for farming, forests, meadows, vineyards, and mills and other buildings necessary for the agricultural economy of the peasant. The peasants spent most of their lives working the farms, raising wheat, oats, and other grains, as well as livestock, including chickens, cows, sheep, and pigs. Beyond the individual landholdings of the peasants was the village. This larger community provided some relief from the more onerous burdens of peasant life and tenant farming. Members of the village often worked together, and the more successful free peasants often regulated the daily affairs of the members of the community and arbitrated their disputes. Decisions affecting the village, such as when to plant and to harvest or how to manage the wastelands, were made by the community as a whole.

See also: Agriculture; Anglo-Saxons; Animals; Carolingian Dynasty; Charlemagne; Slaves and Slavery

Bibliography

Bloch, Marc. *French Rural History: An Essay on Its Basic Characteristics.* Trans. Janet Sondheimer. Berkeley: University of California Press, 1966.

Duby, Georges. *The Early Growth of the European Economy: Warriors and Peasants from the Seventh to the Twelfth Century.* Trans. Howard B. Clarke. Ithaca, NY: Cornell University Press, 1979.

Riché, Pierre. *Daily Life in the World of Charlemagne.* Trans. Jo Ann McNamara. Philadelphia: University of Pennsylvania Press, 1983.

Wolfram, Herwig. *The Roman Empire and Its Germanic Peoples.* Trans. Thomas J. Dunlap. Berkeley: University of California Press, 1997.

Wood, Ian. *The Merovingian Kingdoms, 450–751.* London: Longman, 1994.

Penda (d. 654)

Penda was the Mercian king (r. 632/633–654) who transformed his kingdom into a significant power during his lifetime. Penda was a mighty king, who extended his overlordship over much of southern England. Although not a Christian himself, Penda allowed his son, Paeda, to introduce Christianity into the kingdom.

Penda is first mentioned in a passage from the *Anglo-Saxon Chronicle* in the year 628 after the Battle of Cirencester. The passage notes that he made an agreement with the West Saxons in which the Mercians annexed territory along the river Severn. At that time Penda was most likely not yet king but a powerful noble of royal lineage. He assumed the kingship after the defeat and death of Edwin, king of Northumbria, in 632. In an alliance with Cadwallon of Gwynedd, a native Briton, Penda invaded Deira, devastated the countryside, and slew Edwin, who had extended his authority over Mercia and other regions. Although now king, Penda was forced to recognize the authority of the new Northumbrian king, Oswald of Bernicia, in 633. For the next eight years Penda was not strong enough to challenge Oswald, but in 641 he rose up against the Northumbrian king and defeated and killed him at the Battle of Maserfelth. Oswald himself was almost immediately recognized as a saint and martyr because of his death at the hands of the pagan Penda.

Following the victory over Oswald, Penda was the greatest king of the English, but he did not attempt to establish himself as overlord of the other kingdoms. He did, however, drive the West Saxon king into exile in 645, following the Saxon king's repudiation of his wife, Penda's sister. He also subjugated the kingdom of East Anglia, and made his son subking of Middle Anglia in 653. And he was recognized as a great power by the other kings, some of whom served in his army. His sole rival was the king of Northumbria, Oswy, though he respected the power of Penda. Oswy, despite being deemed a personal enemy by Penda, married one of his daughters to Penda's son Paeda and sent a son as a hostage to Penda's court. Despite cordial diplomatic arrangements and the marriage tie, Penda and Oswy did eventually go to war. The cause and course of the war remain unclear, but it was likely the result of border struggles between the two kings. According to Bede, Penda marched against Oswy with some 30 legions in an effort to destroy him. In the army, as a testimony of Penda's power, were soldiers and kings of Mercia's neighboring kingdoms. It is likely that Penda enjoyed some success against Oswy, besieging him in a castle and nearly destroying the king and his army. Penda himself demanded and received a significant amount of treasure from Oswy. But at the Battle of Winwaed, near Leeds, on November of 654, Penda was defeated and killed by Oswy, who, according to Bede, had promised God before the battle that if he were victorious, he would consecrate his daughter to the religious life and build monasteries on 12 estates. Following Penda's death, Mercia was subjugated by Oswy, who remained overlord until Penda's son Wulfhere retook the throne.

Penda's reign was important in the history of early Anglo-Saxon England. He established Mercia as a significant power and extended his influence throughout southern England. Although Mercia succumbed to Northumbria after his death, Penda's kingdom remained an important power in the coming generations. Although not a Christian himself, he did allow the introduction of Christianity into kingdoms under his control.

See also: Anglo-Saxons; *Anglo-Saxon Chronicle*; Bede; Mercia

Bibliography

Blair, Peter Hunter. *The World of Bede.* Cambridge: Cambridge University Press, 1990.

Randers-Pehrson, Justine Davis. *Barbarians and Romans: The Birth Struggle of Europe, A.D. 400–700.* Norman: University of Oklahoma Press, 1983.

Stenton, Frank M. *Anglo-Saxon England.* 3rd ed. Oxford: Clarendon, 1971.

Whitelock, Dorothy, ed. *The Anglo-Saxon Chronicle.* Westport, CT: Greenwood, 1986.

Pippin I, Called Pippin of Landen (d. 640)

A leading noble in the Merovingian subkingdom of Austrasia, Pippin rose to prominence in the revolt against the queen, Brunhilde, in 613. He was rewarded for his role with the office of mayor of the palace and exercised great influence on the kingdom during the reigns of Chlotar II and his son Dagobert. With St. Arnulf of Metz, with whom he was joined by the marriage of his daughter and Arnulf's son, Pippin was one of the founders of the Carolingian dynasty. He built up substantial wealth and family connections and laid the groundwork for the later success of the family. Although his efforts were later undermined by the failed coup of his nephew Grimoald, Pippin's achievements did provide the necessary foundation for the family's ultimate triumph. His namesakes, Pippin II and III, restored the family to the office of mayor of the palace, from which they rose to the office of king of the Franks.

Pippin's rise to power was aided by birth and wise marriage alliances. He was from an economically prosperous area of Austrasia, the Meuse River basin, where his family held extensive lands. His position was enhanced by his marriage to Itta, who was the sister of the future bishop of Trier and, according to a contemporary text, was celebrated because of her virtues and wealth. The marriage alliance he forged with Arnulf of Metz, however, proved of even greater value to Pippin and his family. The marriage of his daughter Begga (d. 693) to Arnulf's son Ansegisel (d. 676) drew two powerful families closer together, and the lands of Pippin and Arnulf provided the territorial and economic foundation for the Carolingian family whose rise to prominence began with Pippin.

Already a wealthy and influential landowner, Pippin's status in the kingdom improved dramatically in 613 when he and Arnulf joined with the Merovingian king Chlotar II to overthrow Queen Brunhilde, who had been the effective ruler of Neustria and the bitter rival of Chlotar's mother Fredegund. Successful in his revolt and in reuniting the kingdom, Chlotar rewarded his supporters. Arnulf was made bishop of Metz, and Pippin was made mayor of the palace in Austrasia, where he became the virtual ruler. Pippin's appointment came shortly after Chlotar appointed his young son Dagobert king in Austrasia. Pippin assumed a heavy share of the burden of government and held an office that enabled him to exercise great power in the king's name. Dagobert benefited from the tutelage of Pippin as well. Moreover, Pippin continued to serve the Merovingian dynasty after Chlotar's death in 629. When Dagobert assumed control of the entire Merovingian kingdom, Pippin continued in his position as mayor. According to the seventh-century chronicle of Fredegar, Pippin provided a steadying hand in the early years of Dagobert's reign. The new king, who had ruled so well in Austrasia during his father's lifetime, now became debauched and greedy. Responding to the complaints of the nobles from the subkingdom of Neustria, Pippin reprimanded the young king and restored him to the virtues he exhibited during Chlotar's life.

Although Fredegar recognized Pippin as a wise counselor who loved justice, rival nobles in Austrasia were not so enamored of the mayor and sought to create a break between Pippin and Dagobert. Their efforts were not immediately successful, but Dagobert did gradually move away from his former mentor, and in 633 removed him from the position of mayor. Pippin's loss of office and the efforts to separate him from Dagobert reveal the nature of Merovingian politics in the seventh century. Although still firmly in charge of the kingdom, the Merovingians ruled over a number of aristocratic families that were involved in frequently shifting alliances. For much of his life, however, Pippin had been able to manage these alliances, as his marriage ties suggest, and even after his fall from office he remained a vital force in Austrasia.

After the death of Dagobert in 639, Pippin moved quickly to retake his position as mayor of the palace. According to Fredegar, he ruled prudently and through friendly tips with his vassals. He also strove to have the nobility recognize the new king in Austrasia, Sigebert III, the 10-year-old son of Dagobert. Despite his ability to restore his authority quickly after the death of Dagobert, Pippin did not rule long; he died suddenly in 640. Although he did not long survive Dagobert, Pippin had provided a secure base for his family's future.

See also: Arnulf of Metz, St.; Austrasia; Brunhilde; Carolingian Dynasty; Chlotar II; Dagobert; Fredegar; Fredegund; Grimoald; Merovingian Dynasty; Neustria; Pippin II, Called Pippin of Herstal; Pippin III, Called Pippin the Short

Bibliography

Fouracre, Paul, and Richard A. Gerberding. *Late Merovingian France: History and Hagiography, 640–720.* Manchester, UK: University of Manchester Press, 1996.

James, Edward. *The Franks.* Oxford: Blackwell, 1991.

Riché, Pierre. *The Carolingians: A Family Who Forged Europe.* Trans. Michael Idomir Allen. Philadelphia: University of Pennsylvania Press, 1993.

Wallace-Hadrill, J. M., ed. and trans. *The Fourth Book of the Chronicle of Fredegar with Its Continuations.* London: Nelson, 1960.

Wood, Ian. *The Merovingian Kingdoms, 450–751.* London: Longman, 1994.

Pippin II, Called Pippin of Herstal (d. 714)

Frankish mayor of the palace and virtual leader of the Merovingian kingdom in the late seventh and early eighth centuries. His reign as mayor witnessed the further growth in power of the Carolingian family, and contributed to the ultimate triumph of the dynasty in the time of his descendants Pippin III the Short and Charlemagne. His victory at the Battle of Tertry in 687 solidified his hold on power and reunited the kingdom under the Merovingian king he supported, Theuderic III (d. 691). He held the office of mayor and remained the main authority in the kingdom until his death in 714. He was ultimately succeeded by his son Charles Martel.

Although Pippin was noted, according to the annals written circa 800, for "the strength of his justice, the unconquerable solidity of his bravery and the guidance of his moderation" (Fouracre 1996, 351), his path to power was not an easy one. Despite the success of his grandfathers, Pippin I of Landen and Arnulf of Metz, the second Pippin was faced by powerful opponents and forced to deal with the failed coup of the family's previous leader, Grimoald, who had sought to replace the ruling Merovingian dynasty with a member of his own family. Pippin was also forced to deal with the murder of his father, Ansegisel, who was killed by a rival family after emerging as the leader of the family after Grimoald's failure.

Moreover, in his first contests with the Neustrian mayors of the palace, Pippin, who was an Austrasian noble, was defeated. In 680, he fought a battle against the Neustrian mayor Ebroin and was decisively defeated. The family suffered more than military defeat; Ebroin ordered the murder of Pippin's brother, Martin, who had sought refuge in Laon. A later battle with Ebroin's successor Waratto ended in another defeat for Pippin.

Although he endured some serious defeats early in his career, Pippin ultimately triumphed over his Neustrian rivals. For one thing, the near tyrannical rule of the Neustrian mayors alienated a large portion of the nobility, which turned to Pippin for help. In 687, war again broke out between the Neustrian mayor, now Berchar, and the Austrasians, led by Pippin. At the request of the Neustrian nobility, Pippin led a campaign against Berchar and his king, Theuderic III, and fought a major battle at Tertry. Pippin's victory secured his position, along with that of his family, in the kingdom. He took control of the king and the royal treasury and reunited the kingdom under his authority as mayor of the palace. Pippin and his descendants ruled the Frankish kingdom for the next three centuries, and after 751 they ruled as kings.

From 687 until his death in 714, Pippin was the real power in the Frankish kingdom, even though a member of the Merovingian dynasty continued to reside on the throne. As mayor of the palace, Pippin directed both the internal and external affairs of the realm. To strengthen his own position after the Battle of Tertry, Pippin promoted family members and loyal supporters to key positions in the kingdom. He made one supporter mayor in Neustria, and then later replaced this supporter with his own son, Grimoald. He placed other allies in places of power in Neustria and made other sons, including Drogo who was duke of the Burgundians, officials in other parts of the kingdom. He also arranged marriages between his family and the families of important nobles throughout the kingdom, the most successful of the marriages he arranged being his own earlier marriage to Plectrude, who came from an important family in the area of modern Cologne.

Pippin extended his family's control of the kingdom, but he did not attempt to usurp the Merovingian throne as his uncle Grimoald had. Perhaps learning the lessons of his uncle's failed coup, Pippin continued to install Merovingians on the throne. He ruled first with Theuderic III, and then with Clovis IV (r. 691–695), Childebert III (r. 695–711), and finally Dagobert III (r. 711–715). Although not the *rois fainéants* (do-nothing kings) of popular legend, these kings were clearly the junior partners in the government of the kingdom. Indeed, as the *Annals of Metz* notes, Pippin called the annual meeting of the nobles of the realm and presided over it, after allowing the kings to ask for peace, call for the protection of widows and orphans, and the like.

Among Pippin's many duties was the prosecution of war against external foes and rebellious elements within the kingdom. Although Pippin led the armies, the

Annals of Metz report that the king "ordered the army to be ready for departure on the appointed day" (356), which suggests that the Merovingian kings, with the exception of the infant Clovis, had greater authority than the pro-Carolingian annals allow. Whatever the case, Pippin led a campaign into Aquitaine, the first of many Carolingian forays into that rich region, which had traditionally resisted Frankish authority. Of greater concern to Pippin, however, were affairs on the northern and eastern frontiers of the kingdom. He marched against the Frisians to the north, who had raided Frankish territory and had extensive trade contacts with England. Pippin's success against the Frisians was followed by the colonization of the region by Austrasian nobles and by the construction of churches. Pippin also appointed the Anglo-Saxon missionary Willibrord bishop of the newly conquered region. Although relations between Rome and the Carolingians were formalized only in the reign of Pippin's grandson, the connection with Willibrord, who had close ties to Rome, laid the foundation for the later alliance. Just as his descendants later expanded on ties to Rome, so too they adopted his policy of conquest and conversion of pagan peoples along their eastern frontier.

Pippin also exploited his relationship with the church in the kingdom. His relations with the bishops were sometimes difficult, and he exiled bishops and replaced them with personal allies or family members. Pippin not only appointed bishops to important sees in the kingdom, but also appointed abbots to prominent monasteries. He also endowed monasteries and churches, and established proprietary family churches. His ecclesiastical policy mirrored his political one and was intended to further strengthen his and his family's hold on power. Appointments to office and charitable donations to religious communities were designed to bring the support of the church to Pippin. Toward this end as well, Pippin put churches and monasteries, and their significant wealth, under the control of close allies, and sometimes took territories from the churches and granted the land to his supporters.

By the time of his death on December 16, 714, Pippin had successfully established himself and, to a lesser degree, his family as the most important power in the Frankish kingdom. His death, however, led the kingdom into turmoil, as his wife and children struggled for control of his legacy. Despite the best efforts of his widow, Plectrude, to promote the interests of her grandson, it was the son of one of Pippin's concubines, Charles Martel, who eventually took over his father's legacy and continued the growth of the family's power.

See also: Arnulf of Metz, St.; Austrasia; Carolingian Dynasty; Charlemagne; Charles Martel; Grimoald; Merovingian Dynasty; Neustria; Pippin of Landen; Pippin III, Called Pippin the Short; Plectrude; *Rois Fainéants*; Tertry, Battle of; Saint-Denis, Abbey of

Bibliography

Fouracre, Paul, and Richard A. Gerberding. *Late Merovingian France: History and Hagiography, 640–720.* Manchester, UK: University of Manchester Press, 1996.

Gerberding, Richard, A. *The Rise of the Carolingians and the "Liber Historiae Francorum."* Oxford: Clarendon, 1987.

Halphen, Louis. *Charlemagne and the Carolingian Empire.* Trans. Giselle de Nie. Amsterdam: North-Holland, 1977.

McKitterick, Rosamond. *The Frankish Kingdoms under the Carolingians, 751–987.* London: Longman, 1983.

Riché, Pierre. *The Carolingians: A Family Who Forged Europe.* Trans. Michael Idomir Allen. Philadelphia: University of Pennsylvania Press, 1993.

Wallace-Hadrill, J. M., ed. and trans. *The Fourth Book of the Chronicle of Fredegar with Its Continuations.* London: Nelson, 1960.

Wood, Ian. *The Merovingian Kingdoms, 450–751.* London: Longman, 1994.

Pippin III, Called Pippin the Short (d. 768)

Mayor of the palace and founder of the Carolingian royal dynasty, Pippin laid the foundation for much of Carolingian royal policy and success. Although often overshadowed by his more illustrious son, Charlemagne, Pippin was a great military, political, and religious reformer in his own right. As mayor and king, he imposed his authority on the kingdom and expanded its boundaries. He formalized the alliance with the pope in Rome that had first been attempted during the reign of Pippin's father, Charles Martel. In fact, the alliance was essential for Pippin's elevation to the kingship, as well as for the long-term growth of the Papal States. Both before and after his usurpation of the throne, Pippin was actively involved in the reform of the church. In many ways, Pippin left a lasting and important legacy for Charlemagne and the Carolingian line.

On the death of his father, Charles Martel, in 741, Pippin and his brother Carloman inherited control of the kingdom. Although officially only mayor of the palace, Charles Martel divided control of the kingdom between his two sons as any Frankish king would, having ruled without a Merovingian king during the last three years of his life. Pippin and Carloman inherited the office of mayor and authority over the entire realm. Their succession to power, however, was not achieved without strife. In the opening years of their joint reign, Pippin and Carloman faced widespread opposition, including the revolt of their half brother, Grifo, who had been excluded from the inheritance. Although Grifo failed to gain power, he remained a problem until his death in 753. But Grifo was not the only source of trouble for Pippin and Carloman at the outset of their reign. They faced unrest and rebellion in Aquitaine and Bavaria, as well as from other Frankish noble families who regarded the Carolingians as equals.

In 743, Pippin and Carloman discovered the heir to the Merovingian throne in a monastery and restored him, as Childeric III, to his rightful place as king. The restoration, possibly initiated by Carloman, may have been done to suppress rebellious partisans of the Merovingian dynasty or to establish legitimacy for the Carolingians' position. Whatever the purpose, the restoration of Childeric proved to be only a short-term solution. In 747, after undertaking military campaigns and religious reform with his brother, Carloman retired to the monastery of Mount Soracte near Rome. Pippin moved quickly to restrict Carloman's sons' claims to power and to consolidate his position as mayor. He was now the sole mayor in the kingdom and king in everything but name.

In 750, Pippin took the first of several steps that brought about a revolution in the Frankish kingdom. He sent two of his most trusted advisors, Archbishop Burchard of Würzburg and Abbot Fulrad of St. Denis, to Pope Zachary (r. 741–752) in Rome to ask whether the person with the power or the person with the title should be king. Zachary answered as Pippin had hoped. By turning to the pope, Pippin hoped to gain a higher spiritual sanction than that possessed by the Merovingians, who claimed descent from a sea god. In 751, at an assembly of the leaders of the realm in Soissons, Childeric was deposed and sent to a monastery. At the same time, Pippin was elected king by the nobility and crowned and anointed king by the bishops of the realm, including possibly, Boniface, the papal representative in the kingdom. The ceremony of anointing, of unction, was borrowed from the Hebrew Scriptures and was intended to establish the Carolingians as kings of the new children of Israel.

In 753, Pope Stephen II (r. 752–757) traveled north to meet with Pippin. Fleeing from the advances of the Lombard king Aistulf, Stephen hoped to secure the aid of the Frankish king. The two met at the royal residence of Ponthion to discuss the issue and other things during the winter of 753–754. Stephen received the promise of aid from Pippin, who also supported the pope's claims to various estates in central Italy. The following spring, Pippin met with various nobles to gain support for a campaign against the Lombards to protect the pope. Because of earlier alliances with the Lombards, many nobles were reluctant to agree to the invasion of Italy, but the appearance of Carloman, who had been sent to argue against the pope's request by Aistulf, helped Pippin's cause. In July 754, Stephen upheld his side of the bargain, crowning and anointing Pippin king. Stephen not only crowned Pippin but also crowned and anointed his sons, Charles and Carloman, granted them the imperial title of patrician, and declared that only descendants of Pippin could legitimately rule the Franks. The revolution was now complete. The Carolingians had become the kings of the Franks and, perhaps more importantly, had become close allies of the pope.

Although at first opposed to the invasion of Italy, the nobles agreed at a second council in 755, after Aistulf had refused Pippin's request to honor the pope. Pippin invaded at the head of a large army and defeated the Lombards at Susa before laying siege to the capital of Pavia. Aistulf relented, gave hostages, and agreed to return territory to the pope. Once Pippin had withdrawn, however, Aistulf broke the treaty. In 756, Pippin again invaded, with the enthusiastic support of the nobles, and again laid siege to Pavia and forced Aistulf to submit. Pippin, determined to enforce the agreement, sent Abbot Fulrad to each of the cities Aistulf was to return to the pope to collect keys from them. A list was compiled by Fulrad, which has come to be known as the Donation of Pippin, and deposited on the altar of St. Peter's in Rome. Aistulf's death in 756 and the Lombard political situation thereafter made any return to Italy on Pippin's part unnecessary. But his two invasions strengthened the alliance between Rome and the Carolingians and helped establish the Papal States.

Pippin's campaigns in Italy were not his only foreign military ventures. In fact, he learned of Stephen's journey to the Frankish kingdom in 753 while returning from a campaign in Saxony. He raided Saxony to enforce a treaty that permitted the free movement of Christian missionaries in that region. More important than the Saxon campaign, however, was the reconquest of the duchy of Aquitaine, a region that had been part of the Frankish kingdom in the seventh century. A region of great agricultural wealth, Aquitaine was also the center of opposition to Carolingian power before and after 750. Moreover, Pippin claimed that the duke, Waifar, had violated the integrity of the church. Defense of ecclesiastical and political interests led Pippin to invade the duchy numerous times, including annual campaigns from 760 to 768. In 761, Pippin led a major expedition that saw his triumph over the duke as well as the assassination of Waifar by some of his own men, probably in the pay of Pippin. Although victorious over Waifar in 761, Pippin's conquest of Aquitaine was a painstaking process, in which the king gradually conquered forts and cities and gradually won over Waifar's vassals. To secure his hold on the duchy, Pippin placed his supporters in positions of political power and installed loyal ecclesiastics as abbots of the monasteries in the duchy. Although a revolt occurred shortly after his death, Pippin had restored Frankish control over Aquitaine and was able to include the duchy in his legacy to his sons.

Along with his usurpation and military campaigns, Pippin carried out a number of political and religious reforms. One crucial policy was not a reform: Pippin acquired extensive estates throughout the realm as a means to bolster his power. In fact, the establishment of landed wealth and power was as important for his elevation to the kingship as the coronation by the bishops. The accumulation of land and loyal vassals on that land provided the justification for the usurpation of the throne. Pippin acquired further power through the establishment of control over monasteries throughout the realm, which he used to curtail the power of the aristocratic bishops. One of the most important monasteries of the kingdom and a former Merovingian royal monastery, St. Denis near Paris, became an important supporter of Pippin and his new dynasty, and was important in Pippin's elevation to the kingship. He also reformed royal administration by increasing the use of writing in government and by employing churchmen as administrators. Finally, he commissioned a new edition of the Salic law that exalted the virtues of the Franks and their new royal dynasty.

Pippin was also an active religious reformer both before and after the retirement of his brother in 747. In the early years of his rule as mayor, Pippin recognized the value of reform of the church, which had suffered during the civil wars of the previous generations. Although not as enthusiastic a supporter of the missionary and reform work of Boniface as was his brother Carloman, Pippin nonetheless supported efforts to reform the church in the Frankish kingdom and certainly recognized the value of the devotion to Rome that Boniface preached. After the retirement of Carloman and death of Boniface in 754, Pippin relied increasingly on Chrodegang, bishop and then archbishop of Metz. Although the king promoted the role of the monastery in the Frankish church, especially to limit the power of the bishops, he found an important ally in Chrodegang, who presided over numerous councils with the king during Pippin's reign.

Councils were held at Ver in 755, at Verberie in 756, at Attigny in 760, and at Gentilly in 767, and were intended to reform religious life and organization in the kingdom. Chrodegang encouraged a closer alliance with Rome for the church, incorporating Roman liturgical traditions in the church, and improved ecclesiastical discipline among the clergy, who had been derided by Boniface for their ignorance and immorality. The clergy, according to Boniface, indulged in battle and committed adultery, and one priest could not offer the blessing properly, blessing "in the name of the country and of the daughter." The councils sought to combat these problems, and passed legislation prohibiting clergy from going to war and demanding that monks and nuns renounce wealth and accept stability. The councils of Pippin also sought to improve church organization by prohibiting the establishment of monasteries on private land by lay nobles.

By his death in 768, Pippin had taken control of the kingdom of the Franks, and he was able to pass the kingship on to his two sons, Charles and Carloman. In good Frankish tradition, Pippin divided the kingdom between his two sons. As a counterbalance to that potentially disruptive tradition, however, Pippin had established the traditions in government, the church, and military that his son Charles, or Charlemagne as he came to be known, exploited to such great end. Although he did not adopt all the policies of his father, Charles was nonetheless greatly indebted to his father for the legacy he left behind. Indeed, if Pippin's achievements had been limited to the founding of the Carolingian royal dynasty, he would certainly still be an important figure. But his reform of the Frankish church and government, which also paved the way for the Carolingian Renaissance emerging under Charlemagne, were important for the long-term success of his dynasty. His association with the pope set a precedent for church–state relations that lasted until at least the end of the Middle Ages, and his conquests created a powerful kingdom that his son was able to transform into an empire. Truly, Pippin was a great king.

See also: Aistulf; Boniface, St.; Carolingian Dynasty; Carolingian Renaissance; Charlemagne; Charles Martel; Childeric III; Chrodegang of Metz; Clovis; Donation of Pippin; Merovingian Dynasty; Paris; Rome; Salic Law; Saint-Denis, Abbey of

Bibliography

Davis, Raymond, trans. *The Lives of the Eighth-Century Popes* (Liber Pontificalis): *The Ancient Biographies of Nine Popes from A.D. 715 to A.D. 817.* Liverpool, UK: Liverpool University Press, 1992.

Ganshof, François Louis. *The Carolingians and the Frankish Monarchy.* Trans. Janet Sondheimer. London: Longman, 1971.

James, Edward. *The Franks.* Oxford: Basil Blackwell, 1988.

Llewellyn, Peter. *Rome in the Dark Ages.* New York: Barnes and Noble, 1996.

McKitterick, Rosamond. *The Frankish Kingdoms under the Carolingians, 751–987.* London: Longman, 1983.

Noble, Thomas X. F. *The Republic of St. Peter: The Birth of the Papal State, 680–825.* Philadelphia: University of Pennsylvania Press, 1984.

Riché, Pierre. *The Carolingians: A Family who Forged Europe.* Trans. Michael Idomir Allen. Philadelphia: University of Pennsylvania Press, 1993.

Scholz, Bernhard Walter, trans. *Carolingian Chronicles: Royal Frankish Annals and Nithard's History.* Ann Arbor: University of Michigan Press, 1972.

Wallace-Hadrill, J. M. *The Frankish Church.* Oxford: Clarendon, 1983.

Plectrude (d. after 721)

Wife of the Carolingian mayor of the palace Pippin II of Herstal (d. 714) and, after her husband's death, rival for control of the Frankish kingdom and the Merovingian king with Charles Martel (d. 741), who was Pippin's son by another woman. A member of an important noble family, Plectrude offered Pippin a good marriage alliance and sought to keep control of her power after her husband's death and promote her own heirs to the office of mayor.

Plectrude was from an important noble family that had extensive domains in the area between the Rhine, Meuse, and Moselle Rivers. Her father, Hugobert, was a powerful palace official whose connections and wealth made marriage to Plectrude an attractive proposition. Moreover, she had no brothers, only sisters, and was sure to inherit many of the vast estates of her family, thus making her an even more coveted bride. In 670, Pippin married Plectrude and increased his own power in the north and northwest of the Frankish kingdom as a result. She bore him two sons, Drogo (d. 708) and Grimoald (d. 714), whose marriages further enhanced their father's power. Pippin married the mother of Charles Martel while his first wife still lived, but Plectrude remained the favored and politically prominent wife. She continued by Pippin's side during the rest of his life, signed official documents as his wife, and supported various monasteries in the kingdom, especially Echternach, which was associated with her mother.

Plectrude remained at her husband's side during his life, and she attempted to keep power after his death in 714. Both of her sons had predeceased their father, Grimoald having died only a few months before Pippin, and after her husband's death she promoted Grimoald's son Theodoald to the office of mayor of the palace to the Merovingian king Dagobert III (d. 715). She also took control of Pippin's treasure and imprisoned her stepson Charles Martel to secure Theodoald's position and prevent Charles from seizing power. Her efforts on her grandson's behalf were met with hostility by the part of the nobility opposed to Pippin and his family. According to a contemporary chronicler, Plectrude kept "Charles from the legitimate governance of his father's authority and she herself, with the infant, in a womanly plan, presumed to control the reins of so great a kingdom" (Fouracre 1996, 365). This hostile chronicler continues that because "she had decided to rule with feminine cunning more cruelly than was necessary, she quickly turned the wrath of the Neustrian Franks to the destruction of her grandson" (365). She faced a revolt that ended with Theodoald in flight and a new mayor, Ragamfred, elected in his stead. The new mayor later marched against her in Cologne and seized part of Pippin's legacy. Not only did she face opposition from outside the family, but her stepson, Charles, also rose against her, seized the rest of his father's wealth, and ultimately took control of the kingdom.

See also: Carolingian Dynasty; Charles Martel; Marriage; Merovingian Dynasty; Neustria; Pippin II, Called Pippin of Herstal

Bibliography

Fouracre, Paul, and Richard A. Gerberding. *Late Merovingian France: History and Hagiography, 640–720.* Manchester, UK: University of Manchester Press, 1996.

Fouracre, Paul. *The Age of Charles Martel.* New York: Longman, 2000.

Riché, Pierre. *The Carolingians: A Family Who Forged Europe.* Trans. Michael Idomir Allen. Philadelphia: University of Pennsylvania Press, 1993.

Wallace-Hadrill, J. M., ed. and trans. *The Fourth Book of the Chronicle of Fredegar with Its Continuations.* London: Nelson, 1960.

Wemple, Suzanne. *Women in Frankish Society: Marriage and the Cloister, 500–900.* Philadelphia: University of Pennsylvania Press, 1985.

Poitiers, Battle of. *See* Tours, Battle of

Procopius (c. 490/507–560)

Author of the most important histories of the reign of Justinian and Theodora, Procopius was an eyewitness and participant in the events he describes. Although he was also the author of official histories of Justinian's reign, Procopius is known best for his scandalous and unrelentingly hostile work *The Secret History* (*Anecdota,* or Unpublished Things), which portrayed nearly everyone associated with Justinian in a most negative light. Indeed, his invective against Theodora was so harsh, and nearly pornographic, that the great historian Edward Gibbon wrote that "her arts must be veiled in the obscurity of a learned language," and J. B. Bury described the *Secret History* as an "orgy of hatred." At the same time, Procopius did write very important official histories, including *History of the Wars* (*Polemon,* or *De bellis*) and *On Buildings* (*Peri Ktismaton,* or *De aedificiis*).

Procopius was probably born around 500, as early as 490 and as late as 507, in Caesarea in ancient Palestine (modern Israel). Little is known of his early life, but he probably received an education according to ancient traditions and was learned in the Greek classics. Indeed, as his later works clearly show, he knew the writings of the great historians Herodotus (c. 484–430/420 BC) and Thucydides (460–after 404 BC). He later became a *rhetor,* or attorney, and in 527 joined the staff of the great general Belisarius as a legal advisor. He remained with Belisarius until 540 and joined him on his campaigns against the Persians (527–531), the Vandals (533–534), and the Goths (535–540). He may well have lost the general's favor in 540 and returned to Constantinople after Belisarius captured Ravenna and remained in the imperial capital until his death, although his exact movements are uncertain. He did witness the plague in Constantinople in 542, received the title *illustris* in 560, and may have been prefect of Constantinople in 562–563. Although much remains uncertain about his movements after 542, and even the date of his death is not definitely known, it was after his return from the Gothic campaign that Procopius began to write. He published his great official histories in the 550s and 560s; the *Secret History* was published after his death. Although much is uncertain concerning his life, his literary record remains a significant and lasting achievement.

Procopius's works provide important accounts of the political and military affairs of the day as well as bitterly personal insights into the major figures of his day. Written in Greek, his works draw on Herodotus, Thucydides, and possibly Arrian (d. 180 AD) and reveal his growing disenchantment with Justinian and the members of his court, including Belisarius and, especially, Theodora. His first work, *History of the Wars,* was published in 551 or 552, with an addition in 554 or 557, and covers the emperor Justinian's wars from the 530s to 554. Divided into eight books, the *History* addresses the wars with the Persian Empire (Books 1–2); wars against the Vandals (Books 3–4); and the Gothic Wars (Books 5–7). The eighth book surveys all theaters of war from 550 to 554. The accounts focus on military and political affairs and often include speeches from the participants and other digressions from the main narrative. The work also reveals his belief in Christianity and opposition to doctrinal disputes and, more importantly, his growing disenchantment with Justinian. Despite that developing hostility, Procopius did also write a panegyric to Justinian, possibly commissioned by the emperor, on the emperor's building program.

Published in 560 or 561, although possibly unfinished, *On Buildings* may have been written several years earlier, possibly before the collapse of the dome of the Hagia Sophia in 558. The work describes in important details Justinian's building program throughout the empire. Procopius discusses the numerous fortifications and churches—including the Hagia Sophia, the greatest of all—and supports the ideology of Byzantine imperialism, stressing that Justinian served and was inspired by God. In stark contrast to the portrayal of the emperor in *Buildings, The Secret History* offers a vicious and vindictive portrait of Justinian and Theodora and others. It purports to offer the "true" reasons for the actions of the emperor and empress, who were motivated by greed and a desire for evildoing, and describes them both as demons, a term he meant literally and not as a figure of speech. *The Secret History* does offer some substantial criticisms of Justinian's policies, but it is best known for its purple prose and scurrilous attacks on the empire's leaders. Although written as early as 550, *The Secret History* was not published until after Procopius's death and was lost for centuries, being discovered in the Vatican Library and published in 1632.

See also: Belisarius; Constantinople; Gothic Wars; Justinian; Ostrogoths; Theodora; Vandals

Bibliography

Browning, Robert. *Justinian and Theodora.* Rev. ed. London: Thames and Hudson, 1987.

Bury, John B. *History of the Later Roman Empire: From the Death of Theodosius I to the Death of Justinian.* 2 Vols. 1923. Reprint, New York: Dover, 1959.

Cameron, Averil. *The Mediterranean World in Late Antiquity, A.D. 395–600.* New York: Routledge, 1993.

Cameron, Averil. *Procopius and the Sixth Century.* London: Routledge, 1996.

Evans, James A. S., *Procopius.* New York: Twayne, 1972.

Gibbon, Edward. *The Decline and Fall of the Roman Empire.* New York: Modern Library, 1983.

Procopius. *The History of the Wars; Secret History.* 4 Vols. Trans. H. B. Dewing. Cambridge, MA: Harvard University Press, 1914–1924.

R

Radagaisus. *See* Stilicho

Radegund (c. 525–587)

Merovingian queen and abbess, Radegund stands in stark contrast to other famous sixth-century Merovingian queens such as Brunhilde and Fredegund, who were known for their bloody quest for power and defense of family interests. Unlike them, Radegund renounced the worldly life and rejected an earthly family for a heavenly one. Although married to a Merovingian king, she lived a celibate life and was eventually allowed to leave her husband and found a convent. Her community, in which Radegund accepted a lowly position rather than that of abbess, was well known for its piety, but also for its internal turmoil, brought on by the competition between noble and non-noble members of the convent. Even though she renounced the world, Radegund did not remain completely separate from it, corresponding with bishops, kings, and emperors. She was held in such great esteem by her contemporaries that they wrote two biographies of her, and the sixth-century historian Gregory of Tours included much information about her in his *History of the Franks,* as well as the letter of the foundation of her monastery.

Born to the royal family of the barbarian kingdom of Thuringia in about 525, Radegund was brought into the Merovingian kingdom in 531 when the sons of the first Merovingian king, Clovis, Theuderic I (r. 511–533) and Chlotar I (r. 511–561), destroyed her family's kingdom. Radegund herself described the destruction of the kingdom in an epic poem she wrote, which reveals her sadness over the kingdom's fate and the death of her brother, who was killed by Chlotar sometime after he captured the brother and sister and took them back to his kingdom. Although he already had at least one wife and as many as seven, Chlotar married Radegund in 540 to legitimize his authority in Thuringia. According to one of her biographers, the sixth-century poet Venantius Fortunatus, who was her chaplain, Radegund spent her youth in preparation for her eventual marriage and was well educated, studying the works of St. Augustine of Hippo, St. Jerome, and Pope Gregory the Great, among others. During her marriage to Chlotar, Radegund remained celibate, much to her husband's dismay, but was able to exploit her position for the benefit of others nonetheless. She actively sought to free captives, often paying the ransoms for their release. She also spent lavishly on the poor.

Radegund and King Chlotar from the *Life of Saint Radegund,*
10th–11th century manuscript. (De Agostini/Getty Images)

Her marriage to Chlotar, however, was clearly not meant to last, and at around
550 she left him to found the monastery of the Holy Cross in Poitiers. The accounts
of her separation from her husband are contradictory. According to Venantius Fortunatus, Radegund was allowed to leave her husband because of the murder of her
brother. Chlotar, after killing her brother, not only allowed the separation but sent
her to the bishop of Soissons, who was to consecrate her in the religious life to calm
the situation politically with the bishops of his own kingdom. Her other biographer
and disciple, Baudonivia, writing in the early seventh century, portrayed the whole
affair differently. She wrote that after Radegund had left the king, Chlotar fell into a
fit of despair and desired that his wife return to him. Indeed, he even went to Poitiers
with one of his sons, Sigebert, to take his wife back, but relented in the end and allowed her to take up the religious life. This decision was influenced by Radegund's
connections with numerous bishops of the kingdom, who helped persuade Chlotar
to allow her to live as a nun. Moreover, not only did Chlotar allow her to take the
veil but he also provided a substantial endowment so that she could establish her
new community in Poitiers.

Although the founder of the new religious community, Radegund was not its abbess. As noted in the letter of foundation, preserved by Gregory of Tours, Radegund appointed Lady Agnes as mother superior. Radegund writes, "I submitted myself to her in regular obedience to her authority, after God" (535). Indeed, despite her royal standing, Radegund lived her life at the monastery of the Holy Cross as a regular nun and set the example in pious living for the other nuns in the community to follow. Baudonivia wrote in her biography that Radegund "did not impose a chore unless she had performed it first herself" (Thiébaux 1994, 113). She was also zealous in the performance of her religious duties and was frequently at prayer. Even while resting, Radegund had someone read passages from the Scriptures to her. She also performed acts of extreme self-mortification, and, according to Venantius Fortunatus, sealed herself up in a wall in her monastery near the end of her life and lived there as a hermit until her death.

Radegund lived her life as a simple nun in her community, but she was still royalty. She continued to participate in the life of the kingdom and used her status for the benefit of the community she established. In her foundation letter, she secured the protection of her monastery from the leading bishops of the realm as well as from various Merovingian kings. She also cultivated her relationship with the bishops of the realm, including her biographer, Venantius Fortunatus, and Gregory of Tours, after the initial contacts at the foundation. Her royal status enabled her to acquire a piece of the True Cross (believed to be the cross on which Christ was crucified) from the emperor in Constantinople. This act, which benefited her community, may also have had political overtones. Her correspondence with the emperor and his delivery of the holy relic may have been intended to improve diplomatic ties between the Merovingian dynasty and Byzantine emperors. She also prayed for the various Merovingian kings and often sent them letters of advice, partly in an effort to preserve the peace within the Merovingian kingdom. She also prohibited the marriage of a Merovingian princess, a nun at the convent in Poitiers, to the Visigothic prince Reccared. Indeed, even though she lived the life of a simple nun, Radegund played an important role in the kingdom because of her status as a former Merovingian queen.

See also: Augustine of Hippo, St.; Brunhilde; Fredegund; Gregory of Tours; Gregory I, the Great, Pope; Merovingian Dynasty; Monasticism; Reccared I; Visigoths; Women

Bibliography

Gregory of Tours. *The History of the Franks*. Trans. Lewis Thorpe. Harmondsworth, UK: Penguin, 1974.

Schulenburg, Jane Tibbetts. *Forgetful of Their Sex: Female Sanctity and Society, ca. 500–1100*. Chicago: University of Chicago Press, 1998.

Thiébaux, Marcelle, trans. *The Writings of Medieval Women: An Anthology*. New York: Garland, 1994.

Wemple, Suzanne. *Women in Frankish Society: Marriage and the Cloister, 500–900.* Philadelphia: University of Pennsylvania Press, 1985.

Wood, Ian. *The Merovingian Kingdoms, 450–751.* London: Longman, 1994.

Ravenna

A wealthy city along the Adriatic coast, Ravenna assumed increasing prominence in late antiquity and the early Middle Ages. It was recognized as the imperial capital of the Western Empire in the fifth century and was later the residence of the Ostrogothic ruler of Italy, Theodoric. Following the reconquest of Italy by Justinian, Ravenna became the outpost of Byzantine power in Italy and retained that position into the eighth century. Although its importance declined after that, it remained the home of some of the greatest monuments of late antique and early medieval art and architecture.

Ravenna may have existed first as an Etruscan settlement and was made a Roman city in 49 BC. It grew in importance in the early empire as a result of the construction of the canal connecting the Po River and the city's port of Classis. The city prospered as a result of trade but only later emerged as a major political center. In 402, the emperor Honorius, moving from Milan, made Ravenna the seat of his government, and it remained the capital of the Western Empire throughout the fifth century. Honorius's sister, Galla Placidia, resided there for a time and made the city, which had become a bishopric in the second century, a center of Christian art and culture. Her mausoleum is one of the monuments of early Christian architecture; it is a dome structure that is decorated with yellow marble and covered throughout with mosaics.

Following the fall of the Western Empire in 476, Ravenna retained its position as a working capital and was the seat of the barbarian kings Odovacar and Theodoric. It was at Ravenna that Odovacar made his last stand in his struggle with Theodoric and endured a three year siege before coming to terms with and being murdered by Theodoric. As ruler in Italy, Theodoric made Ravenna the seat of his government and undertook, in traditional Roman fashion, a major building program in the city. An Arian Christian, Theodoric was eager to establish religious structures for his faith even though he was careful not to offend the Catholic population that lived in Ravenna and throughout Italy. Along with a number of secular buildings, a new Arian baptistery was built by Theodoric that was octagonal in design with a dome on top and mosaics throughout. He also built a magnificent two-storey mausoleum that borrowed very little from Byzantine or late Roman traditions and established an independent Gothic style.

In the year 540, Ravenna was recovered by Justinian and his general Belisarius during the emperor's reconquest of Italy. As a result the city's prosperity and importance continued to increase. In the 580s, Ravenna was established as an exarchate, the administrative center of Byzantine political and military power in Italy. In the later sixth and seventh centuries, the emperors in Constantinople sought to direct affairs in Italy and exercise control over the pope through the exarch in Ravenna. The city also served in the empire's struggle with the Lombards, who had invaded Italy in 568. Elevated in political power, Ravenna also benefited from the building programs undertaken by Justinian and his successors. A number of churches begun by Theodoric were completed by Justinian and include dazzling mosaics. The most famous of these churches is San Vitale, which contains a mosaic depiction of Justinian and his wife Theodora and their entourages.

Ravenna's prosperity and importance as a Byzantine provincial capital was threatened by the Lombards who sought to control all of Italy. Lombard kings laid siege to Ravenna, and the city finally fell to the Lombard king Aistulf, whose efforts may have been aided by growing resentment in Italy toward Constantinople because of the emperor's iconoclastic policies. As a result of the conquest of Ravenna, the exarchate was abolished and Byzantine power was restricted to southern Italy. Ravenna's fortunes faded after the conquest, and the pope in Rome sought to establish his authority over the city. Under the Carolingians, the city was freed from the Lombards but granted to the papacy. Although enjoying increased authority in his diocese in the eighth century, the archbishop served as a representative of the pope. Ravenna's influence and independence were further eroded as a result of the deterioration of the port of Classis and the rise of Venice. The history of the archbishops was composed by Agnellus of Ravenna in the ninth century.

See also: Belisarius; Gothic Wars; Honorius; Justinian; Odovacar; Ostorogoths; Theodora; Theodoric

Bibliography

Agnellus of Ravenna. *The Book of the Pontiffs of the Church of Ravenna*. Trans. Deborah M. Deliyannis. Washington, DC: Catholic University of America Press, 2004.

Deliyannis, Deborah M. *Ravenna in Late Antiquity*. Cambridge: Cambridge University Press, 2010.

Simson, Otto von. *Sacred Fortress: Byzantine Art and Statecraft in Ravenna*. Princeton, NJ: Princeton University Press, 1987.

Reccared I (d. 601)

Son of the last Visigothic Arian king of Spain, Leovigild, and brother of the rebellious Hermenegild, Reccared was the first Catholic Christian king of Spain (r. 573/586–601). Although he broke from his father's religion, Reccared built upon

Leovigild's efforts to unify the kingdom under one religious faith. He held an important church council to confirm the place of the new faith in the kingdom and promoted the ideal of sanctified kingship, with the support of the church. He also took great strides to enforce his authority over the Visigothic nobility in Spain and to extend the power of the Visigothic kingdom in Europe through marriage alliances and warfare.

During the reign of Leovigild, both Reccared and his brother Hermenegild played important roles at court. Their father was a successful king who enjoyed victories over other peoples in Spain, including the Byzantines. He also cultivated an almost imperial ideal of kingship in Spain, a legacy Reccared later enjoyed. Reccared and his brother were made coregents with Leovigild in 573, a step designed to strengthen Leovigild's hold in the kingdom and to establish a royal dynasty in Spain. In 578, Leovigild, in imitation of the Roman emperors, founded a new city, now Toledo, which he named Reccopolis after his younger son. Perhaps because of the favoritism shown him by his father, Reccared remained loyal to Leovigild and did not join the rebellion of Hermenegild in 579. Under the influence of his Catholic Merovingian wife, Ingunde, and Leander of Seville, archbishop and older brother of Isidore, Hermenegild converted to Catholic Christianity. Conflict between father and son continued until 584, when the dispute was resolved. The murder of Hermenegild in 585 paved the way for the eventual succession of Reccared to the throne on his father's death in 586.

As king in his own name, Reccared built on the legacy of his father. Even in terms of religion, Reccared can be seen to have continued his father's policies, with the exception that the unifying religion in Visigothic Spain was Catholic Christianity, not Arian Christianity as his father had hoped. In 587 Reccared converted to Catholic Christianity, which brought him and the kingdom in line with the Hispano-Roman population as well as with his sometime rival the Franks. His conversion also found support from the established Catholic church and the pope, Gregory the Great, with whom Reccared began to correspond. Although generally accepted in Spain, Reccared's conversion did meet some opposition from the Arian bishops, who were supported by the king's stepmother, Gosvintha. This opposition notwithstanding, Reccared converted the Visigoths to Catholic Christianity, and to celebrate and confirm his conversion Reccared held a great church council, the Third Council of Toledo, in 589. The council was attended by the five archbishops of Spain, some 50 Catholic bishops, eight former Arian bishops, and many Arian priests and secular nobles. All participants at the council confessed the Nicene Creed, confirming their acceptance of Catholic Christianity, and the council passed a series of laws for the church in Spain. The former Arian bishops were welcomed into the Catholic church and confirmed in their sees. Reccared had successfully unified the kingdom under the banner of religion and was recognized by contemporaries for his great accomplishment.

Reccared's successes were not limited to the sphere of religion. He built on his father's policy of bringing the nobility to heel and asserting royal authority over them. At one point, he uncovered a conspiracy against him led by a leading noble. The rebel was captured and forced to endure the *decalvatio* (which was either the shaving of his head or scalping; the meaning is uncertain), had his right hand chopped off, and was led through Toledo on a donkey to send a warning to other possible rebels. The king also maintained good relations with the papacy and generally prospered in the international arena, especially in his dealings with the Merovingian Franks. His father had arranged a marriage for him with Rigund, the daughter of Chilperic I. But Chilperic's death ended the possibility of the marriage, and the revolt and death of Hermenegild further complicated relationships with the Merovingians. Despite concerns over the fate of Hermenegild's wife and the enmity of Guntram, the most important Merovingian king of the day, Reccared arranged to marry a Merovingian princess. The marriage in fact failed to take place, and Reccared married a Visigothic woman, Baddo. Nevertheless, his ability to arrange the marriage in the first place demonstrates his stature in Merovingian eyes. Moreover, although Guntram approved the marriage, he later attacked Visigothic territory but was easily defeated by Reccared.

Reccared also furthered his father's policy of enhancing the stature of Visigothic kingship, elevating it to almost imperial rank. Indeed, he clearly ruled as an emperor in his kingdom, as had Leovigild. Reccared also organized larger administrative units in the kingdom as subdivisions of an empire. His relationship with the church in Spain also resembled that of a Roman emperor with the church in the empire. Building upon the precedents of his father, Reccared left an important legacy to the Visigothic kingdom in Spain, a legacy that survived the murder of his son and successor, Liuva II, and the end of the dynasty in 603.

See also: Arianism; Chilperic I; Franks; Gregory I, the Great, Pope; Guntram; Hermenegild; Isidore of Seville; Leovigild; Merovingian Dynasty; Toledo; Visigoths

Bibliography

Bury, John B. *History of the Later Roman Empire: From the Death of Theodosius I to the Death of Justinian.* 2 Vols. 1923. Reprint, New York: Dover, 1959.

Collins, Roger. *Early Medieval Spain: Unity in Diversity, 400–1000.* London: Longman, 1983.

Gregory of Tours. *History of the Franks.* Trans. Lewis Thorpe. Harmondsworth, UK: Penguin, 1974.

Heather, Peter. *The Goths.* Oxford: Blackwell, 1996.

Isidore of Seville. *Isidore of Seville's History of the Goths, Vandals, and Suevi.* 2nd rev. ed. Trans. Guido Donini and Gordon B. Ford. Leiden: Brill, 1970.

Thompson, E. A. *The Goths in Spain.* Oxford: Clarendon, 1969.

Wolfram, Herwig. *History of the Goths.* Trans. Thomas J. Dunlap. Berkeley: University of California Press, 1988.

Wolfram, Herwig. *The Roman Empire and Its Germanic Peoples.* Trans. Thomas J. Dunlap. Berkeley: University of California Press, 1997.

Reihengräber. *See* Row-Grave Cemeteries

Religion, Germanic. *See* Germanic Religion

Ricimer (d. 472)

Roman military leader of Germanic descent, Ricimer (in full, Flavius Ricimer) was the power behind the throne in the Western Empire from 456 until his death in 472. Although an Arian Christian and a barbarian and therefore constitutionally unable to hold imperial office, Ricimer, like Stilicho before him, was the real ruler in the Western Empire. He appointed and deposed emperors and struggled against various rivals and usurpers. He also kept Italy safe from attacks by Alans, Ostrogoths, and Vandals. Indeed, his success in the defense of Italy is best illustrated by its fall to the Germanic general Odovacar only four years after Ricimer's death.

The son of parents of royal Suevi and Visigothic descent, Ricimer rose to prominence, as did many Germans of his day, through military service to Rome. Early on in his military career, while in the service of Aëtius, he befriended the future emperor Marjorian. He became a great hero to the Romans in 456, when he successfully defended Italy from a Vandal attack off Sicily and Corsica. His exploits earned him promotion to the office of master of the soldiers. In the same year, Ricimer joined with his friend Marjorian to depose the reigning emperor in the west, Avitus. Marjorian demonstrated the potential to be an effective emperor and suppressed a near revolt in southern Gaul shortly after his ascension. He also enjoyed a victory over the Visigoths in Gaul in 460, but suffered a disastrous defeat at the hands of Gaiseric and the Vandals. Unfortunately, his early display of ability and initiative inspired the enmity of his friend Ricimer. Upon Marjorian's return to Italy from Gaul after his defeat at the hands of the Vandals, Ricimer captured him and executed him in August 461.

Ricimer then became the undisputed master of Italy and parts of the Western Empire. He then promoted a puppet emperor, whom he dominated until 465. The greatest threat to his power came from a general in Gaul, Aegidius, who refused to recognize Ricimer's authority. To counter Aegidius, Ricimer denounced him as a usurper and used barbarian kings in the north against him; his death by poisoning in 464 strengthened Ricimer's hand. The next great threat to his power came in 467 with the arrival of a new emperor, Anthemius, who had been appointed by the Eastern emperor, Leo I. But any possibility of competition was eliminated by the marriage of Ricimer to Anthemius's daughter. The good relations, however, did not last; and the two became rivals fairly quickly, and civil war broke out in 472 after Anthemius's failure in a campaign against Vandal Africa. Ricimer appointed Olybrius emperor and defeated his rival in battle on July 11, 472. Ricimer, however, did not long survive his rival and died on August 18, 472. His death paved the way for further unrest and the establishment of a Germanic kingdom in Italy, but his virtual reign preserved the integrity of imperial Italy from the attacks of Vandals, Visigoths, and other barbarians.

See also: Aëtius; Alans; Arianism; Gundobad; Odovacar; Ostrogoths; Stilicho, Flavius; Vandals; Visigoths

Bibliography

Bury, John B. *History of the Later Roman Empire: From the Death of Theodosius I to the Death of Justinian.* Vol. 1. 1923. Reprint, New York: Dover, 1959.

Dill, Samuel. *Roman Society in Gaul in the Merovingian Age.* 1926. Reprint, London: Allen and Unwin, 1966.

Randers-Pehrson, Justine Davis. *Barbarians and Romans: The Birth Struggle of Europe,* A.D. *400–700.* Norman: University of Oklahoma Press, 1983.

Roderic (d. 711/712)

Generally identified as the last of the Gothic kings of Spain, the Visigoth Roderic was defeated by Tariq ibn Ziyad and his Muslim army from North Africa in 711. Little is known of Roderic's early life, and his reign as king was short lived as a result of the weaknesses of the Visigoth kingdom and the Muslim invasion of 711. In 710, the ruling king Witiza (r. 702–710) died and was to be succeeded by his son Akhila, but a revolt led by the nobles disrupted the succession. Roderic was then offered the throne by the nobles or seized the opportunity and defeated Akhila and his brothers in battle. Although the circumstances are unclear, Roderic became king in either 710 or 711 and faced the challenge of securing his control of Spain. He was faced with challenges in the northeast of Spain from rivals for power and from the Basques who had long opposed Visigothic rule. It was while he was busy in the northeast that Roderic faced an even greater threat, Tariq's invasion from North Africa.

According to legend, Witiza's sons invited Tariq to Spain to defeat Roderic so that they could reclaim the throne. Although unlikely, the legend does reflect that political turmoil in Spain, and it was most likely that Tariq took the opportunity to invade at the worst possible time for Roderic who hurried south to meet the invader. Contemporary accounts note that Roderic led an army of between 50,000 and 100,000, which is clearly an exaggeration, but the armies on both sides were surely substantial. The two armies met in July 711 (or perhaps 712) in the Trans-ductine Promontories, and Roderic was defeated and killed. The Gothic capital, Toledo, fell not long after and by the end of the decade most of Visigothic Spain had fallen to the Muslims.

See also: Toledo; Visigoths

Bibliography

Collins, Roger. *Visigothic Spain 409–711*. Oxford: Wiley-Blackwell, 2004.

Kennedy, Hugh. *Muslim Spain and Portugal: A Political History of al-Andalus.* London: Longman, 1996.

Rois Fainéants (Do-Nothing Kings)

Rois Fainéants is the name traditionally applied to the last of the kings of the Merovingian dynasty. The so-called *rois fainéants,* or do-nothing kings, held the throne from the death of Dagobert in 638 to the deposition of the final Merovingian king, Childeric III, in 751 by Pippin III the Short. Although a fairly common desig-nation, it is a misleading one. The decline of the Merovingian dynasty was neither as dramatic nor as rapid as the name implies. In fact, the Merovingians remained important figures in the Frankish kingdoms until the time of Charles Martel in the early eighth century.

The impression of sudden and extreme Merovingian weakness is primarily the result of the eighth and ninth century sources that tell the tale of the last century of Merovingian rule. Most of these sources were written by those who supported the Carolingian dynasty that replaced the Merovingians in 751. These sources por-trayed the Carolingian kings in the most favorable light and the last of the descen-dants of the first great Frankish king, Clovis (r. 481–511), in the worst light. The most important of these sources is the Life of Charlemagne written by Einhard, a member of Charlemagne's court. According to Einhard the last Merovingian king, Childeric, was a pathetic figure indeed. Childeric possessed little but the title of king, according to Einhard, and sat on the throne playing the role of king with his long hair and flowing beard. He had little wealth, only the income of a small estate and whatever the Carolingian mayors of the palace provided to support him. He would ride in an oxcart to attend the general assembly of the kingdom, at which whatever answers he gave to questions of state or to visiting ambassadors were ini-tiated by the mayor of the palace. Although the real power of Childeric was quite limited, this portrayal clearly exaggerates the relative power of the Merovingian and Carolingian families, and it has cast an inaccurate shadow over the Merovingian kings of the previous century. Einhard and other pro-Carolingian writers developed this image to buttress the claims to the throne of a dynasty that only a generation or so before usurped royal power.

Although the Carolingians exploited their power as mayors of the palace during the late seventh and early eighth centuries, they were not the sole aristocratic family seeking power, and the Merovingian dynasty remained an important part of the power structure in the Frankish kingdoms. The continued strength of the descendants of Clovis is demonstrated by a number of things. The failure of the coup of Grimoald, a Carolingian mayor, in the 650s shows that the Franks were not yet ready for a new royal dynasty. The various aristocratic factions in the three Frankish kingdoms—Austrasia, Burgundy, and Neustria—competed for control of the kingdoms and for access to the kings. The murders of the Merovingian kings Childeric II and Dagobert II in the 670s were due not to their weakness but rather due to their strength and the opposition to their policies. As late as the 720s Merovingian kings issued charters and other royal enactments for the kingdoms that were effectively implemented. In fact, in the early eighth century, when the Carolingians were clearly in the ascendancy, Merovingian kings competed for the support of important monasteries. Perhaps the best example of the lingering prestige of the dynasty as late as the 740s is the appointment by Pippin and Carloman of Childeric III as king. Thus, although the later Merovingian kings were not the equals of Clovis, the founder of the dynasty, they were not the weak and ineffective kings of tradition.

See also: Carolingian Dynasty; Charlemagne; Charles Martel; Childeric III; Clovis; Dagobert; Einhard; Merovingian Dynasty; Pippin III, Called Pippin the Short

Bibliography

Einhard and Notker the Stammerer. *Two Lives of Charlemagne.* Trans. Lewis Thorpe. Harmondsworth, UK: Penguin, 1981.

Rome

The original capital and main center of the Roman Empire, the city of Rome declined in political importance during late antiquity and the early Middle Ages. Suffering during the barbarian invasions and enduring a decline in population and economic importance, Rome emerged as the most important religious center of early medieval Europe and the residence of the pope. The popes were essential in the rebuilding of the city and the construction of important churches and other structures, and the actions of a number of popes throughout the early Middle Ages enhanced the spiritual power and prestige of Rome.

Although Rome would gradually cede its position of preeminence in the Western Empire to Milan and later Ravenna, it was still the great capital of empire at the opening of the fourth century. In the great struggle for authority in the Western Empire, Constantine won control of the west in his victory at the Milvian Bridge in 312. He would, however, move his capital to Constantinople, thus beginning the decline of Rome's imperial authority, but before doing so Constantine contributed to new construction in the city, including the Arch of Constantine, and the transfer or construction of new Christian churches. The basilica of Constantine (later called St. John of the Lateran), was built and bestowed on the pope and construction was begun on Saint Peter's Basilica, replacing the former structure built over what were held to be the relics of St. Peter. He also began work on the funerary monument that would emerge in the 360s as the mausoleum of Santa Constanza, and the mosaics of the mausoleum established important models for Christian art. Leaving Rome for Constantinople, Constantine nonetheless left an important legacy to the city and aided in its conversion to a Christian capital.

Rome's fates declined during the later fourth and fifth centuries as the empire faced the challenge of the barbarian invasions. In the late fourth century, Milan became the main imperial capital of the Western Empire because it held a more geographically desirable location to monitor the frontiers and movements of barbarian peoples. In 410, the Visigoths led by their king Alaric sacked the city, causing profound shock throughout the empire even though Rome was no longer a capital. The Goths did serious damage to many of the buildings of Rome but left most of the churches unharmed, and the churches and that suffered were rebuilt or repaired by the popes who also built lavish new churches. An even more serious assault on the city occurred in 455, when Gaiseric and the Vandals subjected to the city to a sacking lasting some 14 days, the ferocity of which far exceeded the destruction wrought by the Goths. As one consequence of the human disasters inflicted on Rome and is loss of prestige as the capital, the population dropped by the mid-fifth century to some 250,000 from its height of one million two centuries earlier. In the face of this decline, however, Rome's future as the religious capital of the west was beginning to be established. Pope Leo I the Great undertook renovation of the various churches in the city and saved it from destruction at the hands of Attila in 453. His defense of orthodoxy further enhanced the position of Rome as the Christian capital, a position confirmed, with some qualification, at the council of Chalcedon in 451.

During the sixth century Rome's glory faded even further as the population declined to a mere 50,000 as Italy once again became a great battleground. The Gothic Wars launched by the emperor Justinian sought to restore imperial control over Italy, which it did at great cost. Rome itself suffered greatly during the conflict between the Byzantines and Ostrogoths, who had come to control Italy in the late fifth century. The city faced three separate sieges during the conflict and much of its infrastructure, especially the aqueducts that brought water into Rome, were devastated. The Byzantine victory brought Rome back under imperial control and placed it under the exarch in Ravenna who supervised dukes who administered the city. The pope himself recognized imperial authority and sought to cooperate with the emperor and his representative and to ensure the protection of the city. A challenge made all the greater with the arrival of the Lombards in 568 who proceeded to take control of much of the Italian peninsula in the late sixth century. Indeed, throughout the seventh and eighth centuries, Lombard kings threatened the independence of Rome and forced the popes to find a reliable protector.

The character of Rome underwent further changes during the seventh and eighth centuries. The city itself became more clearly defined as a Christian city as the last vestiges of pagan Rome disappeared or were Christianized: the famous temple the Pantheon and the old Roman Senate building were converted into churches. As the city of Saints Peter and Paul and numerous martyrs, Rome developed into an important pilgrimage site as well during this period. It was also during this time that Rome began to emerge as the administrative center of what would become the Papal States. The failure of the emperor to protect the city and the pressure of the Lombards forced the popes to take direct control of the defense and administration of Rome and its environs. A mixed bureaucracy that was both secular and ecclesiastical was developed and, and the local nobility entered more fully into papal service. The involvement of the local nobility would have negative consequences for Rome on occasion as rival aristocratic factions competed for control of the papacy and for access to important patronage positions.

Rome's ability to assume local control in Italy was aided by the pope's alliance with the Carolingian dynasty. The Carolingians benefited from this alliance because it was the pope who essentially approved of Pippin the Short's usurpation of the Frankish throne and because the pope would crown Pippin king and later Carolingians as emperor. The Carolingians provided aid against the Lombards, who were defeated and incorporated into the Carolingian empire by Charlemagne in 774. Pippin confirmed Rome's territorial claims in the Donation of Pippin, which granted papal authority over much of central Italy. The Donation was confirmed by Charlemagne, and Carolingian rulers in the ninth century provided further legal definition of papal authority in Italy and the relationship between Rome and the Carolingians. Papal Rome's territorial claims were given further support by the Donation of Constantine, a forgery of the mid-eighth century that asserts that Constantine gave Pope Sylvester I temporal and territorial authority of the Western Roman Empire. Along with its growing role as the capital of the Papal State, or more formally the Repbulic of St. Peter, Rome experience a phase of new construction as a series of popes erected new churches and expanded the walls and fortifications surrounding the city.

During the ninth and tenth centuries, Rome's fortunes again suffered a setback. The city, along with much of southern Italy, also was forced to endure a new wave of invasions emanating from North Africa. Divisions within the Carolingian empire limited the ability of the Carolingians to protect Rome, and once again local families jockeyed for control of the city and its territories and institutions. The popes of the 10th century are often held to have been among the worst to hold the papal throne and are thought to have been more interested in the pursuit of pleasure and family interests than in the well being of the church. Despite these negative developments, Rome remained the city of Peter and the destination of increasing numbers of pilgrims. From the depths of the 10th century, Rome would emerge in the 11th century to assume once again its leadership of western Europe.

See also: Attila the Hun; Carolingian Dynasty; Charlemagne; Constantine; Donation of Constantine; Donation of Pippin; Gaiseric; Gothic Wars; Gregory I, the Great, Pope; Huns; Justinian; Leo I, the Great, Pope; Lombards; Pippin III, Called Pippin the Short; Vandals

Bibliography

*The Book of Pontiffs (*Liber Pontificalis*): The Ancient Biographies of the First Ninety Roman Bishops to* AD *715.* Raymond Davis, trans. Liverpool, UK: Liverpool University Press, 1989.

Herrin, Judith. *The Formation of Christendom.* Princeton, NJ: Princeton University Press, 1987.

La Rocca, Cristina. *Italy in the Early Middle Ages: 476–1000.* New York: Oxford University Press, 2002.

Llewellyn, Peter. *Rome in the Dark Ages.* New York: Barnes and Noble, 1996.

Noble, Thomas F. X. *The Republic of St. Peter: The Birth of the Papal State, 680–825.* Philadelphia: University of Pennsylvania Press, 1984.

Romulus Augustulus (fifth century)

Last of the Roman emperors of the western part of the empire, Romulus Augustulus, or in full Flavius Momyllus Romulus Augustus, assumed the imperial throne while still a boy and reigned from October 31, 475, until August 28, 476. He was placed on the throne by his father, Orestes, the master of soldiers, who ruled in his name. His reign was cut short by the Germanic warrior, Odovacar. His deposition traditionally has marked the "fall of the Roman Empire"; no emperor reigned over the Western Empire after his fall.

Romulus Augustus, known as Augustulus (little Augustus) because of his youth, was placed on the throne by his father, the powerful and ambitious general Orestes, after Orestes rebelled against the reigning emperor in Italy, Julius Nepos (d. 480). Orestes ruled for nearly a year in the name of his son, but the emperor in Constantinople, Zeno, refused to recognize Romulus as the legitimate emperor in the west. An even more serious problem for Orestes and Romulus arose among the Germanic soldiers who made up such a large part of the Roman army. They demanded equal status with Roman soldiers, which Orestes refused to grant. Odovacar, a leading Germanic prince, did agree to raise the barbarian soldiers' status should he gain power, and a rebellion then broke out against Orestes. He was quickly overpowered and executed at Odovacar's order on August 28, 476. Romulus, however, was spared. A contemporary chronicler noted that Odovacar spared him because of his youth and fair looks and sent him to live out his days in Campania. And it was with his relatives that Romulus Augustulus lived out his life in anonymity.

After deposing Romulus Augustulus, Odovacar returned the imperial seal and other trappings of the imperial office to the emperor Zeno and did not appoint an emperor to rule in the west. The year 476, therefore, has traditionally been seen as the "end" of the Roman Empire. Of course, this view fails to consider several things about the empire. It continued until 1453 in the east with its capital Constantinople. Moreover, although the line of Western Roman emperors came to an end in 476, a number of other Roman traditions continued for some time to come. The language of the former Western Empire, Latin, continued to be the language of learning and government until the end of the Middle Ages. Christianity remained the predominant religion of the west and was gradually made the official religion of the Germanic rulers who rose to power in the old empire. The majority of the population were Roman or descended from Roman citizens, and many vestiges of the old Roman administration were preserved by the barbarian successors of the emperors. Although the deposition of Romulus Augustulus brought an end to the line of emperors in the west, it did not "end" the empire or its influence.

See also: Odovacar; Orestes; Rome; Zeno

Bibliography

Bury, John B. *History of the Later Roman Empire: From the Death of Theodosius I to the Death of Justinian.* 2 Vols. 1923. Reprint, New York: Dover, 1959.

Randers-Pehrson, Justine Davis. *Barbarians and Romans: The Birth Struggle of Europe, A.D. 400–700.* Norman: University of Oklahoma Press, 1983.

Wolfram, Herwig. *The Roman Empire and Its Germanic Peoples.* Trans. Thomas Dunlap. Los Angeles: University of California Press, 1997.

Roncesvalles, Battle of (778)

Although arguably of limited military importance, the battle of Roncesvalles (Roncesvalles or Roncesvaux) is one of the most celebrated conflicts of the early Middle Ages. The episode would contribute to the evolving legend of Charlemagne as the greatest ruler of Christendom and would evolve from a minor skirmish between Charlemagne's rear guard and indigenous mountain people to a titanic struggle between the forces of Islam and Christianity. The battle also provided the framework for one of the greatest of medieval epics, *The Song of Roland*, which took final form in the late 11th century.

The battle of Roncesvalles was fought on August 15, 778, following an unsuccessful invasion of Islamic Spain. Charlemagne had been invited to Spain by the governor of Barcelona, Suleiman ibn al-Arabi, to assist the governor in his struggles with the emir Abd al-Rahman. The campaign was a mixed success; the king took Pamplona, subjugated Navarre, and laid siege to Saragossa, but was more than a little dissatisfied with the support he received from his erstwhile ally, al-Arabi. While besieging Saragossa, Charlemagne was forced to withdraw, having received news of a major Saxon revolt. While crossing the Pyrenees on return to his kingdom, Charlemagne suffered the defeat at Roncesvalles. As both the *Royal Frankish Annals* and Einhard report, the rearguard of Charlemagne's army was ambushed along a narrow mountain pass by the native Basque people. Basque treachery, as Einhard noted, played a role in their success, and both sources noted that the difficulty of the terrain played a role in the defeat of the Franks as did their own heavy armor and the lightness of the Basques's arms. Knowledge of the land enabled the Basques to escape after plundering the baggage train and killing all the soldiers in the rearguard. Einhard lists some of the important figures killed in the attack, including Eggihard, the king's chamberlain, Anslem, count of the palace, and, most notably, Roland, count of the Breton Marches.

Despite this setback, the battle of Roncesvalles did not put an end to Charlemagne's interests along his southern frontier. In later years, he would return in force to preserve his authority over Aquitaine and the south, extend the boundaries of his empire across the Pyrenees, and create the Spanish March. He would enjoy even greater success in literary form. Although still suffering the defeat of his rearguard and the death of his now beloved Roland, according to *The Song of Roland*, Charlemagne would return to defeat his enemies and even take control of much of Spain. The battle itself became the centerpiece of the great conflict between Muslims and Christians in the Middle Ages in which Christians, as God's elect, would triumph. *The Song of Roland* was an important component of the emerging depiction of Muslims in western Christian literature and served to inspire Christian knights of the late 11th century.

See also: Charlemagne; Einhard; Saxons; Widukind

Bibliography

Burgess, Glyn, trans. *The Song of Roland*. London: Penguin Books, 1990.

Einhard and Notker the Stammerer. *Two Lives of Charlemagne*. Trans. David Ganz. London: Penguin Books, 2008.

Scholz, Bernard Walter. *Carolingian Chronicles: Royal Frankish Annals and Nithard's History*. Ann Arbor: University of Michigan Press, 1972.

Rothari (d. 652)

A Lombard king (r. 636–652) and lawgiver, Rothari was a successful warrior and the last of the Arian Lombard kings. His reign continued the anti-Catholic reaction begun by his predecessor, Ariold (626–636), but was noted most for Rothari's codification of the Lombard laws. His reforms of the law reveal the sometimes ambivalent attitude of the Lombards toward the Romans. The law code he created used Roman models, even as Rothari made major assaults on the last section of imperial Italy governed by the Byzantine Empire.

Rothari, according to the Lombard historian Paul the Deacon, was "brave and strong, and followed the path of justice; he did not however, hold the right line of Christian belief, but was stained by the infidelity of the Arian heresy" (193–194). Indeed, like his predecessor, Ariold, Rothari restored the traditional Lombard support for Arianism and continued the reaction against the pro-Catholic policy of Theudelinda. His support for Arian Christianity was intended, as it had been for Ariold, as a means to preserve the identity of the Lombards and distinguish them from the native population of Italy, which was Catholic. The Lombards had long been kept apart from the Italo-Roman population and often took a hard line against the empire. And on these matters Rothari was a traditional Lombard.

The new king followed the model of Ariold in one other significant way, if we are to trust the Frankish historian Fredegar. According to Fredegar, on the death of Ariold, his widow, Gundeberga, was invited by the Lombard nobility to choose a new king and husband, just as her mother, Theudelinda, had done at the death of her first husband, Authari (r. 584–590). Gundeberga asked Rothari to put away his wife and to become her husband and king of the Lombards. Fredegar notes that Rothari married Gundeberga, but kept her locked away in a little room and lived with concubines for several years, until he restored her to her place at the suggestion of the Merovingian king Clovis II (r. 639–657). The similarity with Paul the Deacon's tale of Theudelinda renders this tale suspect, but Rothari did, in fact, marry Gundeberga, probably to preserve the continuity of the monarchy and the stability of the kingdom.

As king, Rothari made two major contributions to the history of the Lombard kingdom. He launched a highly successful assault against imperial Italy in 643, undertaken in concert with attacks on imperial territory by the independent Lombard duke of Beneventum. He conquered parts of the Italian coast as well as the Italian imperial capital of Ravenna in 643, a conquest that seriously hindered Constantinople's ability to influence Italian affairs and, in the long run, forced the papacy to find another protector. Rothari's success against the empire also led to a treaty between the two in 652. The king's second great accomplishment also occurred in 643, when he codified the laws of the Lombards. Known as Rothari's Edict (*Edictus Rothari*), the code of Lombard laws and customs was arranged in 388 chapters and, like the other barbarian law codes of the time, was written in Latin. Among other things, the Edict emphasized the cooperation between the king and the people, as represented in the army and council of nobles. Rothari dealt with manumission of slaves, inheritance, division of property, marriage customs, and the place of women in society in the code. He also sought to eliminate or at least reduce the practice of the vendetta in Lombard society and thereby guarantee peace. Indeed, preservation of the peace was an important goal of the Edict, which legislated on manslaughter and personal injury. Rothari, therefore, was a great king, conqueror, and lawgiver of the Lombards.

See also: Arianism; Franks; Fredegar; Law and Law Codes; Merovingian Dynasty; Paul the Deacon; Theudelinda

Bibliography

Christie, Neil. *The Lombards: The Ancient Langobards.* Oxford: Blackwell, 1998.

Drew, Katherine Fisher, trans. *The Lombard Laws.* Philadelphia: University of Pennsylvania Press, 1973.

Herrin, Judith. *The Formation of Christendom.* Princeton, NJ: Princeton University Press, 1987.

Llewellyn, Peter. *Rome in the Dark Ages.* New York: Barnes and Noble, 1996.

Paul the Deacon. *History of the Lombards.* Trans. William Dudley Foulke. Philadelphia: University of Pennsylvania Press, 1974.

Wallace-Hadrill, J. M. *The Barbarian West, A.D. 400–1000.* New York: Harper and Row, 1962.

Wallace-Hadrill, J. M., ed. and trans. *The Fourth Book of the Chronicle of Fredegar with Its Continuations.* London: Nelson, 1960.

Wolfram, Herwig. *The Roman Empire and Its Germanic Peoples.* Trans. Thomas J. Dunlap. Berkeley: University of California Press, 1997.

Row-Grave Cemeteries

A traditional Germanic burial practice, the row-grave cemeteries (*Reihengräber*) are important archeological finds because of the wealth of material found in them. There are numerous sites in the Rhine River area and northern France from the migration period and in north central Spain dating from the arrival of the Visigoths. The appearance of these cemeteries in Spain is particularly important; they were once thought to provide evidence of settlement patterns for the Spanish Visigoths. Although no longer thought to reveal such patterns, the row-grave cemeteries are important nonetheless, in part because they are not found in Visigothic France or even Ostrogothic Italy.

Numerous row-grave cemeteries have been found in Spain, and they contain important evidence of Visigothic material culture. Roughly 70 of these cemeteries have been found in Spain, including a very large one of 666 burials with about 1,000 bodies in Duraton. Of particular importance are the burials of women, roughly one fifth of whom were buried in traditional Gothic dress. Another important site, at El Carpio de Tajo, has some 285 graves that stretch over several generations for a village of about 50 or 60 people, and about 90 of the sites contain grave goods.

The evidence from these sites presents an uncertain picture about burial practices in the fifth and sixth centuries. It has been suggested that either the graves represent the native Hispano-Roman population emulating the conquerors and including the types of burial goods the Goths would or that the graves containing grave goods are those of the Visigothic lords, who buried their dead with their wealth as a sign of status.

The graves contain important examples of Visigothic dress in the fifth and sixth centuries. The finds at Duraton contain traditional female clothing, which included a cloak attached at the shoulder with a brooch as well as a belt with a large buckle around the waist. The brooches were of fine quality. An especially important pattern was the eagle brooch found in various graves. The eagle may have become popular as a symbol of power that the Visigoths adopted from the Huns and Romans. Although the source of this style for a brooch is unclear, it became popular, and brooches following it were fashioned out of gold and inlaid with precious stones. Also, combs were frequently included among the grave goods and seem to have been an important manufacture among the Goths.

See also: Huns; Ostrogoths; Visigoths

Bibliography

Collins, Roger. *Early Medieval Spain: Unity in Diversity, 400–1000.* New York: St. Martin's, 1995.

Heather, Peter. *The Goths.* Oxford: Blackwell, 1996.

Thompson, E.A. *The Goths in Spain.* Oxford: Clarendon, 1969.

Wolfram, Herwig. *History of the Goths.* Trans. Thomas J. Dunlap. Berkeley: University of California Press, 1988.

Royal Frankish Annals

One of a number of chronicles of the Carolingian period that describe events in the kingdom or in a particular monastery or bishopric, the *Royal Frankish Annals* (in Latin, *Annales regni Francorum,* as they have been called since the 19th century) are the most important record of events in the early generations of the Carolingian dynasty. The *Royal Frankish Annals* are an official, or at least semiofficial, account of the major political, military, and religious events of Carolingian history from 741 to 829. The *Royal Frankish Annals* thus cover events during the reigns of Pippin the Short, Charlemagne, and Louis the Pious, the later part of whose reign is surveyed also in the history of Nithard. The chronicle includes the official Carolingian version of such significant moments as the replacement of the Merovingian line by

Pippin and his coronation in 751, the wars and imperial coronation of Charlemagne, and the early and successful years in the reign of Louis the Pious. The *Royal Frankish Annals* were divided after 829 and continued in the *Annals of St. Bertin,* which surveyed events in the Western Frankish kingdom until 882 and were written in part by Hincmar of Rheims, and the *Annals of Fulda,* which covered the Eastern Frankish kingdom until 887.

The *Royal Frankish Annals* were most likely composed by a number of different authors over a prolonged period. First written in 787 or 788 as part of the general revival of letters, especially history, under Charlemagne, the *Royal Frankish Annals* were written by several distinct hands and can be divided into three or four sections. Like the minor annals of the period, the *Royal Frankish Annals* were divided into year-by-year entries, with short discussions of the major events of each year. The first section of the work, from 787/788 to 793, begins with an entry on the year 741, noting the death of Charles Martel and the elevation of his sons Pippin and Carloman. The entries for the year 741–787/788 were drawn largely from the continuation of the chronicle of Fredegar and the minor annals composed in the various monasteries of the empire, but from 788 on the authors were contemporary with the events they described. The next section covers the period from 793 to 809, and again its author or authors recorded events that they lived through. The final section before the division into two main annals covers the period from 809 to 829; it can be subdivided even further, with a break at 820.

The style of the final section seems to have improved over the earlier sections, and it has been suggested that the author of part of it was the archchaplain of Louis the Pious. But the identity of any of the annalists remains uncertain, although it is likely that the archchaplain of the royal palace had a hand in the composition of the *Royal Frankish Annals* and equally as likely that Einhard did not. Although he is no longer held to be responsible, Einhard was traditionally associated with the revision of the *Royal Frankish Annals* ordered by Louis the Pious. The entries for the years 741–812 were revised to improve the style and were expanded with information from other sources, with the entries for several years being completely or almost completely rewritten. Although written from the Carolingian perspective, the *Royal Frankish Annals* remain one of the most important sources for the events of the Carolingian period.

See also: Carloman, Mayor of the Palace; Carolingian Dynasty; Charlemagne; Charles Martel; Einhard; Fredegar; Hincmar of Rheims; Louis the Pious; Nithard; Pippin III, Called Pippin the Short

Bibliography

Innes, Matthew, and Rosamond McKitterick. "The Writing of History." In *Carolingian Culture: Emulation and Innovation.* Ed. Rosamond McKitterick. Cambridge: Cambridge University Press, 1994, pp. 193–220.

Laistner, Max L.W. *Thought and Letters in Western Europe,* A.D. *500 to 900.* 2nd ed. Ithaca, NY: Cornell University Press, 1976.

McKitterick, Rosamond. *The Frankish Kingdoms under the Carolingians, 751–987.* London: Longman 1983.

Nelson, Janet, trans. *The Annals of St. Bertin: Ninth Century Histories.* Manchester, UK: University of Manchester Press, 1991.

Reuter, Timothy, trans. *The Annals of Fulda: Ninth Century Histories.* Manchester, UK: University of Manchester Press, 1992.

Riché, Pierre. *The Carolingians: A Family Who Forged Europe.* Trans. Michael Idomir Allen. Philadelphia: University of Pennsylvania Press, 1993.

Scholz, Bernhard Walter, trans. *Carolingian Chronicles: Royal Frankish Annals and Nithard's History.* Ann Arbor: University of Michigan Press, 1972.

S

Saint-Denis, Abbey of

Although perhaps best known for its contributions to the development of the Gothic style under the abbot Suger in the 12th century, the monastery of Saint-Denis was an important religious and political center well before that time. Both the Merovingian and Carolingian dynasties forged close associations with the community and members of both dynasties were buried at the monastery.

Established in honor of the martyr and first bishop of Paris, St. Denis (d. 270), the abbey was built over the existing chapel that had been the focus of an intense pilgrimage. The earlier church was replaced by the Merovingian king, Dagobert, who established a Benedictine monastery in 630 on the site of the old structure. According to legend, Dagobert had sought refuge in the church dedicated to Denis and was protected from the wrath of Dagobert's father by the saint. The abbey became one of the most important institutions in Merovingian Gaul and was closely associated with the dynasty. St. Denis, himself, became the patron saint of Gaul, and the community dedicated in his honor became the final resting place of Dagobert, his successors, and many of his predecessors, including Clovis. The abbey grew under the Merovingians, and the dynasty made numerous grants of land and privilege, including exemption from episcopal jurisdiction in 653, to the community throughout the seventh century. The community boasted a great abbatial church, auxiliary churches as well as buildings necessary for the maintenance of the community of monks such as a dormitory, cloister, a refectory as well as workshops and warehouses for storing the produce of the lands owned by St. Denis. Merchants were attracted by the wealth and resources of St. Denis; and each year on October 9 a great trade fair was held at the abbey, whose power and influence grew as a result of the tolls and taxes the monks collected from the trade fair. There was also a library and scriptorium, and the community is sometimes described as being the chancery of the Merovingian kings.

The importance of St. Denis was recognized in turn by the Carolingians who would replace the Merovingian kings in the eighth century. Charles Martel forged contacts with the community during his tenure as mayor of the palace, confirming their close connection by granting property to St. Denis and being buried there. Ties between St. Denis and the Carolingians were strengthened by Martel's son, Pippin, who continued the practice of making grants to the community. In 750, the abbot of St. Denis, Fulrad, was one of the representatives that Pippin sent to the

Construction of the Abbey of Saint-Denis, overseen by the Merovingian king Dagobert I, from *Les Chroniques des France*, 14th century. (The British Library Board)

pope to justify his deposition of the last Merovinginan king, and in 754, Pippin was crowned by the pope, Stephen II, as king of the Franks. Under Pippin, royal patronage of the abbey continued and important new building projects were undertaken. In 750, Fulrad began construction of a new church, which was completed and consecrated in 775. The church was expanded in the early ninth century during the abbacy of Hilduin. In exchange for royal patronage, the monks of St. Denis offered prayers, hymns of praise, and propaganda in support of the Carolingian dynasty. And, as the Merovingians had done, many Carolingian kings were buried at St. Denis.

See also: Carolingian Dynasty; Clovis; Dagobert; Merovingian Dynasty; Monasticism; Pippin III, called Pippin the Short

Bibliography

Crosby, Sumner McKnight. *The Royal Abbey of Saint-Denis from Its Beginnings to the Death of Abbot Suger, 475–1151*. Ed. Pamela Z. Blum. New Haven, CT: Yale University Press, 1987.

Riché, Pierre. *The Carolingians: A Family Who Forged Europe*. Trans. Michael Idomir Allen. Philadelphia: University of Pennsylvania Press, 1993.

Wallace-Hadrill, J. M. *The Long-Haired Kings*. Toronto: University of Toronto Press, 1982.

Salic Law

Legal code traditionally thought to have been compiled under the great Merovingian king Clovis (r. 481–511), the Salic law *(Lex Salica)* is one of the most important of early medieval legal compilations. The importance of the code is the result, in part, of the preeminence of the Franks in the post-Roman world. It remained an important legal source throughout the Merovingian period and was compiled again by the Carolingians. Sections of the law dealing with the right to succession were of great importance in the 14th and 15th centuries. The code in its earliest version contains 65 titles that address a wide variety of legal and social matters, making it a valuable source for early Merovingian history.

The code was, according to the prologue of a later version, originally compiled during the reign of the first Merovingian king. Known as the *Pactus Lex Salicae* to distinguish it from the many later revisions, it is traditionally thought to have been compiled late in the reign of Clovis, possibly between 507 and 511. Although attribution to Clovis comes from a later version, it is likely that the law appeared early in Merovingian history, surely before the death of Clovis, and it was probably commissioned by him. It is a collection of the laws of the Salian Franks, although it does not include all the laws of the Franks. The *Pactus* is the written version of the traditional customs of the Franks, and the codification of these laws in Latin reflects the growing sophistication and stability of the Franks under Clovis and important Frankish contacts with late Roman culture and government. Indeed, this collection of custom and royal edict was most likely codified by a team of Frankish officials and Roman lawyers. Originally compiled before 511, the Salic law was revised and expanded by later Merovingian kings in the later sixth and seventh centuries, and a prologue and epilogue were added in later versions. It was also revised by the Carolingians and was much studied in the eighth and ninth centuries.

The Salic law is not an orderly codification of the law, but a collection of important laws and customs that provide important insights into Merovingian society. One of the most important concerns of the Salic law is the preservation of peace in the Merovingian kingdom, and a number of chapters address social relations. One section addresses the inheritance of private property, and an earlier section specifies the fines to be paid for the theft of a bull. Penalties are imposed for wrongly calling a woman a "harlot" and for calling someone a "hare" or "fox." Another important section concerns the payment of the wergeld (payment made in compensation for taking a life) to the family of deceased. Other parts of the code deal with lesser offences and injuries and routinely impose a fine for these crimes. The penalties are often quite specific, such as a fine of 2500 denars for attempting to poison someone with an arrow, or 1200 denars for striking someone so hard on the head that the brain appears. Rape, murder of women and children, assault and robbery, and housebreaking are other crimes regulated in the Salic law. The law also concerns royal rights and prerogatives and imposes higher fines for crimes against the king, his property, and his agents.

The Salic law also provides insight into the social structures of Merovingian society. One of the most notable things revealed in the code is the social stratification of Frankish society in the sixth and seventh centuries. The penalties vary according to the social rank of the perpetrator and victim, with harsher fines imposed on the lower orders. The code reveals the continued practice of slavery, and a class of freemen and peasants, as well as one of nobles and kings. Moreover, although designed to cover all those living in the Merovingian kingdom, the Salic law originally observed the principle of personality, according to which each person was bound by the laws of his own group. Thus, it imposed different penalties for crimes by Franks and crimes by Romans and provided a legal distinction between Romans and barbarians. Under the Carolingians the law came to apply to all the people of the realm equally, bearing witness to the integration of Franks and Romans into one society.

See also: Carolingian Dynasty; Clovis; Franks; Law and Law Codes; Merovingian Dynasty

Bibliography

Geary, Patrick J. *Before France and Germany: The Creation and Transformation of the Merovingian World.* Oxford: Oxford University Press, 1988.

Rivers, Theodore John, trans. *The Laws of the Salian and Ripuarian Franks.* New York: AMS, 1986.

Wallace-Hadrill, J. M. *The Long-Haired Kings.* Toronto: Toronto University Press, 1982.

Wood, Ian. *The Merovingian Kingdoms, 450–751.* London: Longman, 1994.

Wormald, Patrick. "*Lex Scripta* and *Verbum Regis:* Legislation and Early Germanic Kingship from Euric to Cnut." In *Early Medieval Kingship.* Ed. Peter H. Sawyer and Ian N. Wood. Leeds, UK: School of History, University of Leeds, 1977, pp. 105–38.

Saxon Capitularies

Two laws issued by Charlemagne during his prolonged conquest of Saxony, 772–804, the Saxon Capitularies were intended to promote the conversion of the Saxons to Christianity, which was an essential component of Charlemagne's conquest. The two capitularies, issued about 12 years apart, reveal two different approaches to conversion of the Saxons, approaches determined, in part, by the progress of the conquest of Saxony.

The first capitulary, the *Capitulatio de partibus Saxoniae* (Capitulary concerning the parts of Saxony), was issued by Charlemagne at an assembly at the palace at Paderborn in 785. It was issued shortly after the suppression of the revolt of the Saxon leader Widukind, during a period in which extreme acts of violence and brutality were committed by both sides. Beyond the revolt against Carolingian authority, the

Saxons attacked and destroyed churches and harmed and killed priests and monks who had been engaged in missionary activity. In his turn, Charlemagne not only put down the revolt but also massacred some 4,500 Saxons at Verdun and forcibly moved a large number of Saxons into Frankish territory. Consequently, the Saxon capitulary of 785 was a draconian law that sought to impose Christianity on the Saxons by the same force that Charlemagne applied in imposing Carolingian political authority. The various decrees in the first Saxon capitulary included penalties of death for forced entry into a church, stealing from a church, eating meat during Lent, killing a priest or bishop, and refusing baptism. Death was also imposed on those who follow pagan burial rites, perform human sacrifice, or burn anyone believed to be a witch. Charlemagne also enacted a number of heavy fines in the capitulary, including fines for contracting an unlawful marriage, refusing to baptize an infant, and praying in groves of trees or at springs. The capitulary further demanded payment of the tithe to the church and forbade meetings other than church services on Sundays. Finally, the capitulary of 785 included a number of chapters establishing Carolingian government and administration.

The second capitulary, the *Capitulare Saxonicum* (Capitulary concerning the Saxons), was issued at the new imperial capital of Aachen in 797. This capitulary was also conditioned by events in the conquest of Saxony and also followed a revolt of the Saxons that was mercilessly suppressed by the great king. But the revolt and enactment of the capitulary followed a long missionary and military campaign in Saxony. Indeed, following the first publication of the first Saxon capitulary, Charlemagne continued to engage in the process of evangelization in Saxony that followed the harsh conditions set out in the ruling of 785. His treatment of the Saxons was so harsh that his closest advisor, Alcuin, complained to the king about it. By 797, Charlemagne contended that the conversion of Saxony had been completed, even though the military campaigns continued for several more years. The *Capitulare Saxonicum,* therefore, was shaped to fit the new conditions and was, therefore, a much less harsh law. It offered the milk and honey of the faith rather than the iron of the sword. Although there is no indication that the earlier capitulary was no longer in effect, the capitulary of 797 abandoned the rigid regime of death sentences and instead proposed various fines for any failure to live as a good Christian. Charlemagne's efforts ultimately bore fruit; the region eventually accepted Carolingian rule and the Christian faith, and in the 10th century Saxony was one of the great centers of medieval Christianity as well as of a resurgence of Carolingian political ideas.

See also: Alcuin of York; Capitularies; Carolingian Dynasty; Charlemagne; Franks; Widukind

Bibliography

Ganshof, François Louis. *Frankish Institutions under Charlemagne.* Trans. Bryce Lyon and Mary Lyon. Providence, RI: Brown University Press, 1968.

Halphen, Louis. *Charlemagne and the Carolingian Empire.* Trans. Giselle de Nie. Amsterdam: North-Holland, 1977.

Loyn, Henry R. and John Percival, trans. *The Reign of Charlemagne.* New York: St. Martin's Press, 1975.

McKitterick, Rosamond. *The Carolingians and the Written Word.* Cambridge: Cambridge University Press, 1989.

"Paderborn, 785 (Capitulary concerning the parts of Saxony)" and "Concerning the Saxons, 797." In *Readings in Medieval History.* Ed. Patrick J. Geary. Peterborough, ON: Broadview, 1989, pp. 316–20.

Riché, Pierre. *The Carolingians: A Family Who Forged Europe.* Trans. Michael Idomir Allen. Philadelphia: University of Pennsylvania Press, 1993.

Seville

Located on the Gaudalquivir River in southern Spain, Seville was one of the major centers of the Visigothic kingdom of the early Middle Ages. According to legend, the city was founded by Hercules and archeological evidence established settlement in the region by the ninth-century BCE. In 206 BC, the Romans took the city, which they came to call Hispalis, and it became the administrative and economic center of the Roman province of Baetica. In 428, as Roman power waned in Spain and elsewhere in the west, Seville was taken by the Vandals, who controlled the city until they were displaced by the Visigoths in 461.

The city flourished under Visigothic rule, especially during the sixth century when the bishops Leander and Isidore reigned. It was an important administrative center for the Visigothic kings and the center of revolt led by the Catholic prince Hermenegild against his father the Arian king Leovigild. The city was also declared a metropolitan bishopric. The greatest of the bishops, Isidore of Seville, was one of the leading early medieval scholars and author of the influential *Etymologies* who established Seville's reputation as an intellectual center. In 712, the city was taken by Muslim invaders and renamed Ishbiliya and would be one of the great cultural and political centers of Islamic Spain.

See also: Arianism; Hermenegild; Isidore of Seville; Leovigild; Vandals; Visigoths

Bibliography

Collins, Roger. *Early Medieval Spain: Unity in Diversity, 400–1000.* New York: St. Martin's Press, 1995.

Collins, Roger. *Visigothic Spain 409–711.* Oxford: Wiley-Blackwell, 2004.

King, P. D. *Law and Society in the Visigothic Kingdom.* Cambridge: Cambridge University Press, 1972.

Sigebert. *See* Brunhilde

Sigismund, St. (d. 524)

Sigismund was a Burgundian king (r. 516–523) and saint, whose reign was marked by the introduction of important legal codes and strained relations with the Franks and Ostrogoths. The son of Gundobad and son-in-law of Theodoric the Great, Sigismund was nonetheless a convert from Arian to Catholic Christianity, like his cousin, Clotilda, the wife of the Merovingian king Clovis. Despite his conversion, Sigismund, according to the sixth-century historian of the Franks Gregory of Tours, was the victim of Clotilda's vengeance because Gundobad had allegedly killed Chilperic, her father and Gundobad's brother. Although that remains uncertain, Sigismund was clearly caught between aggressive Frankish and Ostrogothic powers and struggled to preserve his kingdom, in part by styling himself a traditional ally of the Roman Empire and seeking an alliance with the Eastern Empire. He was eventually overthrown and killed.

Although he became king in his own name in 516, Sigismund was an important figure in the kingdom even before that time. He was made coregent by his father Gundobad in 501 and ruled with him until Gundobad's death in 516. Sigismund also played an important role in his father's diplomacy when he married the daughter of the great Ostrogothic king of Italy, Theodoric. His significance extended to religious affairs as well; he converted to Catholic Christianity, from Arian Christianity, by the year 515. His conversion, like that of Clovis not long before, allowed him to cultivate better relations with the Roman people in the kingdom, especially with the bishops. Indeed, Sigismund had very good relations with the Catholic hierarchy in his kingdom, especially with the powerful and influential bishop Avitus, who wrote a number of letters for the king. Sigismund further improved his relationship with the Catholic hierarchy in 515 by his foundation of the monastery of St. Maurice at Agaune, which became one of the more important communities in the Middle Ages. The monks at the house participated in the *laus perennis* (perpetual prayer) so that God would be praised unceasingly.

As king, Sigismund's greatest achievement was the codification and publication of Burgundian and Roman law in 517. Following the traditions of the barbarian successors to the Roman Empire, the Burgundian kingdom followed the legal principle of personality, according to which each person was bound by the laws of his own group. Like the Visigoths before him, Sigismund issued two separate legal codes, one that applied to his people and another that applied to his Roman subjects. The *Lex Gundobad* (Law of Gundobad), or *Liber Constitutionem* (Book of

Constitutions), was issued in its final form, although it was most likely originally prepared during the reign of Sigismund's father. This was a very important legal code, whose influence would last for several centuries. The king also issued the *Lex Romana Burgundionum* (Roman Law of the Burgundians), which was the personal law of his Roman subjects. Although a significant legal code, Sigismund's Roman law did not survive the fall of the kingdom; it was replaced once the kingdom fell to the Merovingian Franks.

Although Sigismund introduced a number of major reforms in the kingdom, he was less successful in international relations. Upon succeeding his father in 516, Sigismund was faced with the challenge posed by the Franks and Ostrogoths. He was fortunate that his marriage to Theodoric's daughter enabled him to at least keep Theodoric from advancing against him. Even though Theodoric was surely displeased by Sigismund's conversion to Christianity, he maintained good relations with the Burgundian king and allowed him to make a pilgrimage to Rome. To improve his situation, though, Sigismund cultivated relations with the Byzantine Empire as a balance to potential threats from the Franks and, especially, the Ostrogoths, whose relations with Constantinople were strained. When he succeeded to the throne, Sigismund also inherited the Roman title of patrician, which his father had held. But good ties with Constantinople were insufficient to save Sigismund from his closer neighbors.

In 522, Theodoric's daughter died, which removed any impediment to Theodoric's invasion of the kingdom. Moreover, relations with the Franks were long difficult, even though his relative, Clotilda, had married Clovis and, according to tradition, converted him to Christianity. Indeed, according to Gregory of Tours, Clotilda encouraged her sons to invade the Burgundian kingdom to avenge the murder of her father by Gundobad. In 522 or 523, Sigismund faced an invasion of both Franks and Ostrogoths, which he could not stop. He was defeated in battle and handed over to the Franks by his own people, who had abandoned him. In 524, he was murdered by the Frankish king, who ordered that Sigismund be thrown in a well. The kingdom preserved its independence for another 10 years before it was finally absorbed by the Franks in 534.

See also: Aryanism; Clotilda, St.; Clovis; Franks; Gregory of Tours; Gundobad; Law and Law Codes; Merovingian Dynasty; Ostrogoths; Theodoric the Great

Bibliography

Drew, Katherine Fisher, trans. *The Burgundian Code: The Book of Constitutions or Law of Gundobad and Additional Enactments.* 1972.

Gregory of Tours. *History of the Franks.* Trans. Lewis Thorpe. Harmondsworth, UK: Penguin, 1974.

Randers-Pehrson, Justine Davis. *Barbarians and Romans: The Birth Struggle of Europe, A.D. 400–700.* Norman: University of Oklahoma Press, 1983.

Wolfram, Herwig. *The Roman Empire and Its Germanic Peoples.* Trans. Thomas J. Dunlap. Berkeley: University of California Press, 1997.

Wood, Ian. *The Merovingian Kingdoms, 450–751.* London: Longman, 1994.

Slaves and Slavery

One of the most pernicious and persistent practices throughout human history, slavery was found everywhere in the ancient Mediterranean and continued in some form into the Middle Ages. Indeed, some scholars have suggested that the continuance of the practice of slavery and holding of slaves—known as *servi* (servants), *ancillae* (maidservants) or *mancipia* (things sold)—was an essential part of ancient society and that only when slavery was ended, and ultimately transformed into serfdom, did the ancient world truly end. Although slavery persisted into late antiquity and the early Middle Ages, it differed from the traditional Roman practice of holding large gangs of agricultural slave laborers. Still, slaves were found performing agricultural labor in late antiquity and the early Middle Ages in significant numbers, even if they were sometimes hard to distinguish from the local free peasants; they were also found at a number of other tasks, including military. Slavery existed among all the peoples that created kingdoms in the former Western Roman Empire, including Franks, Goths, Lombards, and Vandals.

Slavery had been a fundamental component of economy of the Mediterranean in the classical age; in late antiquity, its practice continued to be supported as a natural part of life and was accepted as part of the divinely established order by the church. Indeed, many Christian writers found justification for slavery in the Scriptures, and the great church father, St. Augustine of Hippo, accepted slavery practice in the fifth century by noting that it was the consequence of sin. The church did, however, forbid the enslavement of people who had been baptized, and some deeply pious Christians freed their slaves—for example, the sixth-century pope Gregory the Great who, according to the seventh-century Anglo-Saxon historian Bede, purchased a number of Anglo-Saxon slaves to free them and join them to the church—but there was no great push by the church for the manumission of slaves. Augustine also provides evidence for its ubiquity in the late fourth and fifth centuries, observing that nearly every household possessed slaves. Indeed, the household slave remained an important functionary, and each soldier generally had at least one or two slaves at his service. In the Roman Empire of the fourth and fifth centuries, slaves continued to be used in a number of other places, including mines, quarries, foundries, and weaving factories. They were, of course, also used as laborers on the farms of the empire, but not in great gangs housed in barracks, as they had been during the early days of the empire. They were often given small plots of land to work to encourage their productivity and also to preserve the land as taxable property. In fact, it was forbidden by law to sell a slave without his property. As a result of this, the slave and free peasant became increasingly difficult to distinguish, with the slave better off in some ways than the peasant. In one of his letters, Augustine voiced the concern that the peasant would abandon his place and join the ranks of the slaves.

Despite their many uses, slaves amounted to no more than 10 or 12 percent of the population. Nevertheless, there still existed a lucrative slave trade, which involved commerce in slaves gathered mainly from the frontier areas of the empire in modern western Hungary and Morocco. Slaves were obtained through inheritance, but more by conquest or trade. Indeed, as the various barbarian peoples entered the empire they sold their compatriots or, more often, the people they had conquered. The invasions themselves led to the continued slave trade, as many Roman citizens fell into slavery. Alaric, during the Visigothic invasion of Italy and sack of Rome, captured many slaves. The invasion of Attila and the Huns also led to the capture of many slaves, as did the invasions of the Vandals, Odovacar, and Theodoric the Great.

In the immediate post-Roman world, slavery existed in the various successor kingdoms established by the Germanic peoples who had moved into the empire and its practice was regulated in the law codes issued of these peoples. In their legal code, for example, the Visigoths imposed slavery on those who could not pay fines for crimes they committed, and in Anglo-Saxon England free persons who had sexual relations with slaves were fined by the king. In daily life, slaves were found working the royal estates in Visigothic Spain and as skilled laborers in the household. Slaves also served in the Visigothic army, although their rank and treatment was little improved by their military service. A noblewoman would be flogged and burned alive for having sexual relations with a slave. The same fate awaited the slave, but a free nobleman could father as many slave children as he wished. In the Ostrogothic kingdom of Italy a slave's life was a harsh one, and slavery was primarily rural. Slaves were chattel with very few rights or privileges, who could be killed by their owners or burned alive for having sexual relations with a widow or causing a fire. Slaves could not legally marry and could be transferred at will from one estate to another. They could even be assigned to a peasant, whose treatment could be worse in practice than that of some distant owner.

The practice of slavery continued in Italy after its conquest by the Lombards in the sixth century, and their invasion of the peninsula brought them many slaves, which provided them a larger slave workforce than that of the Goths or Romans before them. Testimony to the size of the slave population in the Lombard kingdom is found in the numerous references to them in Lombard law. A seventh-century law code, the *Leges Rothari* (Laws of King Rothari) identifies the existence of slaves of Germanic and Roman descent. The Roman slaves were often skilled and so valued more highly than their Germanic counterparts, who generally worked the fields as agricultural labor, though both Roman and Germanic slaves did serve as farmhands. Slaves were used for household and agricultural labor, and there was a monastery that owned a large number of female slaves who wove cloth. The life of the slave improved by the time of King Liutprand, in part because of the influence of the church after the conversion of the Lombards to Catholic Christianity. The marriage of slaves was now recognized as legitimate, and slave owners were forbidden from breaking up marriages by selling one of the partners. Other improvements in the treatment of slaves included the practices of giving part of the fine for killing a slave to the slave's family and allowing slaves to be freed so that they could join the clergy.

In the Frankish kingdoms slavery in some form or other existed into the ninth and tenth centuries, but the distinction between a slave and serf became increasingly blurred. There is evidence that slavery existed from the earliest days of the Merovingian dynasty. The Salic law describes certain legal processes involving slaves, and the sixth-century Frankish historian Gregory of Tours tells of the brutal treatment of slaves, including the burying of two alive by the Frankish noble Rauching. Of course, Gregory held Rauching up as an example of the worst treatment of slaves, and not all slaves endured such debased conditions. Indeed, the sixth-century queen Fredegund may have been a slave, or at least a servant at the royal court, and the seventh-century queen (and later saint) Balthild was a slave, even though of royal birth. The extent of slavery during the Merovingian period remains uncertain, however, because of uncertainties in the sources themselves and vagueness in terminology. It is likely, though, that slavery was not that extensive under the Merovingian dynasty, as records from the early days and as well as the later period of the dynasty indicate. The records of bishops at either end of Merovingian history reveal a small percentage of slaves on episcopal estates. Slavery was most likely hereditary or the result of financial difficulties and the need to buy food during famines. Aside from Gregory's tale of Rauching, the evidence suggests that slaves were frequently released from their bondage and that slaves were not poorly treated, in part because of a labor shortage the kingdom suffered, so that both the free peasantry in the countryside and the slaves were most likely well treated.

Slavery surely continued under the Carolingian dynasty, though in a much changed form from classical slavery. There is evidence revealing the transformation of slaves into serfs. The morality of slavery was much discussed by Carolingian scholars, who often borrowed from Augustine and the other church fathers. The most important of the Carolingian scholars, the Anglo-Saxon Alcuin of York, justified slavery in the very terms used by St. Augustine, and others recognized it as a natural part of the divine order of things. There is also much evidence of an active slave trade in the Carolingian Empire, and the trade was carried on by both Jewish and Christian merchants. Slaves came from the border regions of the empire, including Saxony and the Slavic lands, but it was not uncommon for an unfortunate to be captured while traveling the highways and sold into slavery. The conquests of Charlemagne and other Carolingian rulers were another source of slaves, as captives of war who were not ransomed were kept as slaves. The number of slaves was most likely not that great, seldom more than 10 percent on records from the great estates, but there were concentrations of slaves on the estates employed in a variety of occupations. Alcuin, for example, appears to have had large numbers of slaves at work on the monasteries under his control, and records from a number of other great estates indicate that about 10 percent of the workforce was made up of slaves. Carolingian slaves served as traders and bodyguards, but their most important duty was as agricultural laborers. In their role as farmers, the slaves of the Carolingian era show signs of becoming the serfs of the later Middle Ages.

See also: Alaric; Alcuin of York; Anglo-Saxons; Augustine of Hippo, St.; Balthild, St.; Carolingian Dynasty; Franks; Fredegund; Gregory I, the Great, Pope; Gregory of Tours; Liutprand; Lombards; Merovingian Dynasty; Odovacar; Ostrogoths; Salic Law; Theodoric the Great; Vandals; Visigoths

Bibliography

Bede. *Ecclesiastical History of the English People with Bede's Letter to Egbert and Cuthbert's Letter on the Death of Bede.* Trans. Leo Sherley-Price. Harmondsworth, UK: Penguin, 1991.

Bloch, Marc. *French Rural History: An Essay on Its Basic Characteristics.* Trans. Janet Sondheimer. Berkeley: University of California Press, 1966.

Bloch, Marc. *Slavery and Serfdom in the Middle Ages.* Trans. William R. Beer. Berkeley: University of California Press, 1975.

Bonnassie, Pierre. *From Slavery to Feudalism in South-Western Europe.* Trans. Jean Birrell. Cambridge: Cambridge University Press, 1991.

Cameron, Averil. *The Mediterranean World in Late Antiquity, A.D. 395–600.* New York: Routledge, 1993.

Dockès, Pierre. *Medieval Slavery and Liberation.* Trans. Arthur Goldhammer. Chicago: University of Chicago Press, 1982.

Duby, Georges. *The Early Growth of the European Economy: Warriors and Peasants from the Seventh to the Twelfth Century.* Trans. Howard B. Clarke. Ithaca, NY: Cornell University Press, 1974.

Gregory of Tours. *The History of the Franks.* Trans. Lewis Thorpe. Harmondsworth, UK: Penguin, 1974.

Wallace-Hadrill, J. M. *The Barbarian West, A.D. 400–1000.* New York: Harper and Row, 1962.

Wallace-Hadrill, J. M. *The Long-Haired Kings.* Toronto: University of Toronto Press, 1982.

Wood, Ian. *The Merovingian Kingdoms, 450–751.* London: Longman, 1994.

Solidus. *See* Coins and Coinage

Stilicho, Flavius (c. 360–408)

Roman military commander and regent whose career stood in the tradition of Arbogast, the fourth century German soldier who was the power behind the throne, and in contrast to that of the Gothic king Alaric. The son of a Vandal cavalry officer in the service of Rome and a Roman noblewoman, Stilicho fully embraced the empire and its customs, including Catholic Christianity. He had a successful career and was a loyal follower of the emperor Theodosius the Great. As regent for Theodosius's son Honorius, Stilicho faced the increasing pressure of the barbarians on the empire and invasions by Goths led by Alaric and Radagaisus. Although not wholly successful against either king, Stilicho struggled valiantly to preserve the integrity of the Western Empire, even at the cost of nearly losing Britain. His talent for managing his rivals is perhaps best illustrated in the failure of Honorius to prevent the successful invasion of Italy and sack of Rome by Alaric in the years following Stilicho's execution.

The son of a Vandal father and Roman mother, whose marriage required imperial dispensation, Stilicho was marked early on for advancement in the service of the empire. His parents placed him on the roster of the guards of the court as a small boy, where he may have made contact with the future emperor Theodosius. In 383, Stilicho served on an imperial delegation to the Persian king Shapur III (r. 383–388). Upon his return from the embassy to Shapur, Stilicho married Theodosius's favorite niece, Serena, and was raised to the office of master of the stable. By 385, he was made a general and given promotion to the rank of chief of the guard. In 391, the year he first faced Alaric, Stilicho was promoted to a high-ranking post in the Eastern Empire, and in 393 he was made master of both services, the commander-in-chief of the army.

Stilicho's rapid rise, together with the clear favor of the emperor, brought him to the top of the Roman military hierarchy before the death of his patron. His debt to the emperor did not, however, go unpaid; although little is known of his early military career, it is certain that Stilicho played an important, if not decisive, role in the victory over the pretender to the Western Empire Eugenius and his military commander Arbogast in 394. Indeed, Stilicho probably led the attack on the second day of the battle that turned the tide and brought about the defeat of Eugenius and his general. Stilicho was of such importance to the emperor that he set off for the Eastern Empire before Theodosius, who died suddenly on January 17, 395, while on his way there. Stilicho was favored by the emperor one last time when Theodosius on his deathbed entrusted his sons, Honorius and Arcadius, to the care of the Vandal general.

The death of Theodosius left Stilicho the most powerful figure in the empire, even though he was not without rivals and subject to Theodosius's heirs, Honorius in the Western Empire and Arcadius in the Eastern Empire. Indeed, his greatest rival, and personal enemy of long standing, Rufinus, was the commander in chief for Arcadius. And, under Rufinus's direction, Arcadius restricted Stilicho's field of action and ordered that Stilicho, who preparing to challenge Alaric in part of the Eastern Empire, send some of his troops to defend Constantinople against their mutual enemy Alaric and his followers. Ever loyal to the house of Theodosius and the empire, Stilicho yielded to Arcadius's demands, but the troops he sent murdered Rufinus, perhaps at their general's initiative. Stilicho next faced Eutropius, who assumed the position of chief advisor to Arcadius until late 399. The two negotiated control of important border regions between the two halves of the empire and struggled to contain Alaric. At the same time, of course, they struggled for power in the empire, which Eutropius lost in a plot that included an ally of Stilicho in the Eastern Empire.

As the leading military commander in the empire, Stilicho took on the responsibility of protecting it from various barbarian groups and spent much of his career in a complex game of cat and mouse with Alaric. They had served together when Theodosius crushed the usurpation of Eugenius, but they had become rivals as Alaric's demands went unmet by the imperial governments. In 397, Stilicho had the opportunity to destroy Alaric and his army but negotiated a settlement with him, which allowed the Gothic king to trouble the Eastern Empire and Stilicho's rival at the time, Eutropius. Although Alaric abandoned his claims to western territory over the next four years—during which time Stilicho reached the pinnacle of power, assumed the office of consul, and married his daughter, Maria, to Honorius—he invaded Italy in late 401 while Stilicho was engaged with other barbarians. Quickly turning his attention to Alaric by early 402, Stilicho called for reinforcements from Britain and the Rhine frontier to protect Italy. He also gave command to a pagan Alan, who attacked while Alaric and the Goths were celebrating Easter, thus inflicting a severe defeat on him. This was followed by an even more crushing defeat by Stilicho by late summer 402, but Stilicho once again allowed Alaric to survive and receive a military commission from Arcadius. Alaric launched one more assault on the Western Empire in 407, again at a time of crisis for Stilicho, who sought to reach an agreement with his long-term enemy; the attempt failed because of Stilicho's fall.

Stilicho faced other challenges during his career leading the Roman military. In 397–398, he faced the revolt of the Roman count of Africa, which cut off the grain supply to Italy. Stilicho overcame this challenge by importing grain from elsewhere and by sending a powerful army to suppress the unruly governor. The victorious general of that army mysteriously died not long after his victory, and many blamed Stilicho for the death. He made new treaties with the Alemanni and the Franks, and deposed a Frankish king he disliked. More serious than his difficulties in Africa or Gaul was the invasion by the barbarian Radagaisus and a large band of Ostrogoths in 405. This serious breach of the Rhine frontier, perhaps the result of Stilicho's efforts to protect Italy at the expense of the rest of the empire, would lead to Stilicho's downfall. Although he imposed a punishing defeat on Radagaisus near Florence in the summer of 406, Stilicho could not decisively defeat him. Radagaisus remained a threat to Italy for the next several years, to the dismay of Honorius and Stilicho.

The return of Alaric and death of Arcadius further complicated matters for Stilicho. Indeed, competition over the succession to the throne of Arcadius between Stilicho and Honorius, as well as the death of Maria and Stilicho's loss of important imperial territory and failure to inflict final defeats on Alaric and Radagaisus led to his downfall. No longer confident in his general, Honorius ordered the arrest and execution of Stilicho on August 22, 408. Two years later, Alaric sacked the city of Rome.

See also: Alaric; Arbogast; Honorius; Ostrogoths; Theodosius the Great; Vandals; Visigoths

Bibliography

Burns, Thomas S. *Barbarians within the Gates of Rome: A Study of Roman Military Policy and the Barbarians, ca. 375–425 A.D.* Bloomington: University of Indiana Press, 1994.

Bury, John B. *History of the Later Roman Empire: From the Death of Theodosius I to the Death of Justinian.* 2 Vols. 1923. Reprint, New York: Dover, 1959.

Bury, John B. *The Invasion of Europe by the Barbarians.* New York: W. W. Norton, 1967.

Claudian. *Claudian's Fourth Panegyric on the fourth consulate of Honorius.* Ed. and trans. William Barr. Liverpool, UK: Liverpool University Press, 1981.

Heather, Peter. *The Goths.* Oxford: Blackwell, 1996.

Wolfram, Herwig. *The Roman Empire and Its Germanic Peoples.* Trans. Thomas J. Dunlap. Berkeley: University of California Press, 1997.

Zosimus. *New History.* Trans. Ronald T. Ridley. Canberra: Australian Association for Byzantine Studies, 1982.

Strasbourg, Oath of (842)

An agreement between Charles the Bald and Louis the German, the Oath of Strasbourg solidified an alliance between the two kings during the civil wars following the death of Louis the Pious. Subscribed to by the two kings and their followers, the oath marked an important turning point in the struggles with the emperor Lothar. The oath, preserved by the historian Nithard, is also an important linguistic milestone because it was pronounced and recorded in early versions of the Romance and Germanic languages.

Following their victory over their brother Lothar at the Battle of Fontenoy in 841, Charles the Bald and Louis the German met to forge a pact confirming their continued cooperation because Lothar refused to accept peace after his defeat. They met at the city of Strasbourg on February 12, 842, to exchange oaths of loyalty and mutual assistance, declaring also that if they should violate the oath, their followers were released from their oaths to the kings. Louis, as the elder brother, spoke first in Romance, the language of Charles's followers, and swore to aid his brother and treat him as one should his brother on the condition that Charles treat him in the same way. Charles in turn, speaking in the Germanic language (*lingua teudisca*) of his brother's soldiers, made the same oath, and each brother swore not to enter into any agreement with Lothar that might harm the other's interests. The followers of the two kings then swore in their own languages that they would not give any aid to their king if the king violated the oath. The Oath of Strasbourg thus confirmed the pact of friendship and cooperation between Charles and Louis and enabled them to bring Lothar to a settlement in the Treaty of Verdun in 843.

See also: Carolingian Dynasty; Charles the Bald; Fontenoy, Battle of; Lothar; Louis the German; Louis the Pious; Nithard; Verdun, Treaty of

Bibliography

Dutton, Paul Edward. *Carolingian Civilization: A Reader.* Peterborough, ON: Broadview, 1993.

McKitterick, Rosamond. *The Frankish Kingdoms under the Carolingians, 751–987.* London: Longman, 1983.

Nelson, Janet. *Charles the Bald.* London: Longman, 1992.

Riché, Pierre. *The Carolingians: A Family Who Forged Europe.* Trans Michael Idomir Allen. Philadelphia: University of Pennsylvania Press, 1993.

Scholz, Bernhard Walter, trans. *Carolingian Chronicles: Royal Frankish Annals and Nithard's History.* Ann Arbor: University of Michigan Press, 1972.

Sutton Hoo

Site (in England's Somerset region) of one of the most important archeological discoveries for the history of the Anglo-Saxon kingdoms. In 1939 a burial mound was discovered at Sutton Hoo by Basil Brown that revolutionized modern understanding of pre-Christian Anglo-Saxon civilization. The discovery of a burial ship and its possessions from the first quarter or first half of the seventh century transformed the prevalent perception of early East Anglian courts, and Anglo-Saxon royal courts in general, as impoverished and backward centers with few contacts outside England; it revealed a dynamic court life with wide-ranging contacts with the European continent.

Golden buckle from Sutton Hoo, the Anglo-Saxon burial site from the first quarter or first half of the seventh century, British Museum. (De Agostini/Getty Images)

The burial site, noted for its extraordinary richness, is without human remains and may have been a site intended as a memorial rather than a place of interment. Whatever the case, the question of whose burial mound it was remains unanswered. Its close proximity to Rendlesham, the residence of the kings of East Anglia, and its contents have led to the theory that it was a royal burial site. Among those considered to have been buried in the 90-foot open rowing boat at Sutton Hoo are the seventh-century East Anglian kings Raedwald, Earpwald, and Sigeberht.

The mound is remarkable for the number and variety of domestic and imported goods found inside. Among its numerous and luxurious possessions are the traditional burial goods of pre-Christian warriors, including spearheads, a wooden shield covered in leather, two large drinking horns, and a helmet. A sword decorated with gold and garnets is noteworthy for the skilled craftsmanship used in its creation. There is also an extensive cache of jewelry of great quality. Some of the jewelry is also decorated with gold and garnets, thus linking it with workshops in Kent and on the Continent. A gold buckle with interlacing snakes and small animals is both exquisite in design and typical of contemporary Germanic art. The mound also contains a huge whetstone, wooden buckets with silver mounts, a five-stringed musical instrument, fragments of chain mail and textiles of great quality, and an iron battle standard with bulls' heads. Products of foreign provenance in the find include a purse with 37 gold coins from the Continent, a Byzantine salver with four stamps of the emperor Anastasius I (441–518), and a bronze bowl from the eastern Mediterranean.

Although the original find was spectacular, it was not the end of the excavations at Sutton Hoo. Subsequent work has uncovered another 20 burial mounds and 44 burial sites without mounds. The burial sites without mounds reveal that both inhumation and cremation were practiced, and they also contain possible evidence for the practice of human sacrifice. Whatever else is discovered at Sutton Hoo, the original find has contributed greatly to our understanding of this period and demonstrated the extensive contacts that England had with both the Frankish and Byzantine worlds, although more with the former than latter. Sutton Hoo also revealed the wealth and quality craftsmanship of this period of early medieval English history.

See also: Anglo-Saxons

Bibliography

Bruce-Mitford, Rupert L. S. *The Sutton Hoo Ship Burial.* 3 Vols. London: British Museum, 1975–1983.

Carver, Martin. *The Age of Sutton Hoo.* Woodbridge, UK: Boydell, 1992.

Carver, Martin. *Sutton Hoo: Burial Ground of Kings?* Philadelphia: University of Pennsylvania Press, 1998.

Evans, Angela Care. *The Sutton Hoo Ship Burial.* London: British Museum, 1986.

Stenton, Frank M. *Anglo-Saxon England.* 3rd ed. Oxford: Clarendon, 1971.

Synod of Whitby (664)

One of the most important church councils of early English history, the synod held at Streanaeschalch, or Bay of the Beacon (identified with Whitby since the 11th century), determined the shape of Christianity in the Anglo-Saxon kingdoms. The council, held by Oswy, king of Northumbria (r. 655–670), met in 664 (although some prefer the year 663) to resolve the debate over the calculation of Easter initiated by the contact between missionaries from the Celtic church of Ireland and those from the Roman church of southern England.

After the restoration of Roman Catholic Christianity to England by St. Augustine of Canterbury, conflict occurred between the advocates of the Roman faith and those of the Celtic Christian faith. Missionaries of both churches were especially active in the kingdom of Northumbria, whose king, Oswy, accepted the Celtic tradition, whereas his wife, Eanfled, a princess from Kent, was raised in the Roman tradition. Among the various differences between the practices of the two churches was a difference in the method of calculating the date of Easter, with the Celtic church celebrating the feast a week earlier than the Roman church. As a result, Eanfled would continue fasting while her husband was feasting and celebrating the resurrection of Jesus Christ. The divergence in practice in the royal household, which paralleled the divergence in the kingdom, inspired Oswy to hold a council at Streanaeschalch, the monastery of his cousin Abbess Hilda, to resolve the debate.

The council's main focus was to determine the proper means to calculate the date of Easter, but it also was to decide issues concerning liturgy, organization, the tonsure, and other matters of church discipline. Oswy opened the council by observing that all believers in one God should follow one rule and should celebrate the sacraments of heaven in the same way. The spokesman for the Celtic church, St. Colman (c. 605–676), began the debate by arguing that the saintly and pious fathers of his church, including the widely respected St. Columba (c. 521–597), had long determined the date of Easter in the Celtic way, and that these same fathers

Streanaeschalch (Whitby) Abbey in North Yorkshire, England. The abbey was founded in 657 by Hilda, who presided there as abbess until her death in 680. (Dave Bolton)

had learned their method of calculation from John the Apostle. Although the visiting bishop of the West Saxons, Agilbert, had been appointed to defend the Roman cause, he yielded to Wilfrid (634–709), the abbot of Ripon, who spoke the Anglo-Saxon language better. Wilfrid argued that his church's custom came from Rome, the city of the apostles St. Peter and St. Paul. He said also that these customs are followed in Italy, Gaul, Africa, Asia, and Greece—everywhere but Ireland and Scotland. Colman responded by defending the many Irish saints who had followed the Celtic practice, but Wilfrid argued that no matter how saintly the Celtic fathers were they could not take precedence over St. Peter, who had been given the keys to the kingdom of heaven. Hearing this Oswy asked Colman if this were true and if he could make an equal boast about Columba. Learning that Colman could not, Oswy declared, "Then, I tell you, Peter is guardian of the gates of heaven, and I shall not contradict him" (Bede 1981, 192). The king thus accepted the Roman tradition and ensured the ultimate triumph of Roman Catholic Christianity in England.

See also: Anglo-Saxons; Augustine of Canterbury, St.; Bede; Columba, St.

Bibliography

Bede. *Ecclesiastical History of the English People with Bede's Letter to Egbert and Cuthbert's Letter on the Death of Bede.* Trans. Leo Sherley-Price. Harmondsworth, UK: Penguin, 1991.

Blair, Peter Hunter. *The World of Bede.* Cambridge: Cambridge University Press, 1991.

Mayr-Harting, Henry. *The Coming of Christianity to Anglo-Saxon England.* 3rd ed. University Park: Pennsylvania State University Press, 1991.

Stenton, Frank M. *Anglo-Saxon England.* 3rd ed. Oxford: Clarendon, 1971.

T

Tassilo (742–794)

The last semi-independent duke of Bavaria (r. 749–788), Tassilo was a member of the powerful Agilolfing family, which had once been rivals of the Carolingian family for control in the Frankish kingdoms. He claimed a long tradition of successful rule in Bavaria, and he and his family had established good relations with the church in the duchy and endowed numerous monasteries. He had also established important alliances with other peoples, including the Lombards. His downfall came at the hands of his relative Charlemagne, whose expansionistic policies led him to absorb the Bavarian duchy and force Tassilo into retirement at a monastery.

The son of Odilo, duke of Bavaria, Tassilo enjoyed an important political and religious inheritance. The family had long supported the church in Bavaria and could claim the support of the monasteries they had so richly endowed. Tassilo was also the daughter of Chiltrude (d. 754), Charles Martel's daughter and sister of Pippin; even though his mother married Tassilo's father against her brother's wishes, through her Tassilo had some claim to the Carolingian legacy. On his father's death, however, the duchy was seized by Grifo, one of Charles Martel's sons, who raised an unsuccessful rebellion against Martel's heirs, Pippin and Carloman. On the suppression of the revolt, Pippin installed his young Tassilo on the ducal throne of Bavaria, which he held until 788.

As duke, Tassilo maintained an uneasy relationship with Pippin and strove to preserve as much of Bavarian independence as possible in his relations with his powerful uncle. Tassilo actively promoted the church in his duchy and welcomed the advice of the ecclesiastical nobles of the Bavarian church. He also lavished the church with numerous donations and was especially generous to the monasteries of his duchy, including the monasteries of Kremsmünster and Mondsee. His support of the church also included the promotion of missionary activity in neighboring Carinthia, and the successful conversion of the region led to increased political influence for Tassilo in Carinthia. Tassilo also pursued a foreign policy calculated to strengthen his position in relation to the Carolingians. To that end, he formed a marriage alliance with the Lombard king Desiderius. Despite his best efforts at independent action, however, Tassilo remained tied to Pippin. He accompanied the Carolingian king on one of his trips to Italy in support of the pope, and in 757 he swore an oath of allegiance to Pippin and became his vassal.

After the death of Pippin, Tassilo faced the new challenge of dealing with the new Carolingian ruler, Charlemagne. Although Charlemagne's accession was troubled, he quickly took control of the kingdom. Like Tassilo, Charlemagne first married a daughter of Desiderius, but the arrangement fell apart shortly after the death of Charlemagne's brother Carloman. Tassilo wisely chose not to involve himself in the struggle between Charlemagne and Desiderius, but this did little to ease the Carolingian's concerns about the duke of Bavaria. In 781, Charlemagne forced Tassilo to renew the pledge of vassalage he had sworn to Pippin in 757. In 787, concerned at the state of affairs, Tassilo sought the aid of the pope, Hadrian I, who had previously been favorable to the Bavarian duke. But at this point, the pope sided with the king of the Franks rather than the duke of the Bavarians. Failing to gain the support of the pope, Tassilo was forced to renew his oath of allegiance in 787, but, possibly at the urgings of his wife, he continued to intrigue against Charlemagne and began negotiations with the Avars. Informed of this by loyal Bavarian nobles, Charlemagne summoned the duke to the royal court, where Tassilo admitted to acts of treason. He was condemned to death, but in 788 his sentence was commuted to a life of penance in the monastery of Jumièges. With the fall of Tassilo, the duchy of Bavaria was absorbed into the empire of the Franks, becoming a stepping-stone for the Carolingian advance against the Avars in the 790s.

See also: Avars; Carolingian Dynasty; Charlemagne; Charles Martel; Desiderius; Hadrian I, Pope; Lombards; Pippin III, Called Pippin the Short

Bibliography

Einhard and Notker the Stammerer. *Two Lives of Charlemagne.* Trans. Lewis Thorpe. Harmondsworth, UK: Penguin, 1981.

Halphen, Louis. *Charlemagne and the Carolingian Empire.* Trans. Giselle de Nie. Amsterdam: North-Holland, 1977.

McKitterick, Rosamond. *The Frankish Kingdoms under the Carolingians, 751–987.* London: Longman, 1983.

Odegaard, Charles E. *Vassi et Fideles in the Carolingian Empire.* Cambridge, MA: Harvard University Press, 1945.

Riché, Pierre. *The Carolingians: A Family Who Forged Europe.* Trans. Michael Idomir Allen. Philadelphia: University of Pennsylvania Press, 1993.

Scholz, Bernhard Walter, trans. *Carolingian Chronicles: Royal Frankish Annals and Nithard's History.* Ann Arbor: University of Michigan Press, 1972.

Tertry, Battle of (687)

Important battle in the rise of the Carolingian dynasty that helped secure the place of the Carolingians in Austrasia and the Frankish kingdom as a whole.

Although a decisive victory for Pippin II of Herstal, it was not the decisive turning point in Carolingian history that it is often made out to be. The battle did strengthen Pippin's position as mayor of the palace, but it was two generations before another Carolingian, Pippin III the Short, claimed the kingship of the Franks.

During the seventh century, as the fortunes of the Merovingian dynasty declined and the kingdom was once again divided among the later descendants of the first great Merovingian king, Clovis (r. 481–511), into the regions of Austrasia, Neustria, and Burgundy, rival aristocratic factions competed for power against each other and against the Merovingian do-nothing kings (*rois fainéants*), as they have traditionally been called. In the region of Austrasia the descendants of Arnulf of Metz, the sainted bishop and ancestor of the family, had once again taken control of the office of mayor of the palace. In Neustria, the Arnulfing Pippin faced the powerful Ebroin and the Merovingian king Theuderic III. Pippin had been defeated by Ebroin in 680, but he survived his rival, who was assassinated and whose murderers gained asylum at Pippin's court. Ebroin's successor made peace with Pippin but was deposed by his own son, Ghislemar. Both Ghislemar and his successor, Berchar, remained on bad terms with Pippin, and war once again broke out between the mayors of Austrasia and Neustria.

The war broke out as a result of the long-standing hostility between the Austrasian and Neustrian leaders and the civil strife in Neustria. Berchar had alienated many Neustrian nobles, who joined Pippin and invited him to become involved in the struggle in Neustria. According to one near-contemporary, pro-Carolingian account, Pippin asked his followers to join him in war against the Neustrians. Pippin sought war, according to this account, because Theuderic and Berchar rejected his appeals on behalf of the clergy, the Neustrian nobility asked for aid, and he desired to punish the proud king and his mayor. Pippin's followers agreed to join in the war, and after marshalling his troops, Pippin moved along the Meuse River to meet his rival. Theuderic, learning of the advance of Pippin, levied his own troops, and he rejected, on Berchar's advice, any offers of a peaceful settlement from Pippin. Having been rebuffed, Pippin prepared for battle and at dawn on the day of battle at Tertry quietly moved his troops across the river. Theuderic and Berchar, learning that Pippin's camp was empty, moved in to plunder it and were ambushed by Pippin's army. The king and his mayor fled while their troops were massacred. Berchar too was killed while wandering, and Pippin captured Theuderic, along with the royal treasury. The victor at Tertry, Pippin took control of the king and his wealth and united the three kingdoms of Austrasia, Burgundy, and Neustria under his authority. The Battle of Tertry was a significant victory for Pippin and his descendants, but it was only under his son, Charles Martel, and grandson, Pippin the Short, that power was consolidated in Carolingian hands.

See also: Arnulf of Metz, St.; Carolingian Dynasty; Charles Martel; Clovis; Merovingian Dynasty; Pippin II, Called Pippin of Herstal; Pippin III, Called Pippin the Short

Bibliography

Bachrach, Bernard S. *Merovingian Military Organization, 481–751.* Minneapolis: University of Minnesota Press, 1972.

McKitterick, Rosamond. *The Frankish Kingdoms under the Carolingians, 751–987.* London: Longman, 1983.

Riché, Pierre. *The Carolingians: A Family Who Forged Europe.* Trans. Michael Idomir Allen. Philadelphia: University of Pennsylvania Press, 1993.

Thane. *See* Thegn

Thegn

Anglo-Saxon term that evolved from the verb *thegnian,* to serve, *thegn* acquired a more precise definition from the age of Alfred the Great in the ninth century to the end of Anglo-Saxon history in England with the Battle of Hastings in 1066. A thegn was primarily one of the king's retainers, but the term was also used for a servant of the more powerful counts of Anglo-Saxon England, who at times caused difficulties of the Anglo-Saxon kings. In either case, service was rewarded with higher status and territory for the thegn.

Although the term *thegn* appeared only once in Anglo-Saxon laws before the 10th century, it appeared in the *Anglo-Saxon Chronicle* and *Beowulf* and replaced the early Anglo-Saxon term *gesith* (noble) at some point during the early Middle Ages. And whatever term was used, the function of royal servant was one of honor and prestige and was a duty that eventually became hereditary. Indeed, in exchange for service the kings began to grant thegns hereditary rights to lands that had been granted as reward for the services rendered. In this way, the thegns were transformed into a landed nobility, even though the king retained rights over the thegn and his land. Moreover, proximity to the king and the special relationship between the two brought the thegn greater prestige in society. This heightened status was recognized as early as the sixth century by the higher wergeld given the thegn, which was six times or more than that of an ordinary peasant. Thegns were relatively numerous and could be wealthy in their own right or dependent on maintenance from the king.

The basic duty of the thegn was that of service. One of the primary duties, of course, was military service. The thegn was personally called to serve in the king's host as mounted infantry, and refusal to do so could lead to the loss of the thegn's lands. The thegn's other military duties included bringing a certain number of his own men into military service to the king, and building and repairing roads and fortifications. They also had civil obligations, such as standing as witness to the king's charters. Thegns also oversaw administration of the kingdom at the local level and were the king's representatives in the shires, keeping him in touch with local affairs. As the king's men, the thegns also played a role in royal justice on a panel that was a sort of precursor to the modern grand jury.

See also: Alfred the Great; *Anglo-Saxon Chronicle*; Anglo-Saxons; *Beowulf*; Witenagemot

Bibliography

Loyn, Henry R. *Anglo-Saxon England and the Norman Conquest.* 2nd ed. London: Longman, 1991.

Sawyer, Peter H. *From Roman Britain to Norman England.* 2nd ed. London and New York: Routledge, 1998.

Stenton, Frank M. *Anglo-Saxon England.* 3rd ed. Oxford: Clarendon, 1971.

Theoda (fl. 847/848)

Religious prophetess who appeared in the Carolingian Empire from the country of the Alemanni in the mid-ninth century, Theoda (also spelled Theuda or Thiota) preached the coming of the end of the world. She attracted a large following, which was quickly suppressed by the bishop of Mainz. Her appearance, however, challenged Carolingian ideas about the nature of the ministry in the church.

In the year 847 or 848, according to a contemporary chronicler, Theoda appeared in the city of Mainz, arriving from somewhere in Germany. According to the chronicler, Theoda claimed to know many divine mysteries. She preached the coming of the end of the world and declared that it would arrive on the last day of the year. Apparently she was a skilled preacher, because many men and women began to follow her. They offered her gifts and asked her to pray for them. She also inspired many priests, according to the chronicler, to give up their vows and follow her as though she had been sent from heaven. She was quickly brought before a council of bishops of Mainz, who interrogated her about her teachings. When asked about them she admitted that she learned those things from a certain priest and then began to teach them herself. The council denounced her teachings and had her publicly flogged. She accepted the verdict of the council, admitted that she had "irrationally seized" upon the right of preaching, and gave up her ministry in shame. After the council, Theoda disappeared from all records, and her ultimate end is unknown.

See also: Alemanni; Carolingian Dynasty; Franks

Bibliography

McKitterick, Rosamond. *The Frankish Kingdoms under the Carolingians, 751–987.* London: Longman, 1983.

Russell, Jeffery Burton. *Dissent and Reform in the Early Middle Ages.* Berkeley: University of California Press, 1965.

Wemple, Suzanne. *Women in Frankish Society: Marriage and the Cloister, 500–900.* Philadelphia: University of Pennsylvania Press, 1985.

Theodora (d. 548)

Wife and inspiration of the Byzantine emperor Justinian (r. 527–565), who shared his rule and was an important source of strength for him until her death in 548. Although her background was not the usual one for an empress, Theodora rose from humble circumstances to play a critical role in Justinian's reign. She helped him survive the most difficult moment in his reign and played an important role in his religious and military programs. Her death from cancer on June 28, 548, was a terrible blow to the emperor, who was never the same after the loss of his beloved.

Theodora is not only an important figure but, at least in her own time, also a controversial one. She was from most humble beginnings. Her father was the animal trainer for the imperial arena, and she herself performed on the stage. In the late Roman and early Byzantine world, acting on the stage was deemed a most inglorious profession and a bar from marriage to a person of senatorial rank. Moreover, she was forced into prostitution on occasion to support her family, and, according to the sixth-century Byzantine historian and general Procopius, she was an excellent and insatiable prostitute. He notes in his *Secret History* that Theodora, while still a young and underdeveloped girl, acted as a sort of male prostitute and resided in a brothel. When she was older she continued life as a courtesan and would exhibit herself publicly. Procopius says that she would attend parties with 10 men and lie with them in turn, then proceed to lie with the other partygoers, and then lie with their servants. Not only, Procopius tells us, was she incredibly promiscuous but she was also without shame. She would perform a special act in the theater where she would lie almost completely naked, have servants sprinkle barley grains over her private parts, and have geese come along and pick the grains up with their bills.

Procopius's account clearly is an exaggeration and was included in a work not intended for public consumption. Although *The Secret History* offers a gross caricature of the empress, it does contain a kernel of truth—Theodora was an actor and, probably, a prostitute. Her family history was an unfortunate one. Her father, Akakios, the bear keeper for the Green faction—one of two factions in Constantinople that provided charioteers and other performers for the games in the arena and that had extensive support networks throughout the city—died while Theodora was still a girl. Her mother remarried in the hopes that her new husband would be awarded the position. Unfortunately for Theodora, her two sisters, and her mother this did not happen, and only after public pleading by her mother or Theodora and her sisters did their stepfather receive the position. But the award was made by the Blues, the rival faction to the Greens, an action that Theodora never forgot. Life, however, remained difficult, and Theodora performed on the stage, where her sharp wit and talent won her popularity.

Unwilling to settle for the difficult life of the stage, Theodora aimed higher and became the mistress of Hecebolus, a high government minister and governor of a minor province in Africa. Her relationship with Hecebolus brought great changes to her life. She accompanied him to Africa, but their relationship soon soured, as Theodora's biting wit proved too much for the older and duller Hecebolus to endure. She was sent away after a terrible fight and left to her own resources. Procopius says that she turned to prostitution, but again caution should be exercised in accepting his bitter commentary. It is certain that Theodora spent time in Alexandria, where she met a number of leading Monophysite clergy. At this point, under the influence of the pious Monophysites, Theodora underwent a religious conversion and renounced her former way of life. She managed to find her way back to Constantinople, where she established herself in a small house, practicing the honorable and very traditional profession of sewing.

It was at this point that she met Justinian, nephew of the emperor Justin and heir apparent. Despite her rather checkered past, Theodora possessed a number of qualities that attracted Justinian. Not the least of these qualities was her physical beauty. Contemporary accounts comment on her attractiveness, and mosaics and sculpture confirms this. She was petite and had an oval face with large black eyes—features that served her on the stage and before the emperor. But her qualities went far beyond physical beauty; it was her personal qualities that inspired such great love and devotion from Justinian. Even her harshest critic, Procopius, noted that she was very clever and had a biting wit. Indeed, in his *History of the Wars* Procopius presents a most favorable portrait of Theodora that is in stark contrast to the portrait in *The Secret History.* And another contemporary, John Lydus, noted that she was more intelligent than anyone in the world. She also possessed some learning and culture that enabled her to fit in Justinian's world. But more than learning and intelligence, Theodora possessed great self-confidence and nerves of steel. Justinian himself was a man capable of prodigious amounts of work, but he sometimes lacked resolve, and it was Theodora who provided that strength of will.

Justinian, 15 years her senior, was deeply smitten by Theodora and made her his mistress and shortly thereafter planned to marry her. There were several obstacles to the marriage: Theodora's humble birth, the legal barrier against an actor marrying a senator, and the reigning empress, Euphemia, who absolutely forbade the relationship. Theodora was elevated to the patriciate by Justin, Justinian's uncle and the emperor. Euphemia's death in 524 eliminated another of the obstacles to marriage. Justin, lastly, issued a law allowing actors who had renounced their previous lifestyle, had lived honorably, and had received high dignity to marry members of the senatorial aristocracy. In 525 Justinian and Theodora married, and in 527, at the death of Justin, they ascended to the imperial dignity.

In many ways Theodora exercised great influence over her husband and his reign. Her most important moment, however, came during the Nika Revolt in 532, which nearly toppled Justinian's government. The revolt broke out in January on the heels of yet another riot between the Greens and Blues. Violence between the two factions was not uncommon in Constantinople, but this riot took on more serious implications because leaders of the two factions were arrested and condemned to death. The factions were united by the desire to save their leaders and also by dissatisfaction with taxes, bread distribution, and government agents. The government's failure to respond effectively to the demands of the Blues and Greens and unwillingness to release the leaders led to great violence. The factions stormed the City Prefect's palace, killing police and releasing prisoners as they went. Shouting "Nika the Blues! Nika the Greens!" (Nika meaning win or conquer), the rioters destroyed much of the city. The revolt was so serious that the crowds, directed in part by ambitious senators who sought to exploit the situation, proclaimed a rival emperor, the senator Hypatius.

Justinian's efforts to suppress the revolt were half-hearted and ineffective, but more deliberate attempts depended upon palace guards whose loyalty was uncertain. Justinian's personal appearance before the crowd did little but alienate them further. At that crucial moment Justinian seems to have lost his nerve and ordered flight. Theodora stood before her husband's council and made, according to Procopius, the following speech:

> Whether or not a woman should give an example of courage to men, is neither here nor there. At a moment of desperate danger one must do what one can. I think that flight, even if it brings us to safety, is not in our interest. Every man born to see the light of day must die. But that one who has been emperor should become an exile I cannot bear. May I never be without the purple I wear, nor live to see the day when men do not call me "Your Majesty." If you wish safety, my Lord, that is an easy matter. We are rich, and there is the sea, and yonder our ships. But consider whether if you reach safety you may not desire to exchange that safety for death. As for me, I like the old saying, that the purple is the nobles shroud. (Procopius, *History of the Wars* I.24.33–37, cited in Robert Browning, *Justinian and Theodora*, p. 72)

Theodora's strength gave Justinian the resolve he needed, and a plan was hatched by Justinian and his loyal generals. Using German mercenaries, the generals infiltrated the crowd of rebels in the Hippodrome and successfully massacred 30,000 people. The revolt was suppressed. The rival emperor was captured and brought before Justinian, who was about to commute the death sentence of his old friend to permanent exile when Theodora convinced her husband to execute his rival.

The revolt had ended, and Justinian survived, thanks to his loyal generals and, most especially, Theodora.

Theodora's most dramatic impact on Justinian's reign occurred during the Nika Revolt, but she influenced Justinian's domestic and foreign policy throughout their lives together. She clearly had her favorites among Justinian's civil and military staff, and those whom she disliked suffered. She orchestrated the fall of two of his ministers whom she despised. Priscus, an imperial secretary who had enriched himself at public expense, was tonsured and packed away to a monastery by the empress. John of Cappadocia, an imperial financial minister who had risen from humble beginnings, was another victim. Although he was an honorable minister, his methods were brutal, and his deposition was demanded during the Nika Revolt. He was implicated in a plot against Justinian and accused of the murder of a bishop. His methods and possible betrayal of the emperor made him an enemy of Theodora, who forced Justinian to believe the worst about John. Although Theodora struck out ruthlessly against those she thought unfaithful to Justinian and those who, like Hypatius, openly opposed him, Theodora was also an important benefactor. She was a staunch ally of the general Narses, who earned her favor by his defense of Justinian in 532. She protected him and promoted his cause during the wars in Italy. Theodora not only influenced personnel decisions but also presented a more human face to the imperial dignity by her largesse. With Justinian she indulged in acts of charity that were functions of both imperial responsibility and Christian duty. On numerous occasions, Theodora, with and without her husband, made lavish charitable donations. Following the devastating earthquake in Antioch in 528, Justinian and Theodora, all contemporary records attest, sent great amounts of money to help rebuild the city. On a trip to northwestern Asia Minor, Theodora offered large donations to churches along her route. She also took special care of poor young women who had been sold into a life of prostitution. On one occasion she called the owners of the brothels to the court, reprimanded them for their activities, and purchased the girls from them out of her own purse. She returned them to their parents and also established a convent where they could retire.

The empress also played a critical role in religious affairs in the empire. It was her favorite Vigilius who succeeded to the papal throne in 537, although not simply because he was her favorite. She conspired in the elevation of Vigilius to the office of the papacy above all because she thought he would be a more pliable pope on religious matters important to her and the emperor. But more than that she offered protection to an important religious minority in the empire. As the emperor, Justinian was the protector of the faith and defender of orthodoxy. Consequently, he enforced orthodox Christian belief and ordered the persecution of heretics, including the execution of many Manichaeans of high social rank. The empire, however, faced a serious division over the nature of Jesus Christ that threatened imperial unity and relations with Rome. The largest minority sect in the empire was that of the Monophysites, who were particularly numerous in the wealthy and populous region of Syria. Theodora, a devout Monophysite Christian, defended and protected her coreligionists. She encouraged the promotion of Monophysites or their sympathizers to positions of ecclesiastical importance and protected Monophysites in her private chapel. She also may have influenced Justinian's publication of a profession of faith that sought a common ground between orthodox Catholic doctrine and Monophysite doctrine.

Theodora's impact may also have been felt on Justinian's foreign policy. One of the emperor's great dreams was to restore Italy to imperial control, and the situation on the peninsula after the death of the great Gothic king Theodoric in 526 afforded him an opportunity. Theodoric was succeeded by his eight-year-old grandson, Athalaric, under the regency of his mother and Theodoric's daughter, Amalaswintha. The regent was a cultured, educated, and ambitious woman who found herself at odds with much of the Gothic nobility. Facing conspiracy from the nobility, especially after the death of her son, Amalaswintha found an ally in Justinian, whom she nearly visited in Constantinople in 532. For the emperor, a close alliance with Amalaswintha provided an entry into Italian affairs and the possible extension of imperial control. Her talent and royal blood made her an attractive marriage candidate, a fact not lost on anyone in the imperial capital—especially Theodora. The Gothic queen, however, never made the trip east and was eventually imprisoned by her rivals in Italy. It is at this point that the possible influence of Theodora can be seen.

Mosaic of Theodora from the Church of San Vitale, Ravenna, sixth century. (Neil Harrison/ Dreamstime.com)

Justinian sent an envoy to protest the imprisonment, threatening war if anything should happen to the queen. According to Procopius, the envoy received a second message from Theodora, instructing him to inform the Gothic king, Theodohad, that Justinian would do nothing should anything happen to Amalaswintha. And not long after Amalaswintha was murdered. Justinian had his pretext to invade Italy. Theodora provided this pretext, Procopius tells us, out of jealousy, but it is likely that Justinian was aware of the second letter and approved of it. Whether he did or not is conjecture, but clearly he benefited from the letter, just as he benefited from Theodora's inner strength and good political sense throughout their lives together.

See also: Amalaswintha; Belisarius; Gothic Wars; Justinian; Procopius; Theodoric

Bibliography

Browning, Robert. *Justinian and Theodora.* Rev. ed. London: Thames and Hudson, 1987.

Bury, John B. *History of the Later Roman Empire: From the Death of Theodosius I to the Death of Justinian.* Vol. 2. 1923. Reprint, New York: Dover, 1959.

Clark, Gillian. *Women in Late Antiquity: Pagan and Christian Lifestyles.* Oxford: Clarendon, 1993.

Obolensky, Dmitri. *The Byzantine Commonwealth: Eastern Europe, 500–1453.* New York: Praeger, 1971.

Theodoric the Great (c. 451 or 453/454–526)

One of the greatest of the barbarian kings and the greatest of the Gothic kings, Theodoric the Great, or the Amal as he was originally known, reigned over the Ostrogoths from 471 to 526 and ruled an independent Gothic kingdom in Italy from 493 to 526. He assumed power in Italy by defeating a rival barbarian king, Odovacar, and Theodoric's reign was generally recognized for its effectiveness and tolerance. He skillfully managed the relations between his people and the native Roman population and also maintained good relations with the emperors in Constantinople. Theodoric was able to keep the peace in Italy between Ostrogoths and Romans despite important differences in religion—Theodoric and his people were Arian Christians and the native Italians were Catholic Christians. He preserved the best aspects of the administrations of Odovacar and the Romans and worked well with the Senate and Roman nobles. He was an active builder, promoted culture, and patronized the great scholars Boethius and Cassiodorus. His reign, however, was marred in its later years by increasing tension between Goths and Romans, as Catholic Christianity found important new leaders. The situation was worsened by Theodoric's execution of Boethius and his father-in-law, Symmachus, leading Roman senators. Despite the difficulties of his later years, complicated further by the lack of a male heir, Theodoric was one of the greatest kings to rule in the years after the fall of the Western Empire.

The early life of Theodoric is important for his later years, though modern knowledge of it is marked with confusion. One particularly vexing problem about his early years is the date of his birth, which is traditionally given as 456. According to the tradition, Theodoric was born on the day that his family learned the news that his uncle Valamir had been attacked by and had defeated a large band of Huns. But this date is unlikely because it would make Theodoric quite young—indeed, perhaps too young—when he was sent to Constantinople as a hostage and still quite young when he later took control of the kingdom. More recent scholarship has suggested dates of birth as early as 451, which would correspond to the victory of the Ostrogoths and their Roman allies over the Huns at the Battle of the Catalaunian Plains, a date that would make Theodoric a more mature, and politically useful, boy when he was sent to Constantinople. Whatever his exact date of birth, he was born to the royal Amal family and was sent as a hostage in 459/460 as surety for a treaty between the Ostrogoths and Eastern Empire. While at the imperial court, Theodoric learned a great deal and had experiences that shaped his later life. He became aware of rivalries among the Gothic people, and most likely came to fear and hate rival Ostrogothic families who gained preferment at the imperial court. He also witnessed the sophisticated governmental practices of the empire, which he used when he became king of the Ostrogoths and then later ruler in Italy. He also gained a solid, if unspectacular, education, most likely learning to do arithmetic and to read and write.

Theodoric was released from his service as a hostage in the late 460s, after which, at about 469, he returned to his homeland, received control of a subkingdom, and began his ascent to power among the Ostrogoths. Already in 470 he launched campaigns, sometimes in the name of the empire, against his political rivals or to expand his territory. His success in 470 revealed his ambition; the campaign probably took place without his father's permission, and marked, for Theodoric, the start of his independent authority. In the 470s he became an increasingly powerful and important figure in the military and political life of the Eastern Empire. His main Gothic rival, Theodoric Strabo, or the Squinter, rose in the imperial ranks in the 470s and took a prominent part in a revolt against Emperor Zeno. Having fled from the capital in 475, Zeno was able to return thanks to the support from Theodoric of the Amal clan and strike against Strabo, who quickly fell from grace, though he remained a powerful rival to both Theodoric and Zeno. Theodoric the Amal received numerous honors from Zeno and was made commander of East Roman troops. Theodoric's people were made *foederati* (federated allies) of the empire and were given an annual subsidy from the emperor. Despite these achievements, Theodoric still faced a challenge from Strabo, who sometimes was supported by Zeno for fear of an over mighty Theodoric the Amal. Strabo's sudden death in 481 freed his rival's hand. Theodoric was now sole king of the Ostrogoths and a dangerous friend of the empire.

The 470s and early 480s saw important changes in the life of Theodoric and the Roman Empire. Theodoric had become one of the most powerful figures in the Eastern Empire. In 482–483 Theodoric waged a terrible offensive in the empire to force Zeno to come to terms, which the emperor did. Theodoric was rewarded with a consulship for 484, but his term in office was cut short by Zeno's fears that the Ostrogoth had turned against him. Despite his own strength, Theodoric knew that he was no match for the full power of the empire, and events in the Western Empire offered both Theodoric and Zeno a solution to their problematic relationship. In 476 the last of the Western Roman emperors, Romulus Augustulus, and his general, Orestes, were defeated by the German general Odovacar. After defeating his rivals, Odovacar executed Orestes and deposed Romulus and sent him into internal exile. Odovacar also declared the end of the imperial line in Italy and, although recognizing the sovereignty of the emperor in Constantinople, ruled as an independent king in Italy. In 488, following another revolt by Theodoric, Zeno requested that the Ostrogoth invade Italy and restore it to imperial control.

Theodoric's march to Italy was not unimpeded, as other barbarian peoples struggled against him, but he reached Italy by the summer of 489. His rival Odovacar was waiting for him with his army. Theodoric won two victories against Odovacar in August and September of 489. He also welcomed Tufa, one of Odovacar's leading generals, and it seemed that Theodoric would quickly triumph over his enemy. But Odovacar was able to secure himself behind the walls and swamps of Ravenna, and Tufa rejoined Odovacar shortly after leaving, taking with him the Ostrogothic soldiers he commanded on the way to Ravenna. Odovacar then took the offensive and forced Theodoric to withdraw to the city of Pavia. Theodoric, however, managed to break the siege and defeat Odovacar once again, on August 11, 490, with the aid of a large number of Visigoths. Odovacar returned to Ravenna, where Theodoric besieged him. But Ravenna could not be taken, and Theodoric was forced to negotiate with Odovacar. Agreement was reached on February, 493, and Theodoric entered Ravenna on March 5. Apparently he had agreed to share power with Odovacar. On March 15, he welcomed Odovacar at a great banquet, at which Theodoric himself killed Odovacar. The murder of Odovacar was followed by the massacre of his family and supporters. Theodoric had eliminated his rival and then proceeded to take control of Italy.

Theodoric's position remained uncertain for some time, in part because of his desire to be recognized as the ruler in Italy by the emperor in Constantinople. He was anxious to be recognized in the capital of the empire because he portrayed his kingdom as the legitimate successor of the Roman Empire in Italy. He did this for a number of reasons. He certainly had some sentimental attachment to all things Roman as a result of his time as a hostage in Constantinople. He also recognized the importance of being "Roman." That identity meant civilization and defined relations with the nobility in Italy, as well as with the church, a very powerful force.

It was also a means to secure support for his kingdom from the population of Italy, the birthplace of the Roman Empire. He could also use it in his relations with Constantinople, as an instrument to remind the emperor that any violation of the peace between them was a violation of the empire and an offense against God.

Theodoric's status was resolved gradually over the first two decades of his rule in Italy, and in two stages, in 497/498 and in 508, the Ostrogoth gained recognition from the emperor for his independent status as king in Italy. His rule in Italy, from 497 until his death in 526, was a time of peace and prosperity for the peninsula. Moreover, his kingdom became the center of the greatest power in western Europe, as Theodoric established his authority not only over Italy but also over other parts of the old Western Empire. Although his closest rival, the Merovingian king Clovis, managed some success against Theodoric in southwestern France, the Frankish king never really attempted to unseat Theodoric, to whom he was related by marriage. (His sister, Audofleda, married Theodoric and bore the daughter Amalaswintha.) Indeed, marriage alliances constituted one of the tools Theodoric used to enhance his power in the old Western Empire—his sister married the Vandal king in North Africa, and his daughters married a Visigothic king and a Burgundian king. Another instrument in the extension of his power, of course, was his great ability as a general. His defense of the Visigothic kingdom in Spain and subsequent acquisition of the kingdom in 511 revealed his talents as a military leader, as did his campaigns for and against the emperor and against Odovacar.

Although king of Visigothic Spain, Theodoric is best known for his rule of Italy. As the independent ruler of Italy, Theodoric presided over a cultural and economic revival in the peninsula, and his royal court in Ravenna was a great center of intellectual and cultural life. He worked effectively with the Roman nobility, who enjoyed the peace brought by Theodoric and managed to revive the productivity of their estates. Theodoric's equitable distribution of land, which did not overly burden the Roman population of Italy, also stimulated an economic revival. He not only worked well with the nobles but respected and honored the Senate, and in many ways preserved Roman imperial governmental practices. Despite his Arianism, Theodoric remained on good terms with the pope and Catholic church in Italy. Indeed, at one point he was invited to resolve a disputed papal election, and his good relations with the church were critical to his acceptance as the ruler in Italy. He also supported the traditions of Roman law and education in his kingdom. He helped maintain the infrastructure in Italy, restoring many roads and public buildings, and he was also a great builder in his own right. He built a great palace, an octagonal baptistery decorated with brilliant mosaics (including a mosaic of the Trinity which was not common in Arian church decoration), and, most notably, the magnificent mausoleum that still stands in Ravenna today. Finally, Theodoric was a patron of arts and letters. His personal secretary was the prominent Christian writer Cassiodorus, and Theodoric also had close relations with the great intellectual and author, Boethius.

Despite his long and prosperous reign, Theodoric's end was not a happy one, and his great kingdom did not long survive his death. Several events conspired to bring Theodoric's reign to an unfortunate end. His failure to have a male heir made the establishment of a dynasty difficult and caused tensions among the Ostrogoths, which worsened other internal problems. It also undermined his foreign policy and the extension of his power over Spain. Furthermore, his good relations with the church came to an end for two reasons. The election of a new pope, John I (523–526), ended Theodoric's good relations with the papacy, in part because of John's hostility toward Arianism. His relations with the church also worsened because the tensions that existed within the church, between its eastern and western halves, were eased, as the new emperor, Justin (518–527), outlawed Arianism and supported Catholic orthodoxy. Theodoric's Arianism was made to appear even more at odds with the Catholic population by the conversion of Clovis and the Merovingian dynasty to Catholic Christianity. Finally, his good relations with the Senate and Roman nobility were poisoned by an alleged conspiracy of senators in 522. Boethius's defense of his fellow senators implicated him in the plot in the eyes of Theodoric, and as a result, Boethius fell from favor and was executed in 524.

Theodoric the Great, Ostrogothic king, wrongly identified as Justinian. (iStockPhoto.com)

Theodoric died in August 526. According to the sixth-century Byzantine historian Procopius, Theodoric died of typhoid brought on by remorse for the deaths of Boethius and his father-in-law, Symmachus, who was also implicated in the plot against Theodoric. Procopius notes that Theodoric was served fish for dinner one evening and saw in it the face of Symmachus. Theodoric fled to his room frightened by the vision, and then called for a doctor, to whom he disclosed his great dismay over the execution of Symmachus and Boethius.

Theodoric was succeeded by his grandson, Athalaric, whose mother, Amalaswintha, served as a regent during the first part of her son's reign. The problems of Theodoric's last years continued to plague his successor and Amalaswintha. Dissension among the Goths led to her death and the eventual invasion and destruction of the Gothic kingdom by Justinian. A brilliant, tolerant, and effective ruler in many ways, Theodoric could not provide for a lasting settlement in the kingdom he created.

See also: Amalaswintha; Arianism; Boethius; Catalaunian Plains, Battle of the; Clovis; Huns; Justinian; Merovingian Dynasty; Odovacar; Orestes; Ostrogoths; Romulus Augustulus; Visigoths; Zeno

Bibliography

Amory, Patrick. *People and Identity in Ostrogothic Italy, 489–554.* Cambridge: Cambridge University Press, 1997.

Burns, Thomas. *A History of the Ostrogoths.* Bloomington: University of Indiana Press, 1984.

Bury, John B. *History of the Later Roman Empire: From the Death of Theodosius I to the Death of Justinian.* 2 Vols. 1923. Reprint, New York: Dover, 1959.

Cassiodorus. *The Variae of Magnus Aurelius Cassiodorus.* Trans. S.J.B. Barnish. Liverpool, UK: Liverpool University Press, 1992.

Heather, Peter. *The Goths.* Oxford: Blackwell, 1996.

Hodgkin, Thomas. *Theodoric the Goth: the Barbarian Champion of Civilization.* New York: G. P. Putnam, 1983.

Jordanes. *The Gothic History of Jordanes.* Trans. Charles C. Mierow. New York: Barnes and Noble, 1985.

Moorhead, John. *Theodoric in Italy.* Oxford: Clarendon, 1992.

Procopius. *Procopius, with an English Translation by H. B. Dewing.* Cambridge, MA: Harvard University Press, 1962.

Wolfram, Herwig. *The Roman Empire and Its Germanic Peoples.* Trans. Thomas J. Dunlap. Berkeley: University of California Press, 1997.

Wood, Ian. *The Merovingian Kingdoms, 450–751.* London: Longman, 1994.

Theodosian Code

An official compilation of the laws of the Christian emperors of Rome, the Theodosian Code (*Codex Theodosianus*) was an important and influential legal work.

Binding throughout the empire from its publication in the early fifth century, the code would have a direct impact on early Germanic legal codes such as the Visigothic Breviary of Alaric which contains whole selections of the code. The code also enforced the position of Catholic Christianity as the official religion of the empire and imposed harsh restrictions on heretics and Jews living in the empire.

The emperor Theodosius II (401–450) established a commission in 429 to codify imperial legislation that had been issued since the time of the emperor Constantine. Over the next six years, the commission collected a large number of imperial edicts and general laws that would serve as the main body of the code. In 435 Theodosius issued further instructions, ordering the commission to prepare an index to identify the specific legal point at issue. The completed work was divided into 16 books and included more than 2,500 constitutions issued between 312 and 437. Theodosius published his code in Constantinople in 437, declaring that no law issued by the emperors from the time of Constantine and himself would have legal force if it were not in the code. In 438, the code was officially published in Rome.

See also: Breviary of Alaric; Constantine; Visigoths

Bibliography

Harries, Jill and Ian Wood, eds. *The Theodosian code: Studies in the Imperial Law of Late Antiquity*. London: Duckworth Publishers, 2010.

Matthews, John. *Laying Down the Law: A Study of the Theodosian Code*. New Haven, CT: Yale University Press, 2000.

Pharr, Clyde, Theresa Sherrer Davidson, and Mary Brown Pharr, eds. *The Theodosian Code and Novels and the Sirmondian Constitutions*. Princeton, NJ: Princeton University Press, 1952.

Theodosius the Great (347–395)

The last emperor to rule over a united Roman Empire, Theodosius (r. 378–95) was one of the last great Roman emperors. He had success against the Visigoths, whose marauding across the empire following the Battle of Hadrianople in 378 was stopped by the emperor. A staunch Catholic Christian, Theodosius had mix relations with the church. One of its most ardent defenders, Theodosius also came into conflict with the great bishop of Milan, Ambrose.

Born in Spain to the powerful and important general, Theodosius, and his wife, Thermantia, both of whom were Catholic at a time when Arianism was in the ascendancy, Theodosius would follow his father into a military career, joining the senior Theodosius on campaign and becoming a commander in his own right. In 374, however, Theodosius retired from public life, possibly as a result of his father's disgrace and execution. Four years later, Theodosius was recalled from retirement by the emperor Gratian, whose uncle and emperor in the east Valens was killed after the disastrous Battle of Hadrianople. Given command of the army, Theodosius was formally made emperor in the east in 379 and took steps to rebuild the army destroyed at Hadrianople. He enjoyed several victories over the Goths but was unable to destroy them. In 382, following the precedent set by Gratian in 380, Theodoric came to terms with the Goths and settled them as *foederati* (federated allies) along the Danube in Thrace. In this way, the emperors made enemies of the empire into its defenders, and the Goths were obliged by the treaty to serve alongside the Roman military.

Along with his struggles against the Goths, Theodosius was involved with internal conflict over control of the empire itself. Following the death of Gratian in 383, the western half of the empire endured serious unrest from the pretender Magnus Maximus who challenged Gratian's coemperor Valentinian II. In 387, Maximus, having established himself north of Italy invaded the peninsula, forcing Theodosius to act. In 388, the two met at the battle of Poetovio and Maximus was defeated and then executed. Trouble arose again in 392 when Valentinian was found dead in his palace, and the general Arbogast, accused of murdering Valentinian, propped Eugenius up as emperor. In contrast to Theodosius, Arbogast and Eugenius restored the Altar of Victory in Rome and advocated traditional Roman pagan religion. Although they sought recognition for Eugenius from Theodosius, the emperor in the east refused and made his son, Honorius, emperor. In 394, Theodosius defeated and killed Arbogast and Eugenius and unified the empire under his authority. And in 395, Theodosius's sons, Arcadius and Honorius, would succeed to a divided empire.

Theodosius left an important legacy on the history of the church as well as on the empire. His relations with the church were not always smooth, however, and on two occasions he ran into trouble with Ambrose of Milan. In 388, a group of Christians, spurred on by their bishop, destroyed a synagogue in Mesopotamia. The emperor sought to punish the bishop and force him to pay restitution to the members of the synagogue, but the bishop of Milan threatened spiritual penalties is Theodosius imposed the fines. The emperor yielded to the bishop. In a more famous and important incident, Theodosius ordered the massacre of some 7,000 people in Thessalonica in 390 after a riot that threatened imperial authority broke out in the city. Ambrose placed Theodosius under the ban of excommunication and forced the emperor to do penance. Theodosius submitted and provided a precedent for later churchmen who sought to assert the spiritual over the secular power. Despite these conflicts, the relations between Ambrose and Theodosius as well as those between the church and the emperor were generally good. It was Theodosius who helped to finally resolve the dispute that had raged within the church since the time of Constantine over the nature of the godhead. A devout follower of Nicene Christianity, Theodosius supported Catholic over Arian teachings. In 381, he called the first Council of Constantinople, which affirmed

Nicene orthodoxy and declared Arianism a heresy. Confirming Catholic teachings as orthodox for the church, Theodosius declared Catholic Christianity the official religion of the empire in 391. Although he did not force pagans to convert to Christianity, Theodosius abolished pagan priesthoods, forbade pagan rites, closed temples, confiscated their land and transformed the temples into Christian churches.

See also: Ambrose of Milan; Arbogast; Arianism; Constantine; Galla Placidia; Hadrianople, Battle of; Honorius; Visigoths

Bibliography

Freeman, Charles. A.D. *381: Heretics, Pagans, and the Dawn of the Monotheistic State.* New York: Overlook Press, 2009.

Friell, Gerar, and Stephen Williams. *Theodosius: The Empire at Bay.* New York: Routledge, 1998.

Wolfram, Herwig. *The Roman Empire and Its Germanic Peoples.* Trans. Thomas J. Dunlap. Berkeley: University of California Press, 1997.

Theodulf of Orléans (c. 760–820/821)

Court scholar, abbot, and bishop, Theodulf of Orléans was a leading figure in the Carolingian Renaissance during the reign of Charlemagne. Theodulf was perhaps the finest poet and most gifted theologian among Charlemagne's court scholars. He was also the primary author of the *Libri Carolini* (Caroline Books), a *missus dominicus* (emissary) for the king, and a dedicated preacher. During his term in office as bishop of Orléans, he sought to implement the reforms spelled out in Charlemagne's *Admonitio Generalis.*

Theodulf was born in Spain to Visigothic parents in circa 760 and entered Charlemagne's service after the great ruler's extension of his territory into Spain. He became a devoted supporter of the king and his religious and educational reforms. He benefited from his service, being made abbot of two important monasteries and, some time before 798, bishop of Orléans by Charlemagne. Theodulf partook fully in the reform program of Charlemagne, both as bishop and royal agent.

As *missus dominicus* to southern France in 798, Theodulf performed in exemplary fashion, judging cases of law and executing the royal will. He also learned firsthand of the corruption that such officials perpetrated when he was offered gifts by the litigants whose cases he was to arbitrate. Although he did not accept these gifts, Theodulf recognized that others did and worked to eliminate such abuses of power. In similar fashion, as bishop of Orléans he sought to reform ecclesiastical life and discipline, issuing a number of edicts designed to improve religious life in his diocese. He also established schools to educate young boys in his diocese. In the

790s he was called on to write the Carolingian response to the Second Council of Nicaea (787), at which the veneration of icons forbidden under the iconoclastic emperors was restored, and he accordingly prepared the *Libri Carolini,* which contained the Carolingian denunciation of the veneration of icons and a sophisticated philosophy of art. Although authorship was traditionally given to Alcuin, it is now recognized that Theodulf was the author, but with some role held by Alcuin in the production. Theodulf was also probably present at Charlemagne's coronation as emperor on Christmas Day, 800. His service to the Carolingian dynasty continued during the reign of Charlemagne's successor, Louis the Pious. But in 817 Theodulf was implicated in a rebellion against the emperor, although there is little evidence to confirm or deny any role. Louis deposed Theodulf from his office of bishop and exiled him to Angers, where he died in 820 or 821.

Theodulf was, above all, a theologian and poet of great skill. Along with the *Libri Carolini* Theodulf produced treatises, at Charlemagne's invitation, on baptism and the Holy Spirit. He also produced a new edition of the Bible. Even more celebrated than his theological works is his poetry. Theodulf was the finest and most original poet of all the court scholars of Charlemagne's age. His poetry was characterized by elegant Latin and abundant references to classical literature, especially Ovid (43 BC–AD 17), and his poem *Ad Carolum regem* (To Charles the King) is a charming and often satirical portrait of Charlemagne and his scholars. His religious poetry was often pessimistic, however, reflecting on the poor mores of those around him. He revealed his deep appreciation of art in his poetry, an appreciation that is also reflected in the manuscripts illuminated at his scriptorium and in the beautiful mosaics decorating the church he had built at St. Germigny-des-Prés.

See also: Admonitio Generalis; Alcuin of York; Carolingian Renaissance; Charlemagne; Louis the Pious; *Missi Dominici*; Visigoths

Bibliography

Dutton, Paul Edward, ed. *Carolingian Civilization: A Reader.* Peterborough, ON: Broadview, 1993.

Freeman, Ann. "Theodulf of Orléans and the *Libri Carolini.*" *Speculum* 32 (1957): 664–705.

Laistner, Max L. W. *Thought and Letters in Western Europe, A.D. 500 to 900.* 2nd ed. Ithaca, NY: Cornell University Press, 1976.

McKitterick, Rosamond. *The Frankish Kingdoms under the Carolingians, 751–987.* London: Longman, 1983.

Riché, Pierre. *The Carolingians: A Family Who Forged Europe.* Trans. Michael Idomir Allen. Philadelphia: University of Pennsylvania Press, 1993.

Theodulf of Orleans. *The Poetry of Theodulf of Orleans: A Translation and Critical Study.* Ed. and trans. Nikolai A. Alexandro. Ann Arbor: University Microfilms, 1970.

Theudelinda (d. 628)

Bavarian princess, Theudelinda (also spelled Theodelinde) was the wife of two Lombard kings, Authari (r. 584–590) and Agilulf (r. 590–616), and the mother of a third, Adaloald (r. 616–626). A powerful figure in the Lombard kingdom, Theudelinda exercised her influence in the realm for nearly 30 years. She effectively chose the successor to her first husband, Authari, and acted as regent for her son, Adaloald. In frequent correspondence with Pope Gregory the Great, some of which is found in the history of the eighth-century historian Paul the Deacon, she sought to convert the Lombards from Arian Christianity to Catholic Christianity and welcomed Catholic missionaries into the kingdom. Although ultimately the Lombards did adopt Catholic Christianity, her efforts inspired an Arian reaction during the reigns of Ariold (r. 626–636) and Rothari (r. 626–652).

Paul the Deacon recorded a romantic tale of the courtship of Theudelinda by Authari, which involved Authari's anonymous visit to the Bavarian court. The marriage having been arranged between the Lombard and Bavarian kings, Theudelinda was sent to the Lombard kingdom. She wed King Authari at Verona on May 15, 589. Although Authari was a committed Arian, and welcomed few non-Arians to his court, he chose to marry the Catholic Theudelinda. He did so because of long-standing ties between the Lombards and the Bavarians and because of their mutual hostility toward the Franks, who had the Bavarians on the defensive at that time. Theudelinda was also of the ancient Lombard royal line and thus a suitable match for the Lombard king and former duke. Indeed, the marriage benefited both sides, strengthening the Lombard–Bavarian alliance, which successfully halted a Frankish advance in 590 and established a lasting peace with the Franks in 591.

During her marriage to Authari, Theudelinda established herself as a major figure in the kingdom, and she remained so until her death in 628. According to Paul the Deacon, Theudelinda was so highly esteemed by the Lombards that at the death of Authari they allowed her to remain queen and asked her to choose the successor to Authari as her husband and king. In consultation with the Lombard leaders, she chose Agilulf, duke of Turin. During his reign, Theudelinda continued to exercise her influence and corresponded with Pope Gregory. Under her guidance, Agilulf forged a treaty with the pope, one of the greatest landowners in Italy as well as the spiritual leader of Catholic Christians. She also supported the activity of the Irish missionary St. Columban, which not only improved the religious life of the kingdom but also established a connection with lands to the north of Italy. At her husband's death in 616, she was made regent for their son Adaloald, and she remained his coruler even when he reached his majority. His reign and life, however, ended abruptly in 626 amid allegations that he had gone mad. Theudelinda's support for

Catholicism may have been the real reason for the sudden end of Adaloald's reign, but even though an Arian reaction set in after 626, her influence continued with the marriage of her daughter to the new king, Ariold.

Theudelinda was a major political force throughout her life in the Lombard kingdom, but is perhaps best known for her missionary efforts in support of Catholic Christianity. Although somewhat independent minded in her faith and support for the northern Italian bishops against the pope in a doctrinal dispute, Theudelinda was on good terms with the pope. She actively supported the religious life in her kingdom and built a church dedicated to St. John the Baptist at Monza, near Milan, which she richly endowed. She also received lavish gifts from Pope Gregory to be bestowed on the new church. Her support for new religious foundations did not end with Monza, but included the establishment of monasteries at Bobbio and elsewhere. The foundation at Bobbio, one of the most important and influential monasteries of the early Middle Ages, came as the result of her support for the Irish missionary St. Columban. Although in the short run her support for Catholic Christianity failed to counter Lombard Arianism, Theudelinda's efforts in support of the Catholic church were vindicated when the Lombards converted to Catholic Christianity later in the seventh century.

See also: Arianism; Columban, St.; Franks; Gregory I, the Great, Pope; Merovingian Dynasty; Paul the Deacon; Rothari

Bibliography

Christie, Neil. *The Lombards: The Ancient Langobards.* Oxford: Blackwell, 1998.

Herrin, Judith. *The Formation of Christendom.* Princeton, NJ: Princeton University Press, 1987.

Llewellyn, Peter. *Rome in the Dark Ages.* New York: Barnes and Noble, 1996.

Paul the Deacon. *History of the Lombards.* Trans. William Dudley Foulke. Philadelphia: University of Pennsylvania Press, 1974.

Wallace-Hadrill, J. M. *The Barbarian West, A.D. 400–1000.* New York: Harper and Row, 1962.

Wolfram, Herwig. *The Roman Empire and Its Germanic Peoples.* Trans. Thomas J. Dunlap. Berkeley: University of California Press, 1997.

Three-Field System. *See* Agriculture

Tolbiac, Battle of (496)

Battle fought between the Merovingian king of the Franks, Clovis, and the Alemanni about the year 496. According to the sixth-century Frankish historian Gregory of Tours, the battle was the turning point in the reign of Clovis, who converted to

Catholic Christianity following the victory. The traditional chronology of the conversion, however, is now questioned, and it is considered most likely that Clovis did not convert directly to Catholic Christianity from paganism. Although the battle may not have occurred as Gregory described it and may have become confused with the battle at Zülpich some 10 years later, it may still be recognized as an example of the broader policy of conquest and expansion pursued by the greatest Merovingian king.

As recorded in the history of Gregory of Tours, the Battle of Tolbiac involved the Franks and Alemanni; it has generally been dated to around 496. The battle was critical in the religious formation of Clovis and the Merovingian kingdom. As Gregory reported, Clothild, Clovis's Catholic wife, had pleaded with him for several years to accept her faith. She even baptized their first two sons in the Catholic faith, the first dying shortly after baptism and the second surviving only as a result of Clothild's prayers. Despite his wife's missionary efforts, Clovis was not persuaded and preferred to follow the traditional gods of the Franks, who had served him so well until that point. During the Battle of Tolbiac, however, Gregory wrote that Clovis experienced a change of heart. His army was on the point of annihilation when he appealed to his wife's God and swore that if God gave him victory over his enemies he would convert. The tide of battle suddenly turned, and Clovis emerged victorious. Not long after, according to Gregory, Clovis accepted baptism at the hands of St. Remigius, the archbishop of Rheims.

The exact chronology of Clovis's reign and the date of the battle remain uncertain, although the events of his reign most likely did not follow the pattern set by Gregory of Tours. Nevertheless, Gregory's image is still important, because it remained the predominant view of this great king until recent times. Gregory's depiction of the Battle of Tolbiac portrays Clovis as a Christian king, whose conversion in battle resembles the conversion of the Roman emperor Constantine in the fourth century, as recorded by Eusebius of Caesarea. Clovis was, therefore, first and foremost a Christian king whose conversion was effected by the power of God. Although it is likely that the events of Clovis's life did not unfold the way Gregory described them, the description of the Battle of Tolbiac and the broader image established by Gregory provided later kings and ecclesiastics an important precedent to follow.

See also: Alemanni; Clovis; Constantine; Franks; Gregory of Tours; Merovingian Dynasty

Bibliography

Bachrach, Bernard S. *Merovingian Military Organization, 481–751.* Minneapolis: University of Minnesota Press, 1972.

Daly, William M. "Clovis: How Barbaric, How Pagan?" *Speculum* 69 (1994): 619–64.

Geary, Patrick J. *Before France and Germany: The Creation and Transformation of the Merovingian World.* Oxford: Oxford University Press, 1988.

Gregory of Tours. *The History of the Franks.* Trans. Lewis Thorpe. Harmondsworth, UK: Penguin, 1974.

Wallace-Hadrill, John M. *The Long-Haired Kings.* Toronto: Toronto University Press, 1982.

Wood, Ian. *The Merovingian Kingdoms, 450–751.* London: Longman, 1994.

Toledo

Located on the Tagus River in central Iberia, Toledo was the capital and cultural and religious center of Visigothic Spain until it was conquered by the Muslims in the early eighth century. Its natural protections—the city rests atop a bluff and is surrounded by the Tagus River—attracted settlement, and in 193 BC the Romans made it the capital of the province of Carpentia. After the fall of the Roman Empire, the city came under the control of the Visigoths and rose to a position of prominence. Although seized from the Romans by the Alans in the early fifth century, Toledo was taken shortly after and became part of a growing Gothic realm that included parts of Gaul. Expelled from Gaul by Clovis in the early sixth century, the Goths came to focus their power in Spain. Under Leovigild (r. 568/569–586), the kingdom coalesced and Toledo became its capital. Leovigild established his court at Toledo and attempted to impose Arian Christianity on his kingdom at a council held in the city. Although Leovigild's religious policy would fail, the connection of church and kingdom in Toledo would be continued by his son and successor Reccared (r. 586–601).

In 587, Reccared converted to Catholic Christianity and presided over one of a series of 18 councils in Toledo that would be held in the sixth and seventh centuries. The councils demonstrated the close cooperation of the king and the bishops of Spain and legislated on a wide variety of topics including eradicating heresy and paganism, reforming the liturgy, regulating clerical behavior, organizing the ecclesiastical and political hierarchy, and regulating relations between Christians and Jews. Under Reccared, Toledo also became the cultural center of the Visigothic kingdom. The construction of a cathedral was undertaken by the king, and the bishops of the city produced important works of history, law, and theology. The bishops also reformed the liturgy and established the Toledan liturgy as the liturgy of the church in Spain. Toledo grew in importance during the sixth and seventh centuries, and the bishop of Toledo came to be recognized by his fellow bishops as the leader of the church in Spain. After the defeat of the last Gothic king of Spain, Roderic, in 711 by the Muslim invader Tarik ibn Ziyad, Toledo fell to Muslim control and emerged as an important city during the era of Muslim control of Spain and the residence of a large Mozarabic Christian community. Toledo was also known for the production of steel, particularly swords, throughout the Middle Ages.

See also: Alans; Ariansim; Leovigild; Reccared I; Roderic; Visigoths

Bibliography

Collins, Roger. *Early Medieval Spain: Unity in Diversity, 400–1000*. New York: St. Martin's Press, 1995.

Collins, Roger. *Visigothic Spain 409–711*. Oxford: Wiley-Blackwell, 2004.

Kennedya, Hugh. *Muslim Spain and Portugal: A Political History of al-Andalus*. London: Longman, 1996.

Totila (d. 552)

Eventual successor of Witigis as king of the Ostrogoths in Italy and the greatest Gothic military commander since Theodoric the Great, Totila (r. 541–552) led his people for 11 years and mounted a major challenge to Justinian's efforts to conquer Italy and restore it to imperial control. His early and dramatic military victories restored Gothic confidence and rallied them against the Byzantine general Belisarius. Although unable to inflict a total defeat on the Byzantines, Totila effectively wore down imperial resistance until his defeat by Narses and death in battle. His strategy to make the conquest of Italy so bloody and difficult that Justinian would abandon his effort nearly succeeded, but at great cost to the people, cities, and countryside of Italy. Totila's successor, Teja, did not survive long after Totila's death, and the Goths themselves fell to the armies of Justinian in 555.

After the failure of Witigis against the Byzantine armies in Italy, along with the failure of the Goths' efforts to promote Belisarius, the commander of the Byzantine troops in Italy, to the office of western emperor, the Goths fell into a short period of political turmoil, as two Gothic leaders rose to prominence only to fall to political murders. Totila was the nephew of one of these murdered leaders; he was elected king in the fall of 541 with the duty of restoring Gothic authority in Italy. Totila was a skilled commander who was also blessed with some good fortune, which aided him throughout the 540s. The efforts that the Goths had made to promote Belisarius to the imperial dignity made him suspect in Constantinople, and Persian efforts on the empire's eastern frontier limited the number of troops and resources that could be committed to the war in Italy. Moreover, in the spring of 542 Totila won a major battle at Faenza, rallying the Goths to his side. He once again raised a rebellion against the invaders, and imperial armies moved north to contain him and lay siege to Verona. With some 5,000 troops, Totila moved against an imperial force of some 12,000 troops, and in a brilliant tactical move defeated them. His smaller force managed to catch its rival in a pincer movement, and a reserve of 300 Gothic lancers fell on the imperial army's rear at a crucial moment. His ranks swelling to some 20,000 troops, Totila followed this victory with another major success over the imperial army near Florence and a rapid move to southern Italy to lay claim to the entire peninsula.

Totila's fortunes improved even more in 543 as he moved into the south. He managed to enter Naples and treated both the civilian population and the imperial garrison leniently—a clever strategy that gained the support and respect of many in Italy. He repeated this policy of leniency when he took the city of Rome after a siege that lasted from late 545 until December 546. Even the return of Belisarius, who had been recalled to Constantinople after the defeat of Witigis, could not stop the advance of Totila, who hoped that his military victories would force the emperor to negotiate. Although Justinian was unwilling to come to the table, Totila was not without diplomatic successes; he managed to remove the Frankish threat by ceding part of northern Italy to the Merovingian king Theudebert. Totila's next move, however, was not as successful. He led his army north in the spring of 547 against Ravenna, an imperial stronghold, and lost Rome to Belisarius, a loss that undermined confidence in Totila. His failure to retake the city diminished his prestige even more and led to a breakdown in marriage negotiations with the Merovingian Franks. He did, however, manage to retake the city in 549, seize a number of fortresses in 549 and 550, and take the offensive in Dalmatia and Sicily.

Although enjoying a measure of success and forcing the recall of the great Belisarius, Totila was not able to overcome the Byzantine advantage in wealth and soldiers. Justinian refused to negotiate with the Gothic king and would not even meet with the envoys Totila sent to Constantinople. Instead, Justinian responded to Totila's efforts with total war in Italy, and the emperor sent the great general Narses to prosecute the war with renewed vigor. After a successful march into Italy, Narses secured Ravenna and proceeded on to Rome. In July 552, the armies of Totila and Narses clashed at Busta Gallorum, the decisive battle of the war. Although outnumbered, Totila decided to accept battle, hoping that late reinforcements or an unexpected attack would bring him victory. A cavalry charge at the center of the larger imperial force was the main act of the battle. The Gothic cavalry was broken in the assault, the Gothic armies fled from the field, and some 6,000 Gothic soldiers were killed in the rout. Totila died in battle, as did the hopes of any success for the Goths. Although Totila's nephew continued the struggle, the Goths were essentially broken on the field of Busta Gallorum, and the Gothic people disappeared from history by 555, the date of the final Byzantine victory.

See also: Belisarius; Franks; Justinian; Lombards; Merovingian Dynasty; Narses; Ostrogoths; Theodoric the Great; Witigis

Bibliography

Browning, Robert. *Justinian and Theodora.* Rev. ed. London: Thames and Hudson, 1987.

Burns, Thomas. *A History of the Ostrogoths.* Bloomington: University of Indiana Press, 1984.

Bury, John B. *History of the Later Roman Empire: From the Death of Theodosius I to the Death of Justinian.* 2 Vols. 1923. Reprint, New York: Dover, 1959.

Cassiodorus. *The Variae of Magnus Aurelius Cassiodorus.* Trans. S.J.B. Barnish. Liverpool, UK: Liverpool University Press, 1992.

Heather, Peter. *The Goths.* Oxford: Blackwell, 1996.

Procopius. *History of the Wars.* Trans. H. B. Dewing. 1962.

Wolfram, Herwig. *History of the Goths.* Trans. Thomas J. Dunlap. Berkeley: University of California Press, 1988.

Wolfram, Herwig. *The Roman Empire and Its Germanic Peoples.* Trans. Thomas J. Dunlap. Berkeley: University of California Press, 1997.

Tournai

Important early burial site that, like the site at Sutton Hoo for the Anglo-Saxons, offers important evidence for the early Frankish dynasty of the Merovingians. The tomb is that of the second king of the dynasty, Childeric (d. 481), the father of the dynasty's greatest king, Clovis (r. 481–511).

The tomb was discovered in 1653 and given complete and careful descriptions and illustrations by Jean-Jacques Chifflet, an Antwerp doctor. It is most fortunate that Chifflet took such great care to document the artifacts of this discovery; most of them were stolen from the Cabinet des Medailles in Paris in 1831. A few pieces remain but the astonishing collection can only be appreciated by the account by Chifflet. The tomb contained a wide range of burial goods and was clearly identified as Childeric's by a gold signet ring bearing the king's name and his image showing him wearing his hair long (a tradition of the dynasty to come). The find also contained war goods including a spear, his horse's head with its harness, a battleaxe, and two swords exquisitely inlaid with gold and garnets. There was also a hoard of 100 gold coins and 200 silver coins. The burial site contained numerous other items such as a crystal globe, gold buckles, gold belt mounts, and a magnificent cloak embroidered with 300 bees or cicadas of gold and garnet.

Chifflet's discovery is important because of the light it throws on the first Merovingian kings; it suggests something of the contacts and wealth they had. The use of garnets, for example, suggests Gothic influence; it became traditional in Frankish metalwork. The coin hoard and various decorative ornaments suggest contacts with Constantinople and the Eastern Empire. The coins also demonstrate the growing wealth of the emerging dynasty. The grave goods, furthermore, reveal something of the character of Childeric's court. Burial of the horse's head along with certain other goods clearly reveals the pagan character of the king and his court. But he was no wandering Germanic king searching for a livelihood. Instead, he was most likely a settled warrior king who had become an ally of the late Roman Empire. As recent archeological work around the area has shown, the grave at Tournai was close to a Roman cemetery and a Roman road, which suggests the influence of late Roman culture on this early Frankish king.

See also: Anglo-Saxons; Clovis; Merovingian Dynasty; Sutton Hoo

Bibliography

Geary, Patrick. *Before France and Germany: The Creation and Transformation of the Merovingian World.* New York: Oxford University Press, 1988.

Lasko, Peter. *The Kingdom of the Franks: North-West Europe before Charlemagne.* London: Thames and Hudson, 1971.

Wallace-Hadrill, J.M. *The Long-Haired Kings and Other Studies in Frankish History.* Toronto: University of Toronto Press, 1982.

Wood, Ian. *The Merovingian Kingdoms, 450–751.* London: Longman, 1994.

Tours

The most important city of the Touraine in west central France, Tours is some 140 miles southwest of Paris and is located on the Loire River. Tours was a major religious and pilgrimage center during the Middle Ages as well as a leading intellectual center. It was the site of a bishopric and one of the more important monasteries of medieval France. It was the home of St. Martin, one of its first bishops, and Gregory, the historian of the Franks and bishop.

The region around what would become Tours was settled by the Gauls before its incorporation into the Roman Empire as Caesarodunum in the first century of the Common Era. By the fourth century it came to be called Tours and was the leading city of the Roman province of Lugdunum. In the third century the first Christian community and bishop were established there, but not until the arrival of St. Martin, who became bishop in 372 and had established a monastery outside the city a decade earlier, did the town emerge as one of the real centers of the Christian faith in Gaul. Martin himself would be critical to the town's emergence as an important religious center during his lifetime and after when his tomb became an important pilgrimage site, and in the fifth century a great church was built over Martin's tomb. During the barbarian invasions, Tours first fell under the control of the Visigoths and was later made part of the Frankish kingdom by Clovis, who was made a canon of St. Martin. In the late sixth century, Gregory became bishop and actively promoted the town and its patron, St. Martin, and oversaw the restoration of the cathedral, which had been destroyed by fire in 561. Gregory wrote a history of the Merovingians as well as works on the saints, including a book of the miracles of St. Martin. Around the tomb of his predecessor, Gregory built a monastery that became one of the most important and influential in medieval France. The town and its religious establishments grew in power and wealth during the course of the seventh century, and in the eighth century the church and its wealth was the goal of Muslim raiders from Spain.

Somewhere between Tours and Poitiers, the Carolingian mayor Charles Martel defeated the Muslims and turned them back from their movement into the Frankish kingdom. Under the Carolingian kings, the town and its monastery continued to thrive. The monastery at Tours became one of the leading intellectual centers of the Carolingian Renaissance. Charlemagne appointed his close adviser and greatest scholar of the day, Alcuin, the lay abbot of the monastery, and as a result Tours became important in the development of Carolingian minuscule. In the later eighth and ninth centuries, the town suffered repeated attacks by the Vikings, and as a result extensive new fortifications were built around the town, its suburbs, and monastery.

See also: Alcuin; Carolingian minuscule; Carolingian Renaissance; Charlemagne; Clovis; Charles Martel; Gregory of Tours; Martin of Tours, St; Tours, Battle of; Visigoths

Bibliography

Farmer, Sharon. *Communities of Saint Martin: Legend and Ritual in Medieval Tours.* Ithaca, NY: Cornell University Press, 1991.

Gregory of Tours. *The History of the Franks.* Trans. Lewis Thorpe. Harmondsworth, UK: Penguin, 1974.

Mitchell, Kathleen and Ian Wood, eds. *The World of Gregory of Tours.* Leiden: Brill Academic Publishers, 2002.

Tours, Battle of (732)

Battle fought by the Frankish mayor of the palace, Charles Martel, against invading Muslims from Spain on October 25, 732, somewhere between Tours and Poitiers. Although the military importance and technological impact of the battle has been questioned, it was regarded as a major victory for Charles by contemporaries and by the chroniclers of the ninth century who termed Charles "the Hammer" *(Martellus).*

As a result of the Muslim conquest of Spain in the early eighth century, southern Gaul was plagued by frequent Muslim raids into its territory. Although conquest of the territory by the Muslims was unlikely, their raids into Aquitaine and surrounding areas were a serious problem. In the 720s when the Muslims attacked Autun and towns along the Rhone River, the brunt of the fighting was born by the duke of Aquitaine, Odo. In 732 a more serious raid was launched by the emir of Spain, Abd al-Rahman, who swept through Aquitaine and reached Bordeaux and Poitiers. Odo, who suffered defeat at the hands of the invaders, had requested aid from Charles Martel. After sacking the monastery of St. Hilary in Poitiers, the Muslim party moved toward the wealthy monastery of St. Martin of Tours. It was on the way to Tours that Charles Martel met Abd al-Rahman. After a week of minor skirmishes, the main contingents of the Franks and Muslims engaged in a significant struggle in which, one chronicle noted with great exaggeration, 300,000 Muslims were killed. Although the numbers involved were much more modest, the Franks by all accounts withstood the Muslim onslaught and held the field, managing to kill the Muslim general Abd al-Rahman during the battle. The coming of night put an end to the conflict, and both sides retired to their camps. The next morning, Martel and his army discovered that the Muslims had abandoned their encampment and had withdrawn from the field leaving the Franks the opportunity to pillage the tents of their defeated foes.

The battle has acquired much fame, but generally for the wrong reasons. It has often been held that the victory at Tours "saved" Christian Europe from Muslim conquest in the eighth century. But conquest of Gaul and the larger Frankish kingdom by Muslim raiders from Spain was most unlikely to occur. The invasions were attempts to gain plunder but posed no long-term threat. The victory at Tours did end the raids by Muslims from Spain, and helped Charles Martel strengthen his hold on the kingdom. The battle also demonstrated the weakness of Odo, which Charles exploited after the duke's death in 735.

The Battle of Tours is also supposed to have marked a great turning point in the history of military technology. According to the thesis of Lynn White, Jr., the battle marked the introduction of the stirrup to Western Europe, and the use of the stirrup and the mounted shock troop guaranteed the victory of the Franks over the Muslims. This view, however, has been shown to be wrong; there is neither written nor archeological evidence to support White's conclusions.

Although the military and technological importance of the Battle of Tours is often overstated, the battle remains an important moment in Carolingian history. Charles Martel's victory, recognized as a great achievement by those in the eighth and ninth centuries, was significant. The victory at Tours ended Muslim raids from Spain, and later Carolingian rulers were to extend the frontier into Muslim territory. The victory also further demonstrated the talents of Charles Martel as a military leader and allowed him to gain greater authority over the Frankish kingdom and the duchy of Aquitaine.

See also: Carolingian Dynasty; Charles Martel

Bibliography

Bachrach, Bernard S. "Charles Martel, Mounted Shock Combat, the Stirrup, and Feudalism." *Studies in Medieval and Renaissance History* 7 (1970): 47–75.

Contamine, Philippe. *War in the Middle Ages.* Trans. Michael Jones. Oxford: Basil Blackwell, 1984.

Riché, Pierre. *The Carolingians: A Family Who Forged Europe.* Trans. Michael Idomir Allen. Philadelphia: University of Pennsylvania Press, 1993.

White, Lynn, Jr. *Medieval Technology and Social Change.* Oxford: Oxford University Press, 1964.

U

Ulfilas (c. 311–382/383)

Gothic bishop, missionary, and translator, Ulfilas, which means "little wolf" in the Gothic language, was a key figure in the ongoing Christianization of the Goths. He was hailed as the Moses of his age by the emperor Constantius II, and was compared with the prophet Elijah by others. His reputation came from his missionary activity among Goths who remained loyal to their traditional faith, as well as from his standing as tribal leader of the Goths. He also earned this praise because, like Moses, he brought the word of God to his people with his translation of the Bible into the Gothic language. Like the much later translation of the Bible by Martin Luther, that of Ulfilas had an important influence on the development of a language and culture.

Born at around 311, Ulfilas was a third-generation Danubian Goth whose ancestors on his mother's side, at least, may have come from Cappadocia. But he was a true Goth from birth and, despite his name, was probably not of low social origins. Indeed, his apparent education and later career suggest otherwise. From his early years, Ulfilas seems to have been trilingual, learning Greek and Latin along with his native language. He also probably studied rhetoric; at least his later theological and exegetical works suggest such training. His upper-class social origins are suggested also by his membership in a delegation to Constantinople between 332 and 337 representing the Goths before the imperial government. He may have even lived in Constantinople for a while at that time before returning to his homeland.

On a second trip into imperial territory, to Antioch in 341, Ulfilas was consecrated "bishop of the Christians in the Getic land" by Eusebius the bishop of Constantinople. It is likely that his ordination was part of a broader Roman initiative to convert all the Goths, but it also suggests recognition of the minority population of Goths and their need for spiritual leadership. His promotion to bishop also suggests the esteem in which the Romans held Ulfilas, who advanced to the episcopal office after holding only the minor church office of lector. As bishop in the 340s, Ulfilas sought to fulfill the task bestowed on him at his consecration; as a result, he was an active missionary. He not only ministered to his flock effectively but also reached out to non-Christian Goths. His Christianity was the mainstream Christianity of the empire and was influenced by the Arianism of the ruling emperors of the time. Although Ulfilas may not have accepted fully all the tenets of Arianism, he rejected the Nicene Creed and generally held a centrist position between the two extremes.

Whatever the exact nature of his belief, Ulfilas was an effective missionary, and his activities among his fellow Goths may have alienated those who maintained belief in the traditional gods. In the first Gothic persecution of Christians in 348, Ulfilas was expelled, perhaps because of his evangelical zeal, and as a result of his expulsion has been known by the honorary title *confessor.*

He and his followers, for whom he was both a spiritual and secular leader, were settled within the Roman Empire by the emperor, and Ulfilas again assumed his duties as bishop. As bishop in exile from his native land, Ulfilas sought to continue his evangelical and pastoral work, and even indulged in writing theological treatises. He preached in Gothic, Greek, and Latin, and participated in the council of 360, which supported the Arian faith in the empire. His greatest achievement, however, was his translation of the Bible into the Gothic language, probably after 350. He was faced, first, with the challenge of preparing an alphabet for the Gothic tongue, and only after that could he translate Scripture. He most probably translated his Bible from the Greek version commonly used in the fourth century. His translation and missionary activity were a great inspiration to other Goths who carried on his work, and his Bible provided a single source to unify the Goths in language and faith.

In his later years it is likely that Ulfilas opposed Athanaric, who persecuted Christians, and supported his fellow Arian and pro-Roman Goth, Fritigern. But when Fritigern revolted against the empire, Ulfilas was more inclined toward Rome than Fritigern. Indeed, Ulfilas spent his last days in the imperial capital at Constantinople, preparing for the start of a church council on the Arian question. Ulfilas remained committed to his Arian faith, declaring on his deathbed: "There is one eternal, unbegotten, and invisible God, who before time existed alone. Within time he created the Son, the only-begotten God."(Wolfram 1997, 84–85) Although the empire was moving toward Catholic Christianity, it allowed the barbarian peoples to follow the Christianity of their ancestors. Ulfilas had inspired numerous disciples who spread his Arianism to other barbarian peoples, including the Ostrogoths, the Vandals, and possibly the Franks.

See also: Arianism; Athanaric; Fritigern; Visigoths

Bibliography
Heather, Peter. *The Goths.* Oxford: Blackwell, 1996.

Thompson, Edward A. *The Visigoths in the Time of Ulfila.* Oxford: Clarendon, 1966.

Wolfram, Herwig. *History of the Goths.* Trans. Thomas J. Dunlap. Berkeley: University of California Press, 1988.

Wolfram, Herwig. *The Roman Empire and Its Germanic Peoples.* Trans. Thomas J. Dunlap. Berkeley: University of California Press, 1997.

V

Valens (328–378)

Arian Christian Roman emperor (r. 364–378), whose career is noteworthy for his disastrous defeat by the Visigoths at the Battle of Hadrianople, Valens was coemperor with his brother Valentinian I (r. 364–375). Valens ruled in the eastern capital of Constantinople. His reign was marked by successes against the Visigoths and Persians as well as against pretenders to the throne before his final, tragic defeat.

Valens was promoted to the imperial throne on March 28, 364, when he was elevated to the dignity by his brother Valentinian following the death of Emperor Jovian (r. 363–364). He was faced almost immediately by a rebellion, but managed to suppress it and execute its leaders. After defeating his rival for the throne, Valens turned his attention to the defense of the imperial frontiers against pressures from the Goths. In 367 and again in 369, Valens crossed the Danube River, leaving imperial territory, to attack the Goths. He successfully laid waste to Gothic territories and then returned to Constantinople to celebrate his victory and assume the title *Gothicus*. Although the raids did not yield any long-term benefits, they did promote the status of the emperor and force the Goths to come to terms. Valens and the Gothic leader Athanaric agreed to a treaty in September 369, meeting on boats in the middle of the Danube. As part of the agreement, the Romans sealed off the border from Gothic trade with the empire. Valens may also have sought to exploit the intratribal struggles that existed between the Gothic leaders Athanaric and Fritigern by forging a treaty with Fritigern.

Valens's early success against the Visigoths was not, however, repeated later in his reign. With the arrival of the Huns, new pressures were placed on the Roman frontiers and the barbarian peoples living along those frontiers. The Huns were recognized as a major threat by the Visigoths and seriously undermined the authority of Athanaric, who had previously struggled with the Romans and persecuted the Christians in his midst. The weakness of Athanaric and the enormity of the threat of the Huns inspired a large faction of the Goths, led by Fritigern, to petition Valens for entry into the empire as *foederati* (federated allies) in 376. The request was not unprecedented, but the size of the population involved was some 80,000. Despite the great number of people involved, Valens agreed to allow the Goths to cross the boundary and settle in Roman territory, a fateful decision that had a great influence on the subsequent course of events.

Valens had allowed the Goths to enter, and he made promises of food, territory, and administrative help. But none of this came, and in fact the Goths were harassed by local Roman administrators rather than helped. The poor treatment and general suffering caused the Goths to revolt against the Romans, and Valens himself decided to lead the army against the rebels. After some negotiation and poor decision making by Valens, the battle was fought on August 9, 378, at Hadrianople (in modern Turkey). The Romans were overwhelmed and annihilated by the Goths, and Valens died during the battle. The Goths were allowed to settle in the empire by Valens's successor, Theodosius the Great.

See also: Alaric; Arianism; Athanaric; Hadrianople, Battle of; Fritigern; Huns; Visigoths

Bibliography

Ammianus Marcellinus. *The Later Roman Empire (A.D. 354–378).* Trans. Walter Hamilton. Harmondsworth, UK: Penguin, 1986.

Bury, John B. *The Invasion of Europe by the Barbarians.* New York: W. W. Norton, 1967.

Cameron, Averil. *The Later Roman Empire, A.D. 284–430.* Cambridge, MA: Harvard University Press, 1993.

Ferrill, Arthur. *The Fall of the Roman Empire: The Military Explanation.* New York: Thames and Hudson, 1986.

Heather, Peter. *The Goths.* Oxford: Blackwell, 1996.

Wolfram, Herwig. *The Roman Empire and Its Germanic Peoples.* Trans. Thomas J. Dunlap. Berkeley: University of California Press, 1997.

Vandals

One of the barbarian peoples who established successor kingdoms in the deteriorating remnants of the Western Empire in the fifth century. Although active from the early fourth century, the Vandals only established a kingdom of any consequence in the fifth century under their greatest king, Gaiseric, who carved out a kingdom of his own in North Africa. His son and other descendants preserved this kingdom into the sixth century and created one of the more powerful entities in the newly forming post-Roman Mediterranean. The Vandal kingdom ultimately fell to the armies of Justinian in the 530s, as he attempted to reunite the eastern and western parts of the Roman Empire under his authority. The Vandals are perhaps best known for Gaiseric's sack of the city of Rome in 455, and have, since the 18th century, been associated with the term *vandalism.* They acquired a reputation for senseless destruction and violence that is reflected in the modern term, but one that is undeserved and inaccurate.

The early history of the Vandals before their entry into the empire in the fifth century remains a bit unclear. They probably originated in the region of the Baltic Sea or in Scandinavia, and in the first century of the Common Era they moved south and divided into two groups, the Silings and the Hasdings. By the year 300, at the latest, the Vandals seem to have settled in central Europe where they gradually began to make contact with the Roman Empire and other barbarian peoples. These relationships, however, before too long became increasingly complicated, as the Vandals, like other peoples living outside the empire's frontiers, faced increasing pressure from westward-moving Huns or the peoples they displaced. The two groups of Vandals reunited and joined with other barbarian peoples, then were forced from their homeland after losing a struggle against a confederation of Goths. According to one tradition, the Vandals petitioned the emperor Constantine for admittance into the empire as a people. But this version of events is quite unlikely, even though some individual Vandals may have been settled within the empire at that time. They most likely remained somewhere in central Europe, perhaps reaching parts of modern Hungary in the course of the fourth century. As the pressure from the Huns continued to increase, the necessity of moving the tribe increased. By the late fourth and early fifth centuries, the Vandals had become *foederati*, and had joined with the Roman military commander Stilicho against Alaric and the Goths.

This connection with Stilicho, along with competition and cooperation with other barbarian peoples, led to the entry of the Vandals into the empire when they crossed the Rhine River in 406. After an initial setback following the crossing, the Vandals inflicted a crushing defeat on the Frankish allies of Rome who defended the frontier. Following this victory, the Vandals, along with their Alan allies, went from one end of Gaul to the other and caused serious devastation. Thanks to the decline in the power of the Western Empire, the Vandals, like other barbarian peoples, roamed freely in the empire. After two and a half years in Gaul, they marched into Spain, where they divided again in two and attempted to establish themselves.

The period in Spain was pivotal in the history of the Vandals and witnessed the first appearance of their greatest king, Gaiseric. Before the rise of Gaiseric, however, the Vandals enjoyed a measure of success and endured serious setbacks in Spain. By 422, a confederation of Vandals and Alans had conquered southern Spain, but only after being forced south by Visigothic armies sent by Rome. Indeed, a Visigothic army marched into Spain on Rome's behalf, nearly obliterating the Siling Vandal tribe and forcing the Alans and Hasding Vandals together in 418. Forced by the pressure of the Visigoths, the Vandals moved into the south. By 428, the Vandal king Gunderic (r. 406–428) had captured the Roman cities of Cartagena and Seville. But the sack of Seville did not come without great cost, as Gunderic died while the city was being plundered by the Vandals.

At the death of Gunderic, Gaiseric (c. 390–477) assumed the throne, even though Gunderic had male heirs. Gaiseric regularized this succession plan later by establishing that the oldest Hasding male of the royal family should take the throne. Gaiseric was the son of a Vandal king and an unfree woman, possibly a Roman captured in a raid. At the time of succession he was nearly 40, and had a mature son, Huneric, who may have himself been married to a Visigothic princess. Gaiseric was the greatest of the Vandal kings and one of the ablest barbarian kings of his age, equal to the more famous Attila the Hun. Indeed, Gaiseric had great vision. He created a kingdom in Africa that lasted several generations, before falling in the end to Byzantine armies led by Justinian's general Belisarius.

Gaiseric's vision is best revealed by his movement into Africa, which was embroiled in great turmoil at that time. Recognizing the difficulties the imperial government faced because of the ambitions of its general Boniface, in 429 Gaiseric moved all his people, some 80,000 according to tradition, to Africa in a fleet of ships. Once there, Gaiseric moved gradually across the region and threatened Roman authority. According to one account, Boniface had invited Gaiseric to Africa to help against a Gothic army sent to suppress his revolt, but then faced a hostile Gaiseric. Whatever the cause of his movement, Gaiseric reached St. Augustine's city of Hippo in 430 and laid siege to the city that lasted 14 months. Although the town held out against Gaiseric and the siege was lifted, Roman efforts to rescue it failed when Gaiseric defeated an army led by Boniface, who was now back in Rome's good graces. Gaiseric occupied the town after the siege and settled a treaty with the empire in 435 that recognized Vandal control over the territory. Four years later, in 439, Gaiseric violated the treaty by seizing the great capital of Carthage. He was now clearly in control of important parts of Africa, and the empire was forced to deal with that reality.

Gaiseric had established his kingdom in North Africa, and he remained in control there until his death in 477, despite Roman efforts to dislodge him. It must be noted, however, that relations between Gaiseric and the empire were not always hostile. In 442 Gaiseric agreed to a treaty with the Western Empire in which his authority in Africa was recognized by the empire. And he remained on good terms with the western emperor, Valentinian III (d. 455). But when Valentinian was murdered and his daughter Eudocia, who had already been betrothed to Huneric, was forced to marry the new emperor's son, Gaiseric reacted violently. He led his fleet to Italy and sacked Rome, although at the request of Pope Leo I, known as Leo the Great, he did not massacre the population or burn the city down. He later conquered several islands in the western Mediterranean, and in 456 he defeated a fleet sent against him by the eastern emperor. In 474, he settled a treaty with Constantinople recognizing his authority, and in 476 negotiated rights over Sicily with the western emperor, an agreement that was accepted by the emperor's successor, Odovacar. At his death on January 24, 477, Gaiseric was clearly the greatest power in the western Mediterranean. He transformed the tribal group that followed him into a settled people and was the founder of a kingdom that seemed likely to last for a long time to come.

Gaiseric was succeeded by his son Huneric, who had lived a long life and was probably 66 at the time of succession. Little is known of Huneric's early life other than his role as hostage at the imperial court and his marriages. He was married early on, perhaps before his father took the throne, and was betrothed to Eudocia to confirm the treaty of 442. His first wife was accused of attempting to poison Gaiseric and sent back to Visigothic Spain after being mutilated. The marriage of Eudocia to the new emperor's son was an excuse for the sacking of Rome. The two were married the following year. But Huneric's aggressive Arianism alienated his wife, a devout Catholic, who left him for Jerusalem in 472. As king Huneric is perhaps known for his persecution of Catholics in his kingdom, which became quite serious in the last year of his reign. His death in 484 prevented the persecution from doing serious damage to the church in Africa.

Despite the purge of family members that he had earlier carried out, Huneric was succeeded by his nephew Gunthamund (r. 484–496) rather than his own son. And it was at this point that the kingdom began to suffer from serious internal and external difficulties. Indeed, already under Huneric the attempt to keep the succession in one line of the family demonstrated the problems of Gaiseric's succession plan, according to which the oldest of the sons of the male members of the royal family was to inherit the crown. Gunthamund in his turn faced a series of difficulties. Although he did end Huneric's persecution of Catholics, Gunthamund remained a committed Arian, who made little accommodation with the Catholic church, which increasingly alienated the majority Catholic population from the ruling dynasty. He also felt increasing pressure from the native Berbers, who had formerly served Gaiseric. The Vandal king also faced a challenge from Theodoric the Great, who pushed the Vandals out of Sicily. These difficulties continued under Gunthamund's successor Thrasamund (r. 496–523), whose unrelenting Arianism further alienated the Vandals from the Roman population. He also faced the further erosion of Berber support and even threatened war with Theodoric. But good relations prevailed between the Ostrogoths and Vandals, both because of Thrasamund's earlier marriage to Theodoric's daughter and because of the Vandal's realization of Theodoric's power. Hilderic (r. 523–530), the mature son of Huneric, was the next to rule, and unlike his predecessors he took a tolerant line with the Catholics, despite his own continued Arianism. This act endeared him to the Roman population, as did his diplomatic turn toward the empire and away from the Ostrogoths. He was a personal friend of the great emperor Justinian. His diplomatic shift, however, brought him to the brink of war with Theodoric, a war prevented only by Theodoric's death, and his closeness to the empire led to a revolt, which deposed him.

The final Vandal king was Gelimer (r. 530–534), who assumed the throne by a palace coup, which violated Gaiseric's succession plan and the peace treaty with the empire in existence since 474. Indeed, the deposition of Justinian's friend Hilderic angered the emperor on a personal as well as political level. In 533, Justinian sent his great general Belisarius against the Vandals. A combination of Belisarius's military brilliance and Gelimer's miscalculation and willingness to concede battle led to the rapid defeat of the Vandals by a relatively small imperial army. After a series of defeats, Gelimer capitulated in March or April of 534 and was settled in the empire away from his former kingdom. Justinian, thanks to Belisarius, was able to restore Africa to imperial control and also able to take his first step toward reuniting the empire. The Vandal kingdom, although one of the most powerful under Gaiseric, was destroyed; and the Vandal people were absorbed by the empire.

The Vandals had little physical impact on the African countryside, or at least left little evidence of it. They did seize land from the Roman provincials in an effort to secure their own economic base and weaken Roman power. They built little in the way of fortifications and did not establish urban bases from which they could have defended themselves against the Romans. Their lack of building fortifications may have been the result of the Vandals' pride in their navy, which was quite powerful and allowed them to control much of the western Mediterranean and sack Rome in 455. They also left little in terms of a written record of their time in Africa. Unlike other barbarian peoples, the Vandals did not compile a law code, although there was a collection of laws that reveals Roman influence. And all accounts of the Vandals were written by writers from the Eastern Empire, who generally left an unfavorable portrait.

Vandal life in Africa is best captured by the fifth-century Byzantine historian Procopius, in his history of the Vandal wars. He noted that the Vandals spent all their time in the baths or attended the theater. They wore much gold and dressed in elaborate clothes and were entertained by dancers and mimes. Procopius notes also that they indulged in great banquets, with a wide variety of meat, fish, and other foods. They pursued a number of pleasures, including hunting. Finally, it should be noted that the Vandals were committed Arians, who persecuted the native Catholic population. But here too, their stay in Africa had little long-term impact.

See also: Alans; Alaric; Arianism; Augustine of Hippo, St.; Attila the Hun; Belisarius; Huneric; Huns; Gaiseric; Galla Placidia; Jordanes; Justinian; Law and Law Codes; Odovacar; Ostrogoths; Theodoric the Great; Visigoths

Bibliography

Bury, John B. The *Invasion of Europe by the Barbarians.* New York: W. W. Norton, 1967.

Cameron, Averil. *The Mediterranean World in Late Antiquity, A.D. 395–600.* New York: Routledge, 1993.

Clover, Frank M. *The Late Roman West and the Vandals.* London: Variorum, 1993.

Randers-Pehrson, Justine Davis. *Barbarians and Romans: The Birth Struggle of Europe, A.D. 400–700.* Norman: University of Oklahoma Press, 1983.

Todd, Malcolm. *Everyday Life of the Barbarians: Goths, Franks, and Vandals.* London: G. P. Putnam's Sons, 1972.

Victor of Vita: History of the Vandal Persecution. Trans. John Moorhead. Liverpool, UK: Liverpool University Press, 1992.

Wolfram, Herwig. *The Roman Empire and Its Germanic Peoples.* Trans. Thomas J. Dunlap. Berkeley: University of California Press, 1997.

Verdun, Treaty of (843)

A major agreement between the surviving sons of Louis the Pious—Charles the Bald, Lothar, and Louis the German—that brought to a close the civil war that had raged since the death of Louis the Pious in 840. The treaty divided the Carolingian Empire between Charles, Louis, and Lothar, and established the outlines for the later French kingdom and German empire. Although the treaty divided the empire into three administrative realms, it did not necessarily destroy the empire. The brothers worked together for a time, and each of the brothers attempted to establish his authority over the entire realm during the next several decades.

At his death, Louis the Pious was succeeded by his three sons, Charles, Lothar, and Louis the German, and Pippin II, an adult grandson, the son of his deceased son Pippin. The oldest son, Lothar, had lived in relative disgrace in Italy during Louis's later years because of his part in the revolts against his father in the early 830s, but he was reconciled to his father shortly before Louis's death. Lothar was assigned authority over the eastern section of the Frankish kingdom, with the exception of Bavaria, which Louis the German administered. The other surviving son, Charles, was assigned authority over the western part of the Frankish kingdoms, and Pippin laid claim to his father's territory in Aquitaine. Lothar, who held the imperial title along with his rights over the eastern part of the kingdom, rushed north from Italy to establish his authority over the entire realm and worked to undermine the authority of Charles. Charles, in turn, joined with his other half brother, Louis, in an alliance against the ambitious Lothar. The alliance was followed, in 841, by a terrible and bloody battle between the three brothers at Fontenoy near Auxerre in Burgundy, at which Lothar was defeated and forced to flee to Aachen. Louis and Charles sealed the victory over their elder brother by swearing oaths of mutual support at Strasbourg in 842, a compact that was followed by their assault on Lothar in Aachen. With the capture of Aachen, Lothar realized that he was beaten, and thus the three brothers came together to negotiate the organization of the realm.

Negotiations began in June 842, and lasted over a year before a settlement was reached with the Treaty of Verdun, the text of which no longer exists. The discussions between the brothers began near Mücon in an atmosphere of distrust and demands by Lothar for a fair and equitable partition of the realm. As part of the negotiations, which included some 120 participants along with the three kings, a survey of all the lands and possessions of the empire was taken. Lothar's demands, however, backfired, and he ultimately ended with the least defensible section of the realm. The treaty most likely began with a call for divine support, and the final settlement centered around the core realms of Aquitaine, Lombardy, and Bavaria for Charles, Lothar, and Louis, respectively. Along with Aquitaine, Charles received the western kingdom, whose boundary followed a line along several rivers, the Scheldt, Meuse, Saone, and Rhone. Louis received Bavaria and lands east of the Rhine and also some important cities and wine-producing regions on the west bank of the Rhine. Lothar received a middle kingdom, stretching in the north from the traditional Carolingian heartland down into Italy in the south.

Lothar was granted the imperial title but had only nominal authority over his brothers. His most important imperial responsibilities involved obligations in relation to Italy and the pope. Charles and Louis had real power and freedom of action in their own kingdoms, and Charles received an added bonus with the exclusion of Pippin II, his nephew and heir to lands in Aquitaine. The treaty brought an end to terrible fraternal conflict in the Carolingian Empire, and, in the following year, Charles, Louis, and Lothar swore to maintain good fraternal relations and help preserve the peace in each others' kingdoms. The treaty, however, may have been intended only as a short-term solution and a framework to allow for the formation and reformation of the empire.

The rationale for the agreement remains poorly understood, and there are numerous explanations concerning the purpose and meaning of the treaty and its division of the empire. It has been suggested that an effort was made in forging the treaty and configuring the creation of the three kingdoms to appeal to national instincts in the various parts of the empire. Arguing that neither France nor Germany had yet emerged, other scholars have noted the importance of economic considerations, and have cited Lothar's concerns for a fair and equitable division that led to the land survey as support for their view. But already in the ninth century, the historian and member of the royal family Nithard noted that the primary concern of the three brothers was for the welfare of their vassals, a group that was essential to the long-term success of the kings of each region. Whatever the intentions of the three participants in the treaty, the settlement at Verdun set the boundaries of the later medieval kingdoms of France and Germany and provided a framework for the ultimate permanent division of the Carolingian Empire.

See also: Carolingian Dynasty; Charlemagne; Charles the Bald; Fontenoy, Battle of; Lothar; Louis the German; Louis the Pious; Nithard; Strasbourg, Oath of

Bibliography

McKitterick, Rosamond. *The Frankish Kingdoms under the Carolingians, 751–987.* London: Longman, 1983.

Nelson, Janet. *Charles the Bald.* London: Longman, 1992.

Riché, Pierre. *The Carolingians: A Family Who Forged Europe.* Trans. Michael Idomir Allen. Philadelphia: University of Pennsylvania Press, 1993.

Scholz, Bernhard Walter, trans. *Carolingian Chronicles: Royal Frankish Annals and Nithard's History.* Ann Arbor: University of Michigan Press, 1972.

Visigoths

Barbarian people whose migration played an important role in the decline and fall of the Western Roman Empire. The contacts of the Visigoths (literally "west men"; also known as the West Goths or Tervingi) with the Roman Empire may have started as early as the first century, but clearly occurred in the third century when a powerful Gothic kingdom formed along the imperial frontier by the Danube River. These early contacts between the Visigoths and the Romans were often violent and foreshadowed things to come for both Romans and Goths. The Romans were able to smash the Visigothic threat in the third century, only to face a greater one in the fourth and fifth centuries. From their settlements outside the empire, the Visigoths entered the empire as a result of the advance of the Huns. Once inside the empire, the Visigoths became both its defender and attacker. They inflicted a stunning defeat on imperial armies in 378 and pillaged parts of the Eastern Empire before coming to terms with Emperor Theodosius the Great. After the emperor's death, and under the aggressive leadership of Alaric, the Visigoths moved again and sacked Rome in 410. They then moved out of Italy and eventually settled in southwestern France and Spain, where they established one of the most successful kingdoms to form out of the dissolving Western Empire. Although chased from France by the Merovingian king Clovis (r. 481–511), they remained in Spain and established a dynamic civilization that boasted, among other things, the works of the important early seventh-century scholar Isidore of Seville. They also converted to Catholic Christianity from the Arian Christianity that the missionary Ulfilas had disseminated among them in the fourth century. Despite its advanced political and cultural institutions, the kingdom fell in the early eighth century when Muslim invaders conquered most of Spain. But Visigothic civilization continued to influence Christian Europe even after the kingdom's conquest by Islam.

The people who came to be identified as the Visigoths are traditionally thought to have emerged in Scandinavia and then to have moved further south, where they came into contact with the Roman Empire. According to the sixth-century historian Jordanes, "from this island of Scandza, as from a hive of races of a womb of nations, the Goths are said to have come forth long ago under their king, Berig by name" (104). Historians have long accepted this tale of Gothic origins as essentially true, but recent archeological investigation has challenged this view, suggesting instead origin along the Vistula River in Poland. Although the record is uncertain, in part because the Goths were a nonliterate people and left no written records, it is possible that the Goths were involved with hostilities between Romans and barbarians in the first and second centuries. Their distance from the frontier, however, guaranteed that they were not the focus of imperial concerns. The Visigoths, however, eventually moved from their original homeland southward along the Roman frontier along the Danube and caused the Romans increasing difficulty, especially in the dark years of the third century.

In 238, the first Gothic attack on Roman territory occurred, which was followed by further hostilities between the two powers. Over the next several decades, Gothic attacks became an ever greater problem for the empire, and in 251 the Goths defeated a Roman army and killed Emperor Decius. In the next generation, however, Roman emperors Aurelian and Claudius were able to turn the tide, inflicting severe defeats on the Visigoths that nearly wiped them out as a people.

The Visigoths then settled in the region between the Danubian border and the Black Sea and remained good neighbors to the empire for over a century. During this time, the Visigoths had much better relations with the empire. There were frequent trade contacts between the two, as a variety of goods were exchanged, including cattle, clothing, grain, slaves, and wine. It was during this period as well that the Gothic missionary bishop Ulfilas spread Arian Christianity among the Gothic people and converted some of them, despite a fierce reaction against his missionary work by Gothic leaders. Settled life also brought increasing social sophistication and wealth. New social elites emerged, including specialized armed warriors who served Gothic chieftains. The warriors, as revealed from burial sites in modern Denmark, were well armed and carried knives, spears, lances, and other specialized weaponry. Along with the warrior elite there emerged a new ruling elite, as well as a peasant class that was dedicated to farming. Indeed, agriculture became an important economic activity in this period, as did metalworking; a number of brooches worked in a way characteristic of the Goths began appearing at this time.

For much of the fourth century relations between the empire and the Goths were relatively peaceful, but efforts by the empire to extend its influence into Gothic territory strained relations. This situation was worsened by the westward movement of the Huns, who had conquered Ostrogothic territory and were increasing their pressure on the Visigoths. In 376, the pressure from the Huns was so severe that the Visigoths divided into two camps, one led by Athanaric, who had failed to prevent the Huns' advance, and a larger contingent, led by Fritigern, who petitioned Emperor Valens for entry into the empire. The Romans had welcomed barbarian peoples into the empire as *foederati* previously, but not in such great numbers. Traditionally, the number of Goths to cross into the empire in 376 was about 80,000—an overwhelming number that the local administrators could not handle. Indeed, the sheer number was only one of the difficulties that was faced by the Visigoths and the Romans. The Goths' Arianism increased tensions with the predominately Catholic Roman population, and Roman officials failed to provide the food and other materials necessary for survival that had been promised by the emperor. The Goths rose in rebellion and in 378 fought a great battle against Roman armies at Hadrianople, during which Valens was killed and the imperial force was destroyed. For the next several years the Goths had free rein in Roman territory.

In 382, Emperor Theodosius the Great, who had been made eastern emperor in 379 and given command in the Gothic Wars, brought an end to the pillaging of the Goths. He forged a treaty with the Visigoths that granted them land to farm in exchange for service in the Roman military. This treaty held until Theodosius's death in 395 and proved beneficial to the emperor, who employed large numbers of Goths to put down pretenders to the throne, even though he was forced to subdue rebellious Goths on occasion. The death of Theodosius in 395, however, brought about a significant change in the relationship between the two people and the fortunes of both Romans and Visigoths.

The rise of Alaric as leader of the Visigoths in the late 390s resulted in the increasing hostility of the Goths toward the Romans. Alaric himself had received a high-ranking imperial military post but nevertheless launched raids into Italy in the early fifth century. He was stopped by Emperor Honorius's chief military officer, Stilicho. But the murder of Stilicho in 408 at the emperor's order removed this impediment to Alaric's ambitions. Moreover, the emperor refused to grant Alaric further concessions or to honor previous financial obligations, which pushed the Gothic leader to launch another attack on Italy in 410. In August of that year, Alaric sacked the city of Rome—the first time the city had suffered such treatment in 800 years—plundering and pillaging it for three days. The event profoundly shocked the people of the empire and inspired St. Augustine of Hippo's writing of his great work *City of God.* After sacking the city, Alaric led his followers south with the intention of invading Africa. But his efforts failed, and he died shortly thereafter, replaced by Ataulf, who led the Visigoths into Gaul.

During the fifth century the Visigoths regularized their position in Gaul and eventually expanded into Spain. Ataulf's claim to rule in Gaul was uncertain, and relations with the empire took an interesting turn because of his abduction of the emperor's sister Galla Placidia, whom Ataulf married in 414. But Ataulf's death in 415 ended any possibility of one his heirs ascending the imperial throne. His successors returned his widow to the emperor and signed a treaty in 418 in which the Romans recognized Visigothic claims to reside in Gaul between Toulouse and Bordeaux. The treaty was signed by Theodoric I (r. 418–451), who was elected king in 418 and led the Visigoths during their period of settlement and expansion in Gaul. Although probably not recognized as an independent ruler, Theodoric exercised important power over his people and strove to improve its position in the empire. On the one hand, Theodoric remained a loyal ally of the Romans and often led his Visigoths in battle on behalf of the empire. They actively campaigned on behalf of the empire in Spain to prevent other barbarian peoples from conquering that region. They also participated in the great battle fought in 451 against Attila and the Huns on the Catalaunian Plains, where Roman success depended largely on the Visigoths and their king Theodoric, who died in battle. But Theodoric also sought to use any imperial crisis to his advantage and rallied his people on behalf of Galla Placidia in her struggles against the general Aëtius in the 430s. Theodoric also led numerous campaigns in southern Gaul to expand Visigothic control in that part of the empire and attacked its capital, Arles, on several occasions.

Theodoric had laid the foundation for later Visigothic expansion under his sons, who succeeded him in turn after his death in 451. The increasing weakness of the Western Empire also enabled the Visigoths to increase the size of their kingdom, although it should be noted that the Visigothic kingdom was not the picture of governmental stability. Theodoric's first two successors, his sons Thorismund and Theodoric II, were assassinated in 453 and 466, respectively. His third son Euric, however, did reign for some 18 years, and he built upon his father's legacy and Roman weakness to create a great kingdom in southern France and Spain. Breaking the long-standing agreement with the empire, Euric initiated a series of campaigns lasting from 471 to 476 in which he captured most of southern Gaul. At the same time, Euric's armies were extending Visigothic control over all of Spain, and as a result Euric created the most significant successor kingdom of the age.

The kingdom, which Euric passed on to his son Alaric II when he died a natural death in 484, inherited a number of Roman institutions that both Euric and Alaric exploited effectively. A number of administrative and bureaucratic techniques were adopted by these kings for their realm, most importantly Roman tax-gathering practices. They also were influenced by Roman legal traditions. Euric issued a set of laws, possibly the *Code of Euric,* in 473, and Alaric issued the *Breviary of Alaric* in 506.These legal codes, which were influenced by Roman legal traditions and incorporated Roman laws, addressed a wide range of issues, including loans, use of charters, wills, and other matters concerning relations between Romans and Visigoths under their authority. These kings also shaped church history in their kingdom, promoting the Arian faith that the majority of the Visigoths now professed but being careful not to offend their Catholic Roman subjects by persecuting the Catholic church in their realm. Under Euric and Alaric the Visigoths enjoyed their greatest success, but also suffered a significant setback in 507 when Alaric suffered a crushing defeat at the hands of the Merovingian king Clovis at the Battle of Vouillé. This battle, which the sixth-century Frankish historian Gregory of Tours portrays as something of a crusade, forced the Visigoths out of most of Gaul and limited their kingdom to the lands in Spain. But despite this loss and the death of Alaric II, the Visigoths enjoyed nearly another two centuries of success in Spain.

Although the defeat by Clovis was a serious one, it did not end Visigothic power even in all of Gaul. This was due in part to the Visigoths' own king, but also to support from the powerful Ostrogothic king in Italy, Theodoric the Great. Indeed,

Ostrogothic armies in 508 helped push Clovis's armies out of Visigothic territory and allowed Alaric's heirs to preserve part of their former possession in Gaul. But Theodoric's support was not wholly altruistic and formed part of his plan for a greater Gothic kingdom. He extended his authority over Spain and deposed Alaric's heir in favor of a prefect who administered Spain as part of a broader province. Theodoric also transferred the Visigothic treasury to his own capital at Ravenna. This situation was bound to cause dissatisfaction among the Goths in Spain, and after Theodoric's death in 526 the Visigothic royal line was restored when Amalaric, Alaric's son, took the throne.

Amalaric's rule was a short and unhappy one, which involved further military losses to the Merovingian kings and ended with his murder in 531. This abrupt end to his reign was followed by an extended political crisis in the kingdom, despite the lengthy rule of Amalaric's murderer Theudis (r. 531–548). The kingdom was plagued by internal instability brought about by the competition of the nobility for greater power and by the attempts of several nobles to usurp the throne or establish themselves as independent of the king. This situation began to change in the 560s, as the Visigothic kings gradually took back control of the kingdom, and it was Leovigild (r. 568–586) who successfully ended the turmoil and restored royal authority fully during his reign.

Leovigild's reign is noteworthy for several reasons, not the least of which was his restoration of royal power. For much of the first decade of his reign, Leovigild led or sent out military campaigns to suppress rebellious nobles or to conquer rival barbarian or Byzantine powers in Spain. To celebrate his triumph and signal his claims to powers similar to those of the emperors, he founded a city, which he named after his son Reccared. He also forged a marriage alliance with the Merovingians when his son Hermenegild married a Merovingian princess, perhaps building on the marriages of the Visigothic princesses Galswintha and Brunhilde to Merovingian kings. Moreover, Leovigild sought to establish religious uniformity in his kingdom. He promoted the Arian faith, but rather than persecuting Catholic Christians, he sought to convert them by incorporating Catholic practices into the Arian church and moderating Arian theology. His efforts were not that successful; they may even have contributed to Hermenegild's conversion to Catholic Christianity and failed revolt. The religious dilemma, however, was resolved after Leovigild's death by his son Reccared (r. 586–601), who converted to Catholic Christianity and declared it the official faith of the kingdom in 589.

The church Reccared founded was extremely independent and zealous in defense of the faith. Indeed, Reccared himself aggressively promoted the new faith against elements in the kingdom that supported the traditional Arianism of the Visigoths. The church remained independent of Rome and was hostile toward the Jews, an attitude supported by royal legislation against the Jews that cost the kings vital support at the time of the Muslim invasions. On the other hand, the Visigothic church was highly sophisticated, and church and king presided over a flourishing cultural life in Spain in the late sixth and seventh centuries. The most notable contribution was that of Isidore of Seville, but Spain was also characterized by a vigorous monastic life, a high level of ecclesiastical culture, and widespread literacy in Latin (unique at a time when inhabitants of the other barbarian kingdoms were only beginning to learn the language). Remarkable too were the churches built in Visigothic Spain, with their characteristic horseshoe arches and lavish decoration.

Despite the apparent strength of the Visigothic kingdom, the seventh century witnessed the beginning of the end of this dynamic realm. The monarchy continued to be successful and developed an increasingly sophisticated political theory, revealed in the first royal anointing and coronation after Old Testament models among the barbarian peoples, which took place as early as 631, or at least by the time of King Wamba (r. 672–680). But even before Wamba, Visigothic kings had

Votive crown of King Recceswinth, seventh century. (De Agostini/Getty Images)

taken steps to strengthen the monarchy and improve relations between barbarians and Romans. King Chindaswinth (r. 642–653) and his son and successor Recceswinth (r. 653–672) reformed Visigothic law and issued new legal codes that superseded earlier versions, eliminated all distinctions between Romans and Goths, and permitted marriage between the two peoples. Visigothic kings also eliminated the last of their rivals for control of all of Spain. They also continued, however, to pass anti-Semitic legislation, which alienated an important sector of the population. Finally, in the opening decades of the eighth century the Visigoths faced their greatest challenge—Muslim invasion from Africa. In 711, a force of Muslim Berbers led by Tarik defeated a Visigothic army led by King Roderick (r. 710–711) and killed the king. Visigothic resistance continued, but the kingdom was conquered by the Muslims by 725. Although conquered by the Muslims, the influence of the Visigothic kingdom lasted long beyond its disappearance.

See also: Aëtius; Agriculture; Alaric; Arianism; Attila the Hun; Augustine of Hippo, St.; Brunhilde; Clovis; Galla Placidia; Galswintha; Gregory of Tours; Hadrianople, Battle of; Hermenegild; Huns; Isidore of Seville; Jordanes; Law and Law Code; Leovigild; Merovingian Dynasty; Ostrogoths; Reccared I; Stilicho, Flavius; Theodoric the Great; Ulfilas

Bibliography

Bonnassie, Pierre. "Society and Mentalities in Visigothic Spain." In *From Slavery to Feudalism in South-Western Europe.* Trans. Jean Birrell. Cambridge: Cambridge University Press, 1991, pp. 60–103.

Bury, John B. *The Invasions of Europe by the Barbarians.* New York: W. W. Norton, 1967.

Goffart, Walter. *Barbarians and Romans A.D. 418–584: The Techniques of Accommodation.* Princeton, NJ: Princeton University Press, 1980.

Heather, Peter. *The Goths.* Oxford: Blackwell, 1996.

Isidore of Seville. *Isidore of Seville's History of the Goths, Vandals, and Suevi.* 2d rev. ed. Trans. Guido Domini and Gordon B. Ford. Leiden: Brill, 1970.

James, Edward, ed. *Visigothic Spain: New Approaches.* Oxford: Clarendon, 1980.

Jordanes. *The Gothic History of Jordanes.* Trans. Charles C. Mierow. New York: Barnes and Noble, 1985.

King, Peter D. *Law and Society in the Visigothic Kingdom.* Cambridge: Cambridge University Press 1972.

Thompson, Edward A. *The Visigoths in the Time of Ulfila.* Oxford: Clarendon, 1966.

Thompson, Edward A. *The Goths in Spain.* Oxford: Clarendon, 1969.

Wolfram, Herwig. *History of the Goths.* Trans. Thomas J. Dunlap. Berkeley: University of California Press, 1988.

Wolfram, Herwig. *The Roman Empire and Its Germanic Peoples.* Trans. Thomas J. Dunlap. Berkeley: University of California Press, 1997.

Wood, Ian. *The Merovingian Kingdoms, 450–751.* London: Longman, 1994.

Vita Karoli

One of the most important and influential biographies of the Middle Ages, the *Vita Karoli* (Life of Charlemagne) is the life of the great Carolingian king and emperor Charlemagne that was composed by his friend and advisor Einhard. The work survives in 123 manuscripts and became very popular early in its history. It seems to have become a sort of school text for Carolingian students, and it influenced generations of Carolingian scholars and rulers. The work was studied and quoted by such scholars as Lupus of Ferriere, Gottschalk of Orbais, and Walafrid Strabo, who provided an introduction to the work and arranged it into chapters. The biography also seemed to have inspired Charlemagne's grandson, Charles the Bald, who read the work closely and may have quoted it in some of his legislation.

Despite Einhard's assertion that he lacked the skills necessary to write the biography, his work is one of the most important of the Carolingian Renaissance. His writing reveals the extent of his learning and bears clear echoes of many Roman and Christian Latin writers, including Cicero, Julius Caesar, Tacitus, Orosius, and Sulpicius Severus. His greatest debt, however, was to the great Roman biographer, Suetonius, whose *De vita Caesarum* (Lives of the Caesars), particularly his life of Augustus, provided the format and vocabulary for Einhard's work. But Einhard's work was no slavish copy of Suetonius; it was based also on Einhard's intimate knowledge of his subject. The work addresses the major wars of Charlemagne, his diplomatic activities, and building projects. Einhard provides information on the great ruler's family life, including the king's too strong love of his daughters (whom he would not allow to marry), personal appearance, and personality. Einhard also includes discussion of the imperial coronation of Charlemagne and makes the still controversial statement that had Charlemagne known what was going to happen that Christmas day he would have not gone to church. The life concludes with an extended discussion of Charlemagne's death and includes a copy of his will.

The purpose of the biography and its date of composition remain uncertain, and the former is surely conditioned by the latter. Einhard's life is clearly biased in favor of its subject. He notes in his preface that he must write so as not to allow "the most glorious life of this most excellent king, the greatest of all princes of this day, and his wonderful deeds, difficult for people of later times to imitate, to slip into the darkness of oblivion" (52). He offers only passing criticism of the king, and blames rebellions on the nobles or one of Charlemagne's wives rather than on any action of the king. The work is clearly intended to prove the greatness and virtue of its subject. Beyond Einhard's regard for Charlemagne and sense of obligation, it is likely that the work was intended as a commentary on political affairs in the Carolingian Empire after the death of Charlemagne. A letter of 830 establishes that date as the latest it could have been written. And if the biography were written in the late 820s, it was surely a commentary on the difficulties that Louis the Pious faced by that time, as his sons and the nobility began to stir against him. It has also been suggested that the biography was written early in the reign of Louis and within only a few years of Charlemagne's death. Certain internal evidence supports an early composition, and if the work were completed in the late 810s it was intended to support the claim of Louis as Charlemagne's divinely ordained heir to imperial power. The biography also helped define the nature of imperial power for the Carolingians, an issue Louis himself pursued. Whether the life was composed circa 817 or circa 830, it is one of the most important biographies of the Middle Ages, and one that provides an image of the ideal Christian ruler.

See also: Carolingian Renaissance; Charlemagne; Charles the Bald; Einhard; Gottschalk of Orbais

Bibliography

Einhard and Notker the Stammerer. *Two Lives of Charlemagne.* Trans. David Ganz. Harmondsworth, UK: Penguin, 2008.

Ganshof, Francois Louis. "Einhard: Biographer of Charlemagne." In *The Carolingians and the Frankish Monarchy: Studies in Carolingian History.* Ithaca, NY: Cornell University Press, 1971, pp. 1–16.

Innes, Matthew, and Rosamond McKitterick. "The Writing of History." In *Carolingian Culture: Emulation and Innovation,* edited by Rosamond McKitterick. Cambridge: Cambridge University Press, 1994, pp. 193–220.

Laistner, Max L.W. *Thought and Letters in Western Europe,* A.D. *500 to 900.* 2nd ed. Ithaca, NY: Cornell University Press, 1976.

McKitterick, Rosamond. *Charlemagne: The Formation of a European Identity.* Cambridge: Cambridge University Press, 2008.

Vortigern (fl. 425–455)

A king of the Britons, Vortigern assumed power after the Roman withdrawal from the island. According to an early tradition recorded by the *Anglo-Saxon Chronicle,* Bede, and Gildas, Vortigern invited the Saxon kings Hengist and Horsa to England as mercenaries. His invitation led to the eventual conquest of Britons by the Anglo-Saxons, even though the king of the Britons had invited the two leaders to aid the Britons against the Picts and Scots. According to the sixth-century historian Gildas, a great hero arose in the wake of these invasions; that hero was later believed to be King Arthur.

After the last of the Roman armies left the island of England in the early fifth century, the people of the island were forced to find a means to defend themselves from the attacks of the less civilized Picts and Scots to the north. They sought aid from the emperor Honorius in 410, but got little more than the approval to organize their own defense. At around 425, a leader of the Roman-British aristocracy, Vortigern, arose to take control of part of the country and provide for its defense. Called a tyrant or king by Gildas and other early sources, Vortigern acted as a traditional Roman military governor and struggled to protect the Britons from the invaders. He may have attempted to secure aid from the western emperor by writing a letter to the general Aëtius, but any efforts in that regard failed. He did find allies in the Saxon leaders Hengist and Horsa, who, according to the *Anglo-Saxon Chronicle,* were invited during the reigns of the emperors Marcian and Valentinian III, probably between 449 and 456. According to the early sources, the Saxons arrived in three longboats on the eastern side of the island, at a place called Ipwinesfleet according to the *Anglo-Saxon Chronicle,* and they immediately waged war against the Picts and Scots.

Vortigern's plan at first seemed a good one; the Saxons enjoyed great success against the northern invaders at the British king's direction. But Hengist and Horsa soon sent word back to their homeland of their victories and need for help to secure further victory over their enemies. They also informed their kin that "the country was fertile and the Britons cowardly" (Bede 1981, 56). The Saxons were soon joined by large numbers of Germans, including more Saxons and Angles and Jutes. They then turned against the Britons and Vortigern and proceeded to conquer the Britons. According to the *Anglo-Saxon Chronicle,* Vortigern took up the sword against his former allies, and in a battle in 455 Horsa was killed. But despite this loss and continued wars with Vortigern, the Saxons took control of much of the kingdom.

Vortigern's fate is uncertain, but his legacy, according to the early sources, is certain. The king was blamed for the conquest of England by the Anglo-Saxons. In Gildas's view, the king was a proud tyrant whose unwise rule encouraged the conquerors' invasion. Bede developed the earlier accounts of the progress of the Angles, Saxons, and Jutes, noting that it was the sinfulness of the Britons that brought on God's judgment in the conquest by the mercenaries hired by Vortigern.

See also: Aëtius; *Anglo-Saxon Chronicle*; Anglo-Saxons; Bede; Gildas; Hengist and Horsa; Honorius; King Arthur

Bibliography

Bede. *Ecclesiastical History of the English People with Bede's Letter to Egbert and Cuthbert's Letter on the Death of Bede.* Trans. Leo Sherley-Price. Harmondsworth, UK: Penguin, 1991.

Blair, Peter Hunter. *The World of Bede.* Cambridge: Cambridge University Press, 1990.

Gildas. *The Ruin of Britain and Other Works.* Ed. and trans. Michael Winterbottom. London: Phillimore, 1978.

Howe, Nicholas. *Migration and Mythmaking in Anglo-Saxon England.* New Haven, CT: Yale University Press, 1989.

Sawyer, Peter H. *From Roman Britain to Norman England.* 2nd ed. London: Routledge, 1998.

Stenton, Frank M. *Anglo-Saxon England.* 3rd ed. Oxford: Clarendon, 1971.

Whitelock, Dorothy, ed. *The Anglo-Saxon Chronicle.* Westport, CT: Greenwood, 1986.

Vouillé, Battle of (507)

Fought in 507, battle of Vouillé was a major battle between the Merovingian king of the Franks, Clovis, and the Visigothic king in Spain, Alaric II. According to the tradition recorded by the sixth-century Frankish historian Gregory of Tours, Clovis waged the war as a sort of crusade to expel the Arian Visigoths from Gaul, and the battle came well after the conversion of Clovis to Catholic Christianity. Although the relationship between the time of Clovis's conversion and the battle is now open to question, it is certain that Clovis gained the victory over Alaric, who died in the battle, and that it was a key battle in one of the Frankish king's wars of expansion and conquest.

As recorded by Gregory of Tours in his history, Clovis desired to remove the Visigoths from Gaul because of their Arianism. He declared to his ministers that he could not bear the existence of the Visigoths in Gaul. He said further that the Franks should invade the region and that with God's help he would defeat the Visigoths and take over their territory. His followers agreed with the proposal, and the army marched toward Poitiers to meet the forces of Alaric II. Along the way, one of Clovis's soldiers took hay from the monastery of St. Martin of Tours, which the king had expressly forbidden. Upon learning of this, Clovis killed the soldier to maintain the support of the powerful saint. The battle itself took place some 10 miles from Poitiers, according to Gregory. The fighting included hand-to-hand combat and the exchange of volleys of javelins. The Visigoths fled the attack, and, Gregory wrote, "Clovis was the victor, for God was on his side" (153). Clovis killed Alaric while the Goths fled, but two Goths attacked and struck Clovis with their spears on each side. He was saved by his leather corselet; after the battle, he captured several cities and forced the Visigoths from Gaul.

Modern research, however, shows that both the events leading up to the battle and the battle itself were not so simple and clear-cut as Gregory portrayed them. At the very least, it has been argued that Clovis himself converted to Catholic Christianity only late in his life, or at least after the traditional date of 496, and that he was motivated by a number of factors other than crusading zeal when he attacked Alaric II. The two kings had long been in negotiations over a variety of issues, and previous battles had left the Franks defeated. Clovis had also been successful at times against the Visigoths, and he may have attacked in 507 to exact the payment of tribute he was owed by Alaric. There is clear indication that economic issues inspired Clovis. Moreover, there is no hint in Gregory of the international diplomacy that was involved, which was intended to keep Clovis out of southwestern Gaul. The Ostrogothic king of Italy and greatest power in the west, Theodoric the Great, had supported Alaric and threatened to intervene on his side should Clovis attack. Byzantine warships, however, limited Theodoric's ability to maneuver.

The battle itself probably involved a large Frankish infantry, with the king and his retainers mounted, and a Visigothic cavalry of inferior numbers. Rather than fleeing outright as Gregory reports, the skilled cavalry probably made several feigned retreats to trick the Franks, who were too stubborn and well trained to fall for the trick. Whether or not Clovis was responsible for the death of Alaric, at any rate the Visigothic king did die in the battle. Clovis may well have accepted baptism as a Catholic Christian following the victory, and religious motives should not be totally discounted; most likely they did play a role in Clovis's planning, even though not in the way that Gregory portrayed them.

See also: Alaric II; Arianism; Clovis; Franks; Gregory of Tours; Merovingian Dynasty; Ostrogoths; Visigoths; Theodoric the Great

Bibliography

Geary, Patrick J. *Before France and Germany: The Creation and Transformation of the Merovingian World.* Oxford: Oxford University Press, 1988.

Gregory of Tours. *The History of the Franks.* Trans. Lewis Thorpe. Harmondsworth, UK: Penguin, 1974.

Wallace-Hadrill, J. M. *The Long-Haired Kings.* Toronto: Toronto University Press, 1982.

Wolfram, Herwig. *History of the Goths.* Trans. Thomas J. Dunlap. Berkeley: University of California Press, 1988.

Wood, Ian. *The Merovingian Kingdoms, 450–751.* London: Longman, 1994.

Waltharius

A Latin epic poem of 1,456 lines of dactylic hexameter written in the ninth or tenth century, the *Waltharius* tells the story of Walter of Aquitaine and his adventures at the court of Attila the Hun and in his homeland. The exact date and authorship of the poem remain uncertain, but there are three possible candidates: Ekkehard I of St. Gall (d. 973); an unknown Gerald from Alemannia or Bavaria who wrote the 22-line prologue to the poem; or an anonymous scribe who composed the work for his patron, Erckambald, bishop of Strasbourg from 965 to 991. The author, a German speaker, drew from a wide range of Germanic tales in creating his poem, and he also drew extensively on the works of the classical Latin authors Ovid, Statius, and Virgil and the Christian Latin poet Prudentius. The date of composition has ranged from the time of Charlemagne in the early ninth century to the time of his successors in the late ninth century or to the time of the Ottonian emperors in the late tenth century.

The action of the poem begins at the court of Attila the Hun, where Walter along with Hagen the Frank, and Hildegund of Burgundy are hostages taken during Attila's conquest. As they grow to adulthood, the three flee from Attila's court, with Hagen escaping first. Walter concocts an elaborate plan so that he can escape with his beloved Hildegard. A great warrior now, Walter throws a banquet following a successful battle for his Hunnish comrades. Once they have fallen asleep from too much drink, Walter and Hildegund flee to Frankland. The two are met by King Gunther and Hagen and the king's warriors who plan to seize the treasure carried away from the Huns by Walter. The poem's hero fights a series of duels with Gunther's retainers, beating them all before facing the king and Hagen. Although reluctant to attack his friend, Hagen is compelled by obligation to his king, and the three warriors indulge in combat in which Gunther loses a leg, Hagen an eye and six teeth, and Walter his right hand. After the fight, Hagen and Walter are reconciled, and Hagen escorts Gunther to Frankland. Walter and Hildegund continue on to Aquitaine, where they are married and where Walter will rule as king after his father's death.

See also: Attila the Hun; Charlemagne

Bibliography

Kratz, Denis, ed. and trans. *"Waltharius" and "Ruodlieb"*. New York: Garland, 1984.

Laistner, M.L.W. *Thought and Letters in Western Europe A.D. 500 to 900.* 2nd ed. Ithaca, NY: Cornell University Press, 1957.

Magoun, F. P. Jr., and H. M. Smyser, trans. *Walter of Aquitaine: Materials for the Study of his Legend*. New London, CT: Connecticut College, 1950.

Weapons and Armor

One of the more important functions of late antique and early medieval nobles, kings, and emperors was as warriors or war leaders. As a result it was necessary for them to be properly outfitted for battle, and a certain standard in weapons and armor developed. The basic nature of military technology in barbarian Europe was established already in the pre-migration period among the barbarians themselves, as well as by the ancient Romans and others, and involved both offensive and defensive tools. Included in the armory of the barbarian warrior was some form of armor, a shield, thrusting weapons like spears and swords, axes, and bows and arrows. There was also a degree of specialization among the various peoples who invaded the empire.

The weapons used by the early medieval warrior were the descendants of the pre-migration Germanic warrior and his ancient Roman counterpart. Although the tactics employed by Germans and Romans in the use of their weapons differed, the basic outlines of the armaments of the ancient Roman and barbarian soldier were essentially the same. Of course, there was some diversity in the armories of the Romans and of the various Germanic peoples. In fact, it is sometimes suggested that some of the peoples who invaded the Roman Empire were given their names from the weapons that were unique to them. The Saxons were so called because of the long knife, the *saxo* or *seax,* that they used, and the Angles were known for their barbed spear, or *ango*. Similarly, the Huns were known for the *hunnica,* a type of whip, and the Franks for their throwing axe, the *frankisca.*

Along with the various "national" weapons, noble warriors carried a basic complement of implements of destruction, including a sword or a long knife, a spear, an axe, and a bow and arrows. The poorer foot soldiers carried a lesser complement of weapons, which included a spear, shield, and bow and arrows. The difference in weaponry carried by the noble, usually cavalry, warriors and the infantrymen was due in part to expense. Indeed, outfitting a typical noble warrior was quite a costly proposition. The average cost of a helmet was six solidi, and the cost for a sword and scabbard was about seven solidi, the equivalent of six or seven months' wages for the average soldier, or six or seven cows. Clearly, the fully armed and armored warrior in barbarian Europe was usually a wealthy and powerful figure.

The sword was usually one of two kinds: a blade of some three feet, rather than the shorter Roman sword, which measured roughly two feet in length, or the shorter *saxo.* The long sword, or *spata,* was a double-edged blade suitable for thrusting and slashing and general destruction, and the *saxo* was a single-edged blade that was lighter, more easily wielded, and could even be thrown. In the Carolingian age, however, these two types of sword were merged into one, as the *spata* was transformed from a blade of parallel edges that ended in a short point to a blade that gradually tapered to a point. Carolingian swords were also engraved and decorated with gold, silver, or ivory handles, and were so highly prized for their quality that Charlemagne and other Carolingian rulers sought to restrict their export.

The spear or lance was another popular and important weapon; it was such a valuable part of a soldier's armory that Carolingian legislation required monasteries to provide lances as an annual gift to the king. The least expensive weapon in the early medieval armory, it could be used in various ways by either the infantry or cavalry soldier. This weapon, made of ash and sometimes fitted with a metal point, could be used as either a throwing or a thrusting weapon, and contemporary illustrations depict its use in both ways. Throwing spears continued to be used by soldiers as the early Middle Ages progressed, but the lance gradually became primarily a thrusting weapon used by both cavalry and infantry. As a thrusting weapon, the lance could be thrust downward in a stabbing motion or could be thrust upward to knock an opponent off his horse. It was once argued that during the Carolingian period the lance was held under the arm of the mounted warrior who, held in place by a stirrup, could use the full power of the horse against his enemy, creating a force of mounted shock troops. Although the idea is attractive, there is little evidence, either from contemporary illustrations or from archeological discoveries, to support this theory.

Warriors in barbarian Europe were equipped with two other important weapons. The axe was used during this period as a throwing weapon or a slashing weapon, and it was often double-edged and appeared with either a short or long handle. Bows and arrows were also used and were an essential component of the foot soldiers' armory. Carolingian legislation required that infantry troops carry an extra string and 12 arrows as part of their equipment. Throughout the early Middle Ages the bow was a necessary part of the infantry's weaponry, and arrows have been found in the graves of the Merovingian Franks and other barbarian peoples. The Lombards were noted for their use of a composite reflex bow made of wood, horn, and sinew that was glued together to form a more flexible bow, which gave the string more pull. Even though a short, simple bow was commonly used by the Merovingians and Carolingians archers, it was gradually replaced, beginning in the ninth century, by the composite bow.

Along with a wide range of weapons, barbarian warriors of late antiquity and the early Middle Ages had an extensive complement of body armor. Indeed, Charlemagne appeared as the "iron Charles" to his opponents because of his strong will and body armor. The early medieval soldier used a mixture of body armor, helmet, and shield, with the noble warrior possessing more elaborate and expensive defensive armament. Perhaps the most important piece of protective gear was body armor, which appeared in a variety of styles, but was usually called either *brunia* or *lorica* in contemporary sources. One style, generally preferred by the poorer soldiers, was the so-called *lorica squamata*. This was a cloth-covered suit that was popular because it offered protection to the soldier and was relatively affordable for the common foot soldier. Better known was the *lorica hamata*, a suit of mail that offered better protections but was fabulously expensive and therefore affordable only to the wealthier nobles in the army. A shirt of mail was made of interlocking iron rings of the same size and provided its owner great protection in battle. There are also examples of leg armor made of iron, and the hands and arms were protected by armored gloves and armguards. After about 800, the hauberk, or *halsbergen* (German: neck guard) became a common piece of body armor. This was a caped hood that was worn over the head, under the helmet, and either over or under the mail shirt to provide protection for the neck.

Along with armor to protect the body, early medieval combatants wore helmets, which were usually conical and made of several possible materials, to protect their heads and faces. The most common helmet was the *spangenhelm,* so called because its design involved six or more metal strips (*spangen*) that joined the headband to a plate of metal. The framework strips of the helmet were usually of bronze or iron, but a fully iron helmet was rare. The framework was then filled with metal or horn plates. The *spangenhelm* common in the early Middle Ages was most likely based on an original model used by the Huns, and the Ostrogoths designed a distinctive *spangenhelm,* used by the Ostrogothic kings as a diplomatic gift for other rulers.

The final piece of equipment used for protection by all soldiers in barbarian Europe was the shield, which was also probably the least expensive of all offensive and defensive weapons possessed by cavalry and infantry soldiers. Despite its low cost, the shield was a very important piece of equipment, as Carolingian legislation reveals. Charlemagne required that shield makers live in all regions of the empire, and Louis the Pious and Louis the German required that some monasteries include shields in their annual gifts to the ruler. And makers and merchants of shields often accompanied armies when they campaigned. The shield itself was used to protect the soldier from his enemy's blows, and according to contemporary records, it could even protect a soldier from a javelin. The shield was usually made of a sturdy wood and covered with leather, which would keep the shield in one piece even after the wood split under the force of heavy blows. The shield was reinforced with iron or other metal strips and rivets, and it measured roughly three feet in diameter and offered protection from the thigh to the shoulder. Shields might be round or oval; the shield was always concave and had a grip along one side so that it could be held. Some shields had a pointed boss, which allowed the shield to be used as an offensive weapon and thrust against an attacker.

See also: Anglo-Saxons; Carolingian Dynasty; Charlemagne; Franks; Huns; Lombards; Louis the German; Louis the Pious; Merovingian Dynasty; Ostrogoths; Poitiers, Battle of

Bibliography

Bachrach, Bernard S. "Charles Martel, Mounted Shock Combat, the Stirrup, and Feudalism." *Studies in Medieval and Renaissance History* 7 (1970): 47–75.

Bachrach, Bernard S. *Merovingian Military Organization, 481–751.* Minneapolis: University of Minnesota Press, 1972.

Bachrach, Bernard S. *Early Carolingian Warfare: Prelude to Empire.* Philadelphia: University of Pennsylvania Press, 2001.

Contamine, Philippe. *War in the Middle Ages.* Trans. Michael Jones. Oxford: Basil Blackwell, 1984.

Coupland, Simon. "Carolingian Arms and Armor in the Ninth Century." *Viator: Medieval and Renaissance Studies* 21 (1990): 29–50.

DeVries, Kelly. *Medieval Military Technology.* Peterborough, ON: Broadview, 1992.

Ganshof, François Louis. *Frankish Institutions under Charlemagne.* Trans. Bryce Lyon and Mary Lyon. Providence, RI: Brown University Press, 1968.

Martin, Paul. *Arms and Armour from the 9th to the 17th Century.* Trans. René North. Rutland: Tuttle, 1968.

Verbruggen, Jan F. *The Art of Warfare in Western Europe during the Middle Ages: From the Eighth Century to 1340.* 2nd ed. Trans. Sumner Willard and S.C.M. Southern. Woodbridge, UK: Boydell, 1997.

White, Lynn, Jr. *Medieval Technology and Social Change.* Oxford: Oxford University Press, 1964.

Wearmouth. *See* Benedict Biscop

Wessex

One of the major kingdoms of Anlgo-Saxon England, Wessex, or the kingdom of the West Saxons, was the most powerful of the southern Anglo-Saxon kingdoms and included the upper Thames river valley and Berkshire, Dorset, eastern Devon, Hampshire, Somerset, and Wiltshire. Founded by the Gewisse clan of the Anglo-Saxon peoples in the sixth century, Wessex would achieve its greatest heights under King Alfred in the ninth century and would survive until the Norman Conquest of England in 1066.

The kingdom was established, according to the *Anglo-Saxon Chronicle*, by the chieftains of the Gewisse tribe Cerdic (d. 561) and his son Cynric (d. 581) who invaded England in 494 or 495 with five ships of fellow Saxons. Following a period of conquest in which they established themselves over and became kings of Wessex by 519. The line of Cerdic continued to extend the boundaries of Wessex throughout the sixth century, and his successors often shared the kingship. Cerdic's grandson Cealwin (d. 592) won a series of battles against the Britons and is identified by Bede as one of the kings to hold imperium over Britain, to rule as bretwalda. During the early years of the kingdom its rulers extended their power into Sussex and north of the Thames, which would bring them into contact and competition with rival kingdoms including Mercia and Northumbria.

During the seventh and eighth centuries the fortunes of Wessex ebbed and flowed. In the 620s, Penda of Mercia and the kings of Wessex clashed. During the reigns of Cynegils (d. 643), the first Christian king of Wessex, and his son Cwichelm, Penda secured the territories of the subkingdom Hwicce. The West Saxons also lost control of the Isle of Wight and South Hampshire to the Mercians, and the king of Wessex was driven into exile in East Anglia by the Mercians. Under Caedwalla (r. 685–688), however, the kingdom enjoyed a resurgence. He recaptured the Isle of Wight, took control of Sussex, and expanded his authority into Kent. He also converted to Christianity and abdicated so that he could undertake a pilgrimage to Rome to be baptized by the pope. Ine (r. 688–726), Caedwalla's successor, built upon the successes of earlier West Saxon kings. He promulgated a new law code, abolished the practice of establishing sub-king, and appointed earldormen as local representatives of royal power. During his reign, the church expanded in Wessex and a new bishopric was established at Sherbourne. The later years of the eighth century saw the revival of Mercian power and the possible recognition by the kings of Wessex of Mercian overlordship.

The kingdom of the West Saxons achieved its greatest success during the ninth and tenth centuries, especially during the reign of its greatest king Alfred the Great (r. 871–899). The tide began to turn under King Ecgberht (r. 802–838) who won a major victory over the Mercians in 825 at the battle of Ellendum. Ecgberht regained control of Essex, Kent, Surrey, and Sussex. He continued his expansion of the kingdom in 829 by conquering all of Mercia and gained the submission of the Northumbrians. Despite these successes, the West Saxon kingdom and all of England would face a major challenge with the coming of the Danes. Throughout the ninth century, Danish Vikings invaded England, carving out settlements throughout north and central England and defeating rulers in Northumbrian and East Anglia. In the 870s the Danes threatened and nearly overran Wessex but were turned away, thanks to the efforts of Alfred the Great. Alfred himself was forced into exile but managed to return and inflict a stinging defeat on the Danes at the Battle of Eddington in 878 that drove the Danes from Wessex. He also introduced military reforms and established a series of fortified settlements throughout the kingdom to help prepare it for future threats. Alfred secured his position in Wessex and extended his authority over all of England not held by the Danes.

Along with his military and political reforms, Alfred issued a new legal code, translated works by Augustine of Hippo and Boethius into Anglo-Saxon, and commissioned translations into the vernacular of a number of other important Latin works. Alfred's son and grandson consolidated West Saxon control over much of England, incorporating East Anglia, Mercia, and Northumbria into the kingdom and establishing the first true king of the English. Wessex would become an earldom in the late 10th century and would remain an earldom the Danish conqueror Cnut and the last Anglo-Saxon king Harold Godwinson. With the conquest of England by William the Conqueror in 1066, the existence of Wessex as a distinct political unit came to an end and the region became part of the newly created Anglo-Norman kingdom.

See also: Alfred the Great; *Anglo-Saxon Chronicle*; Anglo-Saxons; Bretwalda; Bede; Caedwalla; Mercia; Penda

Bibliography

Campbell, James. *The Anglo-Saxons*. New York: Penguin, 1991.

Cunliffe, Barry. *Wessex to A.D. 1000*. London: Longman, 1993.

Yorke, Barbara. *Kings and Kingdoms of Early Anglo-Saxon England*. New York: Routledge, 1997.

Whitelock, Dorothy, ed. *The Anglo-Saxon Chronicle*. Westport, CT: Greenwood, 1986.

Widukind (d. c. 807)

Widukind was a Westphalian nobleman who led a serious rebellion against Charlemagne. Widukind managed to rally the pagan Saxons against Carolingian religious and political expansion. The severity of his rebellion threatened Carolingian efforts and caused great difficulties for Charlemagne. Widukind's eventual conversion to Christianity was a key moment in the long Carolingian struggle to conquer and convert the Saxon people.

Shortly after his rise to power as king and the death of his brother, Charlemagne began the conquest of Saxony. Although it began as a response to cross-border raiding by the Saxons, the campaign in Saxony quickly turned into a more serious venture. Indeed, Charlemagne began to look upon the conquest and conversion to Christianity of the pagan Saxons as part of his responsibility as king. The conquest of Saxony ended by taking some 30 years to complete (772–804) and involving some of Charlemagne's most terrible actions, including the deportation of large numbers of Saxons from their homeland to the heart of Frankish territory. The Saxons themselves were poorly organized and lacked any unifying institutions, which made the process all the more difficult, especially since they were intent on preserving their independence and religious traditions.

The Saxons struggled to prevent Charlemagne from conquering them, and the most effective leader against Carolingian incursion into Saxony was Widukind. In 778 Widukind, taking advantage of Charlemagne's absence from Saxony to campaign in Spain, led a massive revolt against Carolingian authority. Unifying the Saxons for the moment, Widukind managed to retake important territory along the Rhine River and even planned to attack the important Carolingian monastery of Fulda. Responding with great urgency, Charlemagne returned from Spain to restore order in the region. His generals waged two further campaigns in 779 and 780 to quell the rebellion. In 782, Charlemagne held a great assembly to organize the region and establish religious institutions there. According to the *Royal Frankish Annals,* many Saxons participated in this assembly, but Widukind did not participate because he remained in rebellion.

After Charlemagne's return to his kingdom, Widukind led the Saxons in revolt again and routed the armies established by Charlemagne in Saxony. The churches and monasteries established by the Carolingian king were destroyed, and the priests and monks were attacked and killed. In a great rage, Charlemagne returned and massacred 4,500 Saxons at Verdun in an effort to suppress the rebellion. His efforts failed, and Widukind and his followers struggled on. Charlemagne also issued his first Saxon Capitulary at that time, which sought to impose Christianity on the Saxons by force. Charlemagne's continued pressure on the Saxons in the mid-780s, however, wore Widukind down, and in 785 he submitted to his Carolingian rival. In 785, Widukind and his son accepted baptism. Although the conquest of Saxony took another twenty years to complete, the submission and conversion of Widukind was a significant step in the process and ended the most serious challenge to Charlemagne's conquest.

See also: Carolingian Dynasty; Charlemagne; Franks; Saxon Capitularies

Bibliography

Collins, Roger. *Charlemagne.* Toronto: University of Toronto Press, 1998.

Einhard and Notker the Stammerer. *Two Lives of Charlemagne.* Trans. Lewis Thorpe. Harmondsworth, UK: Penguin, 1981.

Fichtenau, Heinrich. *The Carolingian Empire.* Trans. Peter Munz. Toronto: University of Toronto Press, 1979.

Halphen, Louis. *Charlemagne and the Carolingian Empire.* Trans. Giselle de Nie. Amsterdam: North-Holland, 1977.

McKitterick, Rosamond. *The Frankish Kingdoms under the Carolingians, 751–987.* London: Longman 1983.

Riché, Pierre. *The Carolingians: A Family Who Forged Europe.* Trans. Michael Idomir Allen. Philadelphia: University of Pennsylvania Press, 1993.

Scholz, Bernhard Walter, trans. *Carolingian Chronicles: Royal Frankish Annals and Nithard's History.* Ann Arbor: University of Michigan Press, 1972.

Witenagemot

General council of the Anglo-Saxon kings, also known as the *Witan* (Anglo-Saxon: wise men), that met to witness royal charters and other enactments of the king. The witenagemot (meeting of wise men) was made up of the leading nobles of the realm along with the leading bishops, abbots, and priests of the kingdom. The members of the council, however, were a relatively fluid group who came when called by the king.

Although it was clearly an important institution in Anglo-Saxon England, the witenagemot's origins remain unclear and are known primarily from charter evidence, which becomes less available after the reign of Alfred the Great. No longer identified as the descendant of a Germanic institution or the precursor of the English Parliament, the witenagemot most likely evolved out of the king's need for advice and was based on his ability to call nobles and ecclesiastics to court. The witenagemot was a mobile assembly that came together before the king as he traveled throughout the kingdom. Members of the assembly were generally high-ranking clergy and nobility; thegns also participated, but only when the king's court was in the thegn's territory.

When meeting in the council, the nobles and churchmen came not as representatives of any specific group, but as advisors to the king who knew the law and needs of the land. They worked together with the king to ensure that law and justice was executed throughout the realm. Although he could rule without the members of the witenagemot, the wise king considered consulting with them valuable and was careful to call the council to advise with him. The council did not meet at specific intervals, but was called to meet when the need arose, when the king needed its help to resolve some problem at hand.

See also: Alfred the Great; Anglo-Saxons; Thegn

Bibliography

Loyn, Henry R. *Anglo-Saxon England and the Norman Conquest.* 2nd ed. London: Longmans, 1991.

Loyn, Henry R. *The Governance of Anglo-Saxon England, 500–1087.* London: Edward Arnold, 1984.

Lyon, Bryce. *A Constitutional and Legal History of Medieval England.* 2nd ed. Palo Alto, CA: Stanford University Press, 1980.

Stenton, Frank M. *Anglo-Saxon England.* 3rd ed. Oxford: Clarendon, 1971.

Witigis (fl. 536–540)

Ostrogothic king in Italy from 536 to 540 who led his people against the Byzantine armies sent by Justinian to conquer the peninsula and restore imperial rule there. Although not of the royal line of Theodoric the Great, Witigis was a successful general, whose prominence led to his election as king. He adopted an aggressive strategy against the Byzantine armies led by Belisarius and took the offensive against Byzantine territory outside of Italy. He also pursued diplomatic ties with the Merovingian Franks and the Lombards. His efforts, however, proved fruitless, and he eventually succumbed to Belisarius, whom the Goths hoped to elect as emperor.

On the death of Theodoric's last heir, Theodohad, in 536, the Goths turned to Witigis, who had enjoyed some success in the campaigns against the armies of the Eastern Empire. Theodohad's failure to save the city of Rome led to his death, and the Goths hoped to have someone worthy of Theodoric to take the throne. Witigis, not of the royal line, proclaimed himself a member of Theodoric's family because the deeds he and the great king performed were of similar stature. To confirm his position on the throne, however, Witigis married Amalaswintha's daughter Matasuntha. His own propaganda to the Goths never stressed this marriage, but he did inform Emperor Justinian of the marriage. The new king also suggested that Justinian's purpose in the war, avenging the murder of Amalaswintha, had been fulfilled by the murder of Theodohad and the marriage, which restored Amalaswintha's line to the throne. His argument, however, did not persuade Justinian, and both the emperor and the new Gothic king were fully committed to war.

Shortly after his election as king in late 536, Witigis moved his Gothic armies south to meet Belisarius, who had recently taken possession of the city of Rome. Along with his march on Rome, Witigis secured a peace treaty with the Merovingian king of the Franks that guaranteed that the Franks would not invade Italy and take advantage of the uncertain situation. He also launched a campaign against the Byzantines in Dalmatia. Indeed, Witigis took the initiative in the hopes of ending the invasion of the Byzantines. Upon reaching Rome, Witigis began a siege of the city that lasted almost a year in the hopes of capturing it outright or forcing Belisarius into open battle. Over the next year, the Goths launched repeated assaults on the city walls, often leading to numerous casualties on their side. The Byzantine forces suffered as well, although not only from Gothic attacks but also from shortage of food and the spread of disease. Attempts to find a diplomatic solution failed, and the arrival of Eastern Roman armies forced Witigis to accept a truce in late 537.

Despite his aggressive efforts, Witigis was doomed to failure, and events began to turn against him by early 538. The Dalmatian campaign failed, and Belisarius, no longer hampered by the siege, decided to take the initiative and ordered a cavalry force to attack a nearby town where the families of the Gothic soldiers resided. His plan succeeded; Witigis was forced to break off the siege and returned to the royal city of Ravenna. He then faced a series of attacks by Belisarius and other forces. The Byzantine general began a march north from Rome to defeat his rival. The Alemanni raided northern Italy, and the devastation contributed to famine conditions on the peninsula. Even worse, an imperial army under the command of Narses arrived to aid Belisarius and counter Gothic numeric superiority. But the arrival of Narses offered the Gothic king a glimmer of hope because of the rivalry that existed between Narses and Belisarius, which often paralyzed the Byzantine war effort.

Witigis in 538 and 539 came to the realization that he would not overcome the Byzantines militarily and sought to win through diplomatic negotiations. Here too, however, Witigis was unsuccessful. Indeed, his earlier treaty with the Franks did not prevent the Merovingian king Theudebert from raiding northern Italy in 539. The Goths no longer trusted the Franks and refused further offers of assistance from them. Witigis's efforts to establish an alliance with the Lombards also proved a failure. And as his diplomatic initiatives came to nothing, Witigis faced a resurgent Belisarius, who managed to unite the Roman armies in 539 and lay siege to Ravenna. By 540, the end of Witigis was near, as the Goths started to abandon him. But Ravenna was nearly impregnable, and so the king began negotiations, at first with other barbarian peoples and with the Persians, and then finally with Constantinople. He hoped for a settlement and was willing to accept terms from Justinian. But Belisarius seemed unwilling to come to terms and may have given the Goths the impression that he was willing to accept the imperial dignity from them. The Goths were willing to elevate him to the rank of emperor, and there is some possibility that he seriously considered it. Ultimately, however, Belisarius remained loyal to Justinian, and accepted the surrender of Witigis, entering Ravenna in May 540. The reign of Witigis had come to an end, but the Goths continued the struggle against the Byzantine invaders under the next Gothic king, Totila.

See also: Alemanni; Amalaswintha; Belisarius; Franks; Justinian; Lombards; Merovingian Dynasty; Narses; Ostrogoths; Theodoric the Great; Totila

Bibliography

Browning, Robert. *Justinian and Theodora.* Rev. ed. London: Thames and Hudson, 1987.

Burns, Thomas. *A History of the Ostrogoths.* Bloomington: University of Indiana Press, 1984.

Bury, John B. *History of the Later Roman Empire: From the Death of Theodosius I to the Death of Justinian.* 2 Vols. 1923. Reprint, New York: Dover, 1959.

Cassiodorus. *The Variae of Magnus Aurelius Cassiodorus.* Trans. S.J.B. Barnish. Liverpool, UK: Liverpool University Press, 1992.

Heather, Peter. *The Goths.* Oxford: Blackwell, 1996.

Procopius. *History of the Wars.* Trans. H. B. Dewing. 1979.

Wolfram, Herwig. *History of the Goths.* Trans. Thomas J. Dunlap. Berkeley: University of California Press, 1988.

Wolfram, Herwig. *The Roman Empire and Its Germanic Peoples.* Trans. Thomas J. Dunlap. Berkeley: University of California Press, 1997.

Women

The place of women in late antique and early medieval society was a complex one; women used a variety of strategies to negotiate their way at a time when their legal status was often low. Modern understanding of these strategies and the place of women in barbarian Europe is made difficult by the nature of the sources, which are often limited to the more traditional histories of government and battles. That notwithstanding, a variety of sources—collections of laws, contemporary literature, religious documents, histories—properly approached can provide insights into the lives of women of the time. The vast majority of women, it can safely be said, simply labored. They worked the fields with their peasant brothers, fathers, and husbands, raised children, and tended the family. The small minority, about whom most can be known, also tended to the family, one of the primary duties of all the women of barbarian Europe, but these women also had the opportunity to exercise power as queens and nobles. Furthermore, they could have recourse to a life of religion and often founded or headed communities of religious men and women. Although their history can sometimes be difficult to discern, women in the late antiquity and the early Middle Ages played an important role in society.

The earliest literary record of barbarian women was provided by the Roman historian and moralist, Tacitus (c. 56–117), whose *Germania* provides an account of the status and duties of barbarian women prior to the migration period and its extensive contacts with the Roman Empire. According to Tacitus, Germanic women were especially esteemed and respected in society. They were thought to possess special holiness and powers of prophecy, and were often asked their advice, which was often heeded, on a wide range of matters. Tacitus also notes that women rallied their warrior husbands and fathers in battle by baring their breasts and "making them realize the imminent prospect of enslavement" (108). The Roman historian also provides details concerning the domestic life of women among the premigration Germanic tribes. He notes that their dress differs from that of men in two important ways. Women wear sleeveless outer garments of linen decorated in purple, which expose their arms and shoulders. Tacitus also notes the important role that women play in marriage and family among the Germans. Marital customs were well defined, according to Tacitus, and involved a specific exchange of gifts between husband and wife that defined their relationship as one of partnership and mutual labor. Indeed, as noted in the *Germania,* the gifts included oxen and weapons, indicating that women were involved in farming and warfare. Marriages were strictly monogamous, and women were severely punished for adultery. Women also were responsible for nursing and raising children, and thus played a central role in all aspects of family life.

Unfortunately, Tacitus's description is as much an indictment of Roman values and decadent family life as it is a picture of the status of Germanic women.

Consequently, his assessment must be treated cautiously and is perhaps best understood as commentary on Roman social life. Nevertheless, although his view is colored by his attitudes toward Roman society, it is not without merit and at the very least provides a rough outline of the areas in which women did play a role. In work, family, politics and war, and religious life, women in late antiquity and the early Middle Ages exercised some, often considerable, influence.

The fundamental role for women in barbarian Europe was that of wife and mother, which was true no matter what social rank they held. Their importance in marriage and family was clearly outlined in the numerous legal codes that were compiled throughout the early Middle Ages. Notably, the Salic law defined the value of men and women in society and established different values for women depending upon their age and ability to bear children. One section noted that if a pregnant woman was struck, the fine was 28,000 denars; if a woman of childbearing age was struck, the fine was 24,000 denars; and if a woman past the age childbearing was struck, the fine was only 8,000 denars. In the laws of King Alfred the Great, a fine was assessed for both mother and child if a pregnant woman was killed, and in earlier Anglo-Saxons laws the amount of inheritance a woman was owed from her husband's family was determined by the bearing of children. Moreover, during the Merovingian and early Carolingian dynasties women used childbearing as a means to power. Women of lower status at times married and bore children to powerful figures in the kingdom. And some women, who were not married but still bore children, enjoyed the prestige of having children with nobles and kings. Merovingian queens especially were empowered by the birth of sons, and their prestige as mothers of kings was even greater than their status as wives of kings. Indeed, as late as the age of Charlemagne, the children from illegitimate unions were given rank and status, which enhanced the prestige of their mothers. Clearly, the most important duty of women was to produce children; in the higher social ranks, bearing children was essential for preserving the dynasty and for use later in marriage alliances.

Although the primary duties of women in late antiquity and the early Middle Ages involved the family, high-ranking women could, and often did, exploit their position. In all the successor kingdoms, women played an important political role. Indeed, even in the Roman and Byzantine Empires, women exercised great influence and direct political authority. Constantine's mother, St. Helena, was an important figure in the church during her son's reign and was an influential pilgrim to Jerusalem, where she discovered the True Cross (believed to be the cross on which Christ was crucified). Theodora, Justinian's wife, was the emperor's partner throughout their marriage. She encouraged Justinian to stand his ground during the Nika Revolt in 532, played a key role in Justinian's plans to reconquer Italy, and helped her husband manage the divided church in the empire. Her contemporary, and some would say victim, Amalaswintha, daughter of the Ostrogothic king Theodoric the Great, assumed the regency for her son and continued to be a powerful figure in Ostrogothic Italy until her murder by rival Gothic nobles who opposed her pro-Roman policy. In Lombard Italy, Queen Theudelinda was the real power in the kingdom for three generations, marrying two successive kings and acting as regent for her son. She introduced Catholic Christianity to the kingdom and was a close friend of Pope Gregory I, called the Great.

In the Frankish kingdoms of the Merovingian and Carolingian dynasties, queens also influenced politics. From the very beginning of the Merovingian dynasty, women played a key role in the direction the kingdom took. Clotilda, a Burgundian Catholic princess, according to the sixth-century historian of the Franks Gregory of Tours, convinced her husband Clovis (r. 481–511), the great Merovingian king of the Franks, to convert to Catholic Christianity. Also, according to Gregory, she persuaded one of her sons to invade and conquer the Burgundians in revenge for the reigning king's murder of her father. In subsequent generations, queens continued to play a central role in the political life of the kingdom, and perhaps the two greatest figures were Brunhilde and Fredegund. The career of Fredegund reveals the fluid nature of marriage and rank in the Merovingian kingdom. She may have been a slave woman, and was surely lowborn, yet she married a king and bore him an heir, Chlotar II, who went on to reign in the early seventh century, restoring the dynasty's greatness. Both Brunhilde and Fredegund, furthermore, employed ruthless measures to guarantee their own power and that of their husbands and especially their sons. They indulged in a terrible blood feud during which each sought to kill the other or the husbands, sons, and supporters of her opponent. During the last decade of the sixth and first decade of the seventh century, Brunhilde was the real power in the kingdom.

In the Carolingian period, marriage customs changed, and women had fewer opportunities to rule as Brunhilde and Fredegund did. Nonetheless, leading Carolingian women managed to influence affairs of state. The widow of Pippin II, Plectrude, seized control of her husband's treasury and nearly managed to take control of the kingdom before being defeated by Pippin's son Charles Martel. Bertrada, the widow of Pippin III, called the Short, exercised great influence after her husband's death and remained an esteemed figure during her son's reign. She negotiated a marriage alliance with the Lombards for her son Charlemagne and struggled to keep the peace between her sons Charlemagne and Carloman. Charlemagne married Fastrada, the daughter of a powerful east Frankish count, to gain political influence in the eastern part of the kingdom; he may have kept his daughters close by his side, refusing to let them marry, so that their husbands would not use their connections to the royal line as justification for revolt. The wife of Louis the Pious, Judith, actively promoted her son, Charles the Bald, and was identified by Louis's sons by his first wife as the cause for disruption in the empire. And the noblewoman, Dhuoda, wrote an important manual for her son to teach him the proper behavior at court and as a Christian nobleman. Although women did not often have formal, legal powers, their close proximity to kings, emperors, and other powerful figures provided them the opportunity to influence affairs and even rule themselves.

As Tacitus noted, pre-migration Germanic women were esteemed for their powers of prophecy. In the mid-ninth century, the prophet Theoda gained a significant following when she preached the coming of the end of the world and called for religious reform. She was quickly suppressed by the authorities, and there were few true female prophets in late antiquity and the early Middle Ages. Women did, however, play a key role in religious life, just as they often did in political life. Indeed, many of the same women who influenced politics shaped religious affairs in their kingdoms. Theodora sponsored and protected Monophysite monks and priests and even established a special chapel in the imperial palace where they officiated for her. Theudelinda warmed relations between the Arian Lombards and the Catholic church in Italy, and laid the foundation for the ultimate triumph of Catholic Christianity in the kingdom. According to Gregory of Tours, Clotilda not only convinced Clovis to accept Catholic Christianity, and with him 3,000 of his followers, but also entered a convent after her husband's death.

Brunhilde, despite her violent struggle with Fregedund and hostility toward the Irish saint Columban, supported the mission to England of Augustine of Canterbury and encouraged reforms in the church at the suggestion of Gregory the Great. Moreover, other royal women, including Balthild, wife of the seventh-century Merovingian king Clovis II, and Radegund, a sixth-century Merovingian queen, founded or led communities of religious women. Indeed, one way that queens and aristocratic women could exercise power and influence was through the foundation or endowment of monasteries, for men or women. And the religious life was highly esteemed even by the most ruthless of kings. In their communities, royal women could wield great power over the other nuns, and they also gained power in the wider world because of the economic strength of their house. Moreover, religious women throughout the early Middle Ages ruled over the unique institution of the double monastery—a community of monks and nuns ruled over by an abbess. Although often without much legal authority, women nonetheless played an important role in the political, religious, and social life of late antiquity and the early Middle Ages.

See also: Alfred the Great; Amalaswintha; Anglo-Saxons; Augustine of Canterbury, St.; Bertrada; Brunhilde; Carolingian Dynasty; Charlemagne; Charles the Bald; Charles Martel; Clotilda, St.; Columban, St.; Dhuoda; Fredegund; Gregory I, the Great, Pope; Gregory of Tours; Judith; Justinian; Lombards; Louis the Pious; Marriage; Merovingian Dynasty; Ostrogoths; Plectrude; Radegund; Salic Law; Theodora; Theodoric the Great; Theudelinda

Bibliography

Cameron, Averil. *The Mediterranean World in Late Antiquity,* A.D. *395–600.* New York: Routledge, 1993.

Clark, Gillian. *Women in Late Antiquity: Pagan and Christian Lifestyles.* Oxford: Clarendon, 1993.

Gies, Frances, and Joseph Gies. *Marriage and Family in the Middle Ages.* New York: Harper and Row, 1987.

Gregory of Tours. *History of the Franks.* Trans. Lewis Thorpe. Harmondsworth, UK: Penguin, 1974.

Kirshner, Julius, and Suzanne Wemple, eds. *Women of the Medieval World.* Oxford: Basil Blackwell, 1985.

Leyser, Henrietta. *Medieval Women: A Social History of Women in England, 450–1500.* New York: St. Martin's, 1995.

Schulenburg, Jane Tibbetts. *Forgetful of Their Sex: Female Sanctity and Society, ca. 500–1100.* Chicago: University of Chicago Press, 1998.

Shahar, Shulamith. *The Fourth Estate: A History of Women in the Middle Ages.* New York: Routledge, 1990.

Tacitus. *The Agricola and the Germania.* Trans. H. Mattingly, rev. trans. S. A. Handford. Harmondsworth, UK: Penguin, 1982.

Thiébaux, Marcelle, trans. *The Writings of Medieval Women: An Anthology.* New York: Garland, 1994.

Wemple, Suzanne. *Women in Frankish Society: Marriage and the Cloister, 500 to 900.* Philadelphia: University of Pennsylvania Press, 1981.

Wulfstan. *See* Anglo-Saxons

Z

Zachary, St. (d. 752)

A central figure in the political revolution in the Frankish kingdom, Zachary, or Zacharias, was pope during an important period in the development of the papacy (r. 741–752). He was actively involved in diplomatic affairs during his reign, frequently attending to negotiations with representatives of the Byzantine Empire, the Franks, and the Lombards. He sought to limit Lombard aggression during his reign, but is remembered most for his relations with the powerful Carolingian family. Indeed, it was Zachary's response to a famous question from Pippin that provided the Carolingian with the justification to depose the last of the Merovingian kings. Zachary was also in close correspondence with the great Anglo-Saxon missionary St. Boniface and made an important translation into Greek of the Dialogues of Gregory the Great that was well known in the Byzantine Empire.

Born to a Greek family living in Calabria, possibly in 679, Zachary was eventually ordained a deacon and priest and may have participated in an important church council in Rome in 732 held by his predecessor Gregory III. A portrait in Rome portrays him as a thin and small person, balding and with a reserved air. According to his official biographer, Zachary was "gentle and gracious, adorned with all kindness, a lover of the clergy and all the Roman people" (Davis 1992, 35). He was also "slow to anger and quick to have pity, repaying no one evil for evil, nor taking even merited vengeance, but dutiful and compassionate to everyone" (35). Clearly these virtues, even if they are only the standard traits attributed to all popes by their biographers, would serve the pope well in his often difficult relations with the Lombard rulers of Italy.

Although no longer a threat to Rome because of their Arianism, the now Catholic Lombard kings in Italy still pursued the dream of unifying the peninsula under their authority. Zachary faced this problem almost immediately upon ascending the papal throne, but did not feel bound to follow the policies of Pope Gregory III, who sought an alliance with the Carolingian Franks, and instead found new solutions to the problem. Indeed, he sought to establish a policy of conciliation with King Liutprand (r. 712–744). Liutprand had advanced on the independent southern Lombard duchy of Spoleto. Zachary broke with the duke, who had refused to return Roman territory to the pope. Liutprand quickly brought the duke to heel, but he too was slow to return the territory to Rome. Zachary then went to the Lombard capital, Pavia, where he met the king and made his demands known. Liutprand was so taken by the courage and prestige of the pope that he returned several cities and other important territories to the papacy. He also provided an escort of his nobles to return Zachary to Rome. Although this worked out well for the pope, difficulties with Liutprand continued because the king did not feel bound to respect imperial territory in Italy. His attacks on Ravenna initiated a second papal visit, and again Liutprand made concessions to the pope.

The policy of conciliation toward the Lombards seemed to have born fruit for the papacy, and Zachary was able to continue the policy during the reign of Liutprand's successor, Ratchis (r. 744–749). Indeed, so impressed was Ratchis with the pope that he abandoned efforts to bring all of Italy under his authority and then abdicated and retired to a monastery. Unfortunately, Ratchis's successor, Aistulf (r. 749–756), was perhaps the most bloodthirsty and expansionistic of all the Lombard kings and was less open to Zachary. The pope's death in 752, however, meant that a resolution of the Lombard question would have to wait until the time of his successor. Zachary's relationship with the Lombards did bring a period of peace and stability for Italy and, especially, papal territories on the peninsula.

Zachary was also actively involved in affairs in the north, where important religious reforms and political change benefited from his rule. The great missionary, Boniface, was in frequent correspondence with Zachary, who guided and encouraged the missionary's activities in the Frankish kingdom and Saxony. Shortly after the pope ascended the throne, Boniface wrote to Zachary professing his loyalty and submission to Rome. Boniface also organized the Frankish church and brought it more fully under the influence and authority of Rome. Zachary approved of Boniface's activities, confirmed three new bishoprics Boniface founded, and made Boniface the papal legate in the Frankish realm. The pope also adopted some of the reform initiatives of Boniface, and was in correspondence with the Carolingian mayors, Pippin and Carloman, concerning church councils and church reform in the kingdom.

The correspondence with Boniface and the Carolingian leaders led to the most famous moment of Zachary's reign. Pippin and Carloman, mayors of the palace, were the real powers in the kingdom, and the Merovingian king, Childeric III, served mainly as a figurehead. In 747, Zachary welcomed Carloman to the monastery of Monte Cassino, just north of Rome, after the Carolingian mayor had abdicated and taken monastic vows. Three years later, Pippin, as the sole real power in the Frankish kingdom, sent two high-ranking representatives to the pope with an important message. As the *Royal Frankish Annals* note, Pippin asked the pope "whether it was good or not that the kings of the Franks should wield no power" (Scholz 1972, 39). The pope responded that "it was better to call him king who had royal power than the one who did not" (39), and ordered that Pippin be made king. Having gained the answer he desired, Pippin deposed the last of the Merovingian kings and assumed the throne as the first Carolingian king. Zachary had provided

Pippin with the justification and higher sanction that he needed to usurp the throne, thus surely strengthening the Carolingian's support for the papacy.

See also: Aistulf; Anglo-Saxons; Arianism; Boniface, St.; Carloman, Mayor of the Palace; Carolingian Dynasty; Childeric III; Franks; Gregory I, the Great, Pope; Gregory III, Pope; Liutprand; Lombards; Merovingian Dynasty; Pippin III, Called Pippin the Short; *Royal Frankish Annals*

Bibliography

Christie, Neil. *The Lombards.* Oxford: Blackwell, 1998.

Davis, Raymond, trans. *The Lives of the Eighth-Century Popes* (Liber Pontificalis): *The Ancient Biographies of Nine Popes from A.D. 715 to A.D. 817.* Liverpool, UK: Liverpool University Press, 1992.

Llewellyn, Peter. *Rome in the Dark Ages.* New York: Barnes and Noble, 1993.

McKitterick, Rosamond. *The Frankish Kingdoms under the Carolingians, 751–987.* London: Longman, 1983.

Noble, Thomas F. X. *The Republic of St. Peter: The Birth of the Papal State, 680–825.* Philadelphia: University of Pennsylvania Press, 1984.

Riché, Pierre. *The Carolingians: A Family Who Forged Europe.* Trans. Michael Idomir Allen. Philadelphia: University of Pennsylvania Press, 1993.

Scholz, Bernhard Walter, trans. *Carolingian Chronicles: Royal Frankish Annals and Nithard's History.* Ann Arbor: University of Michigan Press, 1972.

Ullmann, Walter. *A Short History of the Papacy in the Middle Ages.* London: Methuen, 1972.

Zeno (d. 491)

Zeno was an Eastern Roman emperor (r. 474–491) whose reign witnessed the so-called fall of the Roman Empire in 476. His own reign demonstrates the flaw in the traditional argument about the "fall of Rome," and his continued interest in the affairs of Italy after 476 reveals the importance of the entire empire to the emperors in Constantinople. Zeno's reign was marked by the ambitions of a number of generals, both Roman and barbarian, who sought control of Italy. It was also marked by his own efforts to strengthen the position of the Eastern Empire in the face of the advance of various Germanic peoples, and the conclusion of a treaty with the Vandals that was the first of its kind for Rome and the barbarians.

Since 395 the Roman Empire had been ruled by two emperors in two capitals, one in Constantinople and the other in one of several cities in Italy. In the 470s that situation continued, but it was threatened by the powerful and ambitious generals in Italy. In 475, Orestes, the highest ranking officer in the Western Empire, rose up against the emperor Julius Nepos, who fled into exile. Orestes made his son,

Romulus Augustulus, emperor, but Zeno rejected this claim and continued to support Julius Nepos as his legitimate colleague in the west. The situation was complicated for Zeno in the following year when Orestes and Romulus Augustulus were overthrown by Odovacar, a German tribal leader who was serving in the Roman army, who led a revolt of German soldiers against the western emperor. Odovacar executed Orestes but merely deposed Romulus and allowed him to retire with his family. Odovacar also sent word of his actions to Zeno and requested that Zeno grant him the title Patricius (patrician) so that he could rule Italy legitimately. Zeno was told by Odovacar's representatives, who returned the imperial insignia to Zeno, that there should be only one emperor—Zeno—and that Odovacar would rule as his representative. But Zeno stood by his exiled colleague, Julius Nepos, and informed Odovacar that the legitimate authority in the Western Empire was Julius. Nevertheless, Zeno did confer the office of Patricius on Odovacar, and thus began a long period of uncertain relations between the two rulers. The situation was clarified somewhat by the murder of Julius Nepos in 480, but no formal treaty was ever signed by Zeno and Odovacar.

While Odovacar ruled as the imperial representative in Italy, Zeno faced another powerful and ambitious barbarian general, Theodoric the Great, king of the Ostrogoths. Indeed, Zeno was particularly in Theodoric's debt because the Goth rescued the emperor at a critical period in his reign. In 475, the Gothic commander, Theodoric Strabo, forced Zeno from the throne, and with the aid of Theodoric the Great Zeno was able to seize back the imperial throne. Theodoric was richly rewarded for his efforts and promoted in the ranks of the Roman military. But Theodoric also used his position to improve the position of his Gothic peoples and threatened the stability of Zeno's control of the Eastern Empire in the mid-480s. Zeno's resources as emperor, however, turned out to be too great for Theodoric to overwhelm, even though his rebellion was quite serious. Instead, Zeno offered Theodoric the opportunity to march against Odovacar in Italy as the emperor's representative in Italy. Zeno intended to ease the pressures in his own part of the empire and use Theodoric to correct the uncertain situation in Italy. Although the exact nature of the political establishment Theodoric was to create and the relations of Italy and Constantinople that were to follow remain unclear, it is certain that Zeno intended to use Theodoric to end Odovacar's reign in Italy. In fact Theodoric claimed the title of king once he had established himself in Italy, but the murder of Odovacar and the creation of a new Gothic kingdom in Italy took place after Zeno's death. The emperor was, however, responsible for guiding the empire through uncertain times and establishing new and innovative relations with various barbarian peoples.

See also: Odovacar; Orestes; Ostrogoths; Romulus Augustulus; Theodoric the Great; Vandals

Bibliography

Bury, John B. *History of the Later Roman Empire: From the Death of Theodosius I to the Death of Justinian.* 2 Vols. 1923. Reprint, New York: Dover, 1959.

Bury, John B. *The Invasion of Europe by the Barbarians.* New York: W. W. Norton, 1967.

Lot, Ferdinand. *The End of the Ancient World and the Beginning of the Middle Ages.* 1931. Reprint, New York: Harper and Row, 1961.

Randers-Pehrson, Justine Davis. *Barbarians and Romans: The Birth Struggle of Europe, A.D. 400–700.* Norman: University of Oklahoma Press, 1983.

Wolfram, Herwig. *The Roman Empire and Its Germanic Peoples.* Trans. Thomas J. Dunlap. Los Angeles: University of California Press, 1997.

Primary Documents

1. Tacitus's Description of Early Germanic Society

In his work *Germania*, Tacitus (56–117), one of the great historians and moralists of the first century of the Roman Empire, provides one of the best early introductions to the Germanic peoples living on the empire's frontiers. Although, as revealed in the excerpts below, Tacitus offers valuable insights into the political and social structures of the Germans, his account is marred by his dependence on traditional Roman ethnography and his desire to contrast the noble Germans with the corrupt Romans of his day.

7. In the election of kings they have regard to birth; in that of generals, to valor. Their kings have not an absolute or unlimited power; and their generals command less through the force of authority, than of example. If they are daring, adventurous, and conspicuous in action, they procure obedience from the admiration they inspire. None, however, but the priests are permitted to judge offenders, to inflict bonds or stripes; so that chastisement appears not as an act of military discipline, but as the instigation of the god whom they suppose present with warriors. They also carry with them to battle certain images and standards taken from the sacred groves. It is a principal incentive to their courage, that their squadrons and battalions are not formed by men fortuitously collected, but by the assemblage of families and clans. Their pledges also are near at hand; they have within hearing the yells of their women, and the cries of their children. These, too, are the most revered witnesses of each man's conduct, these his most liberal applauders. To their mothers and their wives they bring their wounds for relief, nor do these dread to count or to search out the gashes. The women also administer food and encouragement to those who are fighting.

20. In every house the children grow up, thinly and meanly clad, to that bulk of body and limb which we behold with wonder. Every mother suckles her own children, and does not deliver them into the hands of servants and nurses. No indulgence distinguishes the young master from the slave. They lie together

amidst the same cattle, upon the same ground, till age separates, and valor marks out, the free-born. The youths partake late of the pleasures of love, and hence pass the age of puberty unexhausted: nor are the virgins hurried into marriage; the same maturity, the same full growth is required: the sexes unite equally matched and robust; and the children inherit the vigor of their parents. Children are regarded with equal affection by their maternal uncles as by their fathers: some even consider this as the more sacred bond of consanguinity, and prefer it in the requisition of hostages, as if it held the mind by a firmer tie, and the family by a more extensive obligation. A person's own children, however, are his heirs and successors; and no wills are made. If there be no children, the next in order of inheritance are brothers, paternal and maternal uncles. The more numerous are a man's relations and kinsmen, the more comfortable is his old age; nor is it here any advantage to be childless.

Source: The Germany and the Agricola of Tacitus. The Oxford Translation, with Notes, by Edward Brooks, Jr. Philadelphia: D. McKay, c. 1897, pp. 22–24, 42–43.

2. An Early Crisis of Church and State: Ambrose of Milan's Excommunication of Theodosius

Theodoret (c. 393–457), an influential theologian and historian, provides an account of a pivotal moment in the history of church–state relations in late antiquity—the conflict between the powerful archbishop of Milan, Ambrose, and the emperor Theodosius the Great. Asserting his authority as an archbishop, Ambrose excommunicated Theodosius for the brutal massacre of the people of Thessalonika ordered by the emperor in 390. A devout Christian, Theodosius sought absolution and appeared as a penitent before Ambrose, establishing a precedent for popes and bishops in the Middle Ages that the secular power must submit to the spiritual authority.

What vast power the Christian bishops and clergy were able to assume less than one hundred years after they ceased to be subject to dire persecution, is shown by the following story of the humiliation and penance St. Ambrose, the masterful bishop of Milan, inflicted upon Theodosius I, the last ruler of the undivided Empire.

Thessalonica is a large and populous city, in the province of Macedonia. [In consequence of a sedition there] the anger of the Emperor [Theodosius] rose to the highest pitch, and he gratified his vindictive desire for vengeance by unsheathing the sword most unjustly, and tyrannically against all, slaying the innocent and guilty alike. It is said 7000 perished without any forms of law, and without even having judicial sentence passed upon them; but that, like ears of corn in the time of harvest, they were alike cut down.

When Ambrose [Bishop of Milan] heard of this deplorable catastrophe, he went out to meet the Emperor, who—on his return to Milan—desired as usual to enter the holy church, but Ambrose prohibited his entrance, saying, "You do not reflect, it seems, O Emperor, on the guilt you have incurred by that great massacre; but now that your fury is appeased, do you not perceive the enormity of your crime? You must not be dazzled by the splendor of the purple you wear, and be led to forget the weakness of the body which it clothes. Your subjects, O Emperor, are of the same nature as yourself, and not only so, but are likewise your fellow servants; for there is one Lord and Ruler of all, and He is the Maker of all creatures, whether princes of people. How would you look upon the temple of the one Lord of all? How could you lift up in prayer hands steeped in the blood of so unjust a massacre? Depart then, and do not by a second crime add to the guilt of the first."

The Emperor, who had been brought up in the knowledge of Holy Writ, and who knew well the distinction between the ecclesiastical and the temporal power, submitted to the rebuke, and with many tears and groans returned to his palace. More than eight months after, occurred the festival of our Saviour's birth. The Emperor shut himself up in his palace . . . and shed floods of tears.

[After vain attempts by intermediaries to appease the bishop, Theodosius at last went to Ambrose privately and besought mercy, saying], "I beseech you, in consideration of the mercy of our common Lord, to unloose me from these bonds, and not to shut the door which is opened by the Lord to all that truly repent." [Ambrose stipulated that the Emperor should prove his repentance by recalling his unjust decrees, and especially by ordering] "that when sentence of death or of proscription has been signed against any one, thirty days are to elapse before execution, and on the expiration of that time the case is to be brought again before you, for your resentment will then be calmed [and you can justly decide the issue]." The Emperor listened to this advice, and deeming it excellent, he at once ordered the law to be drawn up, and himself signed the document. St. Ambrose then unloosed his bonds.

The Emperor, who was full of faith, now took courage to enter holy church, [where] he prayed neither in a standing, nor in a kneeling posture, but throwing himself on the ground. He tore his hair, struck his forehead, and shed torrents of tears, as he implored forgiveness of God. [Ambrose restored him to favor, but forbade him to come inside the altar rail, ordering his deacon to say], "The priests alone, O Emperor, are permitted to enter within the barriers by the altar. Retire then, and remain with the rest of the laity. A purple robe makes Emperors, but not priests." . . .

[Theodosius uttered some excuses, and meekly obeyed, praising Ambrose for his spirit, and saying], "Ambrose alone deserves the title of 'bishop.'"

Source: Theodoret. "How St Ambrose Humiliated Theodosius the Great." In *Readings in Ancient History. Vol. II: Rome and the West.* Ed. William Sterns Davis. New York: Allyn and Bacon, 1913, pp. 298–300.

3. Ammianus Marcellinus's Account of the Battle of Hadrianople

The battle of Hadrianople (August 378) was one of the first steps leading toward the "fall of the Roman Empire." Described here by the late Roman historian Ammianus Marcellinus, the battle was a devastating defeat for the emperor Valens, who was overwhelmed by Visigothic forces that he had welcomed into the empire two years earlier. The account of the battle, steeped in references to events from ancient Greek and Roman history, reveals the preparations undertaken by both sides in the days and weeks prior to the battle, as well as the chaos of the struggle and the death of many Roman soldiers and the emperor himself. Ammianus also provides a description of the appearance of Valens and his many flaws and misdeeds as emperor.

10. When the day broke which the annals mark as the fifth of the Ides of August, the Roman standards were advanced with haste, the baggage having been placed close to the walls of Hadrianople, under a sufficient guard of soldiers of the legions; the treasures and the chief insignia of the emperor's rank were within the walls, with the prefect and the principal members of the council.

11. Then, having traversed the broken ground which divided the two armies, as the burning day was progressing towards noon, at last, after marching eight miles, our men came in sight of the waggons of the enemy, which had been stated by the scouts to be all arranged in a circle. According to their custom, the barbarian host raised a fierce and hideous yell, while the Roman generals marshalled their line of battle. The right wing of the cavalry was placed in front; the chief portion of the infantry was kept in reserve.

12. But the left wing of the cavalry, of which a considerable number were still straggling on the road, were advancing with speed, though with great difficulty; and while this wing was deploying, not as yet meeting with any obstacle, the barbarians being alarmed at the terrible clang of their arms and the threatening crash of their shields (since a large portion of their own army was still at a distance, under Alatheus and Saphrax, and, though sent for, had not yet arrived), again sent ambassadors to ask for peace.

13. The emperor was offended at the lowness of their rank, and replied, that if they wished to make a lasting treaty, they must send him nobles of sufficient dignity.

They designedly delayed, in order by the fallacious truce which subsisted during the negotiation to give time for their cavalry to return, whom they looked upon as close at hand; and for our soldiers, already suffering from the summer heat, to become parched and exhausted by the conflagration of the vast plain; as the enemy had, with this object, set fire to the crops by means of burning faggots and fuel. To this evil another was added, that both men and cattle were suffering from extreme hunger.

14. In the meantime Fritigern, being skilful in divining the future, and fearing a doubtful struggle, of his own head sent one of his men as a herald, requesting that some nobles and picked men should at once be sent to him as hostages for his safety, when he himself would fearlessly bring us both military aid and supplies.

15. The proposition of this formidable chief was received with praise and approbation, and the tribune Equitius, a relation of Valens, who was at that time high steward of the palace, was appointed, with general consent, to go with all speed to the barbarians as a hostage. But he refused, because he had once been taken prisoner by the enemy, and had escaped from Dibaltum, so that he feared their vengeful anger; upon this Richomeres voluntarily offered himself, and willingly undertook to go, thinking it a bold action, and one becoming a brave man; and so he set out, bearing vouchers of his rank and high birth.

16. And as he was on his way towards the enemy's camp, the accompanying archers and Scutarii, who on that occasion were under the command of Bacurius, a native of Iberia, and of Cassio, yielded, while on their march, to an indiscreet impetuosity, and on approaching the enemy, first attacked them rashly, and then by a cowardly flight disgraced the beginning of the campaign.

17. This ill-timed attack frustrated the willing services of Richomeres, as he was not permitted to proceed; in the mean time the cavalry of the Goths had returned with Alatheus and Saphrax, and with them a battalion of Alani; these descending from the mountains like a thunderbolt, spread confusion and slaughter among all whom in their rapid charge they came across.

XIII

§ 1. AND while arms and missiles of all kinds were meeting in fierce conflict, and Bellona, blowing her mournful trumpet, was raging more fiercely than usual, to inflict disaster on the Romans, our men began to retreat; but presently, roused by the reproaches of their officers, they made a fresh stand, and the battle increased like a conflagration, terrifying our soldiers, numbers of whom were pierced by strokes from the javelins hurled at them, and from arrows.

2. Then the two lines of battle dashed against each other, like the beaks (or rams) of ships, and thrusting with all their might, were tossed to and fro, like the waves of the sea. Our left wing had advanced actually up to the wagons, with the intent to push on still further if they were properly supported; but they were deserted by the rest of the cavalry, and so pressed upon by the superior numbers of the enemy, that they were overwhelmed and beaten down, like the ruin of a vast rampart. Presently our infantry also was left unsupported, while the different companies became so huddled together that a soldier could hardly draw his sword, or withdraw his hand after he had once stretched it out. And by this time such clouds of dust arose that it was scarcely possible to see the sky, which resounded with horrible cries; and in consequence, the darts, which were bearing death on every side, reached their mark, and fell with deadly effect, because no one could see them beforehand so as to guard against them.

3. But when the barbarians, rushing on with their enormous host, beat down our horses and men, and left no spot to which our ranks could fall back to deploy, while they were so closely packed that it was impossible to escape by forcing a way through them, our men at last began to despise death, and again took to their swords and slew all they encountered, while with mutual blows of battle-axes, helmets and breastplates were dashed in pieces.

4. Then you might see the barbarian towering in his fierceness, hissing or shouting, fall with his legs pierced through, or his right hand cut off, sword and all, or his side transfixed, and still, in the last gasp of life, casting round him defiant glances. The plain was covered with carcasses, strewing the mutual ruin of the combatants; while the groans of the dying, or of men fearfully wounded, were intense, and caused great dismay all around.

5. Amidst all this great tumult and confusion, our infantry were exhausted by toil and danger, till at last they had neither strength left to fight, nor spirits to plan anything; their spears were broken by the frequent collisions, so that they were forced to content themselves with their drawn swords, which they thrust into the dense battalions of the enemy, disregarding their own safety, and seeing that every possibility of escape was cut off from them.

6. The ground, covered with streams of blood, made their feet slip, so that all that they endeavored to do was to sell their lives as dearly as possible; and with such vehemence did they resist their enemies who pressed on them, that some were even killed by their own weapons. At last one black pool of blood disfigured everything, and wherever the eye turned, it could see nothing but piled-up heaps of dead, and lifeless corpses trampled on without mercy.

7. The sun being now high in the heavens, having traversed the sign of Leo, and reached the abode of the heavenly Virgo, scorched the Romans, who were emaciated by hunger, worn out with toil, and scarcely able to support even the weight of their armor. At last our columns were entirely beaten back by the overpowering weight of the barbarians, and so they took to disorderly flight, which is the only resource in extremity, each man trying to save himself as well as he could.

8. While they were all flying and scattering themselves over roads with which they were unacquainted, the emperor, bewildered with terrible fear, made his way over heaps of dead, and fled to the battalions of the Lancearii and the Mattiarii, who, till the superior numbers of the enemy became wholly irresistible, stood firm and immovable. As soon as he saw him, Trajan exclaimed that all hope was lost, unless the emperor, thus deserted by his guards, could be protected by the aid of his foreign allies.

9. When this exclamation was heard, a count named Victor hastened to bring up with all speed the Batavians, who were placed in the reserve, and who ought to have been near at hand, to the emperor's assistance; but as none of them could be found, he too retreated, and in a similar manner Richomeres and Saturninus saved themselves from danger.

10. So now, with rage flashing in their eyes, the barbarians pursued our men, who were in a state of torpor, the warmth of their veins having deserted them. Many were slain without knowing who smote them; some were overwhelmed by the mere weight of the crowd which pressed upon them; and some were slain by wounds inflicted by their own comrades. The barbarians spared neither those who yielded nor those who resisted.

11. Besides these, many half slain lay blocking up the roads, unable to endure the torture of their wounds; and heaps of dead horses were piled up and filled the plain with their carcasses. At last a dark moonless night put an end to the irremediable disaster which cost the Roman state so dear.

12. Just when it first became dark, the emperor being among a crowd of common soldiers, as it was believed—for no one said either that he had seen him, or been near him—was mortally wounded with an arrow, and, very shortly after, died, though his body was never found. For as some of the enemy loitered for a long time about the field in order to plunder the dead, none of the defeated army or of the inhabitants ventured to go to them.

13. A similar fate befell the Cæsar Decius, when fighting vigorously against the barbarians; for he was thrown by his horse falling, which he had been unable to hold, and was plunged into a swamp, out of which he could never emerge, nor could his body be found.

14. Others report that Valens did not die immediately, but that he was borne by a small body of picked soldiers and eunuchs to a cabin in the neighborhood, which was strongly built, with two stories; and that while these unskillful hands were tending his wounds, the cottage was surrounded by the enemy, though they did not know who was in it; still, however, he was saved from the disgrace of being made a prisoner.

XIV

§ 1. SUCH was the death of Valens, when he was about fifty years old, and had reigned rather less than fourteen years. We will now describe his virtues, which were known to many, and his vices.

2. He was a faithful and steady friend—a severe chastiser of ambition—a rigid upholder of both military and civil discipline—always careful that no one should assume importance on account of any relationship to himself; slow both in conferring office, and in taking it away; a very just ruler of the provinces, all of which he protected from injury, as if each had been his own house; devoting singular care to the lessening the burdens of the state, and never permitting any increase of taxation. He was very moderate in the exaction of debts due to the state, but a vehement and implacable foe to all thieves, and to every one convicted of peculations; nor in affairs of this kind was the East, by its own confession, ever better treated under any other emperor.

3. Besides all this, he was liberal with due regard to moderation, of which quality there are many examples, one of which it will be sufficient to mention here:— As in palaces there are always some persons covetous of the possessions of others, if any one petitioned for lapsed property, or anything else which it was usual to apply for, he made a proper distinction between just and unjust claims, and when he gave it to the petitioner, while reserving full liberty to any one to raise objections, he often associated the successful candidate with three or four partners, in order that those covetous suitors might conduct themselves with more moderation, when they saw the profits for which they were so eager diminished by this device.

4. Of the edifices, which in the different cities and towns he either repaired or built from their foundations, I will say nothing (to avoid prolixity), allowing those things to speak for themselves. These qualities, in my opinion, deserve the imitation of all good men. Now let us enumerate his vices.

5. He was an immoderate coveter of great wealth; impatient of labor, he affected an extreme severity, and was too much inclined to cruelty; his

behavior was rude and rough; and he was little imbued with skill either in war or in the liberal arts. He willingly sought profit and advantage in the miseries of others, and was more than ever intolerable in straining ordinary offences into sedition or treason; he cruelly encompassed the death or ruin of wealthy nobles.

6. This also was unendurable, that while he wished to have it appear that all actions and suits were decided according to the law, and while the investigation of such affairs was delegated to judges especially selected as the most proper to decide them, he still would not allow any decision to be given which was contrary to his own pleasure. He was also insulting, passionate, and always willing to listen to all informers, without the least distinction as to whether the charges which they advanced were true or false. And this vice is one very much to be dreaded, even in private affairs of everyday occurrence.

7. He was dilatory and sluggish; of a swarthy complexion; had a cast in one eye, a blemish, however, which was not visible at a distance; his limbs were well set; his figure was neither tall nor short; he was knock-kneed, and rather pot-bellied.

8. This is enough to say about Valens: and the recollection of his contemporaries will fully testify that this account is a true one. But we must not omit to mention that when he had learnt that the oracle of the tripod, which we have related to have been moved by Patricius and Hilanus, contained those three prophetic lines, the last of which is,—

"Ἐν πεδίοισι Μίμαντος ἀλαλκομένοισιν ἄρηα."
    "Repelling murd'rous war in Mimas' plain;"

—he, being void of accomplishments and illiterate, despised them at first; but as his calamities increased, he became filled with abject fear, and, from a recollection of this same prophecy, began to dread the very name of Asia, where he had been informed by learned men that both Homer and Cicero had spoken of the Mountain of Mimas over the town of Erythræ.

9. Lastly,—after his death, and the departure of the enemy, it is said that a monument was found near the spot where he is believed to have died, with a stone fixed into it inscribed with Greek characters, indicating that some ancient noble of the name of Mimas was buried there.

Source: The Roman History of Ammianus Marcellinus. Trans. C.D. Yonge. London: G. Bell and Sons, Ltd., 1911, pp. 609–18.

4. Pope Leo I, the Great, Defends Rome against Attila the Hun

During the fifth century, the forces of Attila the Hun terrorized the Roman Empire and even invaded deep into the heart of Italy. Reaching Rome in 453, Attila was prepared to sack the city, which had already been sacked earlier in the century in 410. He was met outside the gates by Pope Leo the Great, whose persuasive powers and the timely appearance of the spirits of St. Peter and St. Paul alongside the pope convinced Attila to withdraw and leave the city in peace. Prosper, a Christian chronicler, writing about 455, provides an account of Attila's march on Rome and its miraculous defense by the pope and the Apostles.

Now Attila, having once more collected his forces which had been scattered in Gaul [at the battle of Chalons], took his way through Pannonia into Italy. . . . To the emperor and the senate and Roman people none of all the proposed plans to oppose the enemy seemed so practicable as to send legates to the most savage king and beg for peace. Our most blessed Pope Leo—trusting in the help of God, who never fails the righteous in their trials—undertook the task, accompanied by Avienus, a man of consular rank, and the prefect Trygetius. And the outcome was what his faith had foreseen; for when the king had received the embassy, he was so impressed by the presence of the high priest that he ordered his army to five up warfare and, after he had promised peace, he departed beyond the Danube.

In a life of Leo the Great by some later author, whose name is unknown to us, the episode as told by Prosper has been developed into a miraculous tale calculated to meet the taste of the time:

Attila, the leader of the Huns, who was called the scourge of God, came into Italy, inflamed with fury, after he had laid waste with most savage frenzy Thrace and Illyricum, Macedonia and Moesia, Achaia and Greece, Pannonia and Germany. He was utterly cruel in inflicting torture, greedy in plundering, insolent in abuse. . . . He destroyed Aquileia from the foundations and razed to the ground those regal cities, Pavia and Milan; he laid waste many other towns, (1) and was rushing down upon Rome.

Then Leo had compassion on the calamity of Italy and Rome, and with one of the consuls and a large part of the Roman senate he went to meet Attila. The old man of harmless simplicity, venerable in his gray hair and his majestic garb, ready of his own will to give himself entirely for the defense of his flock, went forth to meet the tyrant who was destroying all things. He met Attila, it is said, in the neighborhood of the river Mincio, and he spoke to the grim monarch, saying: "The senate and the people of Rome, once conquerors of the world, now indeed vanquished, come before thee as suppliants. We pray for mercy and deliverance. O Attila, thou king of kings, thou couldst have no greater glory than to see suppliant at thy feet this people before whom once all peoples and kings lay suppliant. Thou hast subdued, O Attila, the whole circle of the lands which it was granted to the Romans, victors over all peoples, to conquer. Now we pray that thou, who hast conquered others, shouldst conquer thyself. The people have felt thy scourge; now as suppliants they would feel thy mercy."

As Leo said these things, Attila stood looking upon his venerable garb and aspect, silent, as if thinking deeply. And lo, suddenly there were seen the apostles Peter and Paul, clad like bishops, standing by Leo, the one on the right hand, the other on the left. They held swords stretched out over his head, and threatened Attila with death if he did not obey the pope's command. Wherefore Attila was appeased by Leo's intercession—he who had rages as one mad. He straightway promised a lasting peace and withdrew beyond the Danube.

Source: "How Pope Leo the Great Saved Rome from Attila." In *Readings in European History, Vol. 1.* Ed. J.H. Robinson. New York: Gin & Company, 1904, pp. 49–51.

5. Augustine of Hippo's Definition of a True Commonwealth

Written in response to the devastating sack of Rome by the Goths in 410, Augustine's *City of God* sought to defend Christianity against the pagans who blamed it for the sack of the city. One of the greatest theologians in the history of the church, Augustine provided a philosophy of history in his great work as well as one of the most substantial commentaries of the faith ever written. In the *City of God*, Augustine developed the idea that there are two cities on earth—an earthly city and a city of God—and that members of the city of God are on pilgrimage in this world on their way to the heavenly city. In this celebrated passage from book X, Augustine addresses the definition of a republic and whether a true republic could ever exist in the world. Although Augustine himself did not believe a true commonwealth could exist in this sinful world, later Christian rulers and theologians, notably the Carolingian kings and their advisors, saw Augustine's work as a blueprint for the establishment of a Christian kingdom.

21. Whether there ever was a Roman republic answering to the definitions of Scipio in Cicero's dialogue.

This, then, is the place where I should fulfill the promise gave in the second book of this work, and explain, as briefly and clearly as possible, that if we are to accept the definitions laid down by Scipio in Cicero's *De Republica,* there never was a Roman republic; for he briefly defines a republic as the weal of the people. And if this definition be true, there never was a Roman republic, for the people's weal was never attained among the Romans. For the people, according to his definition, is an assemblage associated by a common acknowledgement of right and by a community of interests. And what he means by a common acknowledgment of right he explains at large showing that a republic cannot be administered without justice. Where, therefore, there is no true justice there can be no right. For that which is done by right is justly done, and what is unjustly done cannot be done by right. For the unjust inventions of men are neither to be considered nor spoken of as rights; for even they themselves say that right is that which flows from the fountain of justice, and deny the definition which is commonly given by those who misconceive the matter, that right is that which is useful to the stronger party. Thus, where there is not true justice there can be no assemblage of men associated by a common acknowledgment of right, and therefore there can be no people, as defined by Scipio or Cicero; and if no people, then no weal of the people, but only of some promiscuous multitude unworthy of the name of people. Consequently, if the republic is the weal of the people, and there is no people if it be not associated by a common acknowledgment of right, and if there is no rights where there is no justice, then most certainly it follows that there is no republic where there is no justice. Further, justice is that virtue which gives every one his due. Where, then, is the justice of man, when he deserts the true God and yields himself to impure demons? Is this to give every one his due? Or is he who keeps back a piece of ground from the purchaser, and gives it to a man who has no right to it, unjust, while he who keeps back himself from the God who made him, and serves wicked spirits, is just?

This same book, *De Republica*, advocates the cause of justice against injustice with great force and keenness. The pleading for injustice against justice was first heard, and it was asserted that without injustice a republic could neither increase nor even subsist, for it was laid down as an absolutely unassailable position that it is unjust for some men to rule and some to serve; and yet the imperial city to which the republic belongs cannot rule her provinces without having recourse to this injustice. It was replied in behalf of justice, that this ruling of the provinces is just, because servitude may be advantageous to the provincials, and is so when rightly administered, hat is to say, when lawless men are prevented from doing harm. And further, as they became worse and worse so long as they were free, they will improve by subjection. To confirm this reasoning, there is added an eminent example drawn from nature: for "why," it is asked, "does God rule man, the soul, the body, the reason the passions and other vicious parts of the soul?" This example leaves no doubt that, to some, servitude is useful; and indeed, to serve God is useful to all. And it is when the soul serves God that it exercises a right control over the body; and in the soul itself the reason must be subject to God if it is to govern as it ought the passions and other vices. Hence, when a man does not serve God, what justice can we ascribe to him, since in this case his soul cannot exercise a just control over the body, nor his reason over his vices? And if there is no justice in such an individual, certainly there can be none in a community composed of such persons. Here, therefore, there is not that common acknowledgment of right which makes an assemblage of men a people whose affairs we call a republic. And why need I speak of the advantageousness, the common participation in which, according to the definition, makes a people? For although, if you choose to regard the matter attentively, you will see that there is nothing advantageous to those who live godlessly, as every one lives who does not serve God but demons, whose wickedness you may measure by their desire to receives the worship of men though they are most impure spirits, yet what I have said of the common acknowledgment of right is enough to demonstrate that, according to the above definition, there can be no people, and therefore no republic, where there is no justice. For if they assert that in their republic the Romans did not serve unclean spirits, but good and holy gods, must we therefore again reply to this evasion, though already we have said enough, and more than enough, to expose it? He must be an uncommonly stupid, or a shamelessly contentious person, who has read through the foregoing books to this point, and can yet question whether the Romans served wicked and impure demons. But, not to speak of their character, it is written in the law of the true God, "He that scarificeth unto any god save unto the Lord only, he shall be utterly destroyed." He, therefore, who uttered so menacing a commandment decreed that no worship should be given either to good or bad gods.

Source: The Works of Aurelius Augustine, Bishop of Hippo. Vol. II: City of God. Ed. Rev. Marcus Dods, MA. Edinburgh: Murray and Gibb, 1871, Book 19, Chapter 21.

6. Augustine of Hippo's Conversion Experience

Augustine of Hippo, one of the Church Fathers and one of the greatest theologians in the history of the church, left an extensive literary legacy. Along with his meditation on history and philosophy in his *City of God,* Augustine's most famous and influential work was his Confessions. A work of autobiography and a prayer offered to God, Confessions depicts Augustine's spiritual journey toward God and his conversion to Catholic Christianity. The work describes Augustine's early sinful life and his long relationship with a woman who remains anonymous, as well as his interest in classical philosophy, and long adherence to Manichaeanism. The excerpt that follows describes the famous scene where Augustine hears a child's voice calling him to take up and read, which leads him to read the Bible and convert to the Christian faith.

Chapter 11

Thus I was soul-sick, and tormented, accusing myself much more severely than was my wont, rolling and turning myself in my chain, until they were wholly broken, by which I was held. And You, O Lord, pressed upon me in my inward parts by a severe mercy, redoubling the lashes of fear and shame, lest I should again give way, and not bursting that same slight remaining tie, it should recover strength, and bind me the faster. For I said with myself, "Be it done now, be it done now." And as I spoke, I all but enacted it: I all but did it, and did it not: yet I sunk not back to my former state, but kept my stand hard by, and took breath. And I essayed again, and wanted somewhat less of it, and somewhat less, and all but touched, and laid hold of it. Yet I came not at it, nor touched nor laid hold of it, hesitating to die to death and to live to life. The worse whereto I was inured, prevailed more with me than the better whereto I was unused. The very moment where I was to become other than I was, the nearer it approached me, the greater horror did it strike into me, yet did it not strike me back, nor turned me away, but held me in suspense.

The very toys of toys, and vanities of vanities, my ancient temptations, still held me. They plucked my garment, and whispered softly, "Do you cast us off? From that moment shall we no more be with you forever? From that moment shall not this or that be lawful for you forever?" What defilements did they suggest! What shame! And now I much less than half heard them, and not openly showing themselves and contradicting me, but muttering as it were behind my back, and privately plucking me, as I was departing, but to look back on them. Yet they did slow me, so that I hesitated to burst and shake myself free from them, and to spring over whither I was called, a violent habit saying to me, "Think you, can you live without them?"

But now it spoke very faintly. . . .

Chapter 12

But when a deep consideration from the secret bottom of my soul had drawn together and heaped up all my misery in the sight of my heart; there arose a mighty storm, bringing a mighty shower of tears. That I might pour forth wholly, in its natural expressions, I rose from Alypius. Solitude was suggested to me as fitter for the business of weeping, so I retired so far that even his presence could not be a burden to me. Thus was it then with me, and he perceived something of it; for something I suppose I had spoken, wherein the tones of my voice appeared choked with weeping, and so had risen up. He then remained where we were sitting, most extremely astonished. I cast myself down I know not how, under a certain fig-tree, giving full vent to my tears. The floods of mine eyes gushed out an acceptable sacrifice to You Oh God. And, not indeed in these words, yet to this purpose, I spoke much to You: and You, O Lord, how long? how long, Lord, will You be angry for ever? Remember not my former iniquities, for I felt that I was held by them. I sent up these sorrowful words: "How long, how long, tomorrow, and tomorrow? Why not now? Why is there not an end to my uncleanness?"

So was I speaking and weeping in the most bitter contrition of my heart, when, lo! I heard from a neighboring house a voice, as of boy or girl, I know not, chanting, and oft repeating, "Take up and read; Take up and read." Instantly, my countenance altered, I began to think most intently whether children were wont in any kind of play to sing such words, nor could I remember ever to have heard the like. So checking the torrent of my tears, I arose, interpreting it to be no other than a command from God to open the book, and read the first chapter I should find. For I had heard of Antony (the famous Egyptian hermit), that coming in during the reading of the Gospel, he received the admonition, as if what was being read was spoken to him: "Go, sell all that you have, and give to the poor, and you shall have treasure in heaven, and come and follow me." By such oracle he was forthwith converted. Eagerly then I returned to the place where Alypius was sitting, for there had I laid the volume of the Apostle when I left. I seized, opened, and in silence read that section on which my eyes first fell: "Not in rioting and drunkenness, not in chambering and wantonness, not in strife and envying; but put you on the Lord Jesus Christ, and make not provision for the flesh, in concupiscence." No further would I read, nor needed I: for instantly at the end of this sentence, by a light as it were of serenity infused into my heart, all the darkness of doubt vanished away.

Then putting my finger between, or some other mark, I shut the volume, and with a calmed countenance made it known to Alypius. And what was wrought in him, which I knew not, he thus showed me. He asked to see what I had read. I showed him, and he looked even further than I had read, and I knew not what followed. This followed, "him that is weak in the faith, receive," which he applied to himself, and disclosed to me. And by this admonition was he strengthened; without any turbulent delay he joined me. Thence we went in to my mother; we told her; she rejoiced. We related the order in which it took place. She leapt for joy, and triumphed, and blessed You, Who are able to do more than we ask or think. For she perceived that You had given her more for me, than she was wont to beg by her pitiful and most sorrowful groanings. For You converted me to Yourself, so that I sought neither wife, nor any hope of this world, standing in that rule of faith, where You had showed me unto her in a vision, so many years before. And You did convert her mourning into joy, much more plentiful than she had desired.

Source: "Augustine: Conversion (399 CE)." In *World History: Ancient and Medieval Eras.* Santa Barbara, CA: ABC-CLIO, 2012. Web. 6 May 2012.

7. The Anglo-Saxon Conquest of England according to Bede

During the barbarian invasions of the fifth century, numerous Germanic peoples entered the Roman Empire and created independent kingdoms on former Roman territory. In England, the Angles, Saxons, and Jutes were able to establish kingdoms following the

Roman withdrawal. In the eighth century, Bede, one of the greatest of early medieval historians, described how England was conquered by the Anglo-Saxons. Led by the chieftains Hengist and Horsa, the Anglo-Saxons had been invited by the Britons into their country to protect them and maintain order after the Romans withdrew. Hengist and Horsa exploited this opportunity to seize control of the land, which, Bede suggests, was a punishment sent by God for the sins of the Britons.

In the year of our Lord 449, Marcian, the forty-sixth from Augustus, being made emperor with Valentinian, ruled the empire seven years. Then the nation of the Angles, or Saxons, being invited by the aforesaid king, arrived in Britain with three ships of war and had a place in which to settle assigned to them by the same king, in the eastern part of the island, on the pretext of fighting in defence of their country, whilst their real intentions were to conquer it. Accordingly they engaged with the enemy, who were come from the north to give battle, and the Saxons obtained the victory. When the news of their success and of the fertility of the country, and the cowardice of the Britons, reached their own home, a more considerable fleet was quickly sent over, bringing a greater number of men, and these, being added to the former army, made up an invincible force. The newcomers received of the Britons a place to inhabit among them, upon condition that they should wage war against their enemies for the peace and security of the country, whilst the Britons agreed to furnish them with pay. Those who came over were of the three most powerful nations of Germany—Saxons, Angles, and Jutes. From the Jutes are descended the people, of Kent, and of the Isle of Wight, including those in the province of the West-Saxons who are to this day called Jutes, seated opposite to the Isle of Wight. From the Saxons, that is, the country which is now called Old Saxony, came the East-Saxons, the South-Saxons, and the West Saxons. From the Angles, that is, the country which is called Angulus, and which is said, from that time, to have remained desert to this day, between the provinces of the Jutes and the Saxons, are descended the East-Angles, the Midland-Angles, the Mercians, all the race of the Northumbrians, that is, of those nations that dwell on the north side of the river Humber, and the other nations of the Angles. The first commanders are said to have been the two brothers Hengist and Horsa. Of these Horsa was afterwards slain in battle by the Britons, and a monument, bearing his name, is still in existence in the eastern parts of Kent. They were the sons of Victgilsus, whose father was Vitta, son of Vecta, son of Woden; from whose stock the royal race of many provinces trace their descent. In a short time, swarms of the aforesaid nations came over into the island, and the foreigners began to increase so much, that they became a source of terror to the natives themselves who had invited them. Then, having on a sudden entered into league with the Picts, whom they had by this time repelled by force of arms, they began to turn their weapons against their allies. At first, they obliged them to furnish a greater quantity of provisions; and, seeking an occasion of quarrel, protested, that unless more plentiful supplies were brought them, they would break the league, and ravage all the island; nor were they backward in putting their threats into execution. In short, the fire kindled by the hands of the pagans, proved God's just vengeance for the crimes of the people; not unlike that which, being of old lighted by the Chaldeans, consumed the walls and all the buildings of Jerusalem. For here, too, through the agency of the pitiless conqueror, yet by the disposal of the just Judge, it ravaged all the neighbouring cities and country, spread the conflagration from the eastern to the western sea, without any opposition, and overran the whole face of the doomed island. Public as well as private buildings were overturned; the priests were everywhere slain before the altars; no respect was shown for office, the prelates with the people were destroyed with fire and sword; nor were there any left to bury those who had been thus cruelly slaughtered. Some of the miserable remnant, being taken in the mountains, were butchered in heaps. Others, spent with hunger, came forth and submitted themselves to the enemy, to undergo for the sake of food perpetual servitude, if they were not killed upon the spot. Some, with sorrowful hearts, fled beyond the seas. Others, remaining in their own country, led a miserable life of terror and anxiety of mind among the mountains, woods and crags.

Source: Bede's Ecclesiastical History of England: A Revised Translation. Ed. A.M. Seller. London: George Bell and Sons, 1907, Book 1, Chapter 15.

8. Bede's Description of the Life and Works, Including the Conversion of England, of Pope Gregory I, the Great

One of the greatest and most influential of early medieval historians, Bede describes the process of the conversion of the Anglo-Saxon people and the triumph of Christianity in England in his great work of history. One of the key figures in that history was Pope Gregory I, who sent an evangelical mission to England in 595 that would begin the process of spreading the faith there. Bede provides a moving and respectful account of the pope in the following passage and recounts the episode in Gregory's life when the pope first encountered the English people and was inspired to work for their conversion.

Chap. I

AT this time, that is, in the year of our Lord 605, the blessed Pope Gregory, after having most gloriously governed the Roman Apostolic see thirteen years, six months, and ten days, died, and was translated to an eternal abode in the kingdom of Heaven. Of whom, seeing that by his zeal he converted our nation, the English, from the power of Satan to the faith of Christ, it behoves us to discourse more at large in our Ecclesiastical History, for we may rightly, nay, we must, call him our apostle; because, as soon as he began to wield the pontifical power over all the world, and was placed over the Churches long before converted to the true faith, he made our nation, till then enslaved to idols, the Church of Christ, so that concerning him we may use those words of the Apostle; "if he be not an apostle to others, yet doubtless he is to us; for the seal of his apostleship are we in the Lord."

He was by nation a Roman, son of Gordianus, tracing his descent from ancestors that were not only noble, but religious. Moreover Felix, once bishop of the same Apostolic see, a man of great honour in Christ and in the Church, was his forefather, Nor did he show his nobility in religion by less strength of devotion than his parents and kindred. But that nobility of this world which was seen in him, by the help of the Divine Grace, he used only to gain the glory of eternal dignity; for soon quitting his secular habit, he entered a monastery, wherein he began to live with so much grace of perfection that (as he was wont afterwards with tears to testify) his mind was above all transitory things; that he rose superior to all that is subject to change; that he used to think of nothing but what was heavenly; that, whilst detained by the body, he broke through the bonds of the flesh by contemplation; and that he even loved death, which is a penalty to almost all men, as the entrance into life, and the reward of his labors. This he used to say of himself, not to boast of his progress in virtue, but rather to bewail the falling off which he imagined he had sustained through his pastoral charge. Indeed, once in a private conversation with his deacon, Peter, after having enumerated the former virtues of his soul, he added sorrowfully, "But now, on account of the pastoral charge, it is entangled with the affairs of laymen, and, after so fair an appearance of inward peace, is defiled with the dust of earthly action. And having wasted itself on outward things, by turning aside to the affairs of many men, even when it desires the inward things, it returns to them undoubtedly impaired. I therefore consider what I endure, I consider what I have lost, and when I behold what I have thrown away; that which I bear appears the more grievous."

So spake the holy man constrained by his great humility. But it behoves us to believe that he lost nothing of his monastic perfection by reason of his pastoral charge, but rather that he gained greater profit through the labour of converting many, than by the former calm of his private life, and chiefly because, whilst holding the pontifical office, he set about organizing his house like a monastery. And when first drawn from the monastery, ordained to the ministry of the altar, and sent to Constantinople as representative of the Apostolic see, though he now took part in the secular affairs of the palace, yet he did not abandon the fixed course of his heavenly life; for some of the brethren of his monastery, who had followed him to the royal city in their brotherly love, he employed for the better observance of monastic rule, to the end that at all times, by their example, as he writes himself, he might be held fast to the calm shore of prayer, as it were, with the cable of an anchor, whilst he should be tossed up and down by the ceaseless waves of worldly affairs; and daily in the intercourse of studious reading with them, strengthen his mind shaken with temporal concerns. By their company he was not only guarded against the assaults of the world, but more and more roused to the exercises of a heavenly life.

For they persuaded him to interpret by a mystical exposition the book of the blessed Job, which is involved in great obscurity; nor could he refuse to undertake that work, which brotherly affection imposed on him for the future benefit of many; but in a wonderful manner, in five and thirty books of exposition, he taught how that same book is to be understood literally; how to be referred to the mysteries of Christ and the Church; and in what sense it is to be adapted to every one of the faithful. This work he began as papal representative in the royal city, but finished it at Rome after being made pope. Whilst he was still in the royal city, by the help of the grace of Catholic truth, he crushed in its first rise a new heresy which sprang up there, concerning the state of our resurrection. For Eutychius, bishop of that city, taught, that our body, in the glory of resurrection, would be impalpable, and more subtle than wind and air. The blessed Gregory hearing this, proved by force of truth, and by the instance of the Resurrection of our Lord, that this doctrine was every way opposed to the orthodox faith. For the Catholic faith holds that our body, raised by the glory of immortality, is indeed rendered subtle by the effect of spiritual power, but is palpable by the reality of nature; according to the example of our Lord's Body, concerning which, when risen from the dead, He Himself says to His disciples, "Handle Me and see, for a spirit hath not flesh and bones, as ye see Me have." In maintaining this faith, the venerable Father Gregory so earnestly strove against the rising heresy, and with the help of the most pious emperor, Tiberius Constantine, so fully suppressed it, that none has been since found to revive it.

He likewise composed another notable book, the "Liber Pastoralis," wherein he clearly showed what sort of persons ought to be preferred to rule the Church; how such rulers ought to live; with how much discrimination they ought to instruct the different classes of their hearers, and how seriously to reflect every day on their own frailty. He also wrote forty homilies on the Gospel, which he divided equally into two volumes; and composed four books of Dialogues, in which, at the request of his deacon, Peter, he recounted the virtues of the more renowned saints of Italy, whom he had either known or heard of, as a pattern of life for posterity; to the end that, as he taught in his books of Expositions what virtues men ought to strive after, so by describing the miracles of saints, he might make known the glory of those' virtues. Further, in twenty-two homilies, he showed how much light is latent in the first and last parts of the prophet Ezekiel, which seemed the most obscure. Besides which, he wrote the "Book of Answers," to the questions of the holy Augustine, the first bishop of the English nation, as we have shown above, inserting the same book entire in this history; and the useful little "Synodical Book," which he composed with the bishops of Italy on necessary matters of the Church; as well as private letters to certain persons. And it is the more wonderful that he could write so many lengthy works, seeing that almost all the time of his youth, to use his own words, he was frequently tormented with internal pain, constantly enfeebled by the weakness of his digestion, and oppressed by a low but persistent fever. But in all these troubles, forasmuch as he carefully reflected that, as the Scripture testifies, "He scourgeth every son whom He receiveth," the more severely he suffered under those present evils, the more he assured himself of his eternal hope.

Thus much may be said of his immortal genius, which could not be crushed by such severe bodily pains. Other popes applied themselves to building churches or adorning them with gold and silver, but Gregory was wholly intent upon gaining souls. Whatsoever money he had, he took care to distribute diligently and give to the poor, that his righteousness, might endure for ever, and his horn be exalted with honour; so that the words of the blessed Job might be truly said of him, "When the ear heard me, then it blessed me; and when the eye saw me, it gave witness to me: because I delivered the poor that cried, and the fatherless, and him that had none to help him. The blessing of him that was ready to perish came upon me, and I caused the widow's heart to sing for, joy. I put on righteousness, and it clothed me; my judgement was as a robe and a diadem. I was eyes to the blind, and feet was I to the lame. I was a father to the poor; and the cause which I knew not, I searched out. And I brake the jaws of the wicked, and plucked the spoil out of his teeth." And a little after: "If I have withheld," says he, "the poor from their desire; or have caused the eyes of the widow to fail; or have eaten my morsel myself alone, and the fatherless hath not eaten thereof: (for from my youth compassion grew up with me, and from my mother's womb it came forth with me."

To his works of piety and righteousness this also may be added, that he saved our nation, by the preachers he sent hither, from the teeth of the old enemy, and made it partaker of eternal liberty. Rejoicing in the faith and salvation of our race, and worthily commending it with praise, he says, in his exposition of the blessed Job, "Behold, the tongue of Britain, which only knew how to utter barbarous cries, has long since begun to raise the Hebrew Hallelujah to the praise of God! Behold, the once swelling ocean now serves prostrate at the feet of the saints; and its wild upheavals, which earthly princes could not subdue with the sword, are now, through the fear of God, bound by the lips of priests with words alone; and the heathen that stood not in awe of troops of warriors, now believes and fears the tongues of the humble! For he has received a message from on high and mighty works are revealed; the strength of the knowledge of God is given him, and restrained by the fear of the Lord, he dreads to do evil, and with all his heart desires to attain to everlasting grace." In which words the blessed Gregory shows us this also, that St. Augustine and his companions brought the English to receive the truth, not only by the preaching of words, but also by showing forth heavenly signs.

The blessed Pope Gregory, among other things, caused Masses to be celebrated in the churches of the holy Apostles, Peter and Paul, over their bodies. And in the celebration of Masses, he added three petitions of the utmost perfection: "And dispose our days in thy peace, and bid us to be preserved from eternal damnation, and to be numbered in the flock of thine elect."

He governed the Church in the days of the Emperors Mauritius and Phocas, and passing out of this life in the second year of the same Phocas, departed to the true life which is in Heaven. His body was buried in the church of the blessed Apostle Peter before the sacristy, on the 12th day of March, to rise one day in the same body in glory with the rest of the holy pastors of the Church. On his tomb was written this epitaph:

> Receive, Earth, his body taken from thine own; thou canst restore it, when God calls to life. His spirit rises to the stars; the claims of death shall not avail against him, for death itself is but the way to new life. In this tomb are laid the limbs of a great pontiff, who yet lives for ever in all places in countless deeds of mercy. Hunger and cold he overcame with food and raiment, and shielded souls from the enemy by his holy teaching. And whatsoever he taught in word, that he fulfilled in deed, that he might be a pattern, even as he spake words of mystic meaning. By his guiding love he brought the Angles to Christ, gaining armies for the Faith from a new people. This was thy toil, thy task, thy care, thy aim as shepherd, to offer to thy Lord abundant increase of the flock. So, Consul of God, rejoice in this thy triumph, for now thou hast the reward of thy works for evermore.

Nor must we pass by in silence the story of the blessed Gregory, handed down to us by the tradition of our ancestors, which explains his earnest care for the salvation of our nation. It is said that one day, when some merchants had lately arrived at Rome, many things were exposed for sale in the market place, and much people resorted thither to buy: Gregory himself went with the rest, and saw among other wares some boys put up for sale, of fair complexion, with pleasing countenances, and very beautiful hair. When he beheld them, he asked, it is said, from what region or country they were brought? and was told, from the island of Britain, and that the inhabitants were like that in appearance. He again inquired whether those islanders were Christians, or still involved in the errors of paganism, and was informed that they were pagans. Then fetching a deep sigh from the bottom of his heart, "Alas! what pity," said he, "that the author of darkness should own men of such fair countenances; and that with such grace of outward form, their minds should be void of inward grace. He therefore again asked, what was the name of that nation? and was answered, that they were called Angles. "Right," said he, "for they have an angelic face, and it is meet that such should be co-heirs with the Angels in heaven. What is the name of the province from which they are brought?" It was replied, that the natives of that province were called Deiri. (Note: Southern Northumbria) "Truly are they Deira," said he, "saved from wrath, and called to the mercy of Christ. How is the king of that called?" They told him his name was Aelli; and he, playing upon the name, said, "Allelujah, the praise of God the Creator must be sung in those parts."

Then he went to the bishop of the Roman Apostolic see (for he was not himself then made pope), and entreated him to send some ministers of the Word into Britain to the nation of the English, that it might be converted to Christ by them; declaring himself ready to carry out that work with the help of God, if the Apostolic Pope should think fit to have it done. But not being then able to perform this task, because, though the Pope was willing to grant his request, yet the citizens of Rome could not be brought to consent that he should depart so far from the city, as soon as he was himself made Pope, he carried out the long-desired work, sending, indeed, other preachers, but himself by his exhortations and prayers helping the preaching to bear fruit. This account, which we have received from a past generation, we have thought fit to insert in our Ecclesiastical History.

Source: Bede's Ecclesiastical History of England: A Revised Translation. Ed. A.M. Seller. London: George Bell and Sons, 1907, Book 2, Chapter 1.

9. Bede's Account of the Synod of Whitby

In his History of the English Church and People, Bede described the key moments in the conversion of England. One of the most important events in that process, discussed in the following excerpt from Bede's history, was the synod of Whitby, which was held in 663 or 664. It was at this synod, presided over by King Oswy of Northumbria to determine the method of calculating the date of Esater, that the fate of the English church was determined. Representatives of the Celtic church and the church of Rome attended the synod, and Oswy and the council accepted the Roman practice of calculating Easter. The king was swayed by the knowledge that Rome was the city of the Apostles Peter and Paul. Following the council, Celtic practices were replaced by Roman traditions in England.

How the question arose about the due time of keeping Easter, with those that came out of Scotland.

At this time, a great and frequently debated question arose about the observance of Easter; those that came from Kent or Gaul affirming, that the Scots celebrated Easter Sunday contrary to the custom of the universal Church. Among them was a most zealous defender of the true Easter, whose name was Ronan, a Scot by nation, but instructed in the rule of ecclesiastical truth in Gaul or Italy. Disputing with Finan, he convinced many, or at least induced them to make a more strict inquiry after the truth; yet he could not prevail upon Finan, but, on the contrary, embittered him the more by reproof, and made him a professed opponent of the truth, for he was of a violent temper. James, formerly the deacon of the venerable Archbishop Paulinus, as has been said above, observed the true and Catholic Easter, with all those that he could instruct in the better way. Queen Eanfled and her followers also observed it as she had seen it practised in Kent, having with her a Kentish priest who followed the Catholic observance, whose name was Romanus.

Thus it is said to have sometimes happened in those times that Easter was twice celebrated in one year; and that when the king, having ended his fast, was keeping Easter, the queen and her followers were still fasting, and celebrating Palm Sunday. Whilst Aidan lived, this difference about the observance of Easter was patiently tolerated by all men, for they well knew, that though he could not keep Easter contrary to the custom of those who had sent him, yet he industriously labored to practise the works of faith, piety, and love, according to the custom of all holy men; for which reason he was deservedly beloved by all, even by those who differed in opinion concerning Easter, and was held in veneration, not only by less important persons, but even by the bishops, Honorius of Canterbury, and Felix of the East Angles.

But after the death of Finan, who succeeded him, when Colman, who was also sent from Scotland, came to be bishop, a greater controversy arose about the observance of Easter, and other rules of ecclesiastical life. Whereupon this question began naturally to influence the thoughts and hearts of many who feared, lest haply, having received the name of Christians, they might run, or have run, in vain. This reached the ears of the rulers, King Oswy and his son Alchfrid. Now Oswy, having been instructed and baptized by the Scots, and being very perfectly skilled in their language, thought nothing better than what they taught; but Alchfrid, having for his teacher in Christianity the learned Wilfrid, who had formerly gone to Rome to study ecclesiastical doctrine, and spent much time at Lyon with Dalfinus, archbishop of Gaul, from whom also he had received the crown of ecclesiastical tonsure, rightly thought that this man's doctrine ought to be preferred before all the traditions of the Scots. For this reason he had also given him a monastery of forty families, at a place called Inhrypum; which, not long before, he had given for a monastery to those that were followers of the Scots; but forasmuch as they afterwards, being left to their choice, preferred to quit the place rather than alter their custom, he gave it to him, whose life and doctrine were worthy of it.

Agilbert, bishop of the West Saxons, a friend of King Alchfrid and of Abbot Wilfrid, had at that time come into the province of the Northumbrians, and was staying some time among them. At the request of Alchfrid, he made Wilfrid a priest in his aforesaid monastery. He had in his company a priest, whose name was Agatho. Since questions concerning Easter and the tonsure and other ecclesiastical matters persisted, a synod (664) was held in the monastery of Streanaeshalch, which signifies the Bay of the Lighthouse, where the Abbess Hilda, a woman devoted to the service of God, then ruled; and that this question should be decided. The kings, both father and son, came thither, and the bishops, Colman with his Scottish clerks, and Agilbert with the priests Agatho and Wilfrid. James and Romanus were on their side; but the Abbess Hilda and her followers were for the Scots, as was also the venerable Bishop Cedd, long before ordained by the Scots, as has been said above, and he acted in that council as a most careful interpreter for both parties.

King Oswy first made an opening speech, in which he said that it behooved those who served one God to observe one rule of life; and as they all expected the same kingdom in heaven, so they ought not to differ in the celebration of the heavenly mysteries; but rather to inquire which was the truer tradition, that it might be followed by all in common; he then commanded his bishop, Colman, first to declare what the custom was which he observed, and whence it derived its origin. Then Colman said, "The Easter which I keep, I received from my elders, who sent me hither as bishop; all our forefathers, men beloved of God, are known to have celebrated it after the same manner; and that it may not seem to any contemptible and worthy to be rejected, it is the same which the blessed John the Evangelist, the disciple specially beloved of our Lord, with all the churches over which he presided, is recorded to have celebrated."

When he had said thus much, and more to the like effect, the king commanded Agilbert to make known the manner of his observance and to show whence derived from its origin, and on what authority he followed it. Agilbert answered, "I beseech you, let my disciple, the priest Wilfrid, speak in my stead, because we both concur with the other followers of the ecclesiastical tradition that are here present, and he can better and more clearly explain our opinion in the English language, than I can by an interpreter."

Then Wilfrid, being ordered by the king to speak, began thus: "The Easter which we keep, we saw celebrated by all at Rome, where the blessed Apostles, Peter and Paul, lived, taught, suffered, and were buried. We saw the same done by all in Italy and in Gaul, when we traveled through those countries for the purpose of study and prayer. We found it observed in Africa, Asia, Egypt, Greece, and all the world, wherever the Church of Christ is spread abroad, among different nations and tongues, at one and the same time; save only among these and their accomplices in obstinacy, I mean the Picts and the Britons, who foolishly, in these two remote islands of the ocean, and only in part even of them, strive to oppose all the rest of the world."

When he had so said, Colman answered, "It is strange that you choose to call our efforts foolish, when we follow the example of so great an Apostle, who was thought worthy to lean on our Lord's bosom, when all the world knows him to have lived most wisely."

Wilfrid replied, " Far be it from us to charge John with folly, for he literally observed the precepts of the Mosaic Law, whilst the Church was still Jewish in many points, and the Apostles, lest they should give cause of offence to the Jews who were among the Gentiles, were not able at once to cast off all the observances of the Law which had been instituted by God . . . So John, according to the custom of the Law, began the celebration of the feast of Easter, on the fourteenth day of the first month, in the evening, not regarding whether the same happened on a Saturday, or any other weekday. But when Peter preached at Rome, being mindful that our Lord arose from the dead, and gave to the world the hope of resurrection, on the first day of the week, he perceived that Easter ought to be kept after this manner: he always awaited the rising of the moon on the fourteenth day of the first month in the evening, according to the custom and precepts of the Law, even as John did. And when that came, if the Lord's day, then called the first day of the week, was the next day, he began that very evening to celebrate Easter, as we all do at the present time. But if the Lord's day did not fall the next morning after the fourteenth moon, but on the sixteenth, or the seventeenth, or any other moon till the twenty-first, he waited for that, and on the Saturday before, in the evening, began to observe the holy solemnity of Easter. Thus it came to pass, that Easter Sunday was only kept from the fifteenth moon to the twenty-first. Nor does this evangelical and apostolic tradition abolish the Law, but rather fulfill it; the command being to keep the passover from the fourteenth moon of the first month in the evening to the twenty-first moon of the same month in the evening; which observance all the successors of the blessed John in Asia, since his death, and all the Church throughout the world, have since followed; and that this is the true Easter, and the only one to be celebrated by the faithful, was not newly decreed by the council of Nicaea but only confirmed afresh; as the history of the Church informs us.

"Thus it is plain, that you, Colman, neither follow the example of John, as you imagine, nor that of Peter, whose tradition you oppose with full knowledge, and that you neither agree with the Law nor the Gospel in the keeping of your Easter. For John, keeping the Paschal time according to the decree of the Mosaic Law, had no regard to the first day of the week, which you do not practise, seeing that you celebrate Easter only on the first day after the Sabbath. Peter celebrated Easter Sunday between the fifteenth and the twenty-first moon, which you do not practise, seeing that you observe Easter Sunday from the fourteenth to the twentieth moon; so that you often begin Easter on the thirteenth moon in the evening, whereof neither the Law made any mention, nor did our Lord, the Author and Giver of the Gospel, on that day either eat the old passover in the evening, or deliver the Sacraments of the New Testament, to be celebrated by the Church, in memory of His Passion, but on the fourteenth. Besides, in your celebration of Easter, you utterly exclude the twenty-first moon, which the Law ordered to be specially observed. Thus, as I have said before, you agree neither with John nor Peter, nor with the Law, nor the Gospel, in the celebration of the greatest festival."

To this Colman rejoined: "Did the holy Anatolius, much commended in the history of the Church, judge contrary to the Law and the Gospel, when he wrote, that

Easter was to be celebrated from the fourteenth to the twentieth moon? Is it to be believed that our most reverend Father Columba and his successors, men beloved by God, who kept Easter after the same manner, judged or acted contrary to the Divine writings? There were many among them, whose sanctity was attested by heavenly signs and miracles; whom I, for my part, doubt not to be saints, and whose life, customs, and discipline I never cease to follow."

"It is evident," said Wilfrid, "that Anatolius was a most holy, learned, and commendable man; but what have you to do with him, since you do not observe his decrees? For he undoubtedly, following the rule of truth in his Easter, appointed a cycle of nineteen years, which either you are ignorant of, or if you know it, though it is kept by the whole Church of Christ, yet you despise it as a thing of naught. He so computed the fourteenth moon in our Lord's Paschal Feast, that according to the custom of the Egyptians, he acknowledged it to be the fifteenth moon on that same day in the evening; so in like manner he assigned the twentieth to Easter-Sunday, as believing that to be the twenty-first moon, when the sun had set. That you are ignorant of the rule of this distinction is proved by this—that you sometimes manifestly keep Easter before the full moon, that is, on the thirteenth day. Concerning your Father Columba and his followers, whose sanctity you say you imitate, and whose rule and precepts confirmed by signs from Heaven you say that you follow, I might answer, then when many, in the day of judgement, shall say to our Lord, that in His name they have prophesied, and have cast out devils, and done many wonderful works, our Lord will reply, that He never knew them. But far be it from me to speak thus of your fathers, for it is much more just to believe good than evil of those whom we do not know. Wherefore I do not deny those also to have been God's servants, and beloved of God, who with rude simplicity, but pious intentions, have themselves loved Him. Nor do I think that such observance of Easter did them much harm, as long as none came to show them a more perfect rule to follow; for assuredly I believe that, if any teacher, reckoning after the Catholic manner, had come among them, they would have as readily followed his admonitions, as they are known to have kept those commandments of God, which they had learned and knew.

"But as for you and your companions, you certainly sin, if, having heard the decrees of the Apostolic see, nay, of the universal Church, confirmed, as they are, by Holy Scripture, you scorn to follow them. For, though your fathers were holy, do you think that those few men, in a corner of the remotest island, are to be preferred before the universal Church of Christ throughout the world? And if Columba was a holy man and powerful in miracles, yet could he be preferred before the most blessed chief of the Apostles, to whom our Lord said, 'You are Peter, and upon this rock I will build my Church, and the gates of hell shall not prevail against it, and I will give unto you the keys of the kingdom of Heaven?'"

When Wilfrid had ended, the king said, "Is it true, Colman, that these words were spoken to Peter by our Lord?" He answered, "It is true, O king!" Then said he, "Can you show any such power given to your Columba?" Colman answered, "None." Then again the king asked, "Do you both agree in this, without any controversy, that these words were said above all to Peter, and that the keys of the kingdom of Heaven were given to him by our Lord?" They both answered, "Yes." Then the king concluded, "And I also say unto you, that he is the door-keeper, and I will not gainsay him, but I desire, as far as I know and am able, in all things to obey his laws, lest haply when I come to the gates of the kingdom of Heaven, there should be none to open them, he being my adversary who is proved to have the keys." The king having said this, all who were seated there or standing by, both great and small, gave their assent, and renouncing the less perfect custom, hastened to conform to that which they had found to be better.

Source: "Bede: The Synod of Whitby (ca. 663 or 664 CE)." In *World History: Ancient and Medieval Eras.* Santa Barbara, CA: ABC-CLIO, 2012. Web. May 2012.

10.   Charlemagne's Letter Promoting Learning in His Empire

The Letter to Baugulf (*De litteris colendis*) is one of the foundational letters of the Carolingian Renaissance. Issued by the Carolingian ruler Charlemagne sometime between 780 and 800, the circular letter was to be sent to the bishops and abbots of Charlemagne's empire calling on them to promote learning and teaching throughout the realm. This letter was one of the cornerstones of Charlemagne's intellectual and cultural reform that led to the extensive copying of a wide range of classical and Christian Latin works and the production of new works of history and religion and the production of magnificent illuminated manuscripts.

Charles, by the grace of God, King of the Franks and Lombards and Patrician of the Romans, to Abbot Baugulf and to all the congregation, also to the faithful committed to you, we have directed a loving greeting by our ambassadors in the name of omnipotent God.

Be it known, therefore, to your devotion pleasing to God, that we, together with our faithful, have considered it to be useful that the bishoprics and monasteries entrusted by the favor of Christ to our control, in addition, in the culture of letters also ought to be zealous in teaching those who by the gift of God are able to learn, according to the capacity of each individual, so that just as the observance of the rule imparts order and grace to honesty of morals, so also zeal in teaching and learning may do the same for sentences, so that those who desire to please God by living rightly should not neglect to please him also by speaking correctly. For it is written: "Either from thy words thou shalt be justified or from thy words thou shalt be condemned." For although correct conduct may be better than knowledge, nevertheless knowledge precedes conduct. Therefore, each one ought to study what he desires to accomplish, sc) that so much the more fully the mind may know what ought to be clone, as the tongue hastens in the praises of omnipotent God without the hindrances of errors. For since errors should be shunned by all men, so much the more ought they to be avoided as far as possible by those who are chosen for this very purpose alone, so that they ought to be the especial servants of truth.

For when in the years just passed letters were often written to us from several monasteries in which it was stated that the brethren who dwelt there offered up in our behalf sacred and pious prayers, we have recognized in most of these letters both correct thoughts and uncouth expressions; because what pious devotion dictated faithfully to the mind, the tongue, uneducated on account of the neglect of study, was not able to express in the letter without error. Whence it happened that we began to fear lest perchance, as the skill in writing was less, so also the wisdom for understanding the Holy Scriptures might be much less than it rightly ought to be. And we all know well that, although errors of speech are dangerous, far more dangerous are errors of the understanding. Therefore, we exhort you not only not to neglect the study of letters, but also with most humble mind, pleasing to God, to study earnestly in order that you may be able more easily and more correctly to penetrate the mysteries of the divine Scriptures. Since, moreover, images, tropes and similar figures are found in the sacred pages, no one doubts that each one in reading these will understand the spiritual sense more quickly if previously he shall have been fully instructed in the mastery of letters. Such men truly are to be chosen for this work as have both the will and the ability to learn and a desire to instruct others. And may this be done with a zeal as great as the earnestness with which we command it.

For we desire you to be, as it is fitting that soldiers of the church should be, devout in mind, learned in discourse, chaste in conduct and eloquent in speech, so that whosoever shall seek to see you out of reverence of God, or on account of your reputation for holy conduct, just as he is edified by your appearance, may also be instructed by your wisdom, which he has learned from your reading or singing, and may go away joyfully giving thanks to omnipotent God. Do not neglect, therefore, if you wish to have our favor, to send copies of this letter to all your suffragans and fellow-bishops and to all the monasteries. [And let no monk hold courts outside of his monastery or go to the judicial and other public assemblies. Farewell.]

Source: In Boretius, No. 29, p. 78, trans. by D.C. Munro, In University of Pennsylvania. Dept. of History. *Translations and Reprints from the Original Sources of European History.* Published for the Dept. of History of the University of Pennsylvania, Vol. VI, No. 5. Philadelphia: University of Pennsylvania Press, 1900, pp. 12–14.

11. An Inventory of a Carolingian Royal Estate

The following inventory provides a detailed account of the holdings of and crafts practiced on a country estate in the age Charlemagne. The exact location of Asnapium remains unknown, but the estate was most likely one of the smaller royal estates. The very detailed listing of the holdings of the estate represents the type of annual report that the king expected of his servants. It was important that both the king and his steward know what the estate possessed should the king himself visit the estate as he sometimes did during his travels throughout the realm.

We found in the imperial estate of Asnapium a royal house built of stone in the very best manner, having 3 rooms. The entire house was surrounded with balconies and it had 11 apartments for women. Underneath was 1 cellar. There were 2 porticoes. There were 17 other houses built of wood within the courtyard, with a similar number of rooms and fixtures, all well constructed. There was 1 stable, 1 kitchen, 1 mill, 1 granary, and 3 barns.

The yard was enclosed with a hedge and a stone gateway, and above was a balcony from which distributions can be made. There was also an inner yard, surrounded by a hedge, well arranged, and planted with various kinds of trees.

Of vestments: coverings for 1 bed, 1 table-cloth, and 1 towel.

Of utensils: 2 brass kettles, 2 drinking cups, 2 brass cauldrons, 1 iron cauldron, 1 frying pan, 1 grammalin, 1 pair of andirons, 1 lamp, 2 hatchets, 1 chisel, 2 augers, 1 axe, 1 knife, 1 large plane, 1 small plane, 2 scythes, 2 sickles, 2 spades edged with iron, and a sufficient supply of utensils of wood.

Of farm produce: old spelt from last year, 90 baskets which can be made into 450 weight of flour, and 100 measures of barley. From the present year, 110 baskets of spelt, of which 60 baskets had been planted, but the rest we found, 100 measures of wheat, 60 sown, the rest we found, 98 measures of rye all sown, 1,800 measures of barley, 1,100 sown, the rest we found; 430 measures of oats; 1 measure of beans; 12 measures of peas. At 5 mills were found 800 measures of small size. At 4 breweries, 650 measures of small size, 240 given to clergymen, the rest we found. At 2 bridges, 60 measures of salt and 2 shillings. At 4 gardens, 11 shillings. Also honey, 3 measures; about 1 measure of butter; lard, from last year 10 sides; new sides, 200, with fragments and fats; cheese from the present year, 43 weights.

Of cattle: 51 head of larger cattle; 5 three-year-olds; 7 two-year-olds; 7 yearlings; 10 two-year old colts; 8 yearlings; 3 stallions; 16 cows; 2 asses; 50 cows with calves; 20 young bulls; 38 yearling calves; 3 bulls; 260 hogs; 100 pigs; 5 boars; 150 sheep with lambs; 200 yearling lambs; 120 rams; 30 goats with kids; 30 yearling kids; 3 male goats; 30 geese; 80 chickens; 22 peacocks.

Also concerning the manors which belong to the above mansion: in the villa of Grisio we found domain buildings where there are 3 barns and a yard enclosed by a hedge. There were, besides, 1 garden with trees, 10 geese, 8 ducks, 30 chickens.

In another villa we found domain buildings and a yard surrounded by a hedge, and within 3 barns; 1 arpent of vines; 1 garden with trees; 15 geese; 20 chickens.

In a third villa, domain buildings, with 2 barns; 1 granary; 1 garden and 1 yard well enclosed by a hedge.

We found all the dry and liquid measures just as in the palace. We did not find any goldsmiths, silversmiths, blacksmiths, huntsmen, or persons engaged in other services.

The garden herbs which we found were lily, putchuck, mint, parsley, rue, celery, libesticum, sage, savory, juniper, leeks, garlic, tansy, wild mint, coriander, scullions, onions, cabbage, kohlrabi, betony. Trees: pears, apples, medlars, peaches, filberts, walnuts, mulberries, quinces.

Source: Oggs, Frederic Austin. *A Source Book of Mediaeval History.* New York: American Book Company, 1908, pp. 127–29.

12.   Charlemagne's Law Imposing Christianity on the Saxons

The *Capitulatio de Partibus Saxoniae* (785), or first Saxon capitulary, was issued as part of Charlemagne's prolonged conquest and conversion of Saxony, which lasted from 772 to 804. The capitulary, the standard form of legal decree during Charlemagne's reign, was issued shortly after the rebellion of the Saxon leader Widikund and was part of Charlemagne's attempt to impose Carolingian political authority and religious belief on the Saxons. The Saxon capitulary imposed the death penalty for failing to honor Catholic teachings or harming priests or churches and for performing pagan sacrifices and rituals. The severity of the law was recognized and even condemned by contemporaries such as Alcuin. The capitulary, however, did have a more constructive side in that it established Carolingian civil and judicial administration over Saxony.

First, concerning the greater chapters it has been enacted.

It was pleasing to all that the churches of Christ, which are now being built in Saxony and consecrated to God, should not have less, but greater and more illustrious honor, than the fanes of the idols had had.

2. If any one shall have fled to a church for refuge, let no one presume to expel him from the church by violence, but he shall be left in peace until he shall be brought to the judicial assemblage; and on account of the honor due to God and the saints, and the reverence due to the church itself, let his life and all his

members be granted to him. Moreover, let him please his cause as best he can and he shall be judged; and so let him be led to the presence of the lord king, and the latter shall send him where it shall have seemed fitting to his clemency.

3. If any one shall have entered a church by violence and shall have carried off anything in it by force or theft, or shall have burned the church itself, let him be punished by death.

4. If any one, out of contempt for Christianity, shall have despised the holy Lenten fast and shall have eaten flesh, let him be punished by death. But, nevertheless, let it be taken into consideration by a priest, lest perchance any one from necessity has been led to eat flesh.

5. If any one shall have killed a bishop or priest or deacon, let him likewise be punished capitally.

6. If any one deceived by the devil shall have believed, after the manner of the pagans, that any man or woman is a witch and eats men, and on this account shall have burned the person, or shall have given the person's flesh to others to eat, or shall have eaten it himself, let him be punished by a capital sentence.

7. If any one, in accordance with pagan rites, shall have caused the body of a dead man to be burned and shall have reduced his bones to ashes, let him be punished capitally.

8. If any one of the race of the Saxons hereafter concealed among them shall have wished to hide himself unbaptized, and shall have scorned to come to baptism and shall have wished to remain a pagan, let him be punished by death.

9. If any one shall have sacrificed a man to the devil, and after the manner of the pagans shall have presented him as a victim to the demons, let him be punished by death.

10. If any one shall have formed a conspiracy with the pagans against the Christians, or shall have wished to join with them in opposition to the Christians, (1) let him be punished by death; and whosoever shall have consented to this same fraudulently against the king and the Christian people, let him be punished by death.

11. If any one shall have shown himself unfaithful to the lord king, let him be punished with a capital sentence.

12. If any one shall have ravished the daughter of his lord, let him be punished by death.

13. If any one shall have killed his lord or lady, let him be punished in a like manner.

14. If, indeed, for these mortal crimes secretly committed any one shall have fled of his own accord to a priest, and after confession shall have wished to do penance, let him be freed by the testimony of the priest from death.

15. Concerning the lesser chapters all have consented. To each church let the parishioners (2) present a house and two *mansi* (3) of land, and for each one hundred and twenty men, noble and free, and likewise *lili*, let them give to the same church a man-servant and a maid-servant.

16. And this has been pleasing, Christ being propitious, that whencesoever any receipts shall have come into the treasury, either for a breach of the peace or for any penalty of any kind, and in all income pertaining to the king, a tithe shall be rendered to the churches and priests.

17. Likewise, in accordance with the mandate of God, we command that all shall give a tithe of their property and labor to the churches and priests; let the nobles as well as the freemen, and likewise the *lili*, according to that which God shall have given to each Christian, return a part to God.

18. That on the Lord's day no meetings and public judicial assemblages shall be held, unless perchance in a case of great necessity or when war compels it, but all shall go to the church to hear the word of God, and shall be free for prayers or good works. Likewise, also, on the especial festivals they shall devote themselves to God and to the services of the church, and shall refrain from secular assemblies.

19. Likewise, it has been pleasing to insert in these decrees that all infants shall be baptized within a year; and we have decreed this, that if any one shall have despised to bring his infant to baptism within the course of a year, without the advice or permission of the priest, if he is a noble he shall pay 120 *solidi* to the treasury, if a freeman 60, if a *litus* 30.

20. If any one shall have made a prohibited or illegal marriage, if a noble 60 *solidi*, if a freeman 30, if a *litus* 15.

21. If any one shall have made a vow at springs or trees or groves, or shall have made any offering after the manner of the heathen and shall have partaken of a repast in honor of the demons, if he shall be a noble 60 *solidi*, if a freeman 30, if a *litus* 15. If, indeed, they have not the means of paying at once, they shall be given into the service of the church until the *solidi* are paid.

22. We command that the bodies of Saxon Christians shall be carried to the church cemeteries and not to the mounds of the pagans.

23. We have ordered that diviners and soothsayers shall be given to the churches and priests.

24. Concerning robbers and malefactors who shall have fled from one county to another, if any one shall receive them into his power and shall keep them with him for seven nights, except for the purpose of bringing them to justice, let him

pay our ban. Likewise, if a count shall have concealed him and shall be unwilling to bring him forward so that justice may be done and is not able to excuse himself for this, let him lose his office.

25. Concerning a pledge: that no one shall in any way presume to pledge another, and whosoever shall do this shall pay the ban.

26. That no one shall presume to impede any many coming to us to claim justice; and if any one shall have attempted to do this, he shall pay our ban.

27. If any man shall not have been able to find a fidejussor, his property shall be sequestrated until he shall present a fidejussor. If, indeed, he shall have presumed to enter in to his own dwelling in defiance of the ban, he shall forfeit either ten *solidi* or an ox for the violation of the ban itself, and in addition he shall pay the sum for which he was in debt. If, indeed, the fidejussor shall not observe the day fixed, then he shall suffer as much loss as his proportion of the guarantee was; moreover, he who was debtor to the fidejussor shall restore double the loss which he has permitted the fidejussor to incur.

28. Concerning presents and gifts: let no one receive gifts to the detriment of an innocent person; and if any one shall have presumed to do this, he shall pay our ban. And if perchance the count shall have done this (may it not happen!) he shall lose his office.

29. Let all the counts strive to preserve peace and unity with one another; and if perchance any discord or disturbance shall have arisen between them, they shall not on this account neglect either our aid or profit. (4)

30. If any one shall have killed or shall have aided in the murder of a count, his property shall go to the king, and he shall become the serf of the latter.

31. We have granted the authority to the counts within their jurisdiction of inflicting the ban of 60 *solidi* for revenge (*faida*) or the greater crimes; for the lesser crimes, on the other hand, we have fixed the ban of the count at 15 *solidi*.

32. If any one owes an oath to any man whatsoever, let him duly make his oaths to that one at the church on the day appointed; and if he shall have despised to take the oath, let him give a pledge, and let him who was contumacious pay fifteen *solidi*, and afterwards let him fully compound for his act.

33. Concerning perjuries, let it be according to the law of the Saxons. (5)

34. We have forbidden that all the Saxons shall hold public assemblies in general, unless perchance our missus shall have caused them to come together in accordance with our command; but each count shall hold judicial assemblies and administer justice in his jurisdiction. And this shall be cared for by the priests, lest it be done otherwise.

(1) *Vel cum illis in adversitate christianorum perdurare volueril.*

(2) *Pagenses ad ecclesiam recurrentes.*

(3) A *mansus* is, according to Platz, 720 rods long and 30 broad.

(4) Abel substitutes *profectum* for *perfectum*, and this suggestion has been followed in the translation.

(5) Death penalty.

Source: Capitulatio de Partibus Saxoniae. In *Translations and Reprints from the Original Sources of European History.* Vol. VI: *Laws of Charles the Great.* Ed. Dana Carleton Munro. Philadelphia: University of Pennsylvania Press, 1899, pp. 2–5.

13. Excerpts from Einhard's Biography of Charlemagne

Einhard's "Life of Charlemagne" or *Vita Karoli* is one of the most important medieval biographies and one of the great examples of the cultural reform initiated by Charlemagne. Although the exact date of composition of the work remains uncertain, the biography was composed by the 830s and perhaps as early as 817 and, whatever the date, was most likely intended as a commentary on Carolingian politics. Drawing from personal experience and a wide range of classical Latin sources, such as works by Suetonius, Cicero, and Tacitus, the *Vita* provides an eyewitness account of the life of the great Carolingian king and offers insights into his appearance and personality as well as his many conquests and his diplomatic and administrative activities. Einhard's work also raises one of the great questions of Charlemagne's life and reign, whether he knew and welcomed the coronation he received on Christmas Day 800.

SINCE I have taken upon myself to narrate the public and private life, and no small part of the deeds, of my lord and foster-father, the most lent and most justly renowned King Charles, I have condensed the matter into as brief a form as possible. I have been careful not to omit any facts that could come to my knowledge, but at the same time not to offend by a prolix style those minds that despise everything modern, if one can possibly avoid offending by a new work men who seem to despise also the masterpieces of antiquity, the works of most learned and luminous writers. Very many of them, I have no doubt, are men devoted to a life of literary leisure, who feel that the affairs of the present generation ought not to be passed by, and who do not consider everything done today as unworthy of mention and deserving to be given over to silence and oblivion, but are nevertheless seduced by lust of immortality to celebrate the glorious deeds of other times by some sort of composition rather than to deprive posterity of the mention of their own names by not writing at all.

Be this as it may, I see no reason why I should refrain from entering upon a task of this kind, since no man can write with more accuracy than I of events that took place about me, and of facts concerning which I had personal knowledge, ocular demonstration as the saying goes, and I have no means of ascertaining whether or not any one else has the subject in hand.

In any event, I would rather commit my story to writing, and hand it down to posterity in partnership with others, so to speak, than to suffer the most glorious life of this most excellent king, the greatest of all the princes of his day, and his illustrious deeds, hard for men of later times to imitate, to be wrapped in the darkness of oblivion.

But there are still other reasons, neither unwarrantable nor insufficient, in my opinion, that urge me to write on this subject, namely, the care that King Charles bestowed upon me in my childhood, and my constant friendship with himself and his children after I took up my abode at court. In this way he strongly endeared me to himself, and made me greatly his debtor as well in death as in life, so that were I unmindful of the benefits conferred upon me, to keep silence concerning the most glorious and illustrious deeds of a man who claims so much at my hands, and suffer his life to lack due eulogy and written memorial, as if he had never lived, I should deservedly appear ungrateful, and be so considered, albeit my powers are feeble, scanty, next to nothing indeed, and not at all adapted to write and set forth a life that would tax the eloquence of a Tully [note: *Tully* is Marcus Tullius Cicero].

I submit the book. It contains the history of a very great and distinguished man; but there is nothing in it to wonder at besides his deeds, except the fact that I, who am a barbarian, and very little versed in the Roman language, seem to suppose myself capable of writing gracefully and respectably in Latin, and to carry my presumption so far as to disdain the sentiment that Cicero is said in the first book of the *Tusculan Disputations* to have expressed when speaking of the Latin authors. His words are: "It is an outrageous abuse both of time and literature for a man to commit his thoughts to writing without having the ability either to arrange them or elucidate them, or attract readers by some charm of style." This dictum of the famous orator might have deterred me from writing if I had not made up my mind that it was better to risk the opinions of the world, and put my little talents for composition to the test, than to slight the memory of so great a man for the sake of sparing myself.

3. Charlemagne's Accession

Pepin, however, was raised by decree of the Roman pontiff, from the rank of Mayor of the Palace to that of King, and ruled alone over the Franks for fifteen years or more [752–768]. He died of dropsy [Sept. 24, 768] in Paris at the close of the Aquitanian War, which he had waged with William, Duke of Aquitania, for nine successive years, and left his two sons, Charles and Carloman, upon whim, by the grace of God, the succession devolved.

The Franks, in a general assembly of the people, made them both kings [Oct 9, 786] on condition that they should divide the whole kingdom equally between them, Charles to take and rule the part that had to belonged to their father, Pepin, and Carloman the part which their uncle, Carloman had governed. The conditions were accepted, and each entered into the possession of the share of the kingdom that fell to him by this arrangement; but peace was only maintained between them with the greatest difficulty, because many of Carloman's party kept trying to disturb their good understanding, and there were some even who plotted to involve them in a war with each other. The event, however, which showed the danger to have been rather imaginary than real, for at Carloman's death his widow [Gerberga] fled to Italy with her sons and her principal adherents, and without reason, despite her husband's brother put herself and her children under the protection of Desiderius, King of the Lombards. Carloman had succumbed to disease after ruling two years [in fact more than three] in common with his brother and at his death Charles was unanimously elected King of the Franks.

6. Lombard War

After bringing this war to an end and settling matters in Aquitania (his associate in authority had meantime departed this life), he was induced [in 773], by the prayers and entreaties of Hadrian [I, 772–795], Bishop of the city of Rome, to wage war on the Lombards. His father before him had undertaken this task at the request of Pope Stephen [II or III, 752–757], but under great difficulties, for certain leading Franks, of whom he usually took counsel, had so vehemently opposed his design as to declare openly that they would leave the King and go home. Nevertheless, the war against the Lombard King Astolf had been taken up and very quickly concluded [754]. Now, although Charles seems to have had similar, or rather just the same grounds for declaring war that his father had, the war itself differed from the preceding one alike in its difficulties and its issue. Pepin, to be sure, after besieging King Astolf a few days in Pavia, had compelled him to give hostages, to restore to the Romans the cities and castles that he had taken, and to make oath that he would not attempt to seize them again: but Charles did not cease, after declaring war, until he had exhausted King Desiderius by a long siege [773], and forced him to surrender at discretion; driven his son Adalgis, the last hope of the Lombards, not only from his kingdom, but from all Italy [774]; restored to the Romans all that they had lost; subdued Hruodgaus, Duke of Friuli [776], who was plotting revolution; reduced all Italy to his power, and set his son Pepin as king over it. [781]

At this point I should describe Charles' difficult passage over the Alps into Italy, and the hardships that the Franks endured in climbing the trackless mountain ridges, the heaven-aspiring cliffs and ragged peaks, if it were not my purpose in this work to record the manner of his life rather than the incidents of the wars that he waged.

Suffice it to say that this war ended with the subjection of Italy, the banishment of King Desiderius for life, the expulsion of his son Adalgis from Italy, and the restoration of the conquests of the Lombard kings to Hadrian, the head of the Roman Church.

7. Saxon War

At the conclusion of this struggle, the Saxon war, that seems to have been only laid aside for the time, was taken up again. No war ever undertaken by the Frank nation was carried on with such persistence and bitterness, or cost so much labor, because the Saxons, like almost all the tribes of Germany, were a fierce people, given to the worship of devils, and hostile to our religion, and did not consider it dishonorable to transgress and violate all law, human and divine. Then there were peculiar circumstances that tended to cause a breach of peace every day. Except in a few places, where large forests or mountain ridges intervened and made the bounds certain, the line between ourselves and the Saxons passed almost in its whole extent through an open country, so that there was no end to the murders, thefts, and arsons on both sides. In this way the Franks became so embittered that they at last resolved to make reprisals no longer, but to come to open war with the Saxons [772]. Accordingly war was begun against them, and was waged for thirty-three successive years with great fury; more, however, to the disadvantage of the Saxons than of the Franks. It could doubtless have been brought to an end sooner, had it not been for the faithlessness of the Saxons. It is hard to say how often they were conquered, and, humbly submitting to the King, promised to do what was enjoined upon them, without hesitation the required hostages, gave and received the officers sent them from the King. They were sometimes so much weakened and reduced that they promised to renounce the worship of devils, and to adopt Christianity, but they were no less ready to violate these terms than prompt to accept them, so that it is impossible to tell which came easier to them to do; scarcely a year passed from the beginning of the war without such changes on their part. But the King did not suffer his high purpose and steadfastness—firm alike in good and evil fortune—to be wearied by any fickleness on their part, or to be turned from the task that he had undertaken, on the contrary, he never allowed their faithless behavior to go unpunished, but either took the field against them in person, or sent his counts with an army to wreak vengeance and exact righteous satisfaction. At last, after conquering and subduing all who had offered resistance, he took ten thousand of those that lived on the banks of the Elbe, and settled them, with their wives and children, in many different bodies here and there in Gaul and Germany [804]. The war that had lasted so many years was at length ended by their acceding to the terms offered by the King; which were renunciation of their national religious customs and the worship of devils, acceptance of the sacraments of the Christian faith and religion, and union with the Franks to form one people.

8. Saxon War (continued)

Charles himself fought but two pitched battles in this war, although it was long pro-tracted one on Mount Osning [783], at the place called Detmold, and again on the bank of the river Hase, both in the space of little more than a month. The enemy were so routed and overthrown in these two battles that they never afterwards ven-tured to take the offensive or to resist the attacks of the King, unless they were protected by a strong position. A great many of the Frank as well as of the Saxon nobility, men occupying the highest posts of honor, perished in this war, which only came to an end after the lapse of thirty-two years [804]. So many and grievous were the wars that were declared against the Franks in the meantime, and skillfully con-ducted by the King, that one may reasonably question whether his fortitude or his good fortune is to be more admired. The Saxon war began two years [772] before the Italian war [773]; but although it went on without interruption, business else-where was not neglected, nor was t ere any shrinking from other equally arduous contests. The King, who excelled all the princes of his time in wisdom and greatness of soul, did not suffer difficulty to deter him or danger to daunt him from anything that had to be taken up or carried through, for he-had trained himself to bear and endure whatever came, without yielding in adversity, or trusting to the deceitful favors of fortune in prosperity.

9. Spanish Expedition

In the midst of this vigorous and almost uninterrupted struggle with the Saxons, he covered the frontier by garrisons at the proper points, and marched over the Pyr-enees into Spain at the head of all the forces that he could muster. All the towns and castles that he attacked surrendered. And up to the time of his homeward march he sustained no loss whatever; but on his return through the Pyrenees he had cause to rue the treachery of the Gascons. That region is well adapted for ambuscades by reason of the thick forests that cover it; and as the army was advancing in the long line of march necessitated by the narrowness of the road, the Gascons, who lay in ambush [778] on the top of a very high mountain, attacked the rear of the baggage train and the rear guard in charge of it, and hurled them down to the very bottom of the valley. In the struggle that ensued they cut them off to a man; they then plundered the baggage, and dispersed with all speed in every direction under cover of approaching night. The lightness of their armor and the nature of the bat-tle ground stood the Gascons in good stead on this occasion, whereas the Franks fought at a disadvantage in every respect, because of the weight of their armor and the unevenness of the ground. Eggihard, the King's steward; Anselm, Count Pala-tine; and Roland, Governor of the March of Brittany, with very many others, fell in this engagement. This ill turn could not be avenged for the nonce, because the enemy scattered so widely after carrying out their plan that not the least clue could be had to their whereabouts.

18. Private Life

Thus did Charles defend and increase as well, as beautify his, kingdom, as is well known; and here let me express my admiration of his great qualities and his extraordinary constancy alike in good and evil fortune. I will now forthwith proceed to give the details of his private and family life.

19. Private Life (continued) [Charles and the Education of His Children]

The plan that he adopted for his children's education was, first of all, to have both boys and girls instructed in the liberal arts, to which he also turned his own attention. As soon as their years admitted, in accordance with the custom of the Franks, the boys had to learn horsemanship, and to practise war and the chase, and the girls to familiarize themselves with cloth-making, and to handle distaff and spindle, that they might not grow indolent through idleness, and he fostered in them every virtuous sentiment. He only lost three of all his children before his death, two sons and one daughter, Charles, who was the eldest, Pepin, whom he had made King of Italy, and Hruodrud, his oldest daughter, whom he had betrothed to Constantine [VI, 780–802], Emperor of the Greeks. Pepin left one son, named Bernard, and five daughters, Adelaide, Atula, Guntrada, Berthaid and Theoderada. The King gave a striking proof of his fatherly affection at the time of Pepin's death [810]: he appointed the grandson to succeed Pepin, and had the granddaughters brought up with his own daughters. When his sons and his daughter died, he was not so calm as might have been expected from his remarkably strong mind, for his affections were no less strong, and moved him to tears. Again, when he was told of the death of Hadrian [796], the Roman Pontiff, whom he had loved most of all his friends, he wept as much as if he had lost a brother, or a very dear son. He was by nature most ready to contract friendships, and not only made friends easily, but clung to them persistently, and cherished most fondly those with whom he had formed such ties. He was so careful of the training of his sons and daughters that he never took his meals without them when he was at home, and never made a journey without them; his sons would ride at his side, and his daughters follow him, while a number of his body-guard, detailed for their protection, brought up the rear. Strange to say, although they were very handsome women, and he loved them very dearly, he was never willing to marry any of them to a man of their own nation or to a foreigner, but kept them all at home until his death, saying that he could not dispense with their society. Hence, though other-wise happy, he experienced the malignity of fortune as far as they were concerned; yet he concealed his knowledge of the rumors current in regard to them, and of the suspicions entertained of their honor.

22. Personal Appearance

Charles was large and strong, and of lofty stature, though not disproportionately tall (his height is well known to have been seven times the length of his foot); the upper part of his head was round, his eyes very large and animated, nose a little long, hair fair, and face laughing and merry. Thus his appearance was always stately and dignified, whether he was standing or sitting; although his neck was thick and somewhat short, and his belly rather prominent; but the symmetry of the rest of his body concealed these defects. His gait was firm, his whole carriage manly, and his voice clear, but not so strong as his size led one to expect. His health was excellent, except during the four years preceding his death, when he was subject to frequent fevers; at the last he even limped a little with one foot. Even in those years he consulted rather his own inclinations than the advice of physicians, who were almost hateful to him, because they wanted him to give up roasts, to which he was accustomed, and to eat boiled meat instead. In accordance with the national custom, he took frequent exercise on horseback and in the chase, accomplishments in which scarcely any people in the world can equal the Franks. He enjoyed the exhalations from natural warm springs, and often practised swimming, in which he was such an adept that none could surpass him; and hence it was that he built his palace at Aix-la-Chapelle, and lived there constantly during his latter years until his death. He used not only to invite his sons to his bath, but his nobles and friends, and now and then a troop of his retinue or body guard, so that a hundred or more persons sometimes bathed with him.

23. Dress

He used to wear the national, that is to say, the Frank, dress-next his skin a linen shirt and linen breeches, and above these a tunic fringed with silk; while hose fastened by bands covered his lower limbs, and shoes his feet, and he protected his shoulders and chest in winter by a close-fitting coat of otter or marten skins. Over all he flung a blue cloak, and he always had a sword girt about him, usually one with a gold or silver hilt and belt; he sometimes carried a jewelled sword, but only on great feast-days or at the reception of ambassadors from foreign nations. He despised foreign costumes, however handsome, and never allowed himself to be robed in them, except twice in Rome, when he donned the Roman tunic, chlamys, and shoes; the first time at the request of Pope Hadrian, the second to gratify Leo, Hadrian's successor. On great feast-days he made use of embroidered clothes, and shoes bedecked with precious stones; his cloak was fastened by a golden buckle, and he appeared crowned with a diadem of gold and gems: but on other days his dress varied little from the common dress of the people.

24. Habits

Charles was temperate in eating, and particularly so in drinking, for he abominated drunkenness in anybody, much more in himself and those of his household; but he could not easily abstain from food, and often complained that fasts injured his health. He very rarely gave entertainments, only on great feast-days, and then to large numbers of people. His meals ordinarily consisted of four courses, not counting the roast, which his huntsmen used to bring in on the spit; he was more fond of this than of any other dish. While at table, he listened to reading or music. The subjects of the readings were the stories and deeds of olden time: he was fond, too, of St. Augustine's books, and especially of the one entitled "City of God."

He was so moderate in the use of wine and all sorts of drink that he rarely allowed himself more than three cups in the course of a meal. In summer after the midday meal, he would eat some fruit, drain a single cup, put off his clothes and shoes, just as he did for the night, and rest for two or three hours. He was in the habit of awaking and rising from bed four or five times during the night. While he was dressing and putting on his shoes, he not only gave audience to his friends, but if the Count of the Palace told him of any suit in which his judgment was necessary, he had the parties brought before him forthwith, took cognizance of the case, and gave his decision, just as if he were sitting on the Judgment-seat. This was not the only business that he transacted at this time, but he performed any duty of the day whatever, whether he had to attend to the matter himself, or to give commands concerning it to his officers.

25. Studies

Charles had the gift of ready and fluent speech, and could express whatever he had to say with the utmost clearness. He was not satisfied with command of his native language merely, but gave attention to the study of foreign ones, and in particular was such a master of Latin that he could speak it as well as his native tongue; but he could understand Greek better than he could speak it. He was so eloquent, indeed, that he might have passed for a teacher of eloquence. He most zealously cultivated the liberal arts, held those who taught them in great esteem, and conferred great honors upon them. He took lessons in grammar of the deacon Peter of Pisa, at that time an aged man. Another deacon, Albin of Britain, surnamed Alcuin, a man of Saxon extraction, who was the greatest scholar of the day, was his teacher in other branches of learning. The King spent much time and labour with him studying rhetoric, dialectics, and especially astronomy; he learned to reckon, and used to investigate the motions of the heavenly bodies most curiously, with an intelligent scrutiny. He also tried to write, and used to keep tablets and blanks in bed under his pillow, that at leisure hours he might accustom his hand to form the letters; however, as he did not begin his efforts in due season, but late in life, they met with ill success.

28. Charlemagne Crowned Emperor

When he made his last journey thither, he also had other ends in view. The Romans had inflicted many injuries upon the Pontiff Leo, tearing out his eyes and cutting out his tongue, so that he had been comp lied to call upon the King for help [Nov 24, 800]. Charles accordingly went to Rome, to set in order the affairs of the Church, which were in great confusion, and passed the whole winter there. It was then that he received the titles of Emperor and Augustus [Dec 25, 800], to which he at first had such an aversion that he declared that he would not have set foot in the Church the day that they were conferred, although it was a great feast-day, if he could have foreseen the design of the Pope. He bore very patiently with the jealousy which the Roman emperors showed upon his assuming these titles, for they took this step very ill; and by dint of frequent embassies and letters, in which he addressed them as brothers, he made their haughtiness yield to his magnanimity, a quality in which he was unquestionably much their superior.

32. Omens of Death

Very many omens had portended his approaching end, a fact that he had recognized as well as others. Eclipses both of the sun and moon were very frequent during the last three years of his life, and a black spot was visible on the sun for the space of seven days. The gallery between the basilica and the palace, which he had built at great pains and labor, fell in sudden ruin to the ground on the day of the Ascension of our Lord. The wooden bridge over the Rhine at Mayence, which he had caused to be constructed with admirable skill, at the cost of ten years' hard work, so that it seemed as if it might last forever, was so completely consumed in three hours by an accidental fire that not a single splinter of it was left, except what was under water. Moreover, one day in his last campaign into Saxony against Godfred, King of the Danes, Charles himself saw a ball of fire fall suddenly from the heavens with a great light, just as he was leaving camp before sunrise to set out on the march. It rushed across the clear sky from right to left, and everybody was wondering what was the meaning of the sign, when the horse which he was riding gave a sudden plunge, head foremost, and fell, and threw him to the ground so heavily that his cloak buckle was broken and his sword belt shattered; and after his servants had hastened to him and relieved him of his arms, he could not rise without their assistance. He happened to have a javelin in his hand when he was thrown, and this was struck from his grasp with such force that it was found lying at a distance of twenty feet or more from the spot. Again, the palace at Aix-la-Chapelle frequently trembled, the roofs of whatever buildings he tarried in kept up a continual crackling noise, the basilica in which he was afterwards buried was struck by lightning, and the gilded ball that adorned the pinnacle of the roof was shattered by the thunderbolt and hurled upon the bishop's house adjoining. In this same basilica, on the margin of the cornice that ran around the interior, between the upper and lower tiers of arches, a legend was inscribed in red letters, stating who was the builder of the temple, the last words of which were Karolus Princeps. The year that he died it was remarked by some, a few months before his decease, that the letters of the word Princeps were so effaced as to be no longer decipherable. But Charles despised, or affected to despise, all these omens, as having no reference whatever to him.

33. Will

It had been his intention to make a will, that he might give some share in the inheritance to his daughters and the children of his concubines; but it was begun too late and could not be finished. Three years before his death, however, he made a division of his treasures, money, clothes, and other movable goods in the presence of his friends and servants, and called them to witness it, that their voices might insure the ratification of the disposition thus made. He had a summary drawn up of his wishes regarding this distribution o his property, the terms and text of which are as follows:

"In the name of the Lord God, the Almighty Father, Son, and Holy Ghost. This is the inventory and division dictated by the most glorious and most pious Lord Charles, Emperor Augustus, in the 811th year of the Incarnation of our Lord Jesus Christ, in the 43d year of his reign in France and 37th in Italy, the 11th of his empire, and the 4th Indiction, which considerations of piety and prudence have determined him, and the favor of God enabled him, to make of his treasures and money ascertained this day to be in his treasure chamber. In this division he is especially desirous to provide not only that the largess of alms which Christians usually make of their possessions shall be made for himself in due course and order out of his wealth, but also that his heirs shall be free from all doubt, and know clearly what belongs to them, and be able to share their property by suitable partition without litigation or strife. With this intention and to this end he has first divided all his substance and movable goods ascertained to be in his treasure chamber on the day aforesaid in gold, silver, precious stones, and royal ornaments into three lots and has subdivided and set off two of the said lots into twenty-one parts, keeping the third entire. The first two lots have been thus subdivided into twenty one parts because there are in his kingdom twenty-one" recognized metropolitan cities, and in order that each archbishopric may receive by way of alms, at the hands of his heirs

and friends, one of the said parts, and that the archbishop who shall then administer its affairs shall take the part given to it, and share the same with his suffragans
in such manner that one third shall go to the Church, and the remaining two thirds
be divided among the suffragans. The twenty-one parts into which the first two
lots are to be distributed, according to the number of recognized metropolitan cities, have been set apart one from another, and each has been put aside by itself in
a box labeled with the name of the city for which it is destined. The names of the
cities to which this alms or largess is to be sent are as follows: Rome, Ravenna,
Milan, Friuli, Grado, Cologne, Mayence, Salzburg, Treves, Sens, Besançon, Lyons,
Rouen, Rheims, Arles, Vienne, Moutiers-en-Tarantaise, Embrun, Bordeaux, Tours,
and Bourges. The third lot, which he wishes to be kept entire, is to be bestowed as
follows: While the first two lots are to be divided into the parts aforesaid, and set
aside under seal, the third lot shall be employed for the owner's daily needs, as property which he shall be under no obligation to part with in order to the fulfillment
of any vow, and this as long as he shall be in the flesh, or consider it necessary for
his use. But upon his death, or voluntary-renunciation of the affairs of this world,
this said lot shall be divided into four parts, and one thereof shall be added to the
aforesaid twenty-one parts; the second shall be assigned to his sons and daughters,
and to the sons and daughters of his sons, to be distributed among them in just and
equal partition; the third, in accordance with the custom common among Christians, shall be devoted to the poor; and the fourth shall go to the support of the men
servants and maid servants on duty in the palace. It is his wish that to this said third
lot of the whole amount, which consists, as well as the rest, of gold and silver shall
be added all the vessels and utensils of brass iron and other metals together with
the arms, clothing, and other movable goods, costly and cheap, adapted to divers
uses, as hangings, coverlets, carpets, woolen stuffs leathern articles, pack-saddles,
and whatsoever shall be found in his treasure chamber and wardrobe at that time, in
order that thus the parts of the said lot may be augmented, and the alms distributed
reach more persons. He ordains that his chapel-that is to say, its church property,
as well that which he has provided and collected as that which came to him by inheritance from his father shall remain entire, and not be dissevered by any partition
whatever. If, however, any vessels, books or other articles be found therein which
are certainly known not to have been given by him to the said chapel, whoever wants
them shall have them on paying their value at a fair estimation. He likewise commands that the books which he has collected in his library in great numbers shall be
sold for fair prices to such as want them, and the money received therefrom given
to the poor. It is well known that among his other property and treasures are three
silver tables, and one very large and massive golden one. He directs and commands
that the square silver table, upon which there is a representation of the city of Constantinople, shall be sent to the Basilica of St. Peter the Apostle at Rome, with the
other gifts destined therefore; that the round one, adorned with a delineation of the

city of Rome, shall be given to the Episcopal Church at Ravenna; that the third, which far surpasses the other two in weight and in beauty of workmanship, and is made in three circles, showing the plan of the whole universe, drawn with skill and delicacy, shall go, together with the golden table, fourthly above mentioned, to increase that lot which is to be devoted to his heirs and to alms.

Charles' son Louis who by the grace of God succeeded him, after examining this summary, took pains to fulfill all its conditions most religiously as soon as possible after his father's death.

Source: Einhard: The Life of Charlemagne. Trans. Samuel Epes Turner. New York: Harper & Brothers, 1880.

14. Eusebius' Description of the Battle of the Milvian Bridge and the Conversion of Constantine

One of the major turning points in late antiquity and the rise of Byzantine and early medieval civilization was the conversion of the emperor Constantine to Christianity in 312. According to his friend, the bishop Eusebius, the emperor's conversion, as described in the following excerpt from Eusebius' biography of Constantine, was inspired by a miracle. Informed of this miracle by the emperor himself, Eusebius explains that on the eve of the battle of the Milvian Bridge, which would bring the winner control of the Western Roman Empire, Constantine saw a sign in the sky with the words proclaiming "Conquer by this." The vision was confirmed by a visit from Jesus Christ while the emperor slept that night, and on the following day he ordered his troops into battle bearing the sign, and was victorious.

Chapter XXVII

Being convinced, however, that he needed some more powerful aid than his military forces could afford him, on account of the wicked and magical enchantments which were so diligently practiced by the tyrant, he sought Divine assistance, deeming the possession of arms and a numerous soldiery of secondary importance, but believing the co-operating power of Deity invincible and not to be shaken. He considered, therefore, on what God he might rely for protection and assistance. While engaged in this enquiry, the thought occurred to him, that, of the many emperors who had preceded him, those who had rested their hopes in a multitude of gods, and served them with sacrifices and offerings, had in the first place been deceived by flattering predictions, and oracles which promised them all prosperity, and at last had met with an unhappy end, while not one of their gods had stood by to warn them of the impending wrath of heaven; while one alone who had pursued an entirely opposite course, who had condemned their error, and honored the one Supreme God during his whole life, had formal I him to be the Saviour and Protector of his empire, and the Giver of every good thing. Reflecting on this, and well weighing the fact that they who had trusted in many gods had also fallen by manifold forms of death, without leaving behind them either family or offspring, stock, name, or memorial among men: while the God of his father had given to him, on the other hand, manifestations of his power and very many tokens: and considering farther that those who had already taken arms against the tyrant, and had marched to the battle-field under the protection of a multitude of gods, had met with a dishonorable end (for one of them had shamefully retreated from the contest without a blow, and the other, being slain in the midst of his own troops, became, as it were, the mere sport of death (4)); reviewing, I say, all these considerations, he judged it to be folly indeed to join in the idle worship of those who were no gods, and, after such convincing evidence, to err from the truth; and therefore felt it incumbent on him to honor his father's God alone.

Chapter XXVIII

ACCORDINGLY he called on him with earnest prayer and supplications that he would reveal to him who he was, and stretch forth his right hand to help him in his present difficulties. And while he was thus praying with fervent entreaty, a most marvelous sign appeared to him from heaven, the account of which it might have been hard to believe had it been related by any other person. But since the victorious emperor himself long afterwards declared it to the writer of this history, when he was honored with his acquaintance and society, and confirmed his statement by an oath, who could hesitate to accredit the relation, especially since the testimony of after-time has established its truth? He said that about noon, when the day was already beginning to decline, he saw with his own eyes the trophy of a cross of light in the heavens, above the sun, and bearing the inscription, CONQUER BY THIS. At this sight he himself was struck with amazement, and his whole army also, which followed him on this expedition, and witnessed the miracle.

Chapter XXIX

He said, moreover, that he doubted within himself what the import of this apparition could be. And while he continued to ponder and reason on its meaning, night suddenly came on; then in his sleep the Christ of God appeared to him with the same sign which he had seen in the heavens, and commanded him to make a likeness of that sign which he had seen in the heavens, and to use it as a safeguard in all engagements with his enemies.

Chapter XXX

AT dawn of day he arose, and communicated the marvel to his friends: and then, calling together the workers in gold and precious stones, he sat in the midst of them, and described to them the figure of the sign he had seen, bidding them represent it in gold and precious stones. And this representation I myself have had an opportunity of seeing.

Chapter XXXI

Now it was made in the following manner. A long spear, overlaid with gold, formed the figure of the cross by means of a transverse bar laid over it. On the top of the whole was fixed a wreath of gold and precious stones; and within this, the symbol of the Saviour's name, two letters indicating the name of Christ by means of its initial characters, the letter P being intersected by X in its centre: and these letters the emperor was in the habit of wearing on his helmet at a later period. From the cross-bar of the spear was suspended a cloth, a royal piece, covered with a profuse embroidery of most brilliant precious stones; and which, being also richly interlaced with gold, presented an indescribable degree of beauty to the beholder. This banner was of a square form, and the upright staff, whose lower section was of great length, bore a golden half-length portrait of the pious emperor and his children on its upper part, beneath the trophy of the cross, and immediately above the embroidered banner.

The emperor constantly made use of this sign of salvation as a safeguard against every adverse and hostile power, and commanded that others similar to it should be carried at the head of all his armies.

Chapter XXXII

These things were done shortly afterwards. But at the time above specified, being struck with amazement at the extraordinary vision, and resolving to worship no other God save Him who had appeared to him, he sent for those who were acquainted with the mysteries of His doctrines, and enquired who that God was, and what was intended by the sign of the vision he had seen. They affirmed that He was God, the only begotten Son of the one and only God: that the sign which had appeared was the symbol of immortality, and the trophy of that victory over death which He had gained in time past when sojourning on earth. They taught him also the causes of His advent, and explained to him the true account of His incarnation. Thus he was instructed in these matters, and was impressed with wonder at the divine manifestation which had been presented to his sight. Comparing, therefore, the heavenly vision with the interpretation given, he found his judgment confirmed; and, in the persuasion that the knowledge of these things had been imparted to him by Divine teaching, he determined thenceforth to devote himself to the reading of the Inspired writings.

Source: Philip Schaff and Henry Wace, eds. *From Nicene and Post-Nicene Fathers.* Second Series, Vol. 1. Trans. Ernest Cushing Richardson. Buffalo, NY: Christian Literature Publishing Co., 1890.

15. Gildas's Version of the Conquest of Britain by the Anglo-Saxons

Writing in the 540s, Gildas, a monk and Briton, left a dramatic account of the conquest of Britain by the Anglo-Saxons. One of the earliest sources for the invasion of Britain, Gildas's work, *The Ruin of Britain,* describes the conquest in starkly moral terms. As the passage below demonstrates, Gildas saw the Britons as a sinful and foolish people who brought about their own ruin by inviting the Saxons to serve as their protectors but were instead conquered by them. For Gildas, this was a punishment from God, and his explanation of events helped shape Bede's account of the conquest of Britain. Gildas's history also contributed to the emergence of the legend of King Arthur. Although Gildas does not mention him by name, his account of the battle of Badon Hill would become part of the later legend of Arthur.

§23. Then all the councilors, together with that proud tyrant Gurthrigern [Vortigern], the British king, were so blinded, that, as a protection to their country, they sealed its doom by inviting in among them (like wolves into the sheep-fold), the fierce and impious Saxons, a race hateful both to God and men, to repel the invasions of the northern nations. Nothing was ever so pernicious to our country, nothing was ever so unlucky. What palpable darkness must have enveloped their minds—darkness desperate and cruel! Those very people whom, when absent, they dreaded more than death itself, were invited to reside, as one may say, under the selfsame roof. Foolish are the princes, as it is said, of Thafneos, giving counsel to unwise Pharaoh. A multitude of whelps came forth from the lair of this barbaric lioness, in three cyuls, as they call them, that is, in three ships of war, with their sails wafted by the wind and with omens and prophecies favourable, for it was foretold by a certain soothsayer among them, that they should occupy the country to which they were sailing three hundred years, and half of that time, a hundred and fifty years, should plunder and despoil the same. They first landed on the eastern side of the island, by the invitation of the unlucky king, and there fixed their sharp talons, apparently to fight in favour of the island, but alas! more truly against it. Their mother-land, finding her first brood thus successful, sends forth a larger company of her wolfish offspring, which sailing over, join themselves to their bastard-born comrades. From that time the germ in iniquity and root of contention planted their poison amongst us, as we deserved, and shot forth into leaves and branches. The barbarians being thus introduced as soldiers into the island, to encounter, as they falsely said, any dangers in defence of their hospitable entertainers, obtain an allowance of provisions, which, for some time being plentifully bestowed, stopped their doggish mouths. Yet they complain that their monthly supplies are not furnished in sufficient abundance, and they industriously aggravate each occasion of quarrel, saying that unless more liberality is shown them, they will break the treaty and plunder the whole island. In a short time, they follow up their threats with deeds.

§26. After this, sometimes our countrymen, sometimes the enemy, won the field, to the end that our Lord might in this land try after his accustomed manner these his Israelites, whether they loved him or not, until the year of the siege of Bath-hill, when took place also the last almost, though not the least slaughter of our cruel foes, which was (as I am sure) forty-four years and one month after the landing of the Saxons, and also the time of my own nativity. And yet neither to this day are the cities of our country inhabited as before, but being forsaken and overthrown, still lie desolate; our foreign wars having ceased, but our civil troubles still remaining. For as well the remembrance of such a terrible desolation of the island, as also of the unexpected recovery of the same, remained in the minds of those who were eyewitnesses of the wonderful events of both, and in regard thereof, kings, public magistrates, and private persons, with priests and clergymen, did all and every one of them live orderly according to their several vocations. But when these had departed out of this world, and a new race succeeded, who were ignorant of this troublesome time, and had only experience of the present prosperity, all the laws of truth and justice were so shaken and subverted, that no so much as a vestige or remembrance of these virtues remained among the above-named orders of men, except among a very few who, compared with the great multitude which were daily rushing headlong down to hell, are accounted so small a number, that our reverend mother, the church, scarcely beholds them, her only true children, reposing in her bosom; whose worthy lives, being a pattern to all men, and beloved of God, inasmuch as by their holy prayers, as by certain pillars and most profitable supporters, our infirmity is sustained up, that it may not utterly be broken down, I would have no one suppose I intended to reprove, if forced by the increasing multitude of offences, I have freely, aye, with anguish, no so much declared as bewailed the wickedness of those who are become servants, not only to their bellies, but also to the devil rather than to Christ, who is our blessed God, world without end.

Source: *Six Old English Chronicles*. Trans. J.A. Giles. London: Henry G. Bohn, 1848, pp. 310–11; 313–14.

16. A Letter from Pope Gregory III to Charles Martel Seeking Aid against the Lombards

During the sixth and seventh centuries, the papacy depended on the Byzantine emperors for protection and support, especially against the Lombards, who sought to unify Italy under their authority. In the eighth century, however, the Byzantine inability to protect Rome against its enemies and Byzantine Iconclasm forced Pope Gregory III to find a new defender. In the following letter, Gregory petitions Charles Martel, the Carolingian mayor of the palace, for aid against the Lombards. Martel was unable to provide direct assistance, but Gregory's appeal enhanced the prestige of Martel's family and was the first step in creating a formal alliance between the papacy and the Carolingians.

Pope Gregory to his most excellent son, Charles, sub-king.

In our great affliction we have thought it necessary to write to you a second time, believing that you are a loving son of St. Peter, the prince of apostles, and of ourselves, and that out of reverence for him you would obey our commands to defend the church of God and his chosen people. We can now no longer endure the persecution of the Lombards, for they have taken from St. Peter all his possessions, even those which were given him by you and your fathers. These Lombards hate and oppress us because we sought protection from you; for the same reason also the church of St. Peter is despoiled and desolated by them. But we have intrusted a more complete account of all our woes to your faithful subject, our present messenger, and he will relate them to you. You, oh son, will receive favor from the same prince of apostles here and in the future life in the presence of God, according as you render speedy aid to his church and to us, that all people may recognize the faith and love and singleness of purpose which you display in defending St. Peter and us and his chosen people. For by doing this you will attain lasting fame on earth and eternal life in heaven.

Source: Oliver J. Thatcher and Edgar Holmes McNeal, eds. *A Source Book for Medieval History. Selected Documents Illustrating the History of Europe in the Middle Ages.* New York: Charles Scribner's Sons, 1905, p. 101 (#43).

17. Gregory of Tours: Clovis and the Vase of Soissons

The early history of the Merovingian Franks was compiled by the bishop and historian Gregory of Tours in the late sixth century. His account has largely shaped the modern understanding of Clovis (d. 511) and the other early Merovingian kings, and modern scholars are only beginning to understand and decipher Gregory's agenda in shaping that history. In his depiction of Clovis, Gregory portrayed a brutal but effective ruler who, even before his conversion to Christianity, honored the church. The following passage from Gregory's History of the Franks, demonstrates Clovis's respect for the church as well as competing ideas of kingship—one in which the king is the sovereign authority and the other in which he is first among equals.

At this time [A.D. 486] the army of Clovis pillaged many churches, for he was still sunk in the errors of idolatry. The soldiers had borne away from a church, with all the other ornaments of the holy ministry, a vase of marvelous size and beauty. The bishop of this church sent messengers to the king, begging that if the church might not recover any other of the holy vessels, at least this one might be restored. The king, bearing these things, replied to the messenger: "Follow thou us to Soissons, for there all things that have been acquired are to be divided. If the lot shall give me this vase, I will do what the bishop desires."

When be had reached Soissons, and all the booty had been placed in the midst of the army, the king pointed to this vase, and said: "I ask you, O most valiant warriors, not to refuse to me the vase in addition to my rightful part," Those of discerning mind among his men answered, "O glorious king, all things which we see are thine, and we ourselves are subject to thy power; now do what seems pleasing to thee, for none is strong enough to resist thee." When they had thus spoken one of the soldiers, impetuous, envious, and vain, raised his battle-axe aloft and crushed the vase with it, crying, "Thou shalt receive nothing of this unless a just lot give it to thee." At this all were stupefied.

The king bore his injury with the calmness of patience, and when he had received the crushed vase he gave it to the bishop's messenger, but be cherished a hidden wound in his breast. When a year had passed he ordered the whole army to come fully equipped to the Campus Martius and show their arms in brilliant array—But when he had reviewed them all he came to the breaker of the vase, and said to him, "No one bears his arms so clumsily as thou; for neither thy spear, nor thy sword, nor thy ax is ready for use." And seizing his ax, he cast it on the ground. And when the soldier had bent a little to pick it up the king raised his hands and crushed his head with his own ax. "Thus," he said, "didst thou to the vase at Soissons."

Source: From the accounts translated in J. H. Robinson. *Readings in European History.* Boston, MA: Ginn, 1905, pp. 51–55.

18. Gregory of Tours: The Conversion of Clovis

Along with his portrayal of Clovis as a violent and successful warrior, Gregory of Tours describes the Frankish king's conversion to Christianity. In the following passage, Clovis, after several appeals from his wife Clotilda, petitioned Jesus Christ for aid in a battle the king was losing. His victory and subsequent instruction by the bishop of Rheims, Remigius, secured Clovis's conversion to Christianity and the conversion of many of his followers. Gregory's obvious references to the conversion of the emperor Constantine make the account suspect, and Gregory's efforts to portray Clovis as a Catholic king were part of the bishop's attempt to remind the fractious kings of his own day of their obligations to the church and to maintaining order. Moreover, most scholars now think that Clovis converted to Arian Christianity first before accepting the Catholic faith, which made him the first of the Catholic barbarian kings.

30

The queen did not cease to urge him to recognize the true God and cease worshipping idols. But he could not be influenced in any way to this belief, until at last a war arose with the Alamanni, in which he was driven by necessity to confess what before he had of his free will denied. It came about that as the two armies were fighting fiercely, there was much slaughter, and Clovis's army began to be in danger of destruction. He saw it and raised his eyes to heaven, and with remorse in his heart he burst into tears and cried: "Jesus Christ, whom Clotilda asserts to be the son of the living God, who art said to give aid to those in distress, and to bestow victory on those who hope in thee, I beseech the glory of thy aid, with the vow that if thou wilt grant me victory over these enemies, and I shall know that power which she says that people dedicated in thy name have had from thee, I will believe in thee and be baptized in thy name. For I have invoked my own gods but, as I find, they have withdrawn from aiding me; and therefore I believe that they possess no power, since they do not help those who obey them. I now call upon thee, I desire to believe thee only let me be rescued from my adversaries." And when he said thus, the Alamanni turned their backs, and began to disperse in flight. And when they saw that their king was killed, they submitted to the dominion of Clovis, saying: "Let not the people perish further, we pray; we are yours now." And he stopped the fighting, and after encouraging his men, retired in peace and told the queen how he had had merit to win the victory by calling on the name of Christ. This happened in the fifteenth year of his reign.

31

Then the queen asked saint Remigius, bishop of Rheims, to summon Clovis secretly, urging him to introduce the king to the word of salvation. And the bishop sent for him secretly and began to urge him to believe in the true God, maker of heaven and earth, and to cease worshipping idols, which could help neither themselves nor any one else. But the king said: "I gladly hear you, most holy father; but there remains one thing: the people who follow me cannot endure to abandon their gods; but I shall go and speak to them according to your words." He met with his followers, but before he could speak the power of God anticipated him, and all the people cried out together:/ "O pious king, we reject our mortal gods, and we are ready to follow the immortal God whom Remi preaches." This was reported to the bishop, who was greatly rejoiced, and bade them get ready the baptismal font. The squares were shaded with tapestried canopies, the churches adorned with white curtains, the baptistery set in order, the aroma of incense spread, candles of fragrant odor burned brightly, and the whole shrine of the baptistery was filled with a divine fragrance: and the Lord gave such grace to those who stood by that they thought they were placed amid the odors of paradise. And the king was the first to ask to be baptized by the bishop. Another Constantine advanced to the baptismal font, to terminate the disease of ancient leprosy and wash away with fresh water the foul spots that had long been borne. And when he entered to be baptized, the saint of God began with ready speech: "Gently bend your neck, Sigamber; worship what you burned; burn what you worshipped." The holy bishop Remi was a man of excellent wisdom and especially trained in rhetorical studies, and of such surpassing holiness that he equalled the miracles of Silvester. For there is extant a book of his life which tells that he raised a dead man. And so the king confessed all-powerful God in the Trinity, and was baptized in the name of the Father, Son and holy Spirit, and was anointed with the holy ointment with the sign of the cross of Christ. And of his army more than 3000 were baptized. His sister also, Albofled, was baptized, who not long after passed to the Lord. And when the king was in mourning for her, the holy Remigius sent a letter of consolation which began in this way: "The reason of your mourning pains me, and pains me greatly, that Albofled your sister, of good memory, has passed away. But I can give you this comfort, that her departure from the world was such that she ought to be envied rather than be mourned." Another sister also was converted, Lanthechild by name, who had fallen into the heresy of the Arians, and she confessed that the Son and the Holy Spirit were equal to the Father, and was anointed.

Source: Gregory of Tours. *History of the Franks.* Translated by Ernest Brehaut (extended selections). Records of Civilization 2. New York: Columbia University Press, 1916, Chapters 30–31.

19. An Account of the Battle of Tours by a Spanish Christian Chronicler

In his chronicle written in Islamic Spain sometime after 750, Isidore of Beja reports on the battle of Tours (also known as the battle of Poitiers) of 732. Although no longer recognized as the decisive battle between Islam and Western Christianity, the battle is nonetheless significant. At the battle, the Carolingian mayor Charles Martel stopped a major Muslim raiding party and established his reputation as "the Hammer." The Muslims managed to withdraw from their camp but their progress into France was cut short and the contest between the Muslims and Franks was ever after limited to the southern part of the realm. The passage also reveals the medieval Christian practice of identifying Muslims with the derogatory labels "Saracens" or "Ishmaelites."

Then Abdrahman, [the Muslim emir] seeing the land filled with the multitude of his army, crossed the Pyrenées, and traversed the defiles [in the mountains] and the plains, so that he penetrated ravaging and slaying clear into the lands of the Franks. He gave battle to Duke Eudes (of Aquitaine) beyond the Garonne and the Dordogne, and put him to flight—so utterly [was he beaten] that God alone knew the number of the slain and wounded. Whereupon Abdrahman set in pursuit of Eudes; he destroyed palaces, burned churches, and imagined he could pillage the basilica of St. Martin of Tours. It is then that he found himself face to face with the lord of Austrasia, Charles, a mighty warrior from his youth, and trained in all the occasions of arms.

For almost seven days the two armies watched one another, waiting anxiously the moment for joining the struggle. Finally they made ready for combat. And in the shock of the battle the men of the North seemed like unto a sea that cannot be moved. Firmly they stood, one close to another, forming as it were a bulwark of ice; and with great blows of their swords they hewed down the Arabs. Drawn up in a band around their chief, the people of the Austrasians carried all before them. Their tireless hands drove their swords down to the breasts [of the foe].

At last night sundered the combatants. The Franks with misgivings, lowered their blades, and beholding the numberless tents of the Arabs, prepared themselves for another battle the next day. Very early, when they issued from their retreat, the men of Europe saw the Arab tents ranged still in order, in the same place where they had set up their camp. Unaware that they were utterly empty, and fearful lest within the phalanxes of the Saracens were drawn up for combat, they sent out spies to ascertain the facts. These spies discovered that all the squadrons of the "Ishmaelites" had vanished. In fact, during the night they had fled with the greatest silence, seeking with all speed their home land. The Europeans, uncertain and fearful, lest they were merely hidden in order to come back [to fall upon them] by ambushments, sent scouting parties everywhere, but to their great amazement found nothing. Then without troubling to pursue the fugitives, they contented themselves with sharing the spoils and returned right gladly to their own country.

Source: William Stearns Davis. *Readings in Ancient History. Illustrative Extracts from the Sources.* Vol II: *Rome and the West.* Boston: Allyn and Bacon, 1912–1913, pp. 362–64.

20. Excerpts from Jordanes's *Getica*

In the sixth century, the Goth Jordanes wrote *De origine actibusque Getarum* (On the Origins and Deeds of the Getae), a history of the Gothic peoples. Commonly known as the *Getica*, Jordanes's history provides an important but flawed account of the early history of the Goths and their impact on and assimilation into the Roman Empire. Drawing from a wide range of classical sources, and heavily indebted to the now lost history of the Goths by Cassiodorus, Jordanes's work reflects Roman anthropology and the formation of a people. The work also drew from the oral traditions of the Goths and provides insights into how they saw themselves. Despite its flaws, the *Getica* provides important information on the movement of a wide range of barbarian peoples, including the Goths, Huns, and Franks. It also describes some of the most influential figures of late antiquity, including Alaric, Attila the Hun, Justinian, and Theodoric.

Preface

Though it had been my wish to glide in my little boat by the shore of a peaceful coast and, as a certain writer says, to gather little fishes from the pools of the ancients, you, brother Castalius, bid me set my sails toward the deep. You urge me to leave the little work I have in hand, that is, the abbreviation of the Chronicles, and to condense in my own style in this small book the twelve volumes of the Senator on the origin and deeds of the Getae (i.e., the Goths) from the old days to the present day, descending through the generations of the kings.

Truly a hard command, and imposed by one who seems unwilling to realize the burden of the task. Nor do you note this, that my utterance is too slight to fill so magnificent a trumpet of speech as his. But above every burden is the fact that I have no access to his books that I may follow his thought. Still—and let me lie not—I have in times past read the books a second time by his steward's loan for a three days' reading. The words I recall not, but the sense and the deeds related I think I retain entire.

To this I have added fitting matters from some Greek and Latin histories. I have also put in an introduction and a conclusion, and have inserted many things of my own authorship. Wherefore reproach me not, but receive and read with gladness what you have asked me to write. If I have omitted anything that you remember, do you as a neighbor to our race add to it, praying for me, dearest brother. The Lord be with you. Amen.

The United Goths

4. Now from this island of Scandza, as from a hive of races or a womb of nations, the Goths are said to have come forth long ago under their king, Berig by name.

As soon as they disembarked from their ships and set foot on the land, they straightway gave their name to the place. And even today it is said to be called Gothiscandza. Soon they moved from here to the abodes of the Ulmerugi, who then dwelt on the shores of Ocean, where they pitched camp, joined battle with them and drove them from their homes. Then they subdued their neighbors, the Vandals, and thus added to their victories. But when the number of the people increased greatly and Filimer, son of Gadaric, reigned as king—about the fifth since Berig—he decided that the army of the Goths with their families should move from that region. In search of suitable homes and pleasant places they came to the land of Scythia, called Oium in that tongue. Here they were delighted with the great richness of the country, and it is said that when half the army had been brought over, the bridge whereby they had crossed the river fell in utter ruin, nor could anyone thereafter pass to or fro. For the place is said to be surrounded by quaking bogs and an encircling abyss, so that by this double obstacle nature has made it inaccessible. And even today one may hear in that neighborhood the lowing of cattle and may find traces of men, if we are to believe the stories of travelers, although we must grant that they hear these things from afar.

This part of the Goths, which is said to have crossed the river and entered with Filimer into the country of Oium, came into possession of the desired land, and there they soon came upon the race of the Spali, joined battle with them and won the victory. Thence the victors hastened to the farthest part of Scythia, which is near the sea of Pontus (i.e. the Black Sea); for so the story is generally told in their early songs, in almost historic fashion. Ablabius also, a famous chronicler of the Gothic race, confirms this in his most trustworthy account. Some of the ancient writers also agree with the tale. Among these we may mention Josephus, a most reliable relator of annals, who everywhere follows the rule of truth and unravels from the beginning the origin of causes; but why he has omitted the beginnings of the race of the Goths, of which I have spoken, I do not know. He barely mentions Magog of that stock, and says they were Scythians by race and were called so by name. . . .

The Huns

24. But after a short space of time, as Orosius relates, the race of the Huns, fiercer than ferocity itself, flamed forth against the Goths. We learn from old traditions that their origin was as follows: Filimer, King of the Goths, son of Gadaric the Great, who was the fifth in succession to hold the rule of the Getae after their departure from the island of Scandza—and who, as we have said, entered the land of Scythia with his tribe—found among his people certain witches, whom he called in his native tongue Haliurunnae. Suspecting these women, he expelled them from the midst of his race and compelled them to wander in

solitary exile afar from his army. There the unclean spirits, who beheld them as they wandered through the wilderness, joined them and begat this savage race, which dwelt at first in the swamps—a stunted, foul and puny tribe, scarcely human, and having no language save one which bore but slight resemblance to human speech. Such was the descent of the Huns who came to the country of the Goths.

This cruel tribe, as Priscus the historian relates, settled on the farther bank of the Maeotic swamp. They were fond of hunting and had no skill in any other art. After they had grown to a nation, they disturbed the peace of neighboring races by theft and rapine. At one time, while hunters of their tribe were as usual seeking for game on the farthest edge of Maeotis, they saw a doe unexpectedly appear to their sight and enter the swamp, acting as guide of the way; now advancing and again standing still. The hunters followed and crossed on foot the Maeotic swamp, which they had supposed was impassable as the sea. Presently the unknown land of Scythia disclosed itself and the doe disappeared. Now in my opinion the evil spirits, from whom the Huns are descended, did this from envy of the Scythians. And the Huns, who had been wholly ignorant that there was another world beyond Maeotis, were now filled with admiration for the Scythian land. As they were quick of mind, they believed that this path, utterly unknown to any age of the past, had been divinely revealed to them. They returned to their tribe, told them what had happened, praised Scythia and persuaded the people to hasten thither along the way they had found by the guidance of the doe. As many as they captured, when they thus entered Scythia for the first time, they sacrificed to Victory. The remainder they conquered and made subject to themselves.

Like a whirlwind of nations they swept across the great swamp and at once fell upon the Alpidzuri, Alcildzuri, Itimari, Tuncarsi and Boisci, who bordered on that part of Scythia. The Alans also, who were their equals in battle, but unlike them in civilization, manners and appearance, they exhausted by their incessant attacks and subdued. For by the terror of their features they inspired great fear in those whom perhaps they did not really surpass in war. They made their foes flee in horror because their swarthy aspect was fearful, and they had, if I may call it so, a sort of shapeless lump, not a head, with pin-holes rather than eyes. Their hardihood is evident in their wild appearance, and they are beings who are cruel to their children on the very day they are born. For they cut the cheeks of the males with a sword, so that before they receive the nourishment of milk they must learn to endure wounds.

Hence they grow old beardless and their young men are without comeliness, because a face furrowed by the sword spoils by its scars the natural beauty of a beard. They are short in stature, quick in bodily movement, alert horsemen, broad shouldered, ready in the use of bow and arrow, and have firm-set necks which are ever erect in pride. Though they live in the form of men, they have the cruelty of wild beasts.

The Divided Goths: Visigoths

25. The Visigoths were terrified as their kinsmen had been, and knew not how to plan for safety against the race of the Huns. After long deliberation by common consent they finally sent ambassadors into Romania to the Emperor Valens, brother of Valentinian, the elder Emperor, to say that if he would give them part of Thrace or Moesia to keep, they would submit themselves to his laws and commands. That he might have greater confidence in them, they promised to become Christians, if he would give them teachers who spoke their language. When Valens learned this, he gladly and promptly granted what he had himself intended to ask. He received the Getae into the region of Moesia and placed them there as a wall of defense for his kingdom against other tribes. And since at that time the Emperor Valens, who was infected with the Arian perfidy, had closed all the churches of our party, he sent as preachers to them those who favored his sect. They came and straightway filled a rude and ignorant people with the poison of their heresy. Thus the Emperor Valens made the Visigoths Arians rather than Christians. Moreover, from the love they bore them, they preached the gospel both to the Ostrogoths and to their kinsmen the Gepidae, teaching them to reverence this heresy, and they invited all people of their speech everywhere to attach themselves to this sect. They themselves as we have said, crossed the Danube and settled Dacia Ripensis, Moesia and Thrace by permission of the Emperor.

26. Soon famine and want came upon them, as often happens to a people not yet well settled in a country. Their princes and the leaders who ruled them in place of kings, that is Fritigern, Alatheus and Safrac, began to lament the plight of their army and begged Lupicinus and Maximus, the Roman commanders, to open a market. But to what will not the "cursed lust for gold" compel men to assent? The generals, swayed by avarice, sold them at a high price not only the flesh of sheep and oxen, but even the carcasses of dogs and unclean animals, so that a slave would be bartered for a loaf of bread or ten pounds of meat. When their goods and chattels failed, the greedy trader demanded their sons in return for the necessities of life. And the parents consented even to this, in order to provide for the safety of their children, arguing that it was better to lose liberty than life; and indeed it is better that one be sold, if he will be mercifully fed, than that he should be kept free only to die.

Now it came to pass in that troublesome time that Lupicinus, the Roman general, invited Fritigern, a chieftain of the Goths, to a feast and, as the event revealed, devised a plot against him. But Fritigern, thinking no evil, came to the feast with a few followers. While he was dining in the praetorium he heard the dying cries of his ill-fated men, for, by order of the general, the soldiers were slaying his companions who were shut up in another part of the house. The loud cries of the dying fell upon ears already suspicious, and Fritigern at once perceived the treacherous trick. He drew his sword and with great courage dashed quickly from the banqueting-hall, rescued his men from their threatening doom and incited them to slay the Romans. Thus these valiant men gained the chance they had longed for—to be free to die in battle rather than to perish of hunger—and immediately took arms to kill the generals Lupicinus and Maximus. Thus that day put an end to the famine of the Goths and the safety of the Romans, for the Goths no longer as strangers and pilgrims, but as citizens and lords, began to rule the inhabitants and to hold in their own right all the northern country as far as the Danube.

Alaric

29. But after Theodosius, the lover of peace and of the Gothic race, had passed from human cares, his sons began to ruin both empires by their luxurious living and to deprive their Allies, that is to say the Goths, of the customary gifts. The contempt of the Goths for the Romans soon increased, and for fear their valor would be destroyed by long peace, they appointed Alaric king over them. He was of a famous stock, and his nobility was second only to that of the Amali, for he came from the family of the Balthi, who because of their daring valor had long ago received among their race the name *Baltha,* that is, "The Bold." Now when this Alaric was made king, he took counsel with his men and persuaded them to seek a kingdom by their own exertions rather than serve others in idleness. In the consulship of Stilicho and Aurelian he raised an army and entered Italy, which seemed to be bare of defenders, and came through Pannonia and Sirmium along the right side. Without meeting any resistance, he reached the bridge of the river Candidianus at the third milestone from the royal city of Ravenna. . . . .

30. But as I was saying, when the army of the Visigoths had come into the neighborhood of this city, they sent an embassy to the Emperor Honorius, who dwelt within. They said that if he would permit the Goths to settle peaceably in Italy, they would so live with the Roman people that men might believe them both to be of one race; but if not, whoever prevailed in war should drive out the other, and the victor should henceforth rule unmolested. But the Emperor Honorius feared to make either promise. So he took counsel with his Senate and considered how he might drive them from the Italian borders. He finally decided that Alaric and his race, if they were able to do so, should be allowed to seize for their own home the provinces farthest away, namely, Gaul and Spain. For at this time he had almost lost them, and moreover they had been devastated by the invasion of Gaiseric, King of the Vandals. The grant was confirmed by an imperial rescript, and the Goths, consenting to the arrangement, set out for the country given them.

When they had gone away without doing any harm in Italy, Stilicho treacherously hurried to Pollentia, a city in the Cottian Alps. There he fell upon the unsuspecting Goths in battle, to the ruin of all Italy and his own disgrace.

The Goths enter Rome (410–411)

When the Goths suddenly beheld him, at first they were terrified. Soon regaining their courage and arousing each other by brave shouting, as is their custom, they turned to flight the entire army of Stilicho and almost exterminated it. Then forsaking the journey they had undertaken, the Goths with hearts full of rage returned again to Liguria whence they had set out. When they had plundered and spoiled it, they also laid waste Aemilia, and then hastened toward the city of Rome along the Flaminian Way, which runs between Picenum and Tuscia, taking as booty whatever they found on either hand. When they finally entered Rome, by Alaric's express command they merely sacked it and did not set the city on fire, as wild peoples usually do, nor did they permit serious damage to be done to the holy places. . . .

Attila the Hun

35. Now this Attila was the son of Mundiuch, and his brothers were Octar and Ruas who are said to have ruled before Attila, though not over quite so many tribes as he. After their death he succeeded to the throne of the Huns, together with his brother Bleda. In order that he might first be equal to the expedition he was preparing, he sought to increase his strength by murder. Thus he proceeded from the destruction of his own kindred to the menace of all others. But though he increased his power by this shameful means, yet by the balance of justice he received the hideous consequences of his own cruelty. Now when his brother Bleda, who ruled over a great part of the Huns, had been slain by his treachery, Attila united all the people under his own rule. Gathering also a host of the other tribes which he then held under his sway, he sought to subdue the foremost nations of the world—the Romans and the Visigoths. His army is said to have numbered five hundred thousand men. He was a man born into the world to shake the nations, the scourge of all lands, who in some way terrified all mankind by the dreadful rumors noised abroad concerning him. He was haughty in his walk, rolling his eyes hither and thither, so that the power of his proud spirit appeared in the movement of his body. He was indeed a lover of war, yet restrained in action, mighty in counsel, gracious to suppliants and lenient to those who were once received into his protection. He was short of stature, with a broad chest and a large head; his eyes were small, his beard thin and sprinkled with gray; and he had a flat nose and a swarthy complexion, showing the evidences of his origin.

And though his temper was such that he always had great self-confidence, yet his assurance was increased by finding the sword of Mars, always esteemed sacred among the kings of the Scythians . . . .

Gaiseric, King of the Vandals, and the Huns

36. Now when Gaiseric, King of the Vandals, whom we mentioned shortly before, learned that his mind was bent on the devastation of the world, he incited Attila by many gifts to make war on the Visigoths, for he was afraid that Theodorid, King of the Visigoths, would avenge the injury done to his daughter. She had been joined in wedlock with Huneric, the son of Gaiseric, and at first was happy in this union. But afterwards he was cruel even to his own children, and because of the mere suspicion that she was attempting to poison him, he cut off her nose and mutilated her ears. He sent her back to her father in Gaul thus despoiled of her natural charms. So the wretched girl presented a pitiable aspect ever after, and the cruelty which would stir even strangers still more surely incited her father to vengeance.

Attila, therefore, in his efforts to bring about the wars long ago instigated by the bribe of Gaiseric, sent ambassadors into Italy to the Emperor Valentinian to sow strife between the Goths and the Romans, thinking to shatter by civil discord those whom he could not crush in battle. He declared that he was in no way violating his friendly relations with the Empire, but that he had a quarrel with Theodorid, King of the Visigoths. As he wished to be kindly received, he filled the rest of the letter with the usual flattering salutations, striving to win credence for his falsehood. In like manner he dispatched a message to Theodorid, King of the Visigoths, urging him to break his alliance with the Romans and reminding him of the battles to which they had recently provoked him. Beneath his great ferocity he was a subtle man, and fought with craft before he made war.

Then the Emperor Valentinian sent an embassy to the Visigoths and their king Theodorid, with this message: "Bravest of nations, it is the part of prudence for us to unite against the lord of the earth who wishes to enslave the whole world; who requires no just cause for battle, but supposes whatever he does is right. He measures his ambition by his might. License satisfies his pride. Despising law and right, he shows himself an enemy to Nature herself. And thus he, who clearly is the common foe of each, deserves the hatred of all. Pray remember—what you surely cannot forget—that the Huns do not overthrow nations by means of war, where there is an equal chance, but assail them by treachery, which is a greater cause for anxiety. To say nothing about ourselves, can you suffer such insolence to go unpunished? Since you are mighty in arms, give heed to your own danger and join hands with us in common. Bear aid also to the Empire, of which you hold a part. If you would learn how such an alliance should be sought and welcomed by us, look into the plans of the foe."

The Battle of the Catalaunian Plains and the Defeat of the Huns

On the side of the Romans stood the Patrician Aëtius, on whom at that time the whole Empire of the West depended; a man of such wisdom that he had assembled warriors from everywhere to meet them on equal terms. Now these were his auxiliaries: Franks, Sarmatians, Armoricians, Liticians, Burgundians, Saxons, Riparians, Olibriones (once Romans soldiers and now the flower of the allied forces), and some other Celtic or German tribes. And so they met in the Catalaunian Plains . . . The two hosts bravely joined battle. Nothing was done under cover, but they contended in open fight. What just cause can be found for the encounter of so many nations, or what hatred inspired them all to take arms against each other? It is proof that the human race lives for its kings, for it is at the mad impulse of one mind a slaughter of nations takes place, and at the whim of a haughty ruler that which nature has taken ages to produce perishes in a moment. . . .

38. The armies met, as we have said, in the Catalaunian Plains. The battle field was a plain rising by a sharp slope to a ridge, which both armies sought to gain; for advantage of position is a great help. The Huns with their forces seized the right side, the Romans, the Visigoths and their allies the left, and then began a struggle for the yet untaken crest. Now Theodorid with the Visigoths held the right wing and Aëtius with the Romans the left. They placed in the centre Sangiban (who, as said before, was in command of the Alans), thus contriving with military caution to surround by a host of faithful troops the man in whose loyalty they had little confidence. For one who has difficulties placed in the way of his flight readily submits to the necessity of fighting.

On the other side, however, the battle line of the Huns was arranged so that Attila and his bravest followers were stationed in the center. In arranging them thus the king had chiefly his own safety in view, since by his position in the very midst of his race he would be kept out of the way of threatening danger. The innumerable peoples of the different tribes, which he had subjected to his sway, formed the wings. Amid them was conspicuous the army of the Ostrogoths under the leadership of the brothers Valamir, Thiudimer and Vidimer, nobler even than the king they served, for the might of the family of the Amali rendered them glorious. The renowned king of the Gepidae, Ardaric, was there also with a countless host, and because of his great loyalty to Attila, he shared his plans . . . Attila might well feel sure that they would fight against the Visigoths, their kinsmen. Now the rest of the crowd of kings (if we may call them so) and the leaders of various nations hung upon Attila's nod like slaves, and when he gave a sign even by a glance, without a murmur each stood forth in fear and trembling, or at all events did as he was bid. Attila alone was king of all kings over all and concerned for all.

So then the struggle began for the advantage of position we have mentioned. Attila sent his men to take the summit of the mountain, but was outstripped by Thorismud and Aëtius, who in their effort to gain the top of the hill reached higher ground and through this advantage of position easily routed the Huns as they came up. . . .

At dawn on the following day, when the Romans saw the fields were piled high with bodies and that the Huns did not venture forth, they thought the victory was theirs, but knew that Attila would not flee from the battle unless overwhelmed by a great disaster. Yet he did nothing cowardly, like one that is overcome, but with clash of arms sounded the trumpets and threatened an attack. He was like a lion pierced by hunting spears, who paces to and fro before the mouth of his den and dares not spring, but ceases not to terrify the neighborhood by his roaring. Even so this warlike king at bay terrified his conquerors. Therefore the Goths and Romans assembled and considered what to do with the vanquished Attila. They determined to wear him out by a siege, because he had no supply of provisions and was hindered from approaching by a shower of arrows from the bowmen placed within the confines of the Roman camp. But it was said that the king remained supremely brave even in this extremity and had heaped up a funeral pyre of horse trappings, so that if the enemy should attack him, he was determined to cast himself into the flames, that none might have the joy of wounding him and that the lord of so many races might not fall into the hands of his foes. . . .

In this most famous war of the bravest tribes, one hundred and sixty five thousand are said to have been slain on both sides, leaving out of account fifteen thousand of the Gepidae and Franks, who met each other the night before the general engagement and fell by wounds mutually received, the Franks fighting for the Romans and the Gepidae for the Huns.

Now when Attila learned of the retreat of the Goths, he thought it a ruse of the enemy—for so men are wont to believe when the unexpected happens—and remained for some time in his camp. But when a long silence followed the absence of the foe, the spirit of the mighty king was aroused to the thought of victory and the anticipation of pleasure, and his mind turned to the old oracles of his destiny. . . .

42. But Attila took occasion from the withdrawal of the Visigoths, observing what he had often desired—that his enemies were divided. At length feeling secure, he moved forward his array to attack the Romans. . . .

Attila and Pope Leo the Great at Rome

Attila's mind had been bent on going to Rome. But his followers, as the historian Priscus relates, took him away, not out of regard for the city to which they were hostile, but because they remembered the case of Alaric, the former king of the Visigoths. They distrusted the good fortune of their own king, inasmuch as Alaric did not live long after the sack of Rome, but straightway departed this life. Therefore while Attila's spirit was wavering in doubt between going and not going, and he still lingered to ponder the matter, an embassy came to him from Rome to seek peace. Pope Leo himself came to meet him in the Ambuleian district of the Veneti at the well-traveled ford of the river Mincius. Then Attila quickly put aside his usual fury, turned back on the way he had advanced from beyond the Danube and departed with the promise of peace. . . .

The Death of Attila

49. Shortly before he (i.e., Attila) died, as the historian Priscus relates, he took in marriage a very beautiful girl named Ildico, after countless other wives, as was the custom of his race. He had given himself up to excessive joy at his wedding, and as he lay on his back, heavy with wine and sleep, a rush of superfluous blood, which would ordinarily have flowed from his nose, streamed in deadly course down his throat and killed him, since it was hindered in the usual passages. Thus did drunkenness put a disgraceful end to a king renowned in war. On the following day, when a great part of the morning was spent, the royal attendants suspected some ill and, after a great uproar, broke in the doors. There they found the death of Attila accomplished by an effusion of blood, without any wound, and the girl with downcast face weeping beneath her veil. Then, as is the custom of that race, they plucked out the hair of their heads and made their faces hideous with deep wounds, that the renowned warrior might be mourned, not by effeminate wailings and tears, but by the blood of men. . . .

The End of Attila's Domain and the Independence of the Ostrogoths and Others

50. After they had fulfilled these rites, a contest for the highest place arose among Attila's successors—for the minds of young men are wont to be inflamed by ambition for power—and in their rash eagerness to rule they all alike destroyed his empire. Thus kingdoms are often weighed down by a superfluity rather than by a lack of successors. For the sons of Attila were clamoring that the nations should be divided among them equally and that warlike kings with their peoples should be apportioned to them by lot like a family estate. When Ardaric, king of the Gepidae, learned this, he became enraged because so many nations were being treated like slaves of the basest condition, and was the first to rise against the sons of Attila. Good fortune attended him, and he effaced the disgrace of servitude that rested upon him. For by his revolt he freed not only his own tribe, but all the others who were equally oppressed; since all readily strive for that

which is sought for the general advantage. They took up arms against the destruction that menaced all and joined battle with the Huns in Pannonia, near a river called Nedao. There an encounter took place between the various nations Attila had held under his sway. Kingdoms with their peoples were divided, and out of one body were made many members not responding to a common impulse. Being deprived of their head, they madly strove against each other. They never found their equals ranged against them without harming each other by wounds mutually given. And so the bravest nations tore themselves to pieces. For then, I think, must have occurred a most remarkable spectacle, where one might see the Goths fighting with pikes, the Gepidae raging with the sword, the Rugi breaking off the spears in their own wounds, the Suebi fighting on foot, the Huns with bows, the Alans drawing up a battle-line of heavy-armed and the Heruli of light-armed warriors. . . .

Now when the Goths saw the Gepidae defending for themselves the territory of the Huns and the people of the Huns dwelling again in their ancient abodes, they preferred to ask for lands from the Roman Empire, rather than invade the lands of others with danger to themselves. So they received Pannonia, which stretches in a long plain, being bounded on the east by Upper Moesia, on the south by Dalmatia, on the west by Noricum and on the north by the Danube. This land is adorned with many cities, the first of which is Sirmium and the last Vindobona. But the Sauromatae, whom we call Sarmatians, and the Cemandri and certain of the Huns dwelt in Castra Martis, a city given them in the region of Illyricum. Of this race was Blivila, Duke of Pentapolis, and his brother Froila and also Bessa, a Patrician in our time. The Sciri, moreover, and the Sadagarii and certain of the Alans with their leader, Candac by name, received Scythia Minor and Lower Moesia. Paria, the father of my father Alanoviiamuth (that is to say, my grandfather), was secretary to this Candac as long as he lived. To his sister's son Gunthigis, also called Baza, the Master of the Soldiery, who was the son of Andag the son of Andela, who was descended from the stock of the Amali, I also, Jordanes, although an unlearned man before my conversion, was secretary. The Rugi, however, and some other races asked that they might inhabit Bizye and Arcadiopolis. Hernac, the younger son of Attila, with his followers, chose a home in the most distant part of Lesser Scythia. Emnetzur and Ultzindur, kinsmen of his, won Oescus and Utus and Almus in Dacia on the bank of the Danube, and many of the Huns, then swarming everywhere, betook themselves into Romania, and from them the Sacromontisi and the Fossatisii of this day are said to be descended.

Ulfilas, Apostle to the Goths

51. There were other Goths also, called the Lesser, a great people whose priest and primate was Ulfilas, who is said to have taught them to write. And today they are in Moesia, inhabiting the Nicopolitan region as far as the base of

Mount Haemus. They are a numerous people, but poor and unwarlike, rich in nothing save flocks of various kinds and pasture-lands for cattle and forests for wood. Their country is not fruitful in wheat and other sorts of grain. Certain of them do not know that vineyards exist elsewhere, and they buy their wine from neighboring countries. But most of them drink milk.

The Rise of Theodoric

Now after no great time King Valamir and his brothers Thiudimer and Vidimer sent an embassy to the Emperor Marcian, because the usual gifts which they received like a New Year's present from the Emperor, to preserve the compact of peace, were slow in arriving . . . From the Goths the Romans received as a hostage of peace Theodoric, the young child of Thiudimer, whom we have mentioned above. He had now attained the age of seven years and was entering upon his eighth. While his father hesitated about giving him up, his uncle Valamir convinced him to do it, hoping that peace between the Romans and the Goths might thus be assured. Therefore Theodoric was given as a hostage by the Goths and brought to the city of Constantinople to the Emperor Leo and, being a goodly child, deservedly gained the imperial favor. . . .

55. After a certain time, when the wintry cold was at hand, the river Danube was frozen over as usual. Thiudimer, King of the Goths, saw that it was frozen, he led his army across the Danube and appeared unexpectedly to the Suebi from the rear. Now this country of the Suebi has on the east the Baiovari, on the west the Franks, on the south the Burgundians and on the north the Thuringians. Into a place thus fortified King Thiudimer led his army in the winter-time and conquered, plundered and almost subdued the race of the Suebi as well as the Alamanni, who were mutually banded together. Thence he returned as victor to his own home in Pannonia and joyfully received his son Theodoric, once given as hostage to Constantinople and now sent back by the Emperor Leo with great gifts. Now Theodoric had reached man's estate, for he was eighteen years of age and his boyhood was ended. So he summoned certain of his father's adherents and took to himself from the people his friends and retainers—almost six thousand men. With these he crossed the Danube, without his father's knowledge, and marched against Babai, King of the Sarmatians, who had just won a victory over Camundus, a general of the Romans, and was ruling with insolent pride. Theodoric came upon him and slew him, and taking as booty his slaves and treasure, returned victorious to his father. Next he invaded the city of Singidunum, which the Sarmatians themselves had seized, and did not return it to the Romans, but reduced it to his own sway. . . .

56. Soon after these events, King Thiudimer was seized with a mortal illness in the city of Cyrrhus. He called the Goths to himself, appointed Theodoric his son as heir of his kingdom and presently departed this life.

Theodoric, King of the Ostrogoths

57. When the Emperor Zeno heard that Theodoric had been appointed king over his own people, he received the news with pleasure and invited him to come and visit him in the city, appointing an escort of honor. Receiving Theodoric with all due respect, he placed him among the princes of his palace. After some time Zeno increased his dignity by adopting him as his son-at-arms and gave him a triumph in the city at his expense. Theodoric was made Consul Ordinary also, which is well known to be the supreme good and highest honor in the world. Nor was this all, for Zeno set up before the royal palace an equestrian statue to the glory of this great man.

Theodoric Sets Out for Rome

Now while Theodoric was in alliance by treaty with the Empire of Zeno and was himself enjoying every comfort in the city, he heard that his tribe, dwelling as we have said in Illyricum, was not altogether satisfied or content. So he chose rather to seek a living by his own exertions, after the manner customary to his race, rather than to enjoy the advantages of the Roman Empire in luxurious ease while his tribe lived in want. After pondering these matters, he said to the Emperor: "Though I lack nothing in serving your Empire, yet if Your Piety deem it worthy, be pleased to hear the desire of my heart." And when as usual he had been granted permission to speak freely, he said: "The western country, long ago governed by the rule of your ancestors and predecessors, and that city which was the head and mistress of the world—wherefore is it now shaken by the tyranny of the Torcilingi and the Rugi? Send me there with my race. Thus if you but say the word, you may be freed from the burden of expense here, and, if by the Lord's help I shall conquer, the fame of Your Piety shall be glorious there. For it is better that I, your servant and your son, should rule that kingdom, receiving it as a gift from you if I conquer, than that one whom you do not recognize should oppress your Senate with his tyrannical yoke and a part of the republic with slavery. For if I prevail, I shall retain it as your grant and gift; if I am conquered, Your Piety will lose nothing—nay, as I have said, it will save the expense I now entail." Although the Emperor was grieved that he should go, yet when he heard this he granted what Theodoric asked, for he was unwilling to cause him sorrow. He sent him forth enriched by great gifts and commended to his charge the Senate and the Roman People.

Therefore Theodoric departed from the royal city and returned to his own people. In company with the whole tribe of the Goths, who gave him their unanimous consent, he set out for Hesperia. He went in straight march through Sirmium to the places bordering on Pannonia and, advancing into the territory of Venetia as far as the bridge of the Sontius, encamped there. When he had halted there for some time to rest the bodies of his men and pack-animals, Odoacer sent an armed force against him, which he met on the plains of Verona and destroyed with great slaughter . . . He frequently harassed the army of the Goths at night, sallying forth stealthily with his men, and this not once or twice, but often; and thus he struggled for almost three whole years. But he labored in vain, for all Italy at last called Theodoric its lord and the Empire obeyed his nod. But Odoacer, with his few adherents and the Romans who were present, suffered daily from war and famine in Ravenna. Since he accomplished nothing, he sent an embassy and begged for mercy. Theodoric first granted it and afterwards deprived him of his life.

Theodoric Rules in Italy

It was in the third year after his entrance into Italy, as we have said, that Theodoric, by advice of the Emperor Zeno, laid aside the garb of a private citizen and the dress of his race and assumed a costume with a royal mantle, as he had now become the ruler over both Goths and Romans. He sent an embassy to Lodoin, King of the Franks, and asked for his daughter Audefleda in marriage. Lodoin freely and gladly gave her, and also his sons Celdebert and Heldebert and Thiudebert, believing that by this alliance a league would be formed and that they would be associated with the race of the Goths. But that union was of no avail for peace and harmony, for they fought fiercely with each other again and again for the lands of the Goths; but never did the Goths yield to the Franks while Theodoric lived. . . .

58. Now he sent his Count Pitza, chosen from among the chief men of his kingdom, to hold the city of Sirmium. He got possession of it by driving out its king Thrasaric, son of Thraustila, and keeping his mother captive. Thence he came with two thousand infantry and five hundred horsemen to aid Mundo against Sabinian, Master of the Soldiery of Illyricum, who at that time had made ready to fight with Mundo near the city named Margoplanum, which lies between the Danube and Margus rivers, and destroyed the Army of Illyricum. For this Mundo, who traced his descent from the Attilani of old, had put to flight the tribe of the Gepidae and was roaming beyond the Danube in waste places where no man tilled the soil. He had gathered around him many outlaws and ruffians and robbers from all sides and had seized a tower called Herta, situated on the bank of the Danube. There he plundered his neighbors in wild license and made himself king over his vagabonds. Now Pitza came upon him when he

was nearly reduced to desperation and was already thinking of surrender. So he rescued him from the hands of Sabinian and made him a grateful subject of his king Theodoric. . . .

The Death of Theodoric

59. When he had reached old age and knew that he should soon depart this life, he called together the Gothic counts and chieftains of his race and appointed Athalaric as king. He was a boy scarce ten years old, the son of his daughter Amalasuentha, and he had lost his father Eutharic. As though uttering his last will and testament Theodoric adjured and commanded them to honor their king, to love the Senate and Roman People and to make sure of the peace and good will of the Emperor of the East, as next after God.

They kept this command fully so long as Athalaric their king and his mother lived, and ruled in peace for almost eight years. But as the Franks put no confidence in the rule of a child and furthermore held him in contempt, and were also plotting war, he gave back to them those parts of Gaul which his father and grandfather had seized. He possessed all the rest in peace and quiet. Therefore when Athalaric was approaching the age of manhood, he entrusted to the Emperor of the East both his own youth and his mother's widowhood. But in a short time the ill-fated boy was carried off by an untimely death and departed from earthly affairs. His mother feared she might be despised by the Goths on account of the weakness of her sex. So after much thought she decided, for the sake of relationship, to summon her cousin Theodahad from Tuscany, where he led a retired life at home, and thus she established him on the throne. But he was unmindful of their kinship and, after a little time, had her taken from the palace at Ravenna to an island of the Bulsinian Lake where he kept her in exile. . . .

The End of Gothic Rule in Italy

60. When Justinian (d. 565), the Emperor of the East, heard this, he was aroused as if he had suffered personal injury in the death of his wards. Now at that time he had won a triumph over the Vandals in Africa, through his most faithful Patrician Belisarius. Without delay he sent his army under this leader against the Goths at the very time when his arms were yet dripping with the blood of the Vandals. This sagacious general believed he could not overcome the Gothic nation, unless he should first seize Sicily. Accordingly he did so. As soon as he entered Trinacria, the Goths, who were besieging the town of Syracuse, found that they were not succeeding and surrendered of their own accord to Belisarius, with their leader Sinderith. When the Roman general reached Sicily,

Theodahad sought out Evermud, his son-in-law, and sent him with an army to guard the strait which lies between Campania and Sicily and sweeps from a bend of the Tyrrhenian Sea into the vast tide of the Adriatic. . . .

Meanwhile the Roman army crossed the strait and marched toward Campania. They took Naples and pressed on to Rome. Now a few days before they arrived, King Vitiges had set forth from Rome, arrived at Ravenna and married Mathesuentha, the daughter of Amalasuentha and grand-daughter of Theodoric, the former king. While he was celebrating his new marriage and holding court at Ravenna, the imperial army advanced from Rome and attacked the strongholds in both parts of Tuscany . . . When Vitiges heard the news, he raged like a lion and assembled all the host of the Goths. He advanced from Ravenna and harassed the walls of Rome with a long siege. But after fourteen months his courage was broken and he raised the siege of the city of Rome and prepared to overwhelm Ariminum. Here he was baffled in like manner and put to flight; and so he retreated to Ravenna. When besieged there, he quickly and willingly surrendered himself to the victorious side, together with his wife Mathesuentha and the royal treasure.

And thus a famous kingdom and most valiant race, which had long held sway, was at last overcome in almost its two thousand and thirtieth year by that conqueror of many nations, the Emperor Justinian, through his most faithful consul Belisarius. He gave Vitiges the title of Patrician and took him to Constantinople, where he dwelt for more than two years, bound by ties of affection to the Emperor, and then departed this life. But his consort Mathesuentha was bestowed by the Emperor upon the Patrician Germanus, his cousin. And of them was born a son (also called Germanus) after the death of his father Germanus. This union of the race of the Anicii with the stock of the Amali gives hopeful promise, under the Lord's favor, to both peoples.

Conclusion

And now we have recited the origin of the Goths, the noble line of the Amali and the deeds of brave men. This glorious race yielded to a more glorious prince and surrendered to a more valiant leader, whose fame shall be silenced by no ages or cycles of years; for the victorious and triumphant Emperor Justinian and his consul Belisarius shall be named and known as Vandalicus, Africanus and Geticus (so named for having defeated these peoples).

You who read this, know that I have followed the writings of my ancestors, and have culled a few flowers from their broad meadows to weave a chaplet for him who cares to know these things. Let no one believe that to the advantage of the race of which I have spoken—though indeed I trace my own descent from it—I have added nothing but what I have read or learned by inquiry. Even thus I have not included all that is written or told about them, nor spoken so much to their praise as to the glory of him who conquered them.

Source: Jordanes: *The Origin and Deeds of the Goths,* trans. by Charles C. Mierow, 1908. New Jersey: Princeton University Press, pp. 1–2, 7–9, 38–43, 45–48, 56–62, 65–67, 69, 79–86, 89–90, 92–100.

21. Justinian's Codification of Roman Law

Beginning in 529, the emperor Justinian, with the help of a committee of highly trained lawyers, issued the *Corpus Iuris Civilis* (Body of Civil Law) the most exhaustive codification of Roman law, and one that would reshape legal traditions and political philosophy in the later medieval world. The Corpus was issued in Latin in three collections—Code of Justinian, Digest or Pandects, and Institutes—with a fourth publication, the Novels or new laws of Justinian, issued later in Greek. The Digest, excerpts of which follow, was the second work published, appearing in 530. It is divided into 50 books, which were then divided into chapters, laws, and paragraphs. The Digest offers a systematic approach to the law and became the authoritative commentary on Roman law. The first of the two passages that follow provides the introduction to the Digest, describing Justinian's purpose for the work, its organization and subject matter, and its authority as a legal document. The second excerpt is a list of specific legal questions and the legal authorities on these questions.

On the Confirmation of the Digest

Constitutio Tanta.

In the name of our Lord God Jesus Christ.
The Emperor Caeser Flavius Justinianus Alamannicus Gothicus Francicus Germanicus Anticus Alanicus Vandalicus Africanus pious happy renowned conqueror and triumpher ever Augustus to the Senate and to all peoples.

So great in our behalf is the foresight of Divine Humanity that it ever deigns to support us with eternal acts of liberality. After the Parthian wars were hushed in eternal peace, after the nation of the Vandals was destroyed (1), and Carthage, nay rather all Libya, was again taken into the Roman Empire, then I contrived also that the ancient laws, already bowed down with age, should by my care reach new beauty and come within moderate bounds; a thing which before our command none ever expected or deemed to be at all possible for human endeavour. It was indeed a wondrous achievement when Roman jurisprudence from the time of the building of the city to that of our rule, which period well-nigh reaches to one thousand and four hundred years, had been shaken with intestine war and infected the Imperial legislation with the same mischief, to bring it nevertheless into one harmonious system, so that it should present no contradiction, no repetition and no approach to repetition, and that nowhere should two enactments appear dealing with one question. This was indeed proper for Heavenly Providence, but in no way possible to the weakness of man. We therefore have after our wont fixed our eyes on the aid of Immortality, and, calling on the Supreme Deity, we have desired that God should be made the originator and the guardian of the whole work, and we have entrusted the entire task to Tribonianus, a most distinguished man, Master of the Offices, ex-quaestor of our sacred palace and ex-consul, and we have laid on him the whole service of the enterprise described, so that with other illustrious and most learned colleagues he might fulfil our desire. Besides this, our Majesty, ever investigating and scrutinizing the composition of these men, whensoever anything was found doubtful or uncertain, in reliance on the heavenly Divinity, amended it and reduced it to suitable shape. Thus all has been done by our Lord and God Jesus Christ, who vouchsafed the means of success both to us and to our servants herein. 1. Now the Imperial statutes we have already placed, arranged in twelve books, in the Code which is illuminated with our name. After this, undertaking a very great work, we allowed the same exalted man both to collect together and to submit to certain modifications the very most important works of old times, thoroughly intermixed and broken up as they may almost be called. But in the midst of our careful researches, it was intimated to us by the said exalted person that there were nearly two thousand books written by the old lawyers, are more than three million lines were left us by them, all of which it was requisite to read and carefully consider and out of them to select whatever might be best. This by the grace of Heaven and the favour of the Supreme Trinity, was accomplished in accordance with our instructions such as we gave at the outset to the exalted man above mentioned, so that everything of great importance was collected into fifty books, and all ambiguities were settled, without any refractory passage being left. We gave these books the name of Digest or Pandects, for the reason they have within them all matters of question and the legal decision thereof, having taken to their bosom things collected from all sides, so that they conclude the whole task in the space of about one hundred and fifty thousand lines. We have divided the books into seven parts, not incorrectly nor without reason, but in regard of the nature and use of numbers and in order to make a division of parts in keeping therewith. 2. Accordingly, the first part of the whole frame, which part is called (πρώτη), after the Greek word, comes by itself in four books. 3. The second link has seven books, which are called *de judiciis* (on trials at law). 4. In the third group we have put all that comes under the title *de rebus* (on things), the same having eight books assigned to it. 5. The fourth place, which amounts to a sort of kernel of the whole compilation, takes eight books. This contains everything that relates to hypothec, so that the subject does not differ very much from the *actio pigneratitia* (action to redeem, etc.), and another book is inserted in the same volume which has the Edict of the Edile and the Redhibitorian action and the stipulation for returning double the price received, which is matter of law in case of an *evictio* (recovery of property on the ground of ownership), the fact being that these matters are connected with the subject of purchase and sale, and the aforesaid actions were always closely attendant on those last topics. It is true that, in the scheme of the old Edict, they wandered off into out-of-the-way places widely apart from one another, but by our care they are put in the same group, as it is only right that discussions on almost identical subjects should be put close together. Then another book has been devised by us to follow the two first to deal with interest on money and with *trajectitia pecunia* (bottomry loans), also on documents of title, on witnesses, on proof, and therewith on presumptions, which three separate books are placed close to the portion dealing with things. After these we have assigned a place to the rules laid down anywhere as to betrothals, marriages, and dowries, all which we have set forth within three volumes. On guardianship and curatorship we have composed two books. This framework, consisting of eight books, we have set down in the middle of the whole work, and it contains all the most practical and best expressed rules collected from all quarters. 6. We then come to the fifth article of our Digest, to which the reader will find consigned whatsoever was said of old times on the subject of testaments and codicils, both of ordinary persons and soldiers; this article is called "On Testaments." Next comes the subject of legacies and *fideicommissa* (testamentary trusts), in books five in number. 6a. And as there is nothing so closely bound up with anything else as an account of the *lex Falcidia* with legacies, or of the *Senatusconsultim Trebellianum* with *fideicommissa*, we appropriate two books to these respective subjects, and thus complete the whole fifth part in nine books. We have not thought proper to put anything besides the *Senatusconsultim Trebellianum,* because, as to the stumbling blocks and obscurities of the *Senatusconsultim Pegasianum,* which the very ancients themselves were disgusted with, and their nice and superfluous distinctions, we desire to be rid of them, and we have included all the law we lay down on the subject in the *Trebellianum.* 6b. In all this we have said nothing about *caduca* (escheats), lest a head of law which, in the midst of unprosperous courses and bad times for Rome, grew in importance with public distress, and drew strength from civil war, should remain in our day when our reign is strengthened by Divine favour and a flourishing peace and placed above all nations in the matter of the perils of war, and thus a melancholy reminiscence should be allowed to cast a shadow on a joyful age. 7. Next we have before us the sixth part of the Digest, in which are placed all kinds of *bonorum possessio,* whether they relate to freeborn persons or freedmen, and herein the whole law concerned with degrees of relationship and with connexion by marriage, also statutable heritage and succession *ab intestato* in general and the *Senatusconsultim Trebellianum* or *Orfitianum,* which respectively regulate the succession of children to their mother, and mothers to their children. We have assigned two books to all the varieties of *bonorum possessio* and reduced the whole to a clear and compendious scheme. 7a. After this we take the things laid down by old authors as to *operis novi nuntiatio* (notification of novel structure), as to the *damnum infectum* (apprehended mischief), also for the case of the destruction of buildings or the same being threatened, also as to the keeping off of rainwater; further we take whatever we find provided by statute relating to *publicani* as well as to the making of voluntary gifts both *inter vivos* and *mortis causa*, all which we have put in a single book. 7b. For manumissions and trials as to liberty, these are the subject of another book, (7c) and again on questions as to property and possession there are many discursive passages put in a single volume, (7d) while a further book is assigned to the subject of persons who have suffered judgment or have confessed *in jure* (in the pleadings), also of detention of goods and sales thereof (for insolvency), and as to the preventing of frauds on creditors. 7e. After this, Interdicts are dealt with in the lump, then come *exceptiones* (pleas), and there is again a separate book embracing the subject of lapse of time and obligations and actions; the result being that the above-mentioned sixth part of the whole volume of the Digest is kept within eight books. 8. The seventh and last division of the Digest is made up of six books, and all the law that is met with as to stipulations or verbal obligations, as to sureties and *mandatores* (persons who request an advance to be made to another), also novations, discharges of debt, formal receipts and prætorian stipulations is set down in two volumes, which it was impossible so much as to reckon among the number of ancient books. 8a. After this we have put two terrifying books on the subject of private and extraordinary offences and also of public crimes, in which are described the whole severe treatment and awful penal measures applied to criminals, mixed with which are the provisions which have been made as to incorrigible men who endeavour to conceal themselves and who resist authority also the matter of penalties such as are imposed on condemned persons or remitted and the subject of their property. 8b. Next we have devised a separate book on appeals from judgments delivered by way of deciding either civil or criminal cases, 8c. and whatever else we find devised by the ancients and strictly laid down municipal authorities or with relation to decurions or to public offices or public works or *nundinæ* (right of market), or promises or different kinds of trials or assessments or the meaning of words,—all these are taken into the fiftieth book, which closes the compilation. 9. The whole of the above has been completed by the agency of the eminent man and most learned magistrate Tribonianus, ex-quaestor and ex-consul, a man adorned alike with the arts of eloquence and of legal science, as well as distinguished in practical life, and one who has no greater or dearer object than obedience to our commands: other brilliant and hardworking persons have cooperated, such as Constantinus, that illustrious man, Count of the Sacred Largesses and Master of the Office of Libels and Sacred inquiries, who has long deserved our esteem from his good repute and distinction;

also Theophilus, an illustrious man, a magistrate and learned in the law, who wields admirably the best sway in the law over this brilliant city; Dorotheus, an illustrious man, of great eloquence and quaestorian rank, whom, when he was engaged delivering the law to students in the most brilliant city of Berytus, we, moved by his great reputation and renown, summoned to our presence and made to share in the work in question; again, Anatolius, an illustrious person, a magistrate, who, like the last, was invited to this work when acting as an exponent of law at Brytus, a man who came of an ancient stock, as both his father Leontius and his grandfather Eudoxius left behind them an excellent report in respect of legal learning; also Cratinus, an illustrious person, Count of the Sacred Largesses, who was once a most efficient professor of this revered city. All these were chosen for the above-mentioned work, together with Stephanus, Mena, Prosdocius, Eutolmius, Timotheus, Leonides, Leontius, Plato, Jacobus, Constantinus, Johannes, most learned men, who are of counsel at the supreme seat of the Præfecture, which is at the head of the eastern prætoria, but who derive a testimony to their excellence from all quarters and were chosen by us for the completion of so great a work. Thus, all the above having met together under the guidance of the eminent Tribonianus, so as to accomplish this great work in pursuance of our commission, the whole was by Divine favour completed in fifty books. 10. Herein we had so much respect for ancient authority that we by no means have suffered them to consign to oblivion the names of those learned in the law; everyone of the old lawyers who wrote on law has been mentioned in our Digest; all that we did was to provide that if, in the rules given by them, there appeared to be anything superfluous or imperfect or of small importance, it should be amplified or curtailed to the requisite extent and be reduced to the most correct form; and in many cases of repetition or contradiction what appeared to be better has been set down instead of any other reading and included under one authority thus given to the whole, so that whatever has now been written may appear clearly to be ours and to be composed by our order, none being at liberty to compare the ancient text with what our authority has introduced, as in fact there have been many very important transformations made on the ground of practical utility. It goes as far as this, that where an Imperial enactment is set down in the old books, we have not spared even this, but resolved to correct it and put it in better form; leaving the very names of the old authority, but preserving by our emendations whatever the real sense of the statutes made suitable and necessary. Hence it came to pass that where of old there was any matter of doubt the question has now become quite safe and undisturbed, and no room for hesitation is left. 11. We saw however that the burden of all this mass of knowledge is more than such men are equal to bearing as are insufficiently educated and are standing in the vestibules of law, though on their way towards the secrets thereof, and we therefore were of opinion that a further compendious summaryshould be prepared, so that, thereby tinctured and so to speak imbued with the first elements of the whole subject, they might proceed to the innermost recesses thereof and take in with eyes undazzled the exquisite beauty of the law. We therefore summoned Tribonianus, that eminent man who had been chosen for the direction of the whole work, also Theophilus and Dorotheus, illustrious persons and most eloquent professors, and commissioned them to collect one by one the books composed by old authors in which the first principles were to be found, and thereupon, whatever they found in them that was useful and most to the purpose and polished in every point of view and in accordance with the practice of the present age, all this they were to endeavour to grasp and to put it into four books, so as to lay the first foundations and principles of education in general, and thus enable young men, supported thereon, to be ready for weightier and more perfect rules of law. We instructed them at the same time to bear in mind our own Constitutions as well, which we have issued with a view to the amendment of the law, and, in composing the Institutes, not to omit to insert the same improvement, so that it should be clear both where there had been any doubt previously, and what points had been afterwards established. The whole work, as accomplished by these men, was put before us and read through; whereupon we received it willingly and judged it to be not unworthy of our mind, and we ordered that the books should be equivalent to enactments of our own, as is more plainly declared in our own address which we have placed at the beginning of the whole. 12. The whole frame of Roman law being thus set forth and completed in three divisions, viz. one of the Institutes, one of the Digest or Pandects, and lastly one of the Constitutions, all being concluded in three years, whereas when the work was first taken in hand it was not expected to be finished in ten years, we offered this work too with dutiful intent to Almighty God for the preservation of mankind, and rendered full thanks to the Supreme Deity who vouchsafed us successful waging of war and the enjoyment of honourable peace and the giving of the best laws, not only for our own age, but for all time, both present and future. Therefore we saw it to be necessary that we should make manifest the same system of law to all men, to the end that they should recognise the endless confusion in which the law was, and the judicious and lawful exactitude to which it had been brought, and that they might in future have laws which were both direct and compendious within every one's reach, and of such a nature as to make it easy to possess the books which contained them. Our object was that people should not simply be able by spending a whole mass of wealth to procure volumes containing a superfluous quantity of legal rules, but the means of purchasing at a trifling price should be offered both to rich and poor, a great deal of learning being procurable with a very small outlay. 13. Should it chance that here and there, in so great a collection of legal rules, taken as it is from an immense number of books, some cases of repetition should occur, this no one must be severe upon; it should rather be ascribed first of all to human weakness, which is part of our nature, as indeed it belongs rather to the Deity than to mortal man to have a memory for all things and to come short in nothing, as indeed was said of old. It should also be borne in mind that there are some rules of exceeding brevity in which repetition may be admitted to good purpose, and it has been practised in accordance with our deliberate intent, the fact being that either the rule was so material that it had to be referred to under different heads of inquiry, because the two subjects were connected together, or else, where it was involved in other different inquiries, it was impossible to exclude it from some passages without throwing the whole into confusion. And in these passages, in which there were well-reasoned arguments set forth by the old writers, it would be altogether an unlawyerlike proceeding to cut out and get rid of something that was inserted in one after another, as it would confuse the mind and sound absurd to the ears of anyone to whom it was presented. 14. In like manner, where any provision has been made by Imperial enactment, we have by no means allowed it to be put in the book of the Digest, as the reading of such enactments is all that is wanted; save where this too is done for the same reasons as those for which repetition is admitted. 15. As for any contradiction occurring in this book, none such has any claim to a place in it, nor will any be found, if we consider nicely the grounds of diversity; some special differential feature will be discovered, however obscure, which does away with the imputation of inconsistency, puts a different complexion on the matter and keeps it outside the limits of discrepancy. 16. Again should anything happen to be passed over which, among so many thousand things, was, so to speak, placed in the depth and lying hid, and being fit to be so [placed], [still] was covered with darkness and unavoidably was left out, who could with reason find fault with this, considering in the first place how limited is the mind of mortal man, and secondly the intrinsic difficulty of the case, where the passage, being closely bound up with a number of useless ones, gave the reader no opportunity of detaching it from the rest? It may be added too that it is much better that a few valuable passages should escape notice than that people should be encumbered with a quantity of useless matter. 17. There is one very remarkable fact which comes to light in these books, namely, that the old books, plentiful as they were, are found to be of smaller compass than the more compendious supply now open. The fact is that the men who carried on actions at law in the old days, in spite of the number of rules of law that had been laid down, still only made use of a few of them in the course of the trial, either because of a deficient supply of books, which it was out of their power to procure, or simply owing to their own ignorance; and cases were decided according to the good pleasure of the judge rather than by the letter of the law. In the present compilation, I mean in our Digest, the law is got together from numerous volumes, the very names of which the men of old could not tell, or rather had never heard; and the whole has been composed with an ample supply of matter in such sort that the ancient plenty appears defective while our own compendious collection is very rich. Of this ancient learning Tribouianus, most excellent man, has furnished us with a very large supply of books, a number of which were unknown even to the most erudite men; these were read through, and all the most valuable passages were extracted and found their way into our own excellent work. But the authors of this composition did not peruse those books only from which they took the rules they have set down; they read a great deal more, in which they found nothing of value or nothing new which they could extract and insert in our Digest, and which accordingly they very reasonably rejected. 18. Now whatever is divine is absolutely perfect, but the character of human law is to be constantly hurrying on, and no part of it is there which can abide for ever, as nature is ever eager to produce new forms, so that we fully anticipate that emergencies may hereafter arise which are not enclosed in the bonds of legal rules. Wherever any such case arises, let the August remedy be sought, as in truth God set the Imperial dispensation at the head of human affairs to this end, that it should be in a position, whenever a novel contingency, arrives to meet the same with amendment and arrangement, and to put it under apt form and regulations. We are not the first to enunciate this, it comes of an ancient stock; Julianus himself, that most acute framer of statutes and of the Perpetual Edict, set down in his own writings that wherever anything should turn out defective, the want should be supplied by Imperial legislation. Indeed not only he but the Divine Hadrianus, in the consolidated Edict and the *Senatuscormdtum* which followed it, laid down in the clearest terms that where anything was not found to be set down in the Edict, later authority might meet the defect in accordance with the rules the aims and the analogy thereof. 19. Now therefore, conscript fathers and all men in the whole world, render fullest thanks to the Supreme Divinity, who has kept so greatly beneficial a work for your times: in truth, that of which those of old time were not in the Divine judgment held to be worthy has been vouchsafed to your age. Worship therefore and keep these laws, and let the ancient ones sleep; and let none of you so much as compare them with the former ones, nor, if there be any discrepancy between them, ask any question, seeing that, whatsoever is set down here, we desire that it alone should be observed. Moreover in every trial or other contest, where rules of law have to be enforced, let no one seek to quote or maintain any rule of law save as taken from the above mentioned Institutes or our Digest or Ordinances such as composed and promulgated by us, unless he wish to have to meet a charge of forgery as an adulterator, together with the judge who allows such things to be heard, and to suffer most severe penalties. 20. Lest however it should be unknown to you what those books of old lawyers are from which this composition is taken, we have ordered that this likewise should be set down at the beginning of our Digest, so that it may be quite clear who are the authorities and which are the books written by them, and how many thousands of these there are on which this temple of Roman jurisprudence has been constructed. 20a. Of legal authorities or commentators we have chosen those who were worthy of so great a work as this, and whom older most devoted Emperors did not scorn to admit; we have given all of them one pinnacle of rank, and none is allowed to claim any preeminence for himself. Indeed, seeing that we have laid down that the present laws themselves should be equivalent to enactments issued by us, how should any greater or less importance be attributed to any amongst them where one rank and one authority is vouchsafed to all? 21. One thing there is which, as it seemed good to us at the very beginning, when with the Divine sanction we commissioned the execution of this work, so it seems opportune to us to command now also; this, namely, that no man of those who either at this day are learned in the law or hereafter shall be such shall venture to append any commentary to these laws, save so far as this, that he may translate them into the Greek tongue with the same order and sequence as those in which the Roman text is written, or, as the Greeks call it, κατά πόδα, or if he likes, to make any notes for difficulties in the various titles, he may compose what are commonly called παράτιτλα. Any further interpretations, or rather perversions, of these rules of law we will not allow them to exhibit, for fear lest their long dissertations cause such confusion as to bring some discredit on our legislation. This happened in the case of the old commentators on the *Edictum perpetuum,* for, although that work was composed in a compendious form, these men, by extending in this way and that to divers intents, drew it out beyond all bounds so as to bring almost all Roman law into confusion; and, if we do not put up with *them*, how can we ever allow room for the vain disputes of future generations? If any should venture to do such things, they will themselves be liable to be prosecuted for forgery, but their books will be altogether set at nought. But if, as before said, anything should appear doubtful, this must be by the judges referred to the Imperial Majesty, and the truth be pronounced on the Augustal authority, to which alone it belongs both to make and to interpret laws. 22. We lay down also the same penalty on the ground of forgery for those persons who at any future time should venture to write down our laws by the occult means of ciphers. We desire that everything, the names of authors as well as the titles and numbers of the books, should be plainly given in so many letters and not by means of marks, so that anyone who gets for himself one of these books in which there are marks used in any passage whatever of the book or volume will have to understand that the codex which he owns is useless; if anyone has these objectionable marks in any part of a codex such as described, we decline to allow him to cite any passage therefrom in Court; and a clerk who should venture to write such marks will not only be punished criminally, as already mentioned, but he will also have to give the owner twice the value of the book, if the owner himself either bought such a book or ordered it to be written without notice. This provision has already been issued by us both in a Latin enactment and in Greek and sent to the professors of law. 23. These our laws, which we have set down in these books, I mean the Institutes or Elements and the Digest or Pandects, we desire should be in force from and after our third most happy Consulship, on the third day before the Kalends of January in the present twelfth Indiction, laws which are to hold good for all time to come, and which, while in force together with our own ordinances, may display their own cogency in the Courts in all causes, whether they arise at some future time or are still pending in the Court, because they have not been settled by any judgment or terms of arrangement. Any cases that have been disposed of by judicial decree or set at rest by friendly compromise we do not by any means wish to have stirred up again. We have done well to make a point of bringing out this body of law in our third Consulship, as that Consulship is the happiest one which the favour of Almighty God and of our Lord Jesus Christ has given to our State; in it the Parthian ware were put an end to and consigned to lasting rest, moreover the third division of the world came under our sway, as, after Europe and Asia, all Libya too was added to our dominions, and now a final completion is made of the great work on our law, [so that] all the gifts of Heaven have been poured on our third Consulship. 24. Now therefore let all our judges in their respective jurisdictions take up this law, and both within their own provinces and in this royal city observe and apply it, more especially that distinguished man the Prefect of this revered city. It will be the duty of the three distinguished Pretorian Prefects, the Oriental, the Illyrian, and the Libyan, to make the same known by the exercise of their authority to all those who are subject to their jurisdiction.

Given on the seventeenth day before the Kalends of January in the third Consulship of our Lord Justinianus.

III On Statutes, Decrees of the Senate, and Long Usage

1. Papinianus (*Definitions* 1) A statute (*lex*) is a command of general application, a resolution on the part of learned men, a restraint of offences, committed either voluntarily or in ignorance, a general covenant on the part of the state.

2. Marcianus (*Institutes* 1) The orator Demosthenes himself gives this definition: 'A law (νόμος) is the following:—something which all men ought to obey for many reasons, and chiefly because every law is devised and given by God, but resolved on by intelligent men, a means of correcting offences both intentional and unintentional, a general agreement on the part of the community by which all those living therein ought to order their lives. We may add that Chrysippus the philosopher, a man who professed the highest wisdom of the Stoics, begins his book called περί νόμος (on law) as follows:—"Law is the king of all things, both divine and human, it ought to be the controller, ruler and commander of both the good and the bad, and thus to be a standard as to things just and unjust and" [director of] "beings political by nature, enjoining what ought to be done and forbidding what ought not to be done."

3. Pomponius (*on Sabinus* 25) Laws ought to be laid down, as Theophrastus said, in respect of things which happen for the most part, not which happen against reasonable expectation.

4. Celsus (*Digest* 5) Rules of law are not founded on possibilities which may chance to come to pass on some one occasion,

5. The same (*Digest* 17) since law ought to be framed to meet cases which occur frequently and easily, rather than such as very seldom happen.

6. Paulus (*on Plautius* 17) What occurs once or twice, as Theophrastus says, law-givers pass by.

7. Modestinus (*Rules* 1) The use of a statute is as follows: to command, to prohibit, to permit, to punish.

8. Ulpianus (*on Sabinus* 3) Rules of law are not laid down with respect to particular individuals, but for general application.

9. The same (*on the Edict* 16) Nobody questions that the senate can make law.

10. Julianus (*Digest* 59) Neither statutes nor decrees of the senate can possibly be drawn in such terms as to comprehend every case which will ever arise; it is enough if they embrace such as occur very often.

Source: "On the Confirmation of the Digest" and "On Statues, Decrees of the Senate, and Long Uses." *Digest of Justinian.* Translated by Charles Henry Monro. Cambridge: Cambridge University Press, 1904, pp. xxv–xxvi, 19–23.

22. Charlemagne and a Painted Mouse Humble a Proud Bishop

Writing in the 880s for the Carolingian ruler Charles the Fat, Notker the Stammerer compiled the *Gesta Karoli* (Deeds of Charlemagne), a life of Charlemagne that was intended to provide a model of Christian kingship for the great ruler's descendants. Based on tales Notker heard from one of Charlemagne's warriors, the *Gesta* is often anecdotal, with each episode providing a clear moral concerning proper kingship. As the following passage demonstrates, a true Christian ruler was zealous to humble the proud and ensure that his bishops upheld high moral standards.

16. As we have shown how the most wise Charles exalted the humble, let us now show how he brought low the proud. There was a bishop who sought [81] above measure vanities and the fame of men. The most cunning Charles heard of this and told a certain Jewish merchant, whose custom it was to go to the land of promise and bring from thence rare and wonderful things to the countries beyond the sea, to deceive or cheat this bishop in whatever way he could. So the

Jew caught an ordinary household mouse and stuffed it with various spices, and then offered it for sale to the bishop, saying that he had brought this most precious never-before-seen animal from Judea. The bishop was delighted with what he thought a stroke of luck, and offered the Jew three pounds of silver for the precious ware. Then said the Jew, "A fine price indeed for so precious an article! I had rather throw it into the sea than let any man have it at so cheap and shameful a price." So the bishop, who had much wealth and never gave anything to the poor, offered him ten pounds of silver for the incomparable treasure. But the cunning rascal, with pretended indignation, replied: "The God of Abraham forbid that I should thus lose the fruit of my labor and journeyings." Then our avaricious bishop, all eager for the prize, offered twenty pounds. But the Jew in high dudgeon wrapped up the mouse in the most costly silk and made as if he would depart. Then the bishop, as thoroughly taken in as he deserved [82] to be, offered a full measure of silver for the priceless object. And so at last our trader yielded to his entreaties with much show of reluctance: and, taking the money, went to the emperor and told him everything. A few days later the king called together all the bishops and chief men of the province to hold discourse with him; and, after many other matters had been considered, he ordered all that measure of silver to be brought and placed in the middle of the palace. Then thus he spoke and said:—"Fathers and guardians, bishops of our Church, you ought to minister to the poor, or rather to Christ in them, and not to seek after vanities. But now you act quite contrary to this; and are vain-glorious and avaricious beyond all other men." Then he added: "One of you has given a Jew all this silver for a painted mouse." Then the bishop, who had been so wickedly deceived, threw himself at Charles's feet and begged pardon for his sin. Charles upbraided him in suitable words and then allowed him to depart in confusion.

Source: A.J. Grant, ed. and trans. *Early Lives of Charlemagne by Eginhard and the Monk of St. Gall.* London: Chatto & Windus, 1926, pp. 80–82.

23. Paul the Deacon Explains the Name of the Lombard People

One of the most popular histories of the early Middle Ages, The History of the Lombards by Paul the Deacon provides a narrative of the history of the Lombards, or Langobards, from their origins to the mid-eighth century. In the following passage, Paul explains the origins of the name of the Lombard people.

It is certain, however, that the Langobards were afterwards so called on account of the length of their beards untouched by the knife, whereas at first they had been called Winnili; for according to their language "lang" means "long" and "bart" "beard." Wotan indeed, whom by adding a letter they called Godan is he who among the Romans is called Mercury, and he is worshipped by all the peoples of Germany as a god, though he is deemed to have existed, not about these times, but long before, and not in Germany, but in Greece.

Source: "History of the Langobards by Paul the Deacon." Trans. William Dudley Foulke. In *Translations and Reprints from the Original Sources of European History.* Philadelphia: University of Pennsylvania Press, 1907, Book I, Chapter IX, pp. 17–19.

24. The Lombards Invade Italy on the Invitation of Narses

One of the most important moments in the history of the Lombards, or Langobards as they are called below, was their entry into Italy, where they would settle and establish a kingdom that would last until 774. According to Paul the Deacon in his History of the Lombards, the Lombards were invited into Italy by the Byzantine commander Narses to avenge himself against insults he suffered from the people of Italy and the Byzantine rulers. Although unlikely to have happened this way, this explanation of the arrival of the Lombards was commonly held until modern times.

Now the whole nation of the Goths having been destroyed or overthrown, as has been said, and those also of whom we have spoken having been in like manner conquered, Narses, after he had acquired much gold and silver and riches of other kinds, incurred the great envy of the Romans although he had labored much for them against their enemies, and they made insinuations against him to the emperor Justin and his wife Sophia, in these words, saying, "It would be advantageous for the Romans to serve the Goths rather than the Greeks wherever the eunuch Narses rules and oppresses us with bondage, and of these things our most devout emperor is ignorant: Either free us from his hand or surely we will betray the city of Rome and ourselves to the heathens." When Narses heard this he answered briefly these words: "If I have acted badly with the Romans it will go hard with me." Then the emperor was so greatly moved with anger against Narses that he straightway sent the prefect Longinus into Italy to take Narses' place. But Narses, when he knew these things, feared greatly, and so much was he alarmed, especially by the same empress Sophia, that he did not dare to return again to Constantinople. Among other things, because he was a eunuch, she is said to have sent him this message, that she would make him portion out to the girls in the women's chamber the daily tasks of wool. To these words Narses is said to have given this answer, that he would begin to weave her such a web as she could not lay down as long as she lived.

Therefore, greatly racked by hate and fear, he withdrew to Neapolis (Naples), a city of Campania, and soon sent messengers to the nation of the Langobards, urging them to abandon the barren fields of Pannonia and come and take possession of Italy, teeming with every sort of riches. At the same time he sends many kinds of fruits and samples of which Italy was well supplied. The Langobards receive joyfully the glad tidings which they themselves had also been desiring, and they form high expectations of future advantages. In Italy terrible signs were continually seen at night, that is, fiery swords appeared in heaven gleaming with that blood which was afterwards shed.

Source: "History of the Langobards by Paul the Deacon." Trans. William Dudley Foulke. In *Translations and Reprints from the Original Sources of European History.* Philadelphia: University of Pennsylvania Press, 1907, Book II, Chapter V, pp. 58–61.

25. Priscus's Description of Attila the Hun and His Court

In an influential but now mostly lost work, the historian and diplomat Priscus left a detailed account of the events of his time, including the invasion of the empire by the Huns. An ambassador to the court of Attila in 448, Priscus provides an eyewitness account of the great warrior and his palace and court ritual.

Attila's residence, which was situated here, was said to be more splendid than his houses in other places. It was made of polished boards, and surrounded with wooden enclosures, designed not so much for protection as for appearance sake. The house of the chieftain Onegesius was second only to the king's in splendor and was also encircled with a wooden enclosure, but it was not adorned with towers like that of the king. Not far from the inclosure was a large bath built by Onegesius, who was the second in power among the Scythians. The stones for this bath had been brought from Pannonia, for the barbarians in this district had no stones or trees, but used imported material. . . .

The next day I entered the enclosure of Attila's palace, bearing gifts to his wife, whose name was Kreka. She had three sons, of whom the eldest governed the Acatiri and the other nations who dwell in Pontic Scythia. Within the inclosures were numerous buildings, some of carved boards beautifully fitted together, others of straight planed beams, without carving, fastened on round wooden blocks which rose to a moderate height from the ground. Attila's wife lived here; and, having been admitted by the barbarians at the door, I found her reclining on a soft couch. The floor of the room was covered with woolen mats for walking on. A number of servants stood round her, and maids sitting on the floor in front of her embroidered with colors linen cloths intended to be placed over the Scythian dress for ornament. Having approached, saluted her, and presented the gifts, I went out and walked to the other houses, where Attila was, and waited for Onegesius, who, as I knew, was with Attila. . . .

I saw a number of people advancing, and a great commotion and noise, Attila's egress being expected. And he came forth from the house with a dignified strut, looking round on this side and on that. He was accompanied by Onegesius, and stood in front of the house; and many persons who had lawsuits with one another came up and received his judgment. Then he returned into the house and received ambassadors of barbarous peoples. . . .

[We were invited to a banquet with Attila at three o'clock] When the hour arrived we went to the palace, along with the embassy from the western Romans, and stood on the threshold of the hall in the presence of Attila.

The cupbearers gave us a cup, according to the national custom, that we might pray before we sat down. Having tasted the cup, we proceeded to take our seats, all the chairs being ranged along the walls of the room on either side. Attila sat in the middle on a couch ; a second couch was set behind him, and from it steps led up to his bed, which was covered with linen sheets and wrought coverlets for ornament, such as Greeks and Romans used to deck bridal beds. The places on the right of Attila were held chief in honor—those on the left, where we sat, were only second. . . .

[First the king and his guests pledged one another with the wine.] When this ceremony was over the cupbearers retired, and tables, large enough for three or four, or even more, to sit at, were placed next the table of Attila, so that each could take of the food on the dishes without leaving his seat. The attendant of Attila first entered with a dish of meat, and behind him came the other attendants with bread and viands, which they laid on the tables. A luxurious meal, served on silver plate, had been made ready for us and the barbarian guests, but Attila ate nothing but meat on a wooden trencher. In everything else, too, he showed himself temperate—his cup was of wood, while to the guests were given goblets of gold and silver. His dress, too, was quite simple, affecting only to be clean. The sword he carried at his side, the ratchets of his Scythian shoes, the bridle of his horse were not adorned, like those of the other Scythians, with gold or gems or anything costly.

When the viands of the first course had been consumed, we all stood up, and did not resume our seats until each one, in the order before observed, drank to the health of Attila in the goblet of wine presented to him. We then sat down, and a second dish was placed on each table with eatables of another kind. After this course the same ceremony was observed as after the first. When evening fell torches were lit, and two barbarians coming forward in front of Attila sang songs they had composed, celebrating his victories and deeds of valor in war.

Source: From the account left by Priscus, translated in J.H. Robinson. *Readings in European History.* Boston: Ginn, 1905, pp. 46–49.

26. Procopius Describes the Excesses of Justinian and the Character of the Empress Theodora

One of the most important sources of information for the reign of Justinian and Theodora, Procopius (c. 490/507–560), a servant of the emperor, wrote several histories of Justinian and his wars and building projects. His most famous, or perhaps infamous, work is the *Secret History*, which was written c. 550 but not published until after its author's death. The work contains a vicious and hateful portrait of the emperor and his wife and includes extremely harsh criticism of the two that Procopius feared to include in his official histories. The following excerpts describe the abuses of power by Justinian and, possibly the most notorious passages from the work, the life and rise to power of Theodora.

7. Outrages of the Blues

The people had since long previous time been divided, as I have explained elsewhere, into two factions, the Blues and the Greens. Justinian, by joining the former party, which had already shown favor to him, was able to bring everything into confusion and turmoil, and by its power to sink the Roman state to its knees before him. Not all the Blues were willing to follow his leadership, but there were plenty who were eager for civil war. Yet even these, as the trouble spread, seemed the most prudent of men, for their crimes were less awful than was in their power to commit. Nor did the Green partisans remain quiet, but showed their resentment as violently as they could, though one by one they were continually punished; which, indeed, urged them each time to further recklessness. For men who are wronged are likely to become desperate.

Then it was that Justinian, fanning the flame and openly inciting the Blues to fight, made the whole Roman Empire shake on its foundation, as if an earthquake or a cataclysm had stricken it, or every city within its confines had been taken by the foe. Everything everywhere was uprooted: nothing was left undisturbed by him. Law and order, throughout the State, overwhelmed by distraction, were turned upside down.

First the rebels revolutionized the style of wearing their hair. For they had it cut differently from the rest of the Romans: not molesting the mustache or beard, which they allowed to keep on growing as long as it would, as the Persians do, but clipping the hair short on the front of the head down to the temples, and letting it hang down in great length and disorder in the back, as the Massageti do. This weird combination they called the Hun haircut.

Next they decided to wear the purple stripe on their togas, and swaggered about in a dress indicating a rank above their station: for it was only by ill-gotten money they were able to buy this finery. And the sleeves of their tunics were cut tight about the wrists, while from there to the shoulders they were of an ineffable fullness; thus, whenever they moved their hands, as when applauding at the theater or encouraging a driver in the hippodrome, these immense sleeves fluttered conspicuously, displaying to the simple public what beautiful and well-developed physiques were these that required such large garments to cover them. They did not consider that by the exaggeration of this dress the meagerness of their stunted bodies appeared all the more noticeable. Their cloaks, trousers, and boots were also different: and these too were called the Hun style, which they imitated.

Almost all of them carried steel openly from the first, while by day they concealed their two-edged daggers along the thigh under their cloaks. Collecting in gangs as soon as dusk fell, they robbed their betters in the open Forum and in the narrow alleys, snatching from passersby their mantles, belts, gold brooches, and whatever they had in their hands. Some they killed after robbing them, so they could not inform anyone of the assault.

These outrages brought the enmity of everybody on them, especially that of the Blue partisans who had not taken active part in the discord. When even the latter were molested, they began to wear brass belts and brooches and cheaper cloaks than most of them were privileged to display, lest their elegance should lead to their deaths; and even before the sun went down they went home to hide. But the evil progressed; and as no punishment came to the criminals from those in charge of the public peace, their boldness increased more and more. For when crime finds itself licensed, there are no limits to its abuses; since even when it is punished, it is never quite suppressed, most men being by nature easily turned to error. Such, then, was the conduct of the Blues.

Some of the opposite party joined this faction so as to get even with the people of their original side who had ill-treated them; others fled in secret to other lands, but many were captured before they could get away, and perished either at the hands of their foes or by sentence of the State. And many other young men offered themselves to this society who had never before taken any interest in the quarrel, but were now induced by the power and possibility of insolence they could thus acquire. For there is no villainy to which men give a name that was not committed during this time, and remained unpunished.

Now at first they killed only their opponents. But as matters progressed, they also murdered men who had done nothing against them. And there were many who bribed them with money, pointing out personal enemies, whom the Blues straightway dispatched, declaring these victims were Greens, when as a matter of fact they were utter strangers. And all this went on not any longer at dark and by stealth, but in every hour of the day, everywhere in the city: before the eyes of the most notable men of the government, if they happened to be bystanders. For they did not need to conceal their crimes, having no fear of punishment, but considered it rather to the advantage of their reputation, as proving their strength and manhood, to kill with one stroke of the dagger any unarmed man who happened to be passing by.

No one could hope to live very long under this state of affairs, for everybody suspected he would be the next to be killed. No place was safe, no time of day offered any pledge of security, since these murders went on in the holiest of sanctuaries even during divine services. No confidence was left in one's friends or relatives, for many died by conspiracy of members of their own households. Nor was there any investigation after these deeds, but the blow would fall unexpectedly, and none avenged the victim. No longer was there left any force in law or contract, because, of this disorder, but everything was settled by violence. The State might as well have been a tyranny: not one, however, that had been established, but one that was being overturned daily and ever recommencing.

The magistrates seemed to have been driven from their senses, and their wits enslaved by the fear of one man. The judges, when deciding cases that came up before them, cast their votes not according to what they thought right or lawful, but according as either of the disputants was an enemy or friend of the faction in power. For a judge who disregarded its instruction was sentencing himself to death. And many creditors were forced to receipt the bills they had sent to their debtors without being paid what was due them; and many thus against their will had to free their slaves.

And they say that certain ladies were forced by their own slaves to do what they did not want to do; and the sons of notable men, getting mixed up with these young bandits, compelled their fathers, among other acts against their will, to hand over their properties to them. Many boys were constrained, with their fathers' knowledge, to serve the unnatural desires of the Blues; and happily married women met the same misfortune.

It is told that a woman of no undue beauty was ferrying with her husband to the suburb opposite the mainland; when some men of this party met them on the water, and jumping into her boat, dragged her abusively from her husband and made her enter their vessel. She had whispered to her spouse to trust her and have no fear of any reproach, for she would not allow herself to be dishonored. Then, as he looked at her in great grief, she threw her body into the Bosphorus and forthwith vanished from the world of men. Such were the deeds this party dared to commit at that time in Constantinople.

Yet all of this disturbed people less than Justinian's offenses against the State. For those who suffer the most grievously from evildoers are relieved of the greater part of their anguish by the expectation they will sometime be avenged by law and authority. Men who are confident of the future can bear more easily and less painfully their present troubles; but when they are outraged even by the government what befalls them is naturally all the more grievous, and by the failing of all hope of redress they are turned to utter despair. And Justinian's crime was that he was not only unwilling to protect the injured, but saw no reason why he should not be the open head of the guilty faction; he gave great sums of money to these young men, and surrounded himself with them: and some he even went so far as to appoint to high office and other posts of honor.

9. How Theodora, Most Depraved of all Courtesans, Won His Love

He took a wife: and in what manner she was born and bred, and, wedded to this man, tore up the Roman Empire by the very roots, I shall now relate.

Acacius was the keeper of wild beasts used in the amphitheater in Constantinople; he belonged to the Green faction and was nicknamed the Bearkeeper. This man, during the rule of Anastasius, fell sick and died, leaving three daughters named Comito, Theodora and Anastasia: of whom the eldest was not yet seven years old. His widow took a second husband, who with her undertook to keep up Acacius's family and profession. But Asterius, the dancing master of the Greens, on being bribed by another removed this office from them and assigned it to the man who gave him the money. For the dancing masters had the power of distributing such positions as they wished.

When this woman saw the populace assembled in the amphitheater, she placed laurel wreaths on her daughters' heads and in their hands, and sent them out to sit on the ground in the attitude of suppliants. The Greens eyed this mute appeal with indifference; but the Blues were moved to bestow on the children an equal office, since their own animal-keeper had just died.

When these children reached the age of girlhood, their mother put them on the local stage, for they were fair to look upon; she sent them forth, however, not all at the same time, but as each one seemed to her to have reached a suitable age. Comito, indeed, had already become one of the leading hetaerae [*high class prostitutes*] of the day.

Theodora, the second sister, dressed in a little tunic with sleeves, like a slave girl, waited on Comito and used to follow her about carrying on her shoulders the bench on which her favored sister was wont to sit at public gatherings. Now Theodora was still too young to know the normal relation of man with maid, but consented to the unnatural violence of villainous slaves who, following their masters to the theater, employed their leisure in this infamous manner. And for some time in a brothel she suffered such misuse.

But as soon as she arrived at the age of youth, and was now ready for the world, her mother put her on the stage. Forthwith, she became a courtesan, and such as the ancient Greeks used to call a common one, at that: for she was not a flute or harp player, nor was she even trained to dance, but only gave her youth to anyone she met, in utter abandonment. Her general favors included, of course, the actors in the theater; and in their productions she took part in the low comedy scenes. For she was very funny and a good mimic, and immediately became popular in this art. There was no shame in the girl, and no one ever saw her dismayed: no role was too scandalous for her to, accept without a blush.

She was the kind of comedienne who delights the audience by letting herself be cuffed and slapped on the cheeks, and makes them guffaw by raising her skirts to reveal to the spectators those feminine secrets here and there which custom veils from the eyes of the opposite sex. With pretended laziness she mocked her lovers, and coquettishly adopting ever new ways of embracing, was able to keep in a constant turmoil the hearts of the sophisticated. And she did not wait to be asked by anyone she met, but on the contrary, with inviting jests and a comic flaunting of her skirts herself tempted all men who passed by, especially those who were adolescent.

On the field of pleasure she was never defeated. Often she would go picnicking with ten young men or more, in the flower of their strength and virility, and dallied with them all, the whole night through. When they wearied of the sport, she would approach their servants, perhaps thirty in number, and fight a duel with each of these; and even thus found no allayment of her craving. Once, visiting the house of an illustrious gentleman, they say she mounted the projecting corner of her dining couch, pulled up the front of her dress, without a blush, and thus carelessly showed her wantonness. And though she flung wide three gates to the ambassadors of Cupid, she lamented that nature had not similarly unlocked the straits of her bosom, that she might there have contrived a further welcome to his emissaries.

Frequently, she conceived but as she employed every artifice immediately, a miscarriage was straightway effected. Often, even in the theater, in the sight of all the people, she removed her costume and stood nude in their midst, except for a girdle about the groin: not that she was abashed at revealing that, too, to the audience, but because there was a law against appearing altogether naked on the stage, without at least this much of a fig-leaf. Covered thus with a ribbon, she would sink down to the stage floor and recline on her back. Slaves to whom the duty was entrusted would then scatter grains of barley from above into the calyx of this passion flower, whence geese, trained for the purpose, would next pick the grains one by one with their bills and eat. When she rose, it was not with a blush, but she seemed rather to glory in the performance. For she was not only impudent herself, but endeavored to make everybody else as audacious. Often when she was alone with other actors she would undress in their midst and arch her back provocatively, advertising like a peacock both to those who had experience of her and to those who had not yet had that privilege her trained suppleness.

So perverse was her wantonness that she should have hid not only the customary part of her person, as other women do, but her face as well. Thus those who were intimate with her were straightway recognized from that very fact to be perverts, and any more respectable man who chanced upon her in the Forum avoided her and withdrew in haste, lest the hem of his mantle, touching such a creature, might be thought to share in her pollution. For to those who saw her, especially at dawn, she was a bird of ill omen. And toward her fellow actresses she was as savage as a scorpion: for she was very malicious.

Later, she followed Hecebolus, a Tyrian who had been made governor of Pentapolis, serving him in the basest of ways; but finally she quarreled with him and was sent summarily away. Consequently, she found herself destitute of the means of life, which she proceeded to earn by prostitution, as she had done before this adventure. She came thus to Alexandria, and then traversing all the East, worked her way to Constantinople; in every city plying a trade (which it is safer, I fancy, in the sight of God not to name too clearly) as if the Devil were determined there be no land on earth that should not know the sins of Theodora.

Thus was this woman born and bred, and her name was a byword beyond that of other common wenches on the tongues of all men.

But when she came back to Constantinople, Justinian fell violently in love with her. At first he kept her only as a mistress, though he raised her to patrician rank. Through him Theodora was able immediately to acquire an unholy power and exceedingly great riches. She seemed to him the sweetest thing in the world, and like all lovers, he desired to please his charmer with every possible favor and requite her with all his wealth. The extravagance added fuel to the flames of passion. With her now to help spend his money he plundered the people more than ever, not only in the capital, but throughout the Roman Empire. As both of them had for a long time been of the Blue party, they gave this faction almost complete control of the affairs of state. It was long afterward that the worst of this evil was checked in the following manner.

Justinian had been ill for several days, and during this illness was in such peril of his life that it was even said he had died; and the Blues, who had been committing such crimes as I have mentioned, went so far as to kill Hypatius, a gentleman of no mean importance, in broad daylight in the Church of St. Sophia. The cry of horror at this crime came to the Emperor's ears, and everyone about him seized the opportunity of pointing out the enormity of what was going on in Justinian's absence from public affairs; and they enumerated from the beginning how many crimes had been committed. The Emperor then ordered the Prefect of the city to punish these offenses. This man was one Theodotus, nicknamed the Pumpkin. He made a thorough investigation and was able to apprehend many of the guilty and sentence them to death, though many others were not found out, and escaped. They were destined to perish later, together with the Roman Empire.

Justinian, unexpectedly restored to health, straightway undertook to put Theodotus to death as a poisoner and a magician. But since he had no proof on which to condemn the man, he tortured friends of his until they were compelled to say the words that would wrongfully ruin him. When everyone else stood to one side and only in silence lamented the plot against Theodotus, one man, Proclus the Quaestor, dared to say openly that the man was innocent of the charge against him, and in no way merited death. Thanks to him, Theodotus was permitted by the Emperor to be exiled to Jerusalem. But learning there that men were being sent to do away with him, he hid himself in the church for the rest of his life until he died. And this was the fate of Theodotus.

But after this, the Blues became the most prudent of men. For they ventured no longer to continue their offenses, even though they might have transgressed more fearlessly than before. And the proof of this is, that when a few of them later showed such courage, no punishment at all befell them. For those who had the power to punish, always gave these gangsters time to escape, tacitly encouraging the rest to trample upon the laws.

Source: Procopius: Secret History, trans. by Richard Atwater. Chicago: P. Covici, 1927; New York: Covici Friede, 1927. [Reprinted, Ann Arbor, MI: University of Michigan Press, 1961, with indication that copyright had expired on the text of the translation].

27.   Rebellion against the Emperor Justinian

The Nika Revolt in 532 was one of the great turning points in the reign of Justinian. The revolt was a massive rebellion against the emperor that nearly drove him into exile and threatened his very life. Evolving out of the common violence that often occurred in Constantinople between the factions that supported rival competitors in the arena, the revolt quickly turned against Justinian and led to the election of a new emperor. In his *History of the Wars,* Procopius, an eyewitness to the events, describes the chaos and destruction of the revolt as well as its bloody suppression. He also provides a very different picture of Theodora than he did in his *Secret History.* Here, Theodora inspires her husband to fight back.

XXIV

[Jan. 1, 532] At this same time an insurrection broke out unexpectedly in Byzantium among the populace, and, contrary to expectation, it proved to be a very serious affair, and ended in great harm to the people and to the senate, as the following account will show. In every city the population has been divided for a long time past into the Blue and the Green factions; but within comparatively recent times it has come about that, for the sake of these names and the seats which the rival factions occupy in watching the games, they spend their money and abandon their bodies to the most cruel tortures, and even do not think it unworthy to die a most shameful death. And they fight against their opponents knowing not for what end they imperil themselves, but knowing well that, even if they overcome their enemy in the fight, the conclusion of the matter for them will be to be carried off straightway to the prison, and finally, after suffering extreme torture, to be destroyed. So there grows up in them against their fellow men a hostility which has no cause, and at no time does it cease or disappear, for it gives place neither to the ties of marriage nor of relationship nor of friendship, and the case is the same even though those who differ with respect to these colors be brothers or any other kin. They care neither for things divine nor human in comparison with conquering in these struggles; and it matter not whether a sacrilege is committed by anyone at all against God, or whether the laws and the constitution are violated by friend or by foe; nay even when they are perhaps ill supplied with the necessities of life, and when their fatherland is in the most pressing need and suffering unjustly, they pay no heed if only it is likely to go well with their "faction"; for so they name the bands of partisans. And even women join with them in this unholy strife, and they not only follow the men, but even resist them if opportunity offers, although they neither go to the public exhibitions at all, nor are they impelled by any other cause; so that I, for my part, am unable to call this anything except a disease of the soul. This, then, is pretty well how matters stand among the people of each and every city.

But at this time the officers of the city administration in Byzantium were leading away to death some of the rioters. But the members of the two factions, conspiring together and declaring a truce with each other, seized the prisoners and then straightway entered the prison and released all those who were in confinement there, whether they had been condemned on a charge of stirring up sedition, or for any other unlawful act. And all the attendants in the service of the city government were killed indiscriminately; meanwhile, all of the citizens who were sane-minded were fleeing to the opposite mainland, and fire was applied to the city as if it had fallen under the hand of an enemy. The sanctuary of Sophia and the baths of Zeuxippus, and the portion of the imperial residence from the propylaea as far as the so-called House of Ares were destroyed by fire, and besides these both the great colonnades which extended as far as the market place which bears the name of Constantine, in addition to many houses of wealthy men and a vast amount of treasure. During this time the emperor and his consort with a few members of the senate shut themselves up in the palace and remained quietly there. Now the watchword which the populace passed around to one another was Nika and the insurrection has been called by this name up to the present time.

The praetorian prefect at that time was John the Cappadocian, and Tribunianus, a Pamphylian by birth, was counselor to the emperor; this person the Romans call "quaestor." One of these two men, John, was entirely without the advantages of a liberal education; for he learned nothing while attending the elementary school except his letters, and these, too, poorly enough; but by his natural ability he became the most powerful man of whom we know. For he was most capable in deciding upon what was needful and in finding a solution for difficulties But he became the basest of all men and employed his natural power to further his low designs; neither consideration for God nor any shame before man entered into his mind, but to destroy the lives of many men for the sake of gain and to wreck whole cities was his constant concern. So within a short time indeed he had acquired vast sums of money, and he flung himself completely into the sordid life of a drunken scoundrel; for up to the time of lunch each day he would plunder the property of his subjects, and for the rest of the day occupy himself with drinking and with wanton deeds of lust. And he was utterly unable to control himself, for he ate food until he vomited, and he was always ready to steal money and more ready to bring it out and spend it. Such a man then was John. Tribunianus, on the other hand, both possessed natural ability and in educational attainments was inferior to none of his contemporaries; but he was extraordinarily fond of the pursuit of money and always ready to sell justice for gain; therefore every day, as a rule, he was repealing some laws and proposing others, selling off to those who requested it either favour according to their need.

Now as long as the people were waging this war with each other in behalf of the names of the colours, no attention was paid to the offences of these men against the constitution; but when the factions came to a mutual understanding, as has been said, and so began the sedition, then openly throughout the whole city they began to abuse the two and went about seeking them to kill. Accordingly the emperor, wishing to win the people to his side, instantly dismissed both these men from office. And Phocas, a patrician, he appointed praetorian prefect, a man of the greatest discretion and fitted by nature to be a guardian of justice; Basilides he commanded to fill the office of quaestor, a man known among the patricians for his agreeable qualities and a notable besides.

However, the insurrection continued no less violently under them. Now on the fifth day of the insurrection in the late afternoon the Emperor Justinian gave orders to Hypatius and Pompeius, nephews of the late emperor, Anastasius, to go home as quickly as possible, either because he suspected that some plot was being matured by them against his own person, or, it may be, because destiny brought them to this. But they feared that the people would force them to the throne (as in fact fell out), and they said that they would be doing wrong if they should abandon their sovereign when he found himself in such danger. When the Emperor Justinian heard this, he inclined still more to his suspicion, and he bade them quit the palace instantly. Thus, then, these two men betook themselves to their homes, and, as long as it was night, they remained there quietly.

But on the following day at sunrise it became known to the people that both men had quit the palace where they had been staying. So the whole population ran to them, and they declared Hypatius emperor and prepared to lead him to the marketplace to assume the power. But the wife of Hypatius, Mary, a discreet woman, who had the greatest reputation for prudence, laid hold of her husband and would not let go, but cried out with loud lamentation and with entreaties to all her kinsmen that the people were leading him on the road to death. But since the throng overpowered her, she unwillingly released her husband, and he by no will of his own came to the Forum of Constantine, where they summoned him to the throne; then since they had neither diadem nor anything else with which it is customary for a king to be clothed, they placed a golden necklace upon his head and proclaimed him Emperor of the Romans. By this time the members of the senate were assembling,—as many of them as had not been left in the emperor's residence,—and many expressed the opinion that they should go to the palace to fight. But Origenes, a man of the senate, came forward and spoke as follows: "Fellow Romans, it is impossible that the situation which is upon us be solved in any way except by war. Now war and royal power are agreed to be the greatest of all things in the world. But when action involves great issues, it refuses to be brought to a successful conclusion by the brief crisis of a moment, but this is accomplished only by wisdom of thought and energy of action, which men display for a length of time. Therefore if we should go out against the enemy, our cause will hang in the balance, and we shall be taking a risk which will decided everything in a brief space of time; and, as regards the consequences of such action, we shall either fall down and worship Fortune or reproach her altogether. For those things whose issue is most quickly decided, fall, as a rule, under the sway of fortune. But if we handle the present situation more deliberately, not even if we wish shall we be able to take Justinian in the palace, but he will very speedily be thankful if he is allowed to flee; for authority which is ignored always loses its power, since its strength ebbs away with each day. Moreover we have other palaces, both Placillianae and the palace named from Helen, which this emperor should make his headquarters and from there he should carry on the war and attend to the ordering of all other matters in the best possibly way." So spoke Origenes. But the rest, as a crowd is accustomed to do, insisted more excitedly and though that the present moment was opportune, and not least of all Hypatius (for it was fated that evil should befall him) bade them lead the way to the hippodrome. But some say that he came there purposely, being well-disposed toward the emperor.

Now the emperor and his court were deliberating as to whether it would be better for them if they remained or if they took to flight in the ships. And many opinions were expressed favouring either course. And the Empress Theodora also spoke to the following effect: "As to the belief that a woman out not to be daring among men or to assert herself boldly among those who are holding back from fear, I consider that he present crisis most certainly does not permit us to discuss whether the matter should be regarded in this or in some other way. For in the case of those whose interests have come into the greatest danger nothing else seems best except to settle the issue immediately before them in the best possible way. My opinion then is that the present time, above all others, is inorpportune for flight, even though it bring safety. For while it is impossible for a man who has seen the light not also to die, for one who has been an emperor it is unendurable to be a fugitive. May I never be separated from this purple, and may I not live that day on which those who meet me shall not address me as mistress. If, now, it is your wish to save yourself, O Emperor, there is no difficulty. For we have much money, and there is the sea, here the boats. However consider whether it will not come about after you have been saved that you would gladly exchange that safety to death. For as for myself, I approve a certain ancient saying that royalty is a good burial-shroud." When the queen had spoken thus, all were filled with boldness, and, turning their thoughts towards resistance, they began to consider how they might be able to defend themselves if any hostile forces should come against them. Now the soldiers as a body, including those who were stationed about the emperor's court, were neither well disposed to the emperor nor willing openly to take an active part in fighting, but were waiting for what the future would bring forth. All the hopes of the emperor were centered upon Belisarius and Mundus, of whom the former, Belisarius, had recently returned from the Persian war bringing with him a following which was both powerful and imposing, and in particular he had a great number of spearmen and guards who had received their training in battles and the perils of warfare. Mundus had been appointed general of the Illyrians, and by mere chance had happened to come under summons to Byzantium on some necessary errand, bringing with him Erulian barbarians.

When Hypatius reached the hippodrome, he went up immediately to where the emperor is accustomed to take his place and seated himself on the royal throne from which the emperor was always accustomed to view the equestrian and athletic contests. And from the palace Mundus went out through the gate which, from the circling descent, has been given the name of the Snail. Belisarius meanwhile began at first to go straight up toward Hypatius himself and the royal throne, and when he came to the adjoining structure where there has been a guard of soldiers from of old, he cried out to the soldiers commanding them to open the door for him as quickly as possible, in order that he might go against the tyrant. But since the soldiers had decided to support neither side, until one of them should be manifestly victorious, they pretended not to hear at all and thus put him off. So Belisarius returned to the emperor and declared that the day was lost for them, for the soldiers who guarded the palace were rebelling against him. The emperor therefore commanded him to go to the so-called Bronze Gate and the propylaea there. So Belisarius, with difficulty and not without danger and great exertion, made his way over ground covered by ruins and half-burned buildings, and ascended to the stadium. And when he had reached the Blue Colonnade which is on the right of the emperor's throne, he purposed to go against Hypatius himself first; but since there was a small door there which had been closed and was guarded by the soldiers of Hypatius who were inside, he feared lest while he was struggling in the narrow space the populace should fall upon him, and after destroying both himself and all his followers, should proceed with less trouble and difficulty against the emperor. Concluding, therefore, that he must go against the populace who had taken their stand in the hippodrome—a vast multitude crowding each other in great disorder—he drew his sword from its sheath and, commanding the others to do likewise, with a should he advanced upon them at a run. But the populace, who were standing in a mass and not in order, at the sight of armoured soldiers who had a great reputation for bravery and experience in war, and seeing that they struck out with their swords unsparingly, beat a hasty retreat. Then a great outcry arose, as was natural, and Mundus, who was standing not far away, was eager to join in the fight—for he was a daring and energetic fellow—but he was at a loss as to what he should do under the circumstances; when, however, he observed that Belisarius was in the struggle, he straightway made a sally into the hippodrome through the entrance which they call the Gate of Death. Then indeed from both sides the partisans of Hypatius were assailed with might and main and destroyed. When the rout had become complete and there had already been great slaughter of the populace, Boraedes and Justus, nephews of the Emperor Justinian, without anyone daring to lift a hand against them, dragged Hypatius down from the throne, and, leading him in, handed him over together with Pompeius to the emperor. And there perished among the populace on that day more than thirty thousand. But the emperor commanded the two prisoners to be kept in severe confinement. Then, while Pompeius was weeping and uttering pitiable words (for the man was wholly inexperienced in such misfortunes), Hypatius reproached him at length and said that those who were about to die unjustly should not lament. For in the beginning they had been forced by the people against their will, and afterwards they had come to the hippodrome with no thought of harming the emperor. And the soldiers killed both of them on the following day and threw their bodies into the sea. The emperor confiscated all their property for the public treasury, and also that, of all the other members of the senate who had sided with them. Later, however, he restored to the children of Hypatius and Pompeius and to all others the titles which had formerly held, and as much of their property as he had not happened to bestow upon his friends. This was the end of the insurrection in Byzantium.

Source: History of the Wars. Trans. H.B. Dewing. London: William Heinemann, Ltd., 1914, Book I, Chapter xxiv, pp. 53–57.

28. Procopius's Description of the Hagia Sophia Following Its Reconstruction by Justinian

Following the Nika Revolt, Justinian was faced with the enormous task of rebuilding much of the city of Constantinople. The greatest monument of that construction program is the church of the Hagia Sophia, which remained the most important church of the empire until its conquest in 1453. The historian Procopius offers a moving description of the church from his work *On Buildings*.

The emperor, thinking not of cost of any kind, pressed on the work, and collected together workmen from every land. Anthemius of Tralles, the most skilled in the builder's art, not only of his own but of all former times, carried forward the king's zealous intentions, organized the labors of the workmen, and prepared models of the future construction. Associated with him was another architect [*mechanopoios*] named Isidorus, a Milesian by birth, a man of intelligence, and worthy to carry out the plans of the Emperor Justinian. It is indeed a proof of the esteem with which God regarded the emperor, that he furnished him with men who would be so useful in effecting his designs, and we are compelled to admire the wisdom of the emperor, in being able to choose the most suitable of mankind to execute the noblest of his works. . . .

[The Church] is distinguished by indescribable beauty, excelling both in its size, and in the harmony of its measures, having no part excessive and none deficient; being more magnificent than ordinary buildings, and much more elegant than those which are not of so just a proportion. The church is singularly full of light and sunshine; you would declare that the place is not lighted by the sun from without, but that the rays are produced within itself, such an abundance of light is poured into this church. . . .

Now above the arches is raised a circular building of a curved form through which the light of day first shines; for the building, which I imagine overtops the whole country, has small openings left on purpose, so that the places where these intervals occur may serve for the light to come through. Thus far I imagine the building is not incapable of being described, even by a weak and feeble tongue. As the arches are arranged in a quadrangular figure, the stone-work between them takes the shape of a triangle, the lower angle of each triangle, being compressed where the arches unite, is slender, while the upper part becomes wider as it rises in the space between them, and ends against the circle which rests upon them, forming there its remaining angles. A spherical-shaped dome standing upon this circle makes it exceedingly beautiful; from the lightness of the building, it does not appear to rest upon a solid foundation, but to cover the place beneath as though it were suspended from heaven by the fabled golden chain. All these parts surprisingly joined to one another in the air, suspended one from another, and resting only on that which is next to them, form the work into one admirably harmonious whole, which spectators do not dwell upon for long in the mass, as each individual part attracts the eye to itself.

No one ever became weary of this spectacle, but those who are in the church delight in what they see, and, when they leave, magnify it in their talk. Moreover it is impossible accurately to describe the gold, and silver, and gems, presented by the Emperor Justinian, but by the description of one part, I leave the rest to be inferred. That part of the church which is especially sacred, and where the priests alone are allowed to enter, which is called the Sanctuary, contains forty thousand pounds' weight of silver.

Source: Translated by W. Lethabv and H. Swainson from Procopius. *De Aedificiis*, in *The Church of St. Sophia Constantinople.* New York: MacMillan and Company, 1894, pp. 24–28.

29. Martin of Tours Gives His Cloak to a Poor Beggar

Bishop of Tours and an active preacher and advocate of monasticism, St. Martin was one of the key figures in the early history of Christianity in Gaul. His tomb became one of the great pilgrimage sites in Gaul, and his relics, especially his cloak, were highly venerated sacred objects. One of the most celebrated moments in his life was when he gave part of his cloak to a poor man and then received a vision of Christ who praised Martin for his good deed. This episode was recorded by the historian and hagiographer, Sulpicius Severus (c. 363–425) in his *Life of St. Martin*, one of the most popular and influential of early medieval saints' lives.

Chapter III

Christ appears to St. Martin

ACCORDINGLY, at a certain period, when he had nothing except his arms and his simple military dress, in the middle of winter, a winter which had shown itself more severe than ordinary, so that the extreme cold was proving fatal to many, he happened to meet at the gate of the city of Amiens a poor man destitute of clothing. He was entreating those that passed by to have compassion upon him, but all passed the wretched man without notice, when Martin, that man full of God, recognized that a being to whom others showed no pity, was, in that respect, left to him. Yet, what should he do? He had nothing except the cloak in which he was clad, for he had already parted with the rest of his garments for similar purposes. Taking, therefore, his sword with which he was girt, he divided his cloak into two equal parts, and gave one part to the poor man, while he again clothed himself with the remainder. Upon this, some of the by-standers laughed, because he was now an unsightly object, and stood out as but partly dressed. Many, however, who were of sounder understanding, groaned deeply because they themselves had done nothing similar. They especially felt this, because, being possessed of more than Martin, they could have clothed the poor man without reducing themselves to nakedness. In the following night, when Martin had resigned himself to sleep, he had a vision of Christ arrayed in that part of his cloak with which he had clothed the poor man. He contemplated the Lord with the greatest attention, and was told to own as his the robe which he had given. Ere long, he heard Jesus saying with a clear voice to the multitude of angels standing round—"Martin, who is still but a catechumen, clothed me with this robe." The Lord, truly mindful of his own words (who had said when on earth—"Inasmuch as ye have done these things to one of the least of these, ye have done them unto me"), declared that he himself had been clothed in that poor man; and to confirm the testimony he bore to so good a deed, he condescended to show him himself in that very dress which the poor man had received. After this vision the sainted man was not puffed up with human glory, but, acknowledging the goodness of God in what had been done, and being now of the age of twenty years, he hastened to receive baptism. He did not, however, all at once, retire from military service, yielding to the entreaties of his tribune, whom he admitted to be his familiar tent-companion. For the tribune promised that, after the period of his office had expired, he too would retire from the world. Martin, kept back by the expectation of this event, continued, although but in name, to act the part of a soldier, for nearly two years after he had received baptism.

Source: Sulpicius Severus on the Life of St. Martin. Translation and Notes by Alexander Roberts. From *A Select Library of Nicene and Post-Nicene Fathers of the Christian Church.* Second Series, Volume 11. New York: The Christian Literature Company, 1894.

30. Boniface: An Early Medieval Missionary and Saint

One of the most important of the Anglo-Saxon saints and martyrs, Boniface (c. 675–754) was also a key figure in the reform of the Frankish church and the evangelization of the Saxons on the continent. The Life of Boniface by Willibald offers an overview of the ecclesiastical career and missionary activity of Boniface. Written at the request of Boniface's many friends, the life describes the saint's dedication to God and the faith but lacks the focus on the miraculous commonly found in early medieval hagiography.

Chapter I

How in Childhood He Began to Serve God

THE illustrious and truly blessed life of Saint Boniface the archbishop, and his character, consecrated particularly by imitation of the saints, as I have learned them from the narratives of pious men, who, having zealously attended upon his daily conversation and the way of his piety, handed down to posterity as an example those things which they heard or saw: this life and character I seek, hindered as I am by the darkness of knowledge, to interweave in the meagre warp of this work and to present concisely in the plain garb of history; and from the beginning even unto the end, with the most thorough investigation in my power, to reveal the sanctity of his divine contemplation.

When, in the first bloom of boyhood, his mother had weaned and reared him with a mother's wonted great and anxious care, his father took exceeding great delight in his companionship, and loved him above his brothers. But when he was about four or five years old, it was his passion to enter God's service and to study and toil over the monastic life continually, and his soul panted after that life every day; for already he had subdued unto his spirit all that is transitory and determined to meditate upon the things of eternity rather than those of the present. Indeed, when certain priests, or clerks, had gone out to the lay folk to preach unto them, as is the custom in those countries, and had come to the town and house of the saint's father, presently, so far as the weakness of his tender years permitted, the child began to talk with them of heavenly things, and to ask what would help him and his infirmity for the future.

When thus in protracted meditation he had thought long of heavenly things, and his whole being was straining forward to the future and upward to the things which are on high, at last he laid bare his heart to his father, and asked him to take his desire in good part. His father, astounded at the tidings, rebuked him most vehemently; and, on the one hand, forbade him with threats to abandon him; on the other, incited him with blandishments to the care of worldly business; that he might subdue him to the temporal gain of a transitory inheritance, and, when his own death came, leave him guardian, or rather heir, of his earthly goods. Using the deceitful subtlety of human cunning, he strove in long talks to turn aside the young heart from the fulfillment of the purpose it had formed, and promised, with many a flattering word, that this active life would be more tolerable to the child's tender years than the contemplative life of the monastic warfare: that so he might restrain the boy from the attempt to carry out this purpose; and incite him to the voluptuousness of mundane luxury. But the saint was already in his boyhood filled with God's spirit; and the more his father held him back, the more he took stout heart, and anxiously panted to provide himself a treasure in heaven, and to join himself to the sacred study of letters. And it happened in wondrous wise, as ever the divine compassion is wont to act, that God in his foresight bestowed upon his young soldier consolation in his undertaking and an increase of anxious desire, and a hasty change of mind in the obstinate father: so that at one and the same instant of time sudden sickness crept upon the father, whom the unexpected moment of death already threatened; and the boy's pious desire, long balked, increased most swiftly, and, with the aid of the Lord God, was fulfilled and perfected in its increase.

For the saint's father according to the flesh, when by the wonderful judgment of the dispensation of God great sickness had seized upon him, quickly put away his former obstinacy of heart, made an assembly of the kindred, and of his own free will, but moved by the Lord, directed the boy to the monastery which is called by a name of the ancients Ad-Escancastre, and committed him to an embassy of trusty messengers to deliver to the faithful Wulfhard, who was abbot of that monastery. The little boy, his friends standing beside him, addressed Wulfhard discreetly, and, making his request intelligently, as his parents had taught him aforetime, declared that he had long desired to submit himself to the monastic rule. Forthwith the father of the monastery, after taking counsel with the brethren and receiving their benediction, as the order of the regular life demanded, granted his consent and the fulfillment of the boy's wish. And so the man of God, bereaved of his father according to the flesh, followed the adoptive father of our redemption, and, renouncing the earthly gains of the world, strove to acquire the merchandise of an eternal inheritance: that, according to the veridical voice of truth, by forsaking father, or mother, or lands, or the other things which are of this world, he should receive a hundredfold, and should inherit everlasting life.

Chapter VIII

How Through His Whole Life He Preached Zealously; And with What End He Left This World

FOUR synodal councils were held, where there gathered together bishops and priests, deacons and clerics, and all ecclesiastical ranks, whom Duke Carloman of illustrious memory caused to be summoned under the sovereignty of his kingdom. At these, Boniface, archbishop; ruler of the bishopric of the city of Magontia by the consent and gift of Carloman himself; legate of the Roman church and of the apostolic see, sent first by the holy and venerable bishop of that see, Gregory the Younger, or the Second, to count from the First; then by the honorable Gregory who was the Younger, counting from the Second, or the Third, to count from the First; Boniface, I say, urged that numerous canons and ordinances of the four principal early councils be preserved for the wholesome increase of the heavenly doctrine: in order that, as in the Nicene council, when Constantine Augustus administered the empire of the world, the falsehood of the Arian blasphemy was overthrown; as the assembly of a hundred and fifty fathers, when Theodosius the Elder ruled Constantinople, condemned one Macedonius, who denied that the Holy Spirit is God; as the union of two hundred bishops, assembled at the city of Ephesus under Theodosius the Younger, separated from the Catholic church, with a righteous curse of excommunication, Nestorius, who declared that there are two persons in Christ; and as the council of Chalcedon, an assembly of six hundred and thirty priests, in accordance with the predetermined decision of the fathers bestowed the curse of excommunication upon Eutyches, abbot of the city of Constantinople, and Dioscurus his champion, rebels against the citadel of the Catholic faith: so indeed in Francia, when all the falsehood of the heretics was utterly rooted out and the conspiracy of the wicked destroyed, the power of the divine law might be increased; the synodal canons of the general councils might be received; while at the same time a synodal assembly of bishops of spiritual understanding might meet in accordance with the predetermined prescription of the authentic constitution.

The constant expectation of war, and the hostility and insurrections of the surrounding barbarian tribes, with the attendant attempts of alien robber nations without to destroy the Frankish realm by violence, had prevented the holding of synodal assemblies, or even had caused them to be so wholly forgotten that they were utterly obliterated from present memory and unknown. For it is the nature of the world, that even if it be recruited, it daily suffers damage and decrease within itself; while if it is not thoroughly renewed, it expends itself and vanishes away, and hurries breathlessly to its predestined end. Wherefore in the pilgrimage of this mortal life, if for healing spiritual leaders have ascertained any matters for the common profit of the weak in this world, even if at times these matters have been introduced into the minds of men, they ought to be preserved and most strongly defended by Catholics, and held with minds determined and immovable: lest human oblivion steal upon them, or the enticing delight of worldly enjoyment impede at the instigation of the devil. For this reason our holy bishop of the Lord, moved by sharpest anxiety in this regard, sought to deliver the folk from the baleful beguiling of the crooked serpent, and very often urged Duke Carloman to assemble the synodal meeting: that both to men then living and to later generations the wisdom of spiritual learning might be disclosed and the knowledge of Christianity come, while the snaring of souls was averted.

After he placed a mirror (as it were) of canonical rectitude before all ranks for a pattern of right living, and the way of truth became clearly visible to all, Boniface, being old, weak, and decrepit, presented a plan wholesome for himself and his feebleness, and in accordance with the rule of ecclesiastical management provided a pastoral magistracy for the peoples: that, whether he lived or died, the folk might not lack pastors and their healing care. He promoted to the episcopal order two men of good diligence, Willibald and Burchard, and divided unto them the churches committed to his charge in the innermost parts of the East Franks and the confines of the Bavarians. To Willibald he entrusted the government of his diocese in the place named Haegsted. To Burchard he delegated rank and office in the place called Wirzaburch, and allotted to his province the churches in the borders of the Franks and Saxons and Slavs. And even unto the glorious day of his death he opened without ceasing the narrow way of the heavenly kingdom unto the multitudes.

Pippin, fortunate successor of his brother Carloman, by the grace of God received the royal kingdom of the Franks, and there being now a slight lull in the disorder of the peoples, was raised to the rank of king. Then he began solicitously to fulfill the vows he had sworn unto the Lord, and to restore without delay the synodal ordinances, and to renew the canonical mysteries which his brother in accordance with the exhortation of Saint Boniface the archbishop had faithfully commenced, and to prefer Boniface in friendship and honor, and to obey his precepts in the Lord. But because the saint, oppressed by bodily weakness, was not altogether able to attend the synodal assemblies, he now determined, with the approval and advice of the glorious king, to set a proper minister over his flock. He appointed Lul, his able disciple, to teach the multitude of the great church, and advanced and ordained him to the episcopal rank, and committed to him the inheritance which he had won in Christ by earnest labor. Lul was the trusty comrade in the Lord of his pilgrimage, and was witness both of the suffering and of the consolation.

Now when the Lord wished to deliver his servant from the temptation of this world and to raise him up from the tribulations of the temporal life, then it was determined by the ordinance of the Lord, that, accompanied by the servants of God, he should come to Frisia, which aforetime he had left in body, not in mind: in order that where first he entered upon his active preaching and his profits and rewards began, there also, leaving the world, he might receive the charge of recompense.

He foretold the coming day of his death to Bishop Lul by a marvellous and in a way prophetic forecast, and made known to him with what end he was at last to leave the world, and set before him in order his plans for the building of churches and the teaching of the people. "I desire," said he, "to fulfill the journey set before me. I shall not be able to call myself back from the welcome departing journey. For now the day of my departure is at hand, and the time of my death approaches; now I shall put aside the prison of the body, and return to the prize of the eternal recompense. But do thou, dearest son, conduct to completion the building of churches which I have commenced in Thuringia. Do thou most earnestly recall the people from the trackless waste of error. And do thou complete the construction of the basilica already begun at Fulda, and bring thither my body aged by many hastening years." And having made an end of this discourse, he added to it more words of the following sort, saying: "Son, provide by thy most prudent counsel everything which must be joined to our use in this our journey; but also lay in the chest of my books a linen cloth, wherein my decrepit body may be wrapped."

At this sad speech Bishop Lul could not restrain his sobs, but forthwith wept unrestrainedly. Then Saint Boniface made an end of the conversation and turned to other matters. He did not draw back from the journey which he had undertaken, but,1 after a few days' interval, took travelling companions and went on board ship, and pushed down the Rhine, seeking haven at night time, until he entered the moist fields of the Frisians, and passed in safety across the lake which in their tongue is called Aelmere, and made a round of inspection along shores barren of the divine seed. And after escaping peril and hazard of rivers and the sea and of the great waters, he went safely into danger, and visited the pagan nation of the Frisians, whose land is divided by the intervening waters into many territories and districts, yet in such wise that the different names indicate the property of a single nation. But since it would be tedious to repeat the districts in order, we desire to mention by name only those which are veraciously cited to afford connection to our narrative: that place and language may equally transmit our story of the saint's piety, and disclose the end with which he left this world.

So he traversed all Frisia, and removed the pagan worship and overthrew the erroneous way of heathenism, and earnestly preached the word of God; and, having destroyed the divinity of the heathen temples, he built churches with great zeal. And now he baptized many thousand persons, men and women and little ones, being aided by his fellow soldier and suffragan bishop Eoba, whom he summoned to Frisia to aid the feebleness of his old age, charging him with the bishopric in the city which is called Trecht; and by priests and deacons, of whom these are the names: Wintrung and Walthere and Ethelhere, endowed with the sacerdotal office of the priesthood; Hamund, Scirbald, and Bosa, assigned to the service of Levites; Wacchar and Gundaecer, Illehere and Hathovulf, raised to the conventual order of monks. These with Saint Boniface published widely through the people the seed of eternal life, and, supported by the Lord God, made it known to such an extent, that even as in accordance with the pattern of the apostolic custom they were of one heart and one soul, so they had one and the same martyr's crown, one and the same reward of victory.

After the splendor of faith of which we have spoken dawned through Frisia, and the happy end of our saint's life approached, then, accompanied only by a number of his personal followers, he pitched his tents by the bank of the river which is called Bordne, which is upon the limits of the districts which in the country tongue are called Ostor- and Westeraeche. But because he had appointed unto the people, already scattered far and wide, a holiday of confirmation of the neophytes, and of the laying on of hands by the bishop upon the newly baptized and of their confirmation, every man went unto his own house, that in accordance with the precise command of the holy bishop all might be presented together on the day set for their confirmation.

Wholly opposite was the event. When the appointed day had dawned, and the morning light was breaking after the rising of the sun, then came enemies instead of friends, new lictors instead of new worshippers of the faith; and a vast multitude of foes, armed with spears and shields, rushed with glittering weapons into the camp. Then hastily the attendants sprang forth against them from the camp, and betook themselves to arms on either side, and were eager to defend against the crazy host of the mad folk the sainted martyrs that were to be. But when the man of God heard the onset of the tumultuous throng, immediately he called to his side the band of clerics, and, taking the saints' relics which he was wont to have always with him, came out of the tent. And at once, rebuking the attendants, he forbade combat and battle, saying: "Stop fighting, lads! Give up the battle! For we are taught by the trusty witness of Scripture, that we render not evil for evil, but contrariwise good for evil. Already the long desired day is at hand, and the voluntary time of our departure is near. Therefore be ye comforted in the Lord, and suffer with joy the grace of his permission. Trust on him, and he will release your souls." But also with fatherly speech he incited those standing near, priests and deacons and men of lower rank, trained to God's service, saying: "Men and brethren, be of stout heart, and fear not them who kill the body, since they are not able to slay the soul, which continues without end; but rejoice in the Lord, and fasten to God the anchor of your hope. For straightway he shall render you the reward of perpetual recompense, and shall give you an abode in his heavenly palace with the angels who dwell on high. Do not enslave yourselves to the empty pleasures of this world; be not seduced by the vain flatteries of the Gentiles; but endure firmly here the sudden moment of death, that ye may be able to reign with Christ for all time." While with such exhortation of doctrine he was kindly inciting the disciples to the crown of martyrdom, quickly the mad tumult of pagans rushed in upon them with swords and all the equipment of war, and stained the saints' bodies with propitious gore.

Having worked their will on the mortal flesh of the just, the exultant throng of heathens at once seized the spoils of victory, the fruit of their damnation, and, wasting the camp, shared and plundered the booty. But also they stole the chests, in which were many volumes of books, and the boxes of relics; and, believing themselves enriched by a great abundance of gold and silver, carried away the cases, locked as they were, to the ships. Now in the ships was the daily sustenance of the clerics and attendants, and some wine still left of the same supply. And when they found the beloved drink, the heathens hastily commenced to sate their thirsty maws and to make their stomachs drunken with wine; and at length, through the wonderful direction of almighty God, they took counsel, and began to discuss concerning the booty and spoils that they had taken, and to deliberate how they might mutually share the gold or silver which they had not even seen. While they held wordy discussion over the riches they reckoned so great, again and again dispute and quarrels sprang up; and finally there began such enmity and discord, that insane frenzy divided the raging throng into two factions, and at last they turned the weapons, with which earlier they had murdered the holy martyrs, against each other in merciless strife.

After the most part of the raging throng had been laid low, the survivors ran rejoicing to the wealth gained by the loss of souls and life, while the rivals who opposed them respecting the passionately coveted treasure lay dead. Having broken open the boxes of books, they found volumes instead of gold, and for silver, leaves of divine learning. Thus deprived of the precious reward of gold and silver, they scattered over the meadow some of the books which they found; others they threw away, casting some into the reed thickets of the marshes, hiding the rest each in a different place. But by the grace of almighty God and through the prayers of Saint Boniface the archbishop and martyr, the books were found a long time after, sound and unharmed, and returned by the several discoverers to the house in which even unto this day they are of use for the salvation of souls.

Sad at the loss of the wealth on which they had reckoned, the murderers returned home. After three days' respite, they experienced in their own possessions a greater loss, and also paid life for life in retribution. For the omnipotent Author and Reformer of the world wished to avenge himself on his enemies, and with the zeal of his wonted compassion to take revenge for the blood of saints shed for his sake. Deeply moved by the recent act of mad wickedness, he wished to show openly his wrath, too long deferred, against the idolaters. And as the unexpected tidings of the temporal slaughter of the sainted martyrs flew through the districts and villages and the whole province, and the Christians learned of the corporeal death of the martyrs, they at once collected a very large expeditionary force, and, being warriors prepared to take speedy vengeance, hurried to the boundary. After the lapse of the three days' period mentioned above, they entered the land of the infidels as unharmed but unfriendly guests, and overthrew with prodigious carnage the pagans who came up against them. The pagans were unable to withstand the first onset of the Christian folk, and consequently betook themselves to flight and were slaughtered in great numbers. Fleeing, they lost their lives and household goods and children. But the Christians took as spoil the wives and little ones of the superstitious folk, their menservants also and maidservants, and returned to their own land. And it came to pass in wondrous wise, that the neighboring heathen that survived, shattered by present misfortune, were enlightened by the glory of faith and preferred to shun eternal torment; and, thoroughly terrified by the administration of the divine rebuke, accepted, upon the death of Bishop Boniface, the proof of his doctrine which they rejected while he lived.

With swelling sails and favorable breezes, the body of the sainted bishop, and also those of the other martyrs, were brought after not many days across the sea which is called Aelmere to the above named city of Trecht. There they were deposited and interred, until religious and faithful brethren in the Lord arrived from Magontia, sent by ship by Bishop Lul, the successor of our holy bishop and martyr of Christ, to bring the corpse of the saint to the monastery which he had built during his life, and which is situate on the banks of the river Fulda. Of these brethren there was one, Hadda by name, the promoter of the journey and organizer of the party, who led a life of singular sanctity and peculiar chastity and continence. To him especially, with the brethren who went with him, Bishop Lul entrusted the performance of this embassy and the bringing of the sacred body: that greater honor of devotion might be paid to the venerable saint, and that the witness of many might prevail more in those matters which they heard or saw.

When the honorable brethren of this holy company came to the city of Trecht, a small crowd of the people gathered to oppose them. When the crowd heard how an edict had been issued by glorious King Pippin, the count of the city proclaimed an interdict, and forbade that the body of Bishop Boniface should be removed thence. But the strength of the Almighty is stronger than men's strength. Wherefore immediately, in the presence of all, a marvellous and memorable miracle was heard, wrought through angelic rather than human understanding. The bell of the church, untouched by human hands, was rung, as a token of the admonition of the sacred body; so that all, smitten by sudden fear and terror, were stupefied, and trembled exceedingly, and cried out that the body of this righteous man must be given up. And so at once the body was yielded, and was honorably removed by the aforesaid brethren of sacred memory, and without labor of towers was brought on the thirtieth day after the saint's decease to the abovementioned city of Magontia.

The wonderful providence of almighty God brought it to pass, that on one and the same day, though the time had not been beforehand set and appointed, there assembled unto the funeral of this great man, as if the day had been set and predetermined, not only the ambassadors who brought the sacred body, but also many faithful men and women from distant and widely scattered countries. Moreover the saint's successor in his venerable office, Lul, bishop of the Lord, who at that time was present in the king's palace, came to the city of Magontia as it were at the same hour and moment, though he was altogether ignorant of the occasion, and knew not of the arrival of the sacred body.

And all, strangers and citizens, were oppressed by sorrow and grief, yet rejoiced abundantly and were glad. For in viewing the temporal and bodily death of this great bishop, they grieved, on the one hand, for the loss of his corporeal presence, while on the other hand they believed that he would be protector to them and theirs for all time to come. Wherefore, their hearts torn by these conflicting emotions, the people, with the priests and deacons and every ecclesiastical rank, carried the dead saint to that place which he had determined upon while alive. They prepared a new sarcophagus in the church, and placed the body there with the customary rites of sepulture. And when all was duly performed, they returned to their homes, comforted by the power of faith.

But in the place where they interred the sacred body there was an abundant succession of divine blessings. Through the prayers of the saint, those who came thither possessed by divers infirmities obtained healing remedy of body and mind. Some already moribund in the whole body and almost completely lifeless, at the last breath, were restored to their pristine health. Others, whose eyes were veiled by blindness, received their sight. Yet others, bound fast in the snares of the devil, out of their senses and mad, afterward regained soundness of mind, and, restored to pristine health, gave praise and glorified God: who deigned to adorn and enrich and honor his servant with this great gift, and to glorify him by dazzling miracles made manifest to present and future times and ages, when the fortieth year of his pilgrimage had passed: which year also is reckoned of the incarnation of the Lord the seven hundred and fifty-fifth, and the eighth indiction. Moreover he sat in the episcopacy thirty-six years six months and six days. And so in the manner described above, on the fifth of June, rewarded with the triumph of martyrdom, he departed to the Lord: to whom is honor and glory unto ages of ages. Amen.

Chapter IX

How in the Place Where the Blood of Martyrs Was Shed, A Living Fountain Appeared to Those Who Were Inspecting the Preparations for a Church

HAVING recounted the saint's distinguished deeds in childhood, boyhood, youth, and the prime of life, and even in old age, let us return to those wonders that by the help of the Lord were wrought to declare to mortals the sanctity of the saint's life, after this world's race was run and that life was happily ended; and recall to memory a miracle for folk to remember and repeat. Venerable Bishop Lul told us the story of the miracle even as he learned it from glorious King Pippin, who in turn heard it from eyewitnesses. As Lul related it to us, it was as follows.

In the place where of yore the precious blood of the holy martyr was shed, the church and a great part of the Frisian folk planned to rear high upon a deep foundation an earthen mound. This was because of the vast irruptions of the neap and spring tides, which in alternation disturb the tides of sea and ocean, the lessening of the waters and the floods. On the mound they proposed to raise a church—as was done later—and to erect a habitation of the servants of God in the same place. But when now the mound was wholly finished and the entire work of its erection completed, the residents and inhabitants of that place, having returned home, had some discussion among themselves in regard to the want of fresh water, which throughout almost all Frisia occasions the greatest difficulty both to men and to beasts. Then at length, through the Lord's compassion, a certain man, Abba by name, who in accordance with the edict of glorious King Pippin administered the office of count over that district and place and was director of the work in question, taking comrades with him, mounted, and rode round the hill, and inspected the mound. Suddenly and unexpectedly the steed of an attendant, while merely stamping on the ground, felt it sinking and giving way altogether, and wallowed, its fore legs held fast in the soil, until those who were more active and skillful jumped down very hurriedly from their steeds, and pulled out the horse that was stuck fast in the earth. But at once a miracle stupendous and worthy to behold was made manifest to those who were present. A fountain, exceeding clear beyond the manner of that country, and wondrous sweet and pleasant to the taste, came busting out, and, penetrating through unknown channels, flowed forth, so that it seemed already a very large brook. Astounded by this miracle, they returned home with rejoicing and gladness, and made known to the churches those matters which they had seen.

Source: Robinson, George W., trans. *The Life of Saint Boniface by Willibald.* Cambridge, MA: Harvard University Press, 1916, pp. 27–30, 74–93.

Appendix: Rulers of Early Medieval Europe

Anglo-Saxon Kings of Wessex and England

Cerdic (519–534)

Cynric (534–560)

Ceawlin (560–591)

Ceol (591–597)

Ceolwulf (597–611)

Cynegils (611–643)

Cenwelh (643–674)

Seaxburh (674–676)

Centwine (676–685)

Caedwalla (685–688)

Ine (688–726)

Aethelherd (726–740)

Cuthred (740–756)

Sigeberht (756–757)

Cynewulf (757–786)

Brihtric (786–802)

Egbert (802–839)

Æthelwulf (839–858)

Æthelbald (858–860)

Aethelberht (860–865)

Æthelred (865–871)

Alfred the Great (871–899)

Edward the Elder (899–924)

Æthelstan (924–939, first king of England)

Edmund I (939–946)

Eadred (946–955)

Eadwig (955–959)

Edgar (959–975)

Edward the Martyr (975–978)

Æthelred the Unready (978–1013)

Byzantine Emperors

Zeno (474–491)

Anastasius I (491–518)

Justin I (518–527)

Justinian I (527–565)

Justin II (565–578)

Tiberius II (578–582)

Maurice (582–602)

Phocas (602–610)

Heraclius (610–641)

Constantine III (641)

Constans II (641–668)

Constantine IV (668–685)

Justinian II (685–695, banished)

Leontius (695–698)

Tiberius III (698–705)

Justinian II (restored, 705–711)

Philippicus Bardanes (711–713)

Anastasius II (713–716)

Theodosius III (716–717)

Leo III, the Isaurian (717–741)

Constantine V Copronymus (741–775)

Leo IV (775–780)

Constantine VI (780–797)

Irene (797–802)

Nicephorus I (802–811)

Stauracius (811)

Michael I Rhangabe (811–813)

Leo V (813–820)

Michael II (820–829)

Theophilus (829–842)

Michael III (842–867)

Basil I (867–886)

Leo VI (886–912)

Alexander (912–913)

Constantine VII Porphyrogenitus (913–959)

Romanus I Lecapenus (919–944)

Romanus II (959–963)

Nicephorus II Phocas (963–969)

John I Tzimisces (969–976)

Basil II, the Bulgar slayer (976–1025)

Carolingian Rulers of the Franks

Pippin I (614–628, 640)

Grimoald (640–657)

Out of power (657–680)

Pippin II (mayor of the palace, 680–714)

Charles Martel (mayor of the palace, 714–741)

Carloman (mayor of the palace, 741–747)

Pippin (mayor of the palace, 741–751; king, 751–768)

Carloman (king, 768–771)

Charlemagne (king, 771–800; emperor, 800–814)

Louis the Pious (emperor, 814–840)

Lothar (emperor, 840–855)

Louis II (emperor, 855–875)

West Frankish Kingdom

Charles the Bald (840–875; emperor, 875–877)

Louis the Stammerer (877–879)

Louis III (879–882)

East Frankish Kingdom

Louis the German (840–876)

Charles the Fat (876–887; emperor, 884–887)

Carloman (879–884)

Arnulf (887–899)

Louis the Child (899–911)

Charles the Fat (884–887, deposed)

Odo (not a Carolingian, 888–898)

Charles the Simple (898–922)

Robert I (brother of Odo, 922–923)

Ralph (son-in-law of Robert I, 923–936)

Louis IV, called d'Outremer (936–954)

Lothar (954–986)

Louis V (986–987)

Lombard Kings of Italy

Alboin (560/561–572)

Cleph (572–574)

Interregnum (574–584)

Authari (584–590)

Agilulf (590–616)

Adaloald (616–626)

Ariold (626–636)

Rothari (636–652)

Aripert I (653–661)

Grimoald (662–671)

Perctarit (671–688)

Cuncipert (680–688 coruler, 688–700)

Aripert II (700–712)

Liutprand (712–744)

Ratchis (744–749)

Aistulf (749–756)

Desiderius (757–774)

Merovingian Rulers of the Franks

Merovech (d. 456)

Childeric I (456–481)

Clovis (481–511)

Chlotar I (511–561)

Chlodomer (511–524)

Theuderic (511–533)

Childebert I (511–558)

Theodebert (533–548)

Chilperic I (561–584, Soissons [later, Neustria])

Sigebert I (561–575, Austrasia)

Childebert II (575–595)

Theodebert II (595–612)

Theuderic II (612–613)

Sigebert II (613)

Chlotar II (584–613, Neustria; 613–629, entire kingdom)

Dagobert (629–639)

Clovis II (637–657, Neustria) Sigebert III (632–656)

Chlotar III (655–673)

Childeric II (662–675)

Theuderic III (673–690/91, Neustria)

Dagobert (675–679, Austrasia)

Clovis III (691–694)

Childebert III (694–711)

Dagobert III (711–715)

Chilperic II (715–721, Neustria)

Chlotar IV (717–719, Austrasia)

Theuderic IV (721–737)

Interregnum (737–743)

Childeric III (743–751)

Popes and Antipopes

Sylvester I (314–335)

Mark (336)

Julius I (337–352)

Liberius (352–366)

Felix II (antipope, 355–358)

Damasus I (366–384)

Ursinus (antipope, 366–367)

Siricius (384–399)

Anastasius I (399–401)

Innocent I (401–417)

Zosimus (417–418)

Boniface I (418–422)

Eulalius (antipope, 418–419)

Celestine I (422–432)

Sixtus III (432–440)

Leo I (440–461)

Hilary (461–468)

Simplicius (468–483)

Felix III (II) (483–492)

Gelasius I (492–496)

Anastasius II (496–498)

Symmachus (498–514)

Lawrence (antipope, 498, 501–506, died 507 or 508)

Hormisdas (514–523)

John I (523–526)

Felix IV (III) (526–530)

Dioscorus (antipope, 530)

Boniface II (530–532)

John II (533–535)

Agapetus I (535–536)

Silverius (536–537)

Vigilius (537–555)

Pelagius I (556–561)

John III (561–574)

Benedict I (575–579)

Pelagius II (579–590)

Gregory I (590–604)

Sabinian (604–606)

Boniface III (607)

Boniface IV (608–615)

Deusdedit, later Adeodatus I (615–618)

Boniface V (619–625)

Honorius I (625–638)

Severinus (640)

John IV (640–642)

Theodore I (642–649)

Martin I (649–653)

Eugenius I (654–657)

Vitalian (657–672)

Adeodatus II (672–676)

Donus (676–678)

Agatho (678–681)

Leo II (682–683)

Benedict II (684–685)

John V (685–686)

Conon (686–687)

Theodore (687)

Paschal (687)

Sergius I (687–701)

John VI (701–705)

John VII (705–707)

Sisinnius (708)

Constantine (708–715)

Gregory II (715–731)

Gregory III (731–741)

Zachary (741–752)

Stephen (II) (752)

Stephen II (III) (752–757)

Paul I (757–767)

Constantine (antipope, 767–768)

Philip (antipope, 768)

Stephen III (IV) (768–772)

Hadrian I (772–795)

Leo III (795–816)

Stephen IV (V) (816–817)

Paschal I (817–824)

Eugenius II (824–827)

Valentine (827)

Gregory IV (827–844)

John (antipope, 844)

Sergius II (844–847)

Leo IV (847–855)

Benedict III (855–858)

Anastasius the Librarian
(antipope, 855)

Nicholas I (858–867)

Hadrian II (867–872)

John VIII (872–882)

Marinus I (882–884)

Adrian III (884–885)

Stephen V (VI) (885–891)

Formosus (891–896)

Boniface VI (896)

Stephen VI (VII) (896–897)

Romanus (897)

Theodore II (897)

John IX (898–900)

Benedict IV (900–903)

Leo V (903–904)

Christopher (antipope, 903–904)

Sergius III (904–911)

Anastasius III (911–913)

Lando (913–914)

John X (914–928, died 929)

Leo VI (928)

Stephen VII (VIII) (929–931)

John XI (931–935)

Leo VII (936–939)

Stephen VIII (IX) (939–942)

Marinus II (942–946)

Agapetus II ((946–955)

John XII (955–964)

Leo VIII (963–965)

Benedict V (964, died 966)

John XIII (965–972)

Benedict VI (973–974)

Boniface VII (antipope, 974)

Benedict VII (974–983)

John XIV (983–984)

John XV (985–996)

Gregory V (996–999)

John XVI (antipope, 997–998)

Sylvester II (999–1003)

Bibliography

Primary Sources in Translation

Adomnan. *Adomnan's Life of Columba*. Ed. and trans. Alan O. Anderson and Marjorie O. Anderson. London: T. Nelson, 1961.

Alexander, Michael, trans. *Beowulf*. Harmondsworth, UK: Penguin, 1983.

Ammianus Marcellinus. *Ammianus Marcellinus*. Trans. John C. Rolfe. Cambridge, MA: Harvard University Press, 1971–1972.

Amt, Emilie, ed. *Women's Lives in Medieval Europe*. New York: Routledge, 1993.

Attenborough, Frederick L., ed. and trans. *The Laws of the Earliest English Kings*. Cambridge: Cambridge University Press, 1922.

Augustine. *Concerning the City of God against the Pagans*. Trans. Henry Bettenson. Harmondsworth, UK: Penguin, 1981.

Augustine. *Confessions: Books I–XIII*. Trans. Francis J. Sheed. Indianapolis, IN: Hackett, 1993.

Augustine. *On Christian Doctrine*. Trans. Donald W. Robertson, Jr. New York: Macmillan, 1958.

Bachrach, Bernard S., trans. *Liber historiae Francorum*. Lawrence, KS: Coronado, 1973.

Bede. *Commentary on the Acts of the Apostles*. Trans. Lawrence Martin. Kalamazoo, MI: Cistercian Publications, 1989.

Bede. *Ecclesiastical History of the English Church and People*. Trans. Leo Sherley-Price. Rev. ed. London: Penguin Classics, 1968.

Birks, Peter, and Grant Mcleod, trans. *Justinian's Institutes*. Ithaca, NY: Cornell University Press, 1987.

Boethius. *The Consolation of Philosophy*. Trans. Douglas C. Langston. New York: W. W. Norton &Company, 2009.

Cabaniss, Allen, trans. *Son of Charlemagne: A Contemporary Life of Louis the Pious*. Syracuse, NY: Syracuse University Press, 1961.

Caesarius of Arles: Sermons. Trans. Mary Magdeleine Mueller. 3 Vols. New York: Fathers of the Church, 1956–1973.

Cassiodorus. *The Variae of Magnus Aurelius Cassiodorus.* Trans. S.J.B. Barnish. Liverpool, UK: Liverpool University Press, 1992.

Claudian. *Claudian's Fourth Panegyric on the Fourth Consulate of Honorius.* Ed. and trans. William Barr. Liverpool, UK: Liverpool University Press, 1981.

Colgrave, Bertram, ed. and trans. *The Earliest Life of Gregory the Great, by an Anonymous Monk of Whitby.* Lawrence: University of Kansas Press, 1968.

Davis, Raymond, trans. *The Lives of the Eighth-Century Popes* (Liber Pontificalis): *The Ancient Biographies of Nine Popes from A.D. 715 to A.D. 817.* Liverpool, UK: Liverpool University Press, 1992.

Dhuoda. *Handbook for William: A Carolingian Woman's Counsel for Her Son.* Ed. and trans. Carol Neel. Washington, DC: Catholic University of America Press, 1999.

Drew, Katherine Fisher, trans. *The Burgundian Code: The Book of Constitutions or Law of Gundobad and Additional Enactments.* Philadelphia: University of Pennsylvania Press, 1972.

Drew, Katherine Fisher, trans. *The Lombard Laws.* Philadelphia: University of Pennsylvania Press, 1973.

Dutton, Paul Edward, ed. *Carolingian Civilization: A Reader.* Peterborough, ON: Broadview, 1993.

Einhard. *The Translation and Miracles of the Saints Marcellinus and Peter.* In *Carolingian Civilization: A Reader.* Trans. Paul Edward Dutton. Peterborough, ON: Broadview, 1993, pp. 198–246.

Einhard and Notker the Stammerer. *Two Lives of Charlemagne.* Trans. Lewis Thorpe. Harmondsworth, UK: Penguin, 1981.

Emerton, Ephraim, ed. and trans. *The Letters of Saint Boniface.* New York: Columbia University Press, 2000.

Fisher Drew, Katherine, trans. *The Burgundian Code: Book of Constitutions of Gundobad; Additional Enactments.* Philadelphia: University of Pennsylvania Press, 1972.

Fouracre, Paul, and Richard A. Gerberding. *Late Merovingian France: History and Hagiography, 640–720.* Manchester, UK: University of Manchester Press, 1996.

Fry, Timothy, ed. and trans. *RB 1980: The Rule of Benedict in Latin and English with Notes.* Collegeville, MN: Liturgical Press, 1981.

Geoffrey of Monmouth. *The History of the Kings of Britain.* Trans. Lewis Thorpe. Harmondsworth, UK: Penguin, 1982.

Gildas. *The Ruin of Britain and Other Works.* Ed. and trans. Michael Winterbottom. London: Phillimore, 1978.

Giles, J.A. ed. *Six Old English Chronicles, of which Two are Now First Translated from the Monkish Latin Originals: Ethelwerd's Chronicle; Asser's Life of Alfred; Geoffrey of Monmouth's British History; Gildas; Nennius; and Richard of Cirencester.* London: H.G. Bohn, 1848.

Gregory of Tours. *Gregory of Tours, Glory of the Confessors.* Trans. Raymond Van Dam. Liverpool, UK: Liverpool University Press, 1988.

Gregory of Tours. *Gregory of Tours, Glory of the Martyrs.* Trans. Raymond Van Dam. Liverpool, UK: Liverpool University Press, 1988.

Gregory of Tours. *Gregory of Tours: Life of the Fathers.* 2nd ed. Trans. Edward James. Liverpool, UK: Liverpool University Press, 1991.

Gregory of Tours. *The History of the Franks.* Trans. Lewis Thorpe. Harmondsworth, UK: Penguin, 1974.

Gregory the Great. *Life and Miracles of St. Benedict (Book Two of the Dialogues).* Trans. Odo J. Zimmerman and Benedict Avery. Collegeville, MN: St. John's Abbey Press, 1949.

Head, Thomas, ed. *Medieval Hagiography: An Anthology.* New York: Garland Publishing, Inc., 2000.

Heaney, Seamus, trans. *Beowulf: A New Verse Translation.* New York: Farrar Straus and Giroux, 2000.

Isidore of Seville. *Isidore of Seville's History of the Goths, Vandals, and Suevi.* 2nd rev. ed. Trans. Guido Donini and Gordon B. Ford. Leiden: Brill, 1970.

Jordanes. *The Gothic History of Jordanes in English Version.* Trans. Charles C. Mierow. New York: Barnes and Noble, 1985.

Keynes, Simon, and Michael Lapidge, trans. *Alfred the Great: Asser's Life of King Alfred and Other Contemporary Sources.* Harmondsworth, UK: Penguin, 1983.

Kratz, Denis, ed. and trans. *"Waltharius" and "Ruodlieb."* New York: Garland, 1984.

Larrington, Carolyne. *Women and Writing in Medieval Europe: A Sourcebook.* New York: Routledge, 1995.

Liebeschuetz, J.H.W.G., ed., and Wolfe Liebeschuetz, trans. *Ambrose of Milan: Political Letters and Speeches.* Liverpool, UK: Liverpool University Press, 2010.

Loyn, Henry R., and John Percival. *The Reign of Charlemagne: Documents on Carolingian Government and Administration.* New York: St. Martin's Press, 1975.

Malory, Sir Thomas. *Le Morte d'Arthur.* Ed. Norma Lorre Goodrich. New York: Washington Square Press, 1966.

Marcus, Jacob R. *The Jews in the Medieval World a Source Book: 315–1791.* Cincinnati, OH: Hebrew Union Press, 1999.

McCarthy, Maria Caritas. *The Rule for Nuns of St. Caesarius of Arles: A Translation with Critical Introduction.* Washington, DC: Catholic University of America Press, 1960.

McNamara, Jo Ann, John E. Holberg, and Gordon Whatley, eds. *Sainted Women of the Dark Ages.* Durham, NC: Duke University Press, 1992.

Murphy, G. Roland, trans. *The Heliand: The Saxon Gospel.* Oxford: Oxford University Press, 1992

Nelson, Janet, trans. *The Annals of St. Bertin: Ninth Century Histories.* Manchester, UK: University of Manchester Press, 1991.

Nennius. *Nennius: British History and the Welsh Annals.* Ed. John Morris. Totowa, NJ: Rowman and Littlefield, 1980.

Noble, Thomas F. X. ed. *Charlemagne and Louis the Pious: Lives by Einhard, Notker, Ermoldus, Thegan, and the Astronomer.* University Park, PA: University of Pennsylvania Press, 2009.

Noble, Thomas F. X. and Thomas Head, eds. *Soldiers of Christ: Saints and Saints' Lives from Late Antiquity to the Early Middle Ages.* University Park: Pennsylvania State University Press, 1995.

Paul the Deacon. *History of the Lombards.* Trans. William Dudley Foulke. Philadelphia: University of Pennsylvania Press, 1974.

Pharr, Clyde, Theresa Sherrer Davidson, and Mary Brown Pharr, eds. *The Theodosian Code and Novels and the Sirmondian Constitutsions.* Princeton, NJ: Princeton University Press, 1952.

Procopius. *The History of the Wars; Secret History.* 4 Vols. Ed. and trans. Henry B. Dewing. Cambridge, MA: Harvard University Press, 1914–1940.

Procopius. *Procopius, Vol 7: On Buildings.* Trans. H. B. Dewing and Glanville Downey. Cambridge, MA: Loeb Classical Library, 1940.

Procopius. *Secret History,* ed. and trans. Henry B. Dewing. Cambridge, MA: Harvard University Press, 1914–1940.

Reuter, Timothy, trans. *The Annals of Fulda: Ninth Century Histories.* Manchester, UK: University of Manchester Press, 1992.

Rivers, Theodore J, trans. *Laws of the Alamans and Bavarians.* Philadelphia: University of Pennsylvania Press, 1977.

Rivers, Theodore, J, trans. *The Laws of the Salian and Ripuarian Franks.* New York: AMS, 1986.

Russel, Norman, trans. *The Lives of the Desert Fathers: Historia Monachorum in Aegypto.* Collegeville, MN: Cistercian Publications, 2006.

Silvas, Anna M. *The Asketikon of St. Basil the Great.* Oxford: Oxford University Press, 2005.

Scholz, Bernhard Walter, trans. *Carolingian Chronicles: Royal Frankish Annals and Nithard's History.* Ann Arbor: University of Michigan Press, 1972.

Sulpicius Severus. "Life of Saint Martin of Tours." In *Soldiers of Christ: Saints and Saints' Lives from Late Antiquity and the Early Middle Ages.* Eds. Thomas F. X. Noble and Thomas Head. University Park, PA: Pennsylvania State University Press, 1995, pp. 1–29.

Tacitus. *The Agricola and the Germania*. Trans. H. Mattingly, rev. trans. S.A. Handford. Harmondsworth, UK: Penguin, 1982.

Theodulf of Orléans. *The Poetry of Theodulf of Orleans: A Translation and Critical Study*. Ed. and trans. Nikolai A. Alexandro. Ann Arbor: University Microfilms, 1970.

Thiébaux, Marcelle, ed. and trans. *The Writings of Medieval Women: An Anthology*. 2nd ed. New York: Garland, 1994.

Tilley, Maureen. *Donastist Martyr Stories: The Church in Conflict in North Africa*. Liverpool, UK: Liverpool University Press, 1997.

Victor of Vita: History of the Vandal Persecution. Trans. John Moorhead. Liverpool, UK: Liverpool University Press, 1992.

Wallace-Hadrill, John M., ed. and trans. *The Fourth Book of the Chronicle of Fredegar with Its Continuations*. London: Nelson, 1960.

Watson, Alan. *The Digest of Justinian*. Philadelphia: University of Pennsylvania Press, 1997.

Whitelock, Dorothy, ed. *The Anglo-Saxon Chronicle*. Westport, CT: Greenwood, 1986.

Zosimus. *New History*. Trans. Ronald T. Ridley. Canberra: Australian Association for Byzantine Studies, 1982.

Art and Culture

Backhouse, Janet. *The Lindisfarne Gospels*. Oxford: Phaidon, 1981.

Baker, Peter S., ed. *Beowulf: Basic Readings*. New York: Garland, 1995.

Beckwith, John. *Early Medieval Art*. London: Thames and Hudson, 1969.

Beckwith, John. *Ivory Carvings in Early Medieval England*. London: Harvey Miller, 1972.

Bjork, Robert E., and John D. Niles, eds. *A Beowulf Handbook*. Lincoln: University of Nebraska Press, 1997.

Brown, George Hardin. *Bede the Venerable*. Boston: Twayne, 1987.

Brown, Giles. "Introduction: the Carolingian Renaissance." In *Carolingian Culture: Emulation and Innovation*. Ed. Rosamond McKitterick. Cambridge: Cambridge University Press, 1994, pp. 1–51.

Brown, Michelle. *The Lindisfarne Gospels and the Early Medieval World*. London: British Library, 2010.

Brown, Michelle. *The Lindisfarne Gospels: Society, Spirituality, and the Scribe*. Toronto: University of Toronto Press, 2003.

Brown, Peter. *Augustine of Hippo: A Biography*. Berkeley: University of California Press, 1967.

Cameron, Averil. *Procopius and the Sixth Century*. London: Routledge, 1996.

Chadwick, Henry. *Boethius: The Consolations of Music, Logic, Theology, and Philosophy.* Oxford: Clarendon, 1981.

Chambers, Raymond. W. *Beowulf: An Introduction to the Study of the Poem with a Discussion of the Stories of Offa and Finn.* 3rd ed., supplement by C. L. Wrenn. Cambridge: Cambridge University Press, 1959.

Contreni, John J. "The Carolingian Renaissance: Education and Literary Culture." In *The New Cambridge Medieval History.* Vol. 2. Ed. Rosamond McKitterick. Cambridge: Cambridge University Press, 1995, pp. 709–57.

Cribiore, Raffaella. *The School of Libanius in Late Antique Antioch.* Princeton, NJ: Princeton University Press, 2007.

Crocker, Richard. *The Early Medieval Sequence.* Berkeley: University of California Press, 1976.

Crosby, Sumner McKnight. *The Royal Abbey of Saint-Denis from Its Beginnings to the Death of Abbot Suger, 475–1151.* Ed. Pamela Z. Blum. New Haven: Yale University Press, 1987.

Curtius, Ernst Robert. *European Literature and the Latin Middle Ages.* Trans. Willard R. Trask. 1953. Reprint, with a new epilogue by Peter Goodman, Princeton, NJ: Princeton University Press, 1990.

Davis-Weyer, Caecilia. *Early Medieval Art, 300–1150.* Toronto: Toronto University Press, 1986.

Deane, Herbert. *The Political and Social Ideas of Saint Augustine.* New York: Columbia University Press, 1964.

Duckett, Eleanor Shipley. *Anglo-Saxon Saints and Scholars.* New York: Macmillan, 1947.

Evans, James A. S. *Procopius.* New York: Twayne, 1972.

Farr, Carol Ann. *The Book of Kells: Its Function and Audience.* Toronto: University of Toronto Press, 1997.

Freeman, Ann. "Theodulf of Orléans and the *Libri Carolini.*" *Speculum* 32 (1957): 664–705.

Ganz, David. "Humour as History in Notkers's *Gesta Karoli Magni.*" In *Monks, Nuns, and Friars in Medieval Society.* Eds. E. King, J. Schaefer, and W. Wadley. Sewanee, TN: University of the South Press, 1989, pp. 171–83.

Gibson, Margaret, ed. *Boethius: His Life, Thought, and Influence.* Oxford: Blackwell, 1981.

Grabar, André. *Early Medieval Painting from the Fourth to the Eleventh Century.* Lausanne: Skira, 1957.

Hasenfratz, Robert J. *Beowulf Scholarship: An Annotated Bibliography, 1979–1990.* New York: Garland, 1993.

Henderson, George. "Emulation and Invention in Carolingian Art." In *The New Cambridge Medieval History,* vol. 2. Ed. Rosamond McKitterick. Cambridge: Cambridge University Press, 1995, pp. 248–73.

Hubert, Jean, Jean Porcher, and Wolfgang Fritz Volbach. *The Carolingian Renaissance.* New York: George Braziller, 1970.

Hubert, Jean, Jean Porcher, and Wolfgang Fritz Volbach. *Europe in the Dark Ages.* London: Thames and Hudson, 1969.

Hunt, David, and Jan Willem Drijvers, eds. *The Late Roman World and its Historian: Interpreting Ammianus Marcellinus.* London: Routledge, 1999.

Innes, Matthew, and Rosamond McKitterick. "The Writing of History." In *Carolingian Culture: Emulation and Innovation.* Ed. Rosamond McKitterick. Cambridge: Cambridge University Press, 1994, pp. 193–220.

Kornbluth, Genevra A. *Engraved Gems of the Carolingian Empire.* University Park: Pennsylvania State University Press, 1995.

Lasko, Peter. *Ars Sacra 800–1200.* 2nd ed. New Haven: Yale University Press, 1994.

Lasko, Peter. *The Kingdom of the Franks: Northwest Europe before Charlemagne.* London: Thames and Hudson, 1971.

Lobbedey, U. "Carolingian Royal Palaces: The State of Research from an Architectural Historian's Viewpoint." In *Court Culture in the Early Middle Ages: The Proceedings of the First Alcuin Conference.* Ed. Rosamond McKitterick. Turnhout: Brepols, 2003, pp. 129–54.

Marenbon, John. "Carolingian Thought." In *Carolingian Culture: Emulation and Innovation.* Ed. Rosamond McKitterick. Cambridge: Cambridge University Press, 1994, pp. 171–92.

Mayvaert, Paul. "The Authorship of the 'Libri Carolini': Observations Prompted by a Recent Book." *Revue bénédictine* 89 (1979): 29–57.

McKitterick, Rosamond, ed. *Carolingian Culture: Emulation and Innovation.* Cambridge: Cambridge University Press, 1994.

McKitterick, Rosamond, ed. *The Carolingians and the Written Word.* Cambridge: Cambridge University Press, 1989.

Meehan, Bernard. *The Book of Kells: An Illustrated Introduction to the Manuscript in Trinity College Dublin.* London: Thames and Hudson, 1994.

Mütherich, Florentine, and Joachim E. Gaehde. *Carolingian Painting.* New York: George Braziller, 1976.

Nie, Giselle de. *Views from a Many-Windowed Tower: Studies of Imagination in the Works of Gregory of Tours.* Amsterdam: Rodopi, 1987.

Neese, Lawrence. *Justinian to Charlemagne: European Art, 565–787: An Annotated Bibliography.* Boston: Hall, 1987.

O'Donnell, James J. *Augustine.* Boston: Twayne, 1985.

O'Donnell, James J. *Cassiodorus.* Berkeley: University of California Press, 1979.

Pulliam, Heather. *Word and Image in the Book of Kells.* Dublin: Four Courts Press, 2006.

Randall, Richard H., Jr. *Masterpieces of Ivory from the Walters Art Gallery.* New York: Hudson Hills, 1985.

Riché, Pierre. *Education and Culture in the Barbarian West: From the Sixth to the Eighth Century.* Trans. John Contreni. Columbia: University of South Carolina Press, 1978.

Ross, Marvin, and Philippe Verdier. *Arts of the Migration Period in the Walters Art Gallery.* Baltimore, MD: Walters Art Gallery, 1961.

Snyder, James. *Medieval Art: Painting, Sculpture, Architecture, 4th–14th Century.* New York: Harry Abrams, 1989.

Tolkien, J. R. R. "*Beowulf:* The Monsters and the Critics." *Proceedings of the British Academy* 22 (1936): 245–295.

Van Riel, Gerd, Carlos Steel, and James McEvoy, eds. *Iohannes Scottus Eriugena: The Bible and Hermeneutics.* Leuven: Leuven University Press, 1996.

Wallach, Luitpold. *Alcuin and Charlemagne: Studies in Carolingian History and Literature.* Ithaca, NY: Cornell University Press, 1959.

Wills, Gary. *Saint Augustine.* New York: Penguin, 1999.

England and the Continent in the Early Middle Ages

Arnold, Christopher J. *Roman Britain to Saxon Shore.* Bloomington: Indiana University Press, 1984.

Bachrach, Bernard. *Early Medieval Jewish Policy in Western Europe.* Minneapolis: University of Minnesota Press, 1977.

Bassett, Steven, ed. *The Origins of Anglo-Saxon Kingdoms.* Leicester, UK: Leicester University Press, 1989.

Blair, Peter Hunter. *The World of Bede.* Cambridge: Cambridge University Press, 1990.

Blumenthal, Uta-Renata, ed. *Carolingian Essays: Andrew W. Mellon Lectures in Early Christian Studies.* Washington, DC: Catholic University of America Press, 1983.

Boussard, Jacques. *The Civilization of Charlemagne.* Trans. Frances Partridge. New York: McGraw-Hill Book Company, 1968.

Brown, Peter. *The Rise of Western Christendom: Triumph and Diversity.* Cambridge, MA: Blackwell, 1996.

Bullough, Donald. "*Europae Pater:* Charlemagne and His Achievement in the Light of Recent Scholarship." *English Historical Review* 75 (1970): 59–105.

Cabaniss, Allen. *Agobard of Lyons: Churchman and Critic.* Syracuse, NY: Syracuse University Press, 1953.

Christie, Neil. *The Lombards: The Ancient Langobards.* Oxford: Blackwell, 1998.

Collins, Roger. *Charlemagne.* Toronto: University of Toronto Press, 1998.

Collins, Roger. *Early Medieval Spain: Unity in Diversity, 400–1000.* New York: Longman, 1983.

Collins, Roger. *Visigothic Spain 409–711.* Oxford: Wiley-Blackwell, 2004.

Daly, William M. "Clovis: How Barbaric, How Pagan?" *Speculum* 69 (1994): 619–64.

De Jong, Mayke. *The Penitential State: Authority and Atonement in the Age of Louis the Pious, 814–840.* Cambridge: Cambridge University Press, 2005.

Dill, Samuel. *Roman Society in Gaul in the Merovingian Age.* 1926. Reprint. London: Allen and Unwin, 1966.

Duckett, Eleanor Shipley. *Alcuin, Friend of Charlemagne: His World and His Work.* New York: Macmillan, 1951.

Duckett, Eleanor Shipley. *Carolingian Portraits: A Study in the Ninth Century.* Ann Arbor: University of Michigan Press, 1962.

Dutton, Paul Edward. *The Politics of Dreaming in the Carolingian Empire.* Lincoln: University of Nebraska Press, 1994.

Farmer, David H. *The Age of Bede.* Harmondsworth, UK: Penguin, 1998.

Fichtenau, Heinrich. *The Carolingian Empire.* Trans. Peter Munz. Toronto: University of Toronto Press, 1979.

Fouracre, Paul. *The Age of Charles Martel.* New York: Longman, 2000.

Ganshof, François L. *The Carolingians and the Frankish Monarchy: Studies in Carolingian History.* Trans. Janet L. Sondheimer. London: Longman, 1971.

Geary, Patrick. *Before France and Germany: The Creation and Transformation of the Merovingian World.* Oxford: 1988.

Gerberding, Richard, A. *The Rise of the Carolingians and the "Liber Historiae Francorum."* Oxford: Clarendon, 1987.

Godman, Peter, and Roger Collins, eds. *Charlemagne's Heir: New Perspectives on the Reign of Louis the Pious.* Oxford: Clarendon, 1990.

Goldberg, Eric. *Struggle for Empire: Kingship and Conflict under Louis the German, 817–876.* Ithaca, NY: Cornell University Press, 2009.

Halphen, Louis. *Charlemagne and the Carolingian Empire.* Trans. Giselle de Nie. Amsterdam: North-Holland, 1977.

Hawkes, Jane, and Susan Mills. *Northumbria's Golden Age.* Stroud, UK: Sutton Publishing, Ltd., 1999.

James, Edward. *The Franks.* Oxford: Blackwell, 1991.

James, Edward, ed. *Visigothic Spain: New Approaches.* Oxford: Clarendon, 1980.

Keynes, Simon. "The British Isles: England, 700–900." In *The New Cambridge Medieval History.* Vol. 2. Ed. Rosamond McKitterick. Cambridge: Cambridge University Press, 1995, pp. 18–42.

King, P. D. *Law and Society in the Visigothic Kingdom.* Cambridge: Cambridge University Press, 1972.

Kirby, David P. *The Earliest English Kings.* London: Unwin Hyman, 1991.

Lapidge, Michael. *Bede and His World: The Jarrow Lectures, 1958–1993.* 2 Vols. Aldershot, UK: Variorum, 1994.

Levison, Wilhelm. *England and the Continent in the Eighth Century.* New York: Oxford University Press, 1998.

Llewellyn, Peter. *Rome in the Dark Ages.* New York: Barnes and Noble, 1993.

Loyn, Henry R. *Anglo-Saxon England and the Norman Conquest.* 2nd ed. London: Longman, 1991.

MaClean, Simon. *Kingship and Politics in the Late Ninth Century: Charles the Fat and the End of the Carolingian Empire.* Cambridge: Cambridge University Press, 2003.

McKitterick, Rosamond. *The Frankish Kingdoms under the Carolingians, 751–987.* London: Longman, 1983.

Myres, John N. L. *The English Settlements.* Oxford: Clarendon, 1986.

Nelson, Janet. *Charles the Bald.* London: Longman, 1992.

Neuman de Vegvar, Carol. *The Northumbrian Renaissance: A Study in the Transmission of Style.* Cranbury, NJ: Associated University Presses, 1987.

Noble, Thomas F. X. *Images, Iconoclasm, and the Carolingians.* Philadelphia: University of Pennsylvania Press, 2009.

Noble, Thomas F. X. *The Republic of St. Peter: The Birth of the Papal State, 680–825.* Philadelphia: University of Pennsylvania Press, 1984.

Reuter, Timothy. *Germany in the Early Middle Ages, c. 800–1056.* London: Longman, 1991.

Riché, Pierre. *The Carolingians: A Family Who Forged Europe.* Trans. Michael Idomir Allen. Philadelphia: University of Pennsylvania Press, 1993.

Sawyer, Peter. H. *From Roman Britain to Norman England.* 2nd ed. London and New York, 1998.

Smyth, Alfred P. *King Alfred the Great.* Oxford: Oxford University Press, 1995.

Stenton, Frank M. *Anglo-Saxon England.* 3rd ed. Oxford: Clarendon, 1971.

Sturdy, David J. *Alfred the Great.* London: Constable, 1995.

Sullivan, Richard. *Aix-La-Chapelle in the Age of Charlemagne.* Norman: University of Oklahoma Press, 1974.

Sullivan, Richard E. "The Carolingian Age: Reflections on Its Place in the History of the Middle Ages." *Speculum* 64 (1989): 257–306.

Wallace-Hadrill, John. M. *The Long-Haired Kings.* Toronto: Toronto University Press, 1982.

Wickham, Chris. *Early Medieval Italy: Central Power and Local Society, 400–1000.* Ann Arbor: University of Michigan Press, 1981.

Wood, Ian. *The Merovingian Kingdoms, 450–751.* London: Longman, 1994.

Yorke, Barbara. *Kings and Kingdoms of Early Anglo-Saxon England.* London: Seaby, 1990.

Late Antiquity and the Migration Period

Alcock, Leslie. *Arthur's Britain: History and Archeology, A.D. 367–634.* Harmondsworth, UK: Penguin, 1971.

Amory, *Patrick. People and Identity in Ostrogothic Italy, 489–554.* Cambridge: Cambridge University Press, 1997.

Bachrach, Bernard S. "The Alans in Gaul." *Traditio* 23 (1967): 476–89.

Bachrach, Bernard S. *A History of the Alans in the West, from Their First Appearance in the Sources of Classical Antiquity through the Early Middle Ages.* Minneapolis: University of Minnesota Press, 1973.

Barber, Richard. *The Figure of Arthur.* Totowa, NJ: Rowman and Littlefield, 1972.

Barker, John W. *Justinian and the Later Roman Empire.* Madison: University of Wisconsin Press, 1960.

Barnes, Timothy D. *Ammianus Marcellinus and the Representation of Historical Reality.* Ithaca, NY: Cornell University Press, 1998.

Barnes, Timothy. *Constantine and Eusebius.* Cambridge, MA: Harvard University Press, 1981.

Bassett, Steven, ed. *The Origins of Anglo-Saxon Kingdoms.* Leicester, UK: Leicester University Press, 1989.

Baüml, Franz H., and Marianna. Birnbaum. *Attila: The Man and His Image.* Budapest: Corvina, 1993.

Brown, Peter. *Late Antiquity.* Cambridge, MA: Harvard University Press, 1998.

Brown, Peter. *Society and the Holy in Late Antiquity.* Berkeley: University of California Press, 1982.

Brown, Peter. *The World of Late Antiquity, A.D. 150–750.* London: Thames and Hudson, 1971.

Browning, Robert. *Justinian and Theodora.* London: Thames and Hudson, 1987.

Burckhardt, Jacob. *The Age of Constantine the Great.* Trans. Moses Hadas. Berkeley: University of California Press, 1983.

Burns, Thomas S. *Barbarians within the Gates of Rome: A Study of Roman Military Policy and the Barbarians, ca. 375–425 A.D.* Bloomington: University of Indiana Press, 1994.

Burns, Thomas S. *A History of the Ostrogoths.* Bloomington: Indiana University Press, 1984.

Bursche, Aleksander. *Later Roman-Barbarian Contacts in Central Europe: Numismatic Evidence.* Berlin: Gebr. Mann Verlag, 1996.

Bury, John B. *History of the Later Roman Empire: From the Death of Theodosius I to the Death of Justinian.* Vol. 1. 1923. Reprint, New York: Dover, 1959.

Bury, John B. *The Invasions of Europe by the Barbarians.* New York: W.W. Norton, 1967.

Cameron, Averil. *The Mediterranean World in Late Antiquity, A.D. 395–600.* New York: Routledge, 1993.

Cameron, Averil, and Peter Garnsey, eds. *The Late Empire, A.D. 337–425. Cambridge Ancient History.* Vol. 13. Cambridge: Cambridge University Press, 1998.

Clover, Frank M. *The Late Roman West and the Vandals.* London: Variorum, 1993.

Freeman, Charles. *A.D. 381: Heretics, Pagans, and the Dawn of the Monotheistic State.* New York: Overlook Press, 2009.

Friell, Gerard, and Stephen Williams. *Theodosius: The Empire at Bay.* New York: Routledge, 1998.

Goffart, Walter. *Barbarians and Romans, A.D. 418–584: The Techniques of Accommodation.* Princeton: Princeton University Press, 1980.

Grant, Michael. *Constantine the Great: The Man and His Times.* New York: Charles Scribner's Sons, 1994.

Halsall, Guy. *Barbarian Migrations and the Roman West, 376–568.* Cambridge: Cambridge University Press, 2008.

Heather, Peter. *The Goths.* Oxford: Blackwell, 1996.

Heather, Peter. "Goths and Huns, c. 320–425." In *The Late Empire, A.D. 337–425, vol. 13, The Cambridge Ancient History.* Eds. Averil Cameron and Peter Garnsey. Cambridge: Cambridge University Press, 1998, pp. 487–537.

Herrin, Judith. *The Formation of Christendom.* Princeton, NJ: Princeton University Press, 1987.

Hodgkin, Thomas. *Theodoric the Goth: The Barbarian Champion of Civilization.* New York: G. P. Putnam, 1983.

Honoré, Tony. *Justinian's Digest: Character and Compilation.* Oxford: Oxford University Press, 2010.

Howe, Nicholas. *Migration and Mythmaking in Anglo-Saxon England.* New Haven: Yale University Press, 1989.

Jones, Arnold H. M. *The Later Roman Empire, 284–602: A Social Economic and Administrative Survey.* Baltimore, MD: Johns Hopkins University Press, 1986.

King, Peter. D. *Law and Society in the Visigothic Kingdom.* Cambridge: Cambridge University Press, 1972.

Klingshirn, William E. *Caesarius of Arles: The Making of a Christian Community in Late Antique Gaul.* Cambridge: Cambridge University Press, 1994.

Lot, Ferdinand. *The End of the Ancient World and the Beginnings of the Middle Ages.* New York: Harper and Row, 1961.

Matthews, John. *The Roman Empire of Ammianus Marcellinus.* Baltimore, MD: Johns Hopkins University Press, 1989.

Matthews, John. *Western Aristocracies and Imperial Court, A.D. 364–425.* Oxford: Clarendon, 1998.

McLynn, Neil B. *Ambrose of Milan: Church and Court in a Christian Capital.* Berkeley: University of California Press, 1994.

Metzger, Ernest, ed. *A Companion to Justinian's Institutes.* Ithaca, NY: Cornell University Press, 1999.

Moorhead, John. *Ambrose: Church and Society in the Late Roman World.* New York: Longman, 1999.

Moorhead, John. *Theodoric in Italy.* Oxford: Clarendon, 1992.

Murray, Alexander, ed. *After Rome's Fall: Narrators and Sources of Early Medieval History.* Toronto: University of Toronto Press, 1998.

Obolensky, Dmitri. *The Byzantine Commonwealth: Eastern Europe, 500–1543.* New York: Praeger, 1971.

Radding, Charles and Antonio Ciaralli. *The Corpus Iuris Civilis in the Middle Ages.* Brill: Leiden, 2006.

Randers-Pehrson, Justine Davis. *Barbarians and Romans: The Birth Struggle of Europe, A.D. 400–700.* Norman: University of Oklahoma Press, 1983.

Reynolds, Susan. "Our Forefathers? Tribes, Peoples, and Nations in the Historiography of the Age of Migrations." In *After Rome's Fall: Narrators and Sources of Early Medieval History.* Ed. Alexander Callander Murray. Toronto: University of Toronto Press, 1999, pp. 17–36.

Roth, Norman. *Jews, Visigoths, and Muslims in Medieval Spain.* Leiden: Brill Academic Publishers, 1994.

Rutgers, L. V. *The Jews of Late Ancient Rome.* Leiden: Brill Academic Publishers, 1995.

Schwartz, Seth. *Imperialism and Jewish Society: 200 B.C.E. to 640 C.E. (Jews, Christians, and Muslims from the Ancient to the Modern World).* Princeton, NJ: Princeton University Press, 2004.

Sullivan, Richard. *Heirs of the Roman Empire.* Ithaca, NY: Cornell University Press, 1974.

Thompson, Edward A. *A History of Attila and the Huns.* Oxford: Clarendon, 1948.

Thompson, Edward A. *The Huns.* Oxford: Blackwell, 1995.

Treadgold, Warren. *The History of the Byzantine State and Society.* Stanford, CA: Stanford University Press, 1997.

Ure, Percy N. *Justinian and His Age.* Harmondsworth, UK: Penguin, 1951.

Wallace-Hadrill, John M. *The Barbarian West, A.D. 400–1000.* New York: Harper and Row, 1962.

Wessel, Susan. *Leo the Great and the Spiritual Rebuilding of Rome.* Leiden: Brill Academic Publishers, 2008.

Wolfram, Herwig. *History of the Goths.* Trans. Thomas J. Dunlap. Berkeley: University of California Press, 1988.

Wolfram, Herwig. *The Roman Empire and Its Germanic Peoples.* Trans. Thomas J. Dunlap. Berkeley: University of California Press, 1997.

Van Dam, Raymond. *Leadership and Community in Late Antique Gaul.* Berkeley: University of California Press, 1985.

Military History

Bachrach, Bernard S. "Charles Martel, Mounted Shock Combat, the Stirrup, and Feudalism." *Studies in Medieval and Renaissance History* 7 (1970): 47–75.

Bachrach, Bernard S. *Early Carolingian Warfare: Prelude to Empire.* Philadelphia: University of Pennsylvania Press, 2001.

Bachrach, Bernard S. *Merovingian Military Organization, 481–751.* Minneapolis: University of Minnesota Press, 1972.

Contamine, Philippe. *War in the Middle Ages.* Trans. Michael Jones. Oxford: Basil Blackwell, 1984.

Coupland, Simon. "Carolingian Arms and Armor in the Ninth Century." *Viator: Medieval and Renaissance Studies* 21 (1990): 29–50.

DeVries, Kelly. *Medieval Military Technology.* Peterborough, ON: Broadview, 1992.

Ferrill, Arthur. *The Fall of the Roman Empire: The Military Explanation.* New York: Thames and Hudson, 1986.

Hughes, Ian. *Belisarius: The Last Roman General.* Yardley, PA: Westholme Publishing, 1996.

Le Bohec, Yann. *The Imperial Roman Army.* Trans. Raphael Bate. New York: Routledge, 2000.

Luttwak, Edward. *The Grand Strategy of the Roman Empire.* Baltimore, MD: Johns Hopkins University Press, 1974.

Martin, Paul. *Arms and Armour from the 9th to the 17th Century.* Trans. René North. Rutland: Tuttle, 1968.

Southern, Pat and Karen Ramsey Dixon. *The Late Roman Army.* New Haven: Yale University Press, 1996.

Verbruggen, Jan. F. *The Art of Warfare in Western Europe during the Middle Ages: From the Eighth Century to 1340.* 2nd ed. Trans. Sumner Willard and S.C.M. Southern. Woodbridge, UK: Boydell, 1997.

Regional Studies

Bloch, Herbert. *Monte Cassino in the Middle Ages.* 3 Vols. Cambridge, MA: Harvard University Press, 1988.

Brown, Michelle, and Carol Ann Farr, eds. *Mercia: An Anglo-Saxon Kingdom in Europe*. London: Continuum, 2001.

Clover, F. M. "Felix Karthago." *Dumbarton Oaks Papers* 40 (1986): 1–16.

Cunliffe, Barry. *Wessex to A.D. 1000*. London: Longman, 1993.

Deliyannis, Deborah M. *Ravenna in Late Antiquity*. Cambridge: Cambridge University Press, 2010.

Downey, Glanville. *A History of Antioch in Syria: From Seleucus to the Arab Conquest*. Princeton, NJ: Princeton University Press, 1961.

Freely, John, and Ahmet S. Cakmak. *Byzantine Monuments of Constantinople*. Cambridge: Cambridge University Press, 2009.

Hallenback, Jan T. *Pavia and Rome: The Lombard Monarchy and the Papacy in the Eighth Century*. Philadelphia, PA: American Philosophical Society, 1982.

Harris, Jonathan. *Constantinople: Capital of Byzantium*. Oxford: Continuum Books, 2007.

Holum, Kenneth G., Avner Raban, Robert L. Hohlfelder, and Robert J. Bull. *King Herod's Dream: Caesarea on the Sea*. New York: W. W. Norton and Company, 1988.

Huskinson, Janet, and Isabella Sandwell, eds. *Culture and Society in Later Roman Antioch*. Oxford: Oxbow Books, 2003.

Kondoloeon, Christine, ed. *Antioch: The Lost Ancient City*. Princeton, NJ: Princeton University Press, 2000.

Krautheimer, Richard. *Three Christian Capitals: Topography and Politics*. Berkeley: University of California Press, 1983.

La Rocca, Cristina. *Italy in the Early Middle Ages: 476–1000*. New York: Oxford University Press, 2002.

Levine, Lee. *Caesarea under Roman Rule*. Leiden: Brill, 1975.

Liebeschuetz, J.H.W.G. *Antioch: City and Imperial Administration in the Later Roman Empire*. Oxford: Oxford University Press, 1972.

Raban, Avner, and Kenneth G. Holum, eds. *Caesarea Maritima: A Restrospective after Two Millenia*. Leiden: Brill, 1996.

Sherrard, Philip. *Constantinople: Iconography of a Sacred City*. Oxford: Oxford University Press, 1965.

Trumbull, Stephen. *The Walls of Constantinople AD 324–1453*. Oxford: Osprey Publishing, 2004.

Velay, Phiippe. *From Lutetia to Paris: The Island and the Two Banks*. Paris: CNRS, 1992.

Religion

Barber, Charles. *Figure and Likeness: On the Limits of Representation in Byzantine Iconoclasm*. Princeton, NJ: Princeton University Press, 2002.

Brown, Peter. *The Cult of the Saints: Its Rise and Function in Latin Christianity*. Chicago: University of Chicago Press, 1982.

Brown, Peter.. *Relics and Social Status in the Age of Gregory of Tours.* Reading, UK: University of Reading, 1977.

Brown, Peter.. *Religion and Society in the Age of Augustine.* New York: Harper and Row, 1972.

Bullough, Donald. "Alcuin and the Kingdom of Heaven: Liturgy, Theology, and the Carolingian Age." In *Carolingian Essays.* Ed. Uta-Renate Blumenthal. Washington, DC: Catholic University Press, 1983, pp. 1–69.

Cavadini, J.C. *The Last Christology of the West: Adoptionism in Spain and Gaul, 785–820.* Philadelphia: University of Pennsylvania Press, 1993.

Chazelle, Celia. *The Crucified God in the Carolingian Era: Theology and Art of Christ's Passion.* Cambridge: Cambridge University Press, 2001.

Clarke, Howard B., and Mary Brennen, eds. *Columban and Merovingian Monasticism.* Oxford: British Archeological Reports, 1981.

Cohen, Jeremy. *Living Letters of the Law: Ideas of the Jew in Medieval Christianity.* Berkeley: University of California Press, 1999.

Dumézil, Georges. *Gods of the Ancient Northmen.* Trans. Einer Haugen. Berkeley: University of California Press, 1973.

Dunn, Marilyn. *Emergence of Monasticism: From the Desert Fathers to the Early Middle Ages.* Oxford: Wiley Blackwell, 2003.

Evans, Gillian R. *The Thought of Gregory the Great.* Cambridge: Cambridge University Press, 1988.

Farmer, David Hugh, ed. *Benedict's Disciples.* Leominster, UK: Fowler Wright, 1980.

Fox, Robin Lane. *Pagans and Christians.* New York: Knopf, 1987.

Fredriksen, Paula. *Augustine and the Jews: A Christian Defense of Jews and Judaism.* New York: Doubleday Religion, 2008.

Frend, W.H.C. *The Donatist Church: A Movement of Protest in Roman North Africa.* New York: Oxford University Press, 2000.

Geary, Patrick. *Furta Sacra: Thefts of Relics in the Central Middle Ages.* Rev. ed. Princeton, NJ: Princeton University Press, 1990.

Grimm, Jakob. *Teutonic Mythology.* 4 Vols. Trans. James Stevens Stallybrass. London: Routledge, 1999.

Hanson, Richard P.C. *The Search for the Christian Doctrine of God: The Arian Controversy, 318–381.* Edinburgh: Baker Academic, 1988.

Harmless, J. William. "Monasticism." In *The Oxford Handbook of Early Christian Studies.* Eds. Susan Ashbrook Harvey and David G. Hunter. Oxford: Oxford University Press, 2008, pp. 493–517.

Higham, Nicholas J. *The Convert Kings: Power and Religious Affiliation in Early Anglo-Saxon England.* Manchester, UK: Manchester University Press, 1997.

Hildebrand, Stephen M. *The Trinitarian Theology of Basil of Caesarea: A Synthesis of Greek Thought and Biblical Faith.* Washington, DC: Catholic University Press of America, 2009.

Jolly, Karen Louise. *Popular Religion in Late Saxon England: Elf Charms in Context.* Chapel Hill: University of North Carolina Press, 1996.

Knowles, David. *Christian Monasticism.* New York: McGraw Hill, 1969.

Lawrence, Clifford H. *Medieval Monasticism: Forms of Religious Life in Western Europe in the Middle Ages.* 2nd ed. London: Longman, 1989.

Markus, Robert A. *Gregory the Great and His World.* Cambridge: Cambridge University Press, 1998.

Mayr-Harting, Henry. *The Coming of Christianity to Anglo-Saxon England.* 3rd ed. University Park, PA: Pennsylvania State University Press, 1991.

McKitterick, Rosamond. *The Frankish Church and the Carolingian Reforms, 789–895.* London: Longman, 1977.

Meyvaert, Paul. *Benedict, Gregory, Bede and Others.* London: Variorum Reprints, 1977.

Pelikan, Jaroslav. *The Emergence of the Catholic Tradition.* Vol. 2 of *The Christian Tradition: A History of the Development of Doctrine.* Chicago: University of Chicago Press, 1978.

Pelikan, Jaroslav. *The Growth of Medieval Theology (600–1300).* Vol. 3 of *The Christian Tradition: A History of the Development of Doctrine.* Chicago: University of Chicago Press, 1978.

Polomé, Edgar C. *Essays on Germanic Religion.* Washington, DC: Institute for the Study of Man, 1989.

Radde-Gallwitz, Andrew. *Basil of Caesarea; Gregory of Nyssa, and the Transformation of Divine Simplicity.* Oxford: Oxford University Press, 2009.

Reuter, Timothy, ed. *The Greatest Englishman: Essays on St. Boniface and the Church at Crediton.* Exeter: Paternoster Press, 1980.

Richards, Jeffrey. *Consul of God: The Life and Times of Gregory the Great.* London: Routledge and Kegan Paul, 1980.

Rousseau, Philip. *Basil of Caesarea.* Berkeley: University of California Press, 1998.

Russell, James C. *The Germanization of Early Medieval Christianity: A Socio-historical Approach to Religious Transformation.* Oxford: Oxford University Press, 1994.

Russell, Jeffery Burton. *Dissent and Reform in the Early Middle Ages.* Berkeley: University of California Press, 1965.

Straw, Carol. *Gregory the Great: Perfection in Imperfection.* Berkeley: University of California Press, 1991.

Sullivan, Richard. "What Was Carolingian Monasticism? The Plan of St. Gall and the History of Monasticism." In *After Rome's Fall: Narrators and Sources of Early Medieval History.* Ed. Alexander Callander Murray. Toronto: University of Toronto Press, 1998, pp. 251–87.

Turville-Petre, Edward O. G. *Myth and Religion of the North: The Religion of Ancient Scandinavia.* London: Weidenfeld and Nicholson, 1964.

Ullmann, Walter. *A Short History of the Papacy in the Middle Ages.* London: Methuen, 1972.

Van Dam, Raymond. *Saints and Their Miracles in Late Antique Gaul.* Princeton, NJ: Princeton University Press, 1993.

Wallace-Hadrill, John M. *The Frankish Church.* Oxford: Clarendon, 1983.

Williams, Daniel H. *Ambrose of Milan and the End of the Arian-Nicene Conflict.* Oxford: Oxford University Press, 1995.

Social and Economic History

Blackburn, Mark A. S., ed. *Anglo-Saxon Monetary History: Essays in Memory of Michael Dolley.* Leicester, UK: Leicester University Press, 1986.

Bloch, Marc. *French Rural History: An Essay on Its Basic Characteristics.* Trans. Janet Sondheimer. Berkeley: University of California Press, 1966.

Bloch, Marc. *Slavery and Serfdom in the Middle Ages.* Trans. William R. Beer. Berkeley: University of California Press, 1975.

Bonnassie, Pierre. *From Slavery to Feudalism in South-Western Europe.* Trans. Jean Birrell. Cambridge: Cambridge University Press, 1991.

Bruce-Mitford, Rupert L. S. *The Sutton Hoo Ship Burial.* 3 Vols. London: British Museum, 1975–1983.

Carver, Martin. *The Age of Sutton Hoo.* Woodbridge, UK: Boydell, 1992.

Carver, Martin. *Sutton Hoo: Burial Ground of Kings?* Philadelphia: University of Pennsylvania Press, 1998.

Dockès, Pierre. *Medieval Slavery and Liberation.* Trans. Arthur Goldhammer. Chicago: University of Chicago Press, 1982.

Dolley, Reginald H. Michael, ed. *Anglo-Saxon Coins: Studies Presented to F. M. Stenton.* London: Methuen, 1961.

Duby, Georges, ed. *A History of Private Life.* Vol. 2, *Revelations of the Medieval World.* Trans. Arthur Goldhammer. Cambridge, MA: Harvard University Press, 1988.

Duby, Georges. *The Early Growth of the European Economy: Warriors and Peasants from the Seventh to the Twelfth Century.* Ithaca, NY: Cornell University Press, 1979.

Duby, Georges. *Rural Economy and Country Life in the Medieval West.* Trans. Cynthia Postan. Columbia: University of South Carolina Press, 1968.

Evans, Angela Care. *The Sutton Hoo Ship Burial.* London: British Museum, 1986.

Finberg, Herbert P. R., ed. *Agrarian History of England and Wales.* Vol. 1. Cambridge: Cambridge University Press, 1972.

Ganshof, François Louis. *Frankish Institutions under Charlemagne.* Trans. Bryce Lyon and Mary Lyon. Providence, RI: Brown University Press, 1968.

Gies, Frances, and Joseph Gies. *Marriage and Family in the Middle Ages.* New York: Harper and Row, 1987.

Gladitz, Charles. *Horse Breeding in the Medieval World.* Dublin: Four Courts Press, 1997.

Goody, Jack. *The Development of Family and Marriage in Europe.* Cambridge: Cambridge University Press, 1983.

Grierson, Philip, and Mark Blackburn. *Medieval European Coinage.* Vol. 1, *The Early Middle Ages (5th–10th Centuries).* Cambridge: Cambridge University Press, 1986.

Harvey, John. *Mediaeval Gardens.* Beaverton, OR: Timber, 1981.

Herlihy, David. *Medieval Households.* Cambridge, MA: Harvard University Press, 1985.

Hodges, Richard. *The Anglo-Saxon Achievement: Archeology and the Beginnings of English Society.* London: Duckworth, 1989.

King, Peter D. *Law and Society in the Visigothic Kingdom.* Cambridge: Cambridge University Press, 1972.

Lewit, Tamara. *Agricultural Production in the Roman Economy, A.D. 200–400.* Oxford: Tempus Reparatum, 1991.

Lyon, Bryce. *A Constitutional and Legal History of Medieval England.* 2nd ed. New York: Norton, 1980.

Morrison, Karl F., and Henry Grunthal. *Carolingian Coinage.* New York: American Numismatic Society, 1967.

Munz, Peter. *Life in the Age of Charlemagne.* New York: G. P. Putnam's Sons, 1971.

Odegaard, Charles E. *Vassi et Fideles in the Carolingian Empire.* Cambridge, MA: Harvard University Press, 1945.

Pirenne, Henri. *Mohammed and Charlemagne.* Trans. Bernard Miall. New York: Barnes and Noble, 1992.

Pollock, Frederick, and Frederic W. Maitland. *The History of English Law before the Time of Edward I.* 2nd ed. 2 Vols. London: Cambridge University Press, 1968.

Reynolds, Philip. L. *Marriage in the Western Church: The Christianization of Marriage.* Leiden: Brill, 1994.

Riché, Pierre. *Daily Life in the World of Charlemagne.* Trans. Jo Ann McNamara. Philadelphia: University of Pennsylvania Press, 1983.

Shahar, Shulamith. *Growing Old in the Middle Ages: 'Winter clothes us in shadow and pain.'* Trans. Yael Lotan. New York: Routledge, 1995.

Slicher van Bath, Bernard H. *The Agrarian History of Western Europe: A.D. 500–1850.* Trans. Olive Ordish. London: Arnold, 1963.

Todd, Malcolm. *Everyday Life of the Barbarians: Goths, Franks, and Vandals.* London: G. P. Putnam's Sons, 1972.

Veyne, Paul. *A History of Private Life.* Vol. 1, *From Pagan Rome to Byzantium.* Trans. Arthur Goldhammer. Cambridge, MA: Harvard University Press, 1987.

White, Lynn, Jr. *Medieval Technology and Social Change.* Oxford: Oxford University Press, 1964.

Wormald, Patrick. "*Lex Scripta* and *Verbum Regis:* Legislation and Germanic Kingship from Euric to Cnut." In *Early Medieval Kingship.* Eds. Peter Sawyer and Ian N. Wood. Leeds, UK: University of Leeds Press, 1977, pp. 105–38.

Women

Blamires, Alcuin. *Women Defamed, Women Defended.* Oxford: Oxford University Press, 1990.

Clark, Gillian. *Women in Late Antiquity: Pagan and Christian Lifestyles.* Oxford: Clarendon, 1993.

Damico, Helen, and A. Hennessy, eds. *New Readings on Women in Old English Literature.* Bloomington: Indiana University Press, 1990.

Dronke, Peter. *Women Writers of the Middle Ages: A Critical Study of Texts from Perpetua (d. 203) to Marguerite Porete (d. 1310).* Cambridge: Cambridge University Press, 1984.

Ferrante, Joan M. "Women's Role in Latin Letters from the Fourth to the Early Twelfth Century." In *The Cultural Patronage of Medieval Women.* Ed. June Hall McCash. Athens: University of Georgia Press, 1996, pp. 73–105.

Hollum, Kenneth G. *Theodosian Empresses: Women and Imperial Dominion in Late Antiquity.* Berkeley: University of California Press, 1989.

Jewell, Helen. *Women in Medieval England.* Manchester, UK: Manchester University Press, 1996.

Kirshner, Julius, and Suzanne Wemple, eds. *Women of the Medieval World.* Oxford: Basil Blackwell, 1985.

Leyser, Henrietta. *Medieval Women: A Social History of Women in England, 450–1500.* New York: St. Martin's, 1995.

McCash, June Hall, ed. *The Cultural Patronage of Medieval Women.* Athens: University of Georgia Press, 1996.

Nelson, Janet L. "Queens as Jezebels: The Careers of Brunhild and Balthild in Merovingian History." In *Medieval Women.* Ed. Derek Baker. Oxford: Blackwell, 1978, pp. 31–77.

Schulenburg, Jane Tibbetts. *Forgetful of their Sex: Female Sanctity and Society, ca. 500–1100.* Chicago: University of Chicago Press, 1998.

Shahar, Shulamith. *The Fourth Estate: A History of Women in the Middle Ages.* New York: Routledge, 1990.

Stafford, Pauline. *Queens, Concubines, and Dowagers: The King's Wife in the Early Middle Ages.* Athens: University of Georgia Press, 1983.

Stuard, Susan Mosher, ed. *Women in Medieval Society.* Philadelphia: University of Pennsylvania Press, 1976.

Ward, Elizabeth. "Caesar's Wife: The Career of the Empress Judith, 819–829." In *Charlemagne's Heir: New Perspectives on the Reign of Louis the Pious.* Eds. Peter Godman and Roger Collins. Oxford: Clarendon, 1990, pp. 205–27.

Wemple, Suzanne. *Women in Frankish Society: Marriage and the Cloister, 500 to 900.* Philadelphia: University of Pennsylvania Press, 1981.

Index

Items in **bold** refer to main entries.

About the Author

Michael Frassetto earned his PhD in history at the University of Delaware and was awarded a Fulbright Scholarship to research his dissertation in Berlin in 1989–1990. He teaches medieval and world history at the University of Delaware, La Salle University, and Richard Stockton College, and is the former religion and medieval history editor at the *Encyclopaedia Britannica*. He is the author of *The Great Medieval Heretics* and numerous articles on medieval history. He is also the editor of *Medieval Purity and Piety: Essays on Medieval Clerical Celibacy and Religious Reform*, *Western Views of Islam in Medieval and Early Modern Europe* (with David Blanks), *Christian Attitudes Toward the Jews in the Middle Ages*, and *Heresy and the Persecuting Society in the Middle Ages*.